ROMAN POLANSKI

ODD MAN OUT

ROMAN POLANSKI
ODD MAN OUT

DENIS MEIKLE

Research Associate:
John Hamilton

Reynolds & Hearn Ltd
London

To Joy

who sadly did not live to see this one

First published in 2006 by
Reynolds & Hearn Ltd
61a Priory Road
Kew Gardens
Richmond
Surrey TW9 3DH

© Denis Meikle 2006

A CIP catalogue record for this book is available from the British Library.

ISBN 1 905287 21 6

Designed by Peri Godbold.

Printed and bound in Great Britain by Biddles Ltd, King's Lynn, Norfolk.

ACKNOWLEDGMENTS

Those who helped with the acquisition of materials related to Roman Polanski's films were David Barraclough, Kim Newman, Dick Klemensen and Doug Murray. I thank them all. A special thanks on this occasion goes to John Hamilton, himself the author of an exceptional book on the career of Tony Tenser, who volunteered his services at a late stage and selflessly undertook some of the necessary leg-work. I am also indebted to Blue Underground's Carl Daft and his Polish interviewers, Daniel Horowitz and Karina Kleszczewska.

No book of this kind is possible without input from those who have gone before. I have made use of interviews and articles by journalists on both sides of the Atlantic, most of whom have been credited in the text; to any I may have missed, I offer my apologies and my appreciation.

Other mundane tasks fell, as ever, into the hands of my ever-patient wife Jane, who was herself assisted by my daughter Sarah. My love and thanks go to both.

CONTENTS

For as far back as I can remember,
the line between fantasy and reality has been
hopelessly blurred.

Roman Polanski, *Roman by Polanski* (1983)

Once I had a hideous dream,
There I saw a cloven tree;
It had a dreadful rent and yet,
Ugly as it was, it suited me.

Mephistopheles, *Faust*/Wolfgang von Goethe (1832)

Introduction
A GOTHiC PASSiON

Say it with passion:
   Roman Polanski.
      It is a name which inspires loyalty or loathing in almost equal measure.

To some, it belongs to one of the greatest film directors of all time – to others, it signifies an 'evil, profligate dwarf' (Polanski's own words), still on the run from the authorities for a notorious sex-crime.

Roman Polanski.

He remains one of the most controversial figures of our age, revered in his native France (and across Europe) as an auteur without peer, reviled in the United States (and by the American Right in particular) for having the temerity to try to outwit the justice system of the greatest power on earth.

At its worst, criticism of him smacks of anti-Semitic vitriol, for Polanski was born a Parisian Jew. At best, praise for his films has been lavish indeed, and he has been the recipient of an Oscar for Best Director (for *The Pianist*), as well as numerous Césars, BAFTAs and assorted Lifetime Achievement awards. This is the man whom actor Jack Nicholson called 'a fucking genius'.

Roman Polanski's life has been one of triumph and tragedy. From an upbringing in the ghetto and on the mean streets of post-war Poland, he has scaled the show-business heights to become one of the most lauded film craftsmen of his generation. This is the man who gave the world *Rosemary's Baby* and *Chinatown*.

But sorrow and scandal have never been far from Polanski's side. He was a central figure in one of the most atrocious murder-sprees in criminal history, when his then-wife and unborn child were mercilessly slaughtered by a commune of drug-crazed 'hippies' under the control of self-styled satanic guru Charles Manson. Sorrow, for Polanski, in the wake of this tragedy of unparalleled proportions took the form of unbridled sexual indulgence; scandal came along when his predilection for such casual sexual encounters involved a 13-year-old wannabe actress and model... His fall from grace was spectacular. His public rehabilitation and artistic renaissance have been equally startling.

Polanski's story is every bit as exotic and dramatic as that of the characters in any of his 17 films; he is a living legend. If he were a talentless hack, his oeuvre would have counted for naught against the outrages which he is alleged to have perpetrated against the sensibilities of civilised society. But he has talent in abundance, and he has proved it time and again.

To understand the cinema of Roman Polanski, one must understand the influences which went into creating it. He had witnessed, at age nine, the cold-blooded murder of a frail old Jewish woman at the hands of an SS officer. The killing – by a single bullet to the back – had been sudden and shockingly unexpected; the blood from the wound was all-too real. The experience sent Polanski scuttling off to hide under a stairwell, where he stayed until the trauma subsided. Such events burn indelibly into the memory – from such events are woven the patterns of a life.

Roman Polanski is cinema's prodigal son – its 'Dark Prince', according to a BBC website. He is a creature of sun and shadow, of day and night – a child of the extremes of 20th century excess, be they the horrors of war or the lasciviousness of life in the LA film community. His is a story of high achievement and hubris, and of the price that is sometimes paid for riches and fame in the shallow, transient world of show-biz celebrity. His obsessions, his neuroses, have been writ large on screen for all to see, and for more than 40 years: his protagonists invariably are confident and assured, yet somehow vulnerable in a world which they do not fully understand and in which they ultimately are unable to distinguish fact from fiction, fantasy from reality. The earth spins, and they try frantically to keep themselves from falling off.

Polanski's strengths were also his failings – for which eventually he paid a heavy price. His single-minded determination to succeed brought him wealth and glory... and the very real possibility of irredeemable damnation in the eyes of those who previously had sung his praises to the skies. That he has managed to shrug off even that most outlandish of outcomes and live to tell the tale is a mark of the man.

Roman Polanski set out to be noticed. Some might say that he succeeded too well.

His was, and is, a very Gothic passion.

PROLOGUE

Words light up the screen — white letters on black...

FRIDAY 11 MARCH 1977

An imposing edifice hoves into view, opulence embedded in every stone. It is the Regent Beverly Wilshire Hotel, playground of the stars, and famously situated at 9500 Wilshire Boulevard, Beverly Hills, California. Walking through the foyer towards the entrance in company with a group of friends is Roman Polanski, acclaimed director of *Chinatown* and *Rosemary's Baby*, who has been renting a suite at the hotel for the past several weeks while working on the script of a new film entitled *The First Deadly Sin*.

Polanski has not long returned to America after spending the Christmas holidays in his native Poland, catching up with family and old friends. On this particular evening, he has been invited to the theatre to see Richard Dreyfuss in Erwin Stoff's production of *The Tenth Man*; word on the play is good, but something is nagging at him. He still feels a little uneasy about the outcome of a date on the previous day with a 13-year-old 'wannabe' actress and model named Samantha Jane Gailey, whom he had persuaded to accompany him to actor Jack Nicholson's house in Mulholland Canyon for the purpose of a photo-shoot for a special issue of French *Vogue*. Sensing what he later described to be an 'erotic tension' between them, Polanski had urged drink and a prescription drug on his model before engaging in what he believed was an act of consensual sex.

After driving the girl back to her home in Woodland Hills, Polanski had taken time out to show her mother (and others) a set of slides from the previous shoot. The photos were politely received and favourably commented upon, but their author had noticed a distinct chill in the air as they were being perused. Twenty-four hours later, he remains oblivious to the fact that some gulfs in understanding between East and West are not so easily bridged. (He had shown them shots of Samantha posing topless and had thought nothing of it; her mother, on the other hand, had silently been mortified.) Still, Polanski cannot put his finger on what is troubling him.

Even the drug aspect of the brief liaison is not one which reasonably might inspire cause for concern. Quaaludes (derived from the anti-malarial extract *methaqualone*) were a widely available tranquilliser tab which even teenagers like Samantha were now ingesting with alcohol to 'lude out' and attain a state of drunken euphoria; so widespread was their use, in fact, that they had become second only to marijuana as a depressant 'drug of choice'. No – there could be nothing to worry about in relation to a sexual encounter between consenting parties beside Jack Nicholson's Jacuzzi... Something else must be rotten in the state of Poland. Either that, or he is plagued by a feeling of guilt to which he simply is not prepared consciously to concede. There is a restless mood in the air. A companion asks if he has any Quaalude tabs; he retires to his hotel room to obtain one before rejoining the group.

As he nears the entranceway, Polanski is confronted by a man holding a badge. 'Mr Polanski?' the stranger enquires. Instinctively, Polanski nods. 'LAPD. I have a warrant for your arrest.'

Polanski is taken aback. 'On what charge?' he asks.

The detective pockets his badge. His name is Philip Vannatter; 18 years later, he would feature in another high-profile celebrity court case – that of O J Simpson. He lowers his voice in reply to Polanski's question. 'Statutory rape.'

'Rape...?'

When the enormity of the situation dawns on Polanski, he remembers the Quaalude and tries to dispose of it. A little too obviously. Vannatter takes charge of the evidence. 'I observed Mr Polanski reach into his left coat pocket and remove a small white object that looked to me like a tablet,' the detective was later to testify.

Other detectives appear alongside the first and together they escort Polanski to his room, which is thoroughly searched. While the search is being conducted, the arresting officer reads Polanski his Miranda rights: 'You have the right to remain silent. Anything you say can and will be used against you in a court of law. You have the right to speak to an attorney, and to have an attorney present during any questioning. If you cannot afford a lawyer, one will be provided for you at government expense...'

One of the several officials present introduces himself to Polanski by handing him a business card; he is a deputy District Attorney. A second search warrant covers Jack Nicholson's house in Santa Monica, and Polanski is invited to accompany the police to the scene of the alleged crime.

The search of Nicholson's home, in the reluctant presence of his actress-girlfriend Anjelica Huston, turns up the predictable quantity of recreational drugs. Huston is also arrested. She and Polanski are driven to the West Los Angeles police station, where the director's bail is set at $2500. Polanski pays up and is released to await arraignment.

A new caption:

Los Angeles County Grand Jury hearing, Thursday 24 March 1977

Samantha Gailey is seated in the dock, confused by her sudden celebrity and often visibly upset. Samantha is physically mature for her years but in other respects she is a typical ninth-grader at

Junior High. A voice is heard, softly spoken and patient in tone. It
is that of the deputy District Attorney, Roger Gunsun.

'...*What happened after that?*'

'He started to have intercourse with me.'

'*What do you mean by intercourse?*'

'He placed his penis in my vagina.'

'*What did you say, if anything, before he did that?*'

'I was mostly just on and off saying "no, stop". But I wasn't
fighting really because I, you know, there was no one else there and
I had no place to go.'

'*What did he say, if anything?*'

'He didn't answer me when I said "no." I think he was... he
was saying something, but I wasn't listening to him and I can't
remember...'

The questions become more clinical, each one fading into the
next. Until...

'*Did you resist at that time?*'

'A little bit, but not really because – '

'*Because what?*'

'Because I was afraid of him.'

Freeze-frame.

OFFICE OF DOUGLAS DALTON, ATTORNEY-AT-LAW, FLOWER STREET, LOS ANGELES. FRIDAY 25 MARCH 1977

Polanski sits before an imposing expanse of desk and stares
expectantly at the man who hovers by the window, gazing out at the
urban crawl of downtown LA, 33 floors below; his modest frame
is dwarfed by the desk and the fashionable emptiness of the vast
office in which it resides. The dark-haired Dalton, smart-suited and
sombre in appearance, turns towards his casually-dressed client at
last. 'They've indicted you on six counts of felony,' he says.

Polanski noticeably pales. 'Six...!'

Dalton nods. 'Furnishing a controlled substance to a minor; committing a lewd or lascivious act; having unlawful sexual intercourse; perversion; sodomy; rape by use of drugs.'

Polanski takes a deep breath, shaking his head in disbelief. 'At least we know now what we're up against,' Dalton reassures him. 'And without supporting testimony from Anjelica Huston, placing you in the house and in the room with the Jacuzzi at the time in question, then it could just be the girl's word against yours.'

'When will you know for certain how things are likely to go?' Polanski asks.

Dalton shrugs. 'Couple of days...'

The scene fades as the front pages of several newspapers swirl into view. One in particular holds centre-screen: it is the **Washington Post** *for 26 March 1977.*

POLANSKI INDICTED ON DRUG, RAPE CHARGES

A grand jury has indicted Roman Polanski, director of *Rosemary's Baby* and other macabre movies, on six counts of drugging and raping a 13-year-old girl at actor Jack Nicholson's home. Conviction on the charges lodged Thursday could send Polanski to prison for up to 50 years. Polanski, 43, remained free on $2,000 bail and was given until Tuesday to surrender in Superior Court. Prosecutors said Polanski's attorney told them he would appear before then.'

A phone ringing...

Polanski picks up the receiver. *'Is that Roman?'* The voice is Dalton's. Polanski mumbles an affirmative. *'Bad news, I'm afraid. Huston's been granted immunity from prosecution on the drugs charges if she takes the stand against you... You're to appear before County*

Court Judge Laurence J Rittenband on 15 April, pending trial.'

After further instructions, Dalton rings off. Polanski replaces the receiver. He takes a moment to reflect upon his predicament...

At least until the US opening of *The Tenant* on 11 June 1976, Roman Polanski had been the toast of Hollywood, the king of all he surveyed. While Hitchcock continued to lord it over fellow directors from his suite at Universal, Polanski had been given the biggest, brashest office on the Paramount lot. Projects were his for the picking. But *The Tenant* had not been well received. A deal with Paramount for a new film called *Pirates* (again with Jack Nicholson) had collapsed. His earnings from *Chinatown* had dwindled. Now, he was to be indicted on multiple charges arising from the 'rape' of a minor...

How had it come to this?

In the distance, the sound of marching feet. An army in motion. Jackboots...

1

THE GHETTO

*If we pass all the causes of the German collapse in review, the
ultimate and most decisive remains the failure to recognise the
racial problem and especially the Jewish menace.*

Adolf Hitler, 'Nation and Race', *Mein Kampf Vol 1* (1925)

Roman Polanski had been on the run from authority since
the age of nine.

Born in Paris on 18 August 1933, to émigré Poles
Ryszard and Bula Polanski, the young Raimund (a forename
which his father mistakenly had believed to be French for Roman)
was the second child of the family; Bula had a daughter named
Annette from a previous marriage. Somewhere along the way, his
father had taken the name Polanski in place of his real surname
of Liebling and, for the first six years of his life, little Raimund
(who much preferred Roman, or the affectionate diminutive
'Romek') led what seemed to him to be a carefree and untroubled
existence.

Polanski's father was Jewish – his mother part-Jewish, of Russian
Catholic descent – and unknown to the boy at the time, being born
a Jew in Europe during the 1930s was tantamount to having had
a death-sentence passed on one at birth by some invisible but all-
powerful court.

1933 had turned out to be a pivotal year in the history of the
world. On 30 January, a 44-year-old Austrian-born ex-soldier and
failed commercial artist named Adolf Hitler had been installed as
Chancellor of Germany. Hitler was a holder of the Iron Cross for

valour in battle; he was a rousing and persuasive orator, whose
rise to power had taken ten long years and cost him his liberty
for six months on a charge of treason. He was also quite mad.
His methods had become increasingly brutal, and dissent in the
ranks or opposition to his particular brand of visionary leadership
was ruthlessly quelled by a private army of brown-shirted thugs
known as the SA, or *Sturmabteilung*, led by Ernst Roehm. Less than
a month after Hitler's investiture as Chancellor, the Reichstag,
Germany's parliament building, was set ablaze. Hitler's National
Socialists – *Nazis* for short – blamed the fire on Communist
insurgents, and by 23 March he had persuaded Germany's ailing
President Hindenburg to sign the Enabling Act, which granted his
new Chancellor full dictatorial authority for an initial period of four
years. 'You are now witnessing the beginning of a great epoch in
German history,' Hitler had informed a reporter while watching the
Reichstag burn. 'This fire is the beginning.'

Never a truer word. On 18 August, the day of Roman's birth,
Hitler's new Minister for Enlightenment and Propaganda, Joseph
Goebbels, opened the tenth German Radio Exhibition with the
following declaration: 'A government that has determined to bring
a nation together so that it is once more a centre of power in the
scales of great world events has not only the right, but the duty,
to subordinate all aspects of the nation to its goals, or at least
ensure that they are supportive. It is our dearest wish that science,
industry and the intellectual leadership of German radio from now
on will follow a new path, at the end of which stands our common,
great goal: One People, one Reich, one Will, and a glorious German
future!'

To this end, the Nazi Party had set about two parallel courses of
action: to secretly subvert the constraints of the Treaty of Versailles
and re-arm Germany in readiness for a war of expansion in Europe,
and to seize control of the country's domestic agenda in accordance
with the precepts which the Aryan philosopher in Hitler had
established in his political 'Bible', *Mein Kampf* – ghost-written for

him by the diligent Rudolf Hess while *der Führer* languished in his Landsberg Castle prison.

Mein Kampf ('My Struggle') was in part influenced by the anti-Semitic rantings of American car manufacturer Henry Ford, who believed that the world was under threat from an international Jewish conspiracy. Hitler had begun wholeheartedly to embrace a warped geopolitical outlook which seemed to him to pinpoint the source of the travails under which Germany currently suffered; despite the fact that Jews represented a mere one per cent of the population, *Mein Kampf* postulated the idea that they held disproportionate sway over the country's social and economic affairs, being over-represented in the arts, business and in the make-up of the German Social Democratic Party in particular. Now enabled to put his theories into practice, Chancellor Hitler passed the Nuremberg Laws in September 1935, which stripped German Jews of their citizenship and thus removed them from legal protection.

Sensing the way in which the wind was blowing, Ryszard Polanksi decided that the safest course of action might be for the family to return to their homeland of Poland. In 1937, they did just that, renting a third-floor apartment in a quiet residential street in Krakow, the second city and ancient capital of the country, before it was superseded by Warsaw in 1596. In Germany itself, more affluent Jews had chosen different routes to freedom from potential persecution – many of them emigrating to the United States; among their number were celebrated artists like Thomas Mann, Fritz Lang, Marlene Dietrich, Otto Klemperer and Kurt Weill, as well as psychologist Sigmund Freud and physicist Albert Einstein, who already was ensconced in a post at New Jersey's Princeton University in 1933 before he opted to remain and apply for permanent residency (granted to him in 1935).

By the summer of 1939, the Polanskis had exchanged their Komorowski Street flat in Krakow for a low-rent hideout in Warsaw, some 160 miles further to the north of the border between Poland

and Czechoslovakia (which effectively had fallen into German hands in March) and where Polanski's father felt they would be safer still. But Hitler's armies were now on the march. The Nazi-Soviet Pact of August that year cleared the way for an invasion of Poland. It came on 1 September. Warsaw was bombarded by a force of more than two thousand tanks and a thousand warplanes. The city fell on 28 September, but Britain and France had already decreed their intent to stand by a joint guarantee of Poland's sovereignty. On 3 September, that decree had become a declaration: war in Europe was underway.

Within a month of the invasion, German-occupied Poland was made a protectorate and placed under the control of a civilian 'governor-general' – Nazi Party official Hans Frank – who set up his administration in Wawel Castle in Krakow. Having been forced to flee Warsaw in the meanwhile, the Polanskis had also found themselves once more in Krakow. For a time, it seemed to the young Roman that life for the family was returned to a semblance of normality. However, the outlook was not good: his sister and parents were now required to wear a white armband, emblazoned with the blue Star of David (as were all Jews over the age of 12).

In the Poland of 1939, there were some 60,000 Jews in Krakow alone, out of a total population of almost a quarter of a million; many were settled in Kazimierz, the Jewish Quarter of the city, but as many again lived and worked throughout. With the German army in full control, Frank announced his intention to 'cleanse' Krakow of Jews and, in May 1940, the Nazis commenced a programme of forced 'resettlement'. The Polanskis were moved to a ground-floor apartment in Podgorze Square, to the south of the city, which they had to share with three other families in accordance with the new regulations. One day, Annette Polanski beckoned her stepbrother to the window – a window which until then had looked out onto a quiet street and tree-lined square. Workmen were there, and they appeared to be building some sort of barricade. 'Suddenly it dawned on me: they were walling us in,' Polanski recalled. 'My

Krakow Ghetto

Kazimierz

The Polanskis' apartment block in the Ghetto

Vistula River

Plac Zgody

— *Wall*
— *Gate*
● *German police*
1. *Gate*
2. *Ghetto police station*
3. *Judenrat*
4. *Hospital*
5. *Church*

Rynek Podgorski

Limanowskiego

Rekawka

Podgorze

heart sank; I couldn't stop crying. This was our first real sign that the Germans meant business...' The business they meant was the 'ghettoisation' of Krakow, and it began on 3 March 1941.

In its final form, the Krakow Ghetto covered an area of less than 50 acres; it was comprised of 15 streets and 320 houses, with an available living-space of 3,167 rooms. Windows and doors which previously had faced onto the parts of the city that now lay outside the ghetto perimeter were bricked up to form a 'wall'. Barbed wire was used to cross open roads and four entrances were created, at which armed guards were posted. Into this city-within-a-city were now to be squeezed 15,000 'working' Jews, along with their families, where a mere 3,000 inhabitants had resided before.

The ghetto swarmed with vermin, and nothing could be done about it. The clothing of people you passed in the street was infested with lice, and so were the interiors of trams and shops. Lice crawled over the pavements, up stairways, and dropped from the ceilings of the public offices that had to be visited on so many different kinds of business. Lice found their way into the folds of your newspaper, into your small change; there were even lice on the crust of the loaf you had just bought. And each of these verminous creatures could carry typhus.

Wladislaw Szpilman (writing about the Warsaw Ghetto), *The Pianist* (1946)

The adaptability of human beings is infinite and, once again, when the initial shock of upheaval subsided, life for the Polanskis returned to a new sort of routine. As he was of smaller-than-average build for his age, Roman was able to wander in and out of the Ghetto at will, using a number of breaks in the perimeter fencing. He was thus at liberty to lead something of a normal 'boy's life', exploring his grim surroundings, playing in the militarised streets – though by this juncture, he had been excluded from his former school. But a new emotion had intruded to keep him awake at night: fear. At first, it was intangible and non-specific but, by 1942, it had taken on a form which was all too real. The ghettoising of Krakow's Jews had been only the beginning: the true horror of their situation was now revealed.

Within a year of the establishment of the Ghetto, the Nazis commenced the forced deportation of its inhabitants. In March, some 4,000 Jews were summarily rounded up and led to Plaszow railway station, where they were sent by train to be gassed at the Belzec death-camp, which had opened for business on the 17th as part of Himmler's 'Operation Reinhard'. Belzec had three gas chambers initially, but with the numbers of Jews now expected to arrive from Krakow, the facility was quickly expanded to incorporate six (catering for a thousand people at a time). These first victims were told that they were being shipped out to labour-camps in the Ukraine; some died in transit, many more were simply shot in the streets on the way to the trains. (Belzec was closed down at the end of 1942 – by which time it had exterminated all the Jews in its designated area: a total of 434,508.)

In the circumstances, it was not long before the Krakow Ghetto came alive with rumours about the real intentions of the occupying Nazis. Ryszard Polanski felt that he could do little to save himself or his wife – or even his stepdaughter – all of whom had been appropriately arm-banded and branded as Jews. But he could try to save his son. Accordingly, he had used what remained of his life-savings to bribe a Catholic family to take Roman in with them when the time came, or to find others who were equally willing to do so. The plan had been set in motion; the Wilks were ready and waiting.

On 28 October, a further 4,500 Jews were deported. Six hundred more were killed where they stood. The children from a local orphanage were assembled and shot, along with their teachers and carers. Jews who had thought themselves 'privileged' by virtue of the occupations which had been allocated them were chosen as randomly as the rest. There no longer was doubt in anyone's mind: the Nazis not only meant business, they meant death.

As the population of the Ghetto diminished, so did the Ghetto itself. Buildings were reduced to rubble as they were emptied of their inhabitants and 'walls' moved back, to ominous and imminent purpose. Like a noose of bricks and mortar, the Krakow Ghetto was tightening around the necks of its residents. Where once the Polanskis' apartment had opened out onto Rekawka Street, it was now outside the new perimeter and thus off-limits. Consequently, the family was moved again. During this final phase of the operation, all pretence at resettlement or deportation on behalf of the Ghetto's masters was abandoned; it was allowed to descend into a slum. Food and water were in short supply, and the few thousand Jews who remained were deprived of the means of conducting even a semblance of normal life. All the victims could do was await the fate which inevitably was to be theirs. By the end of 1942, some 13,000 Jews had been forcibly removed from the Ghetto – their last sight of Krakow being assembly points at the Plac Zgody or outside the Optima factory to the south. The more fortunate among them had been picked to work at the Plaszow factories of Oskar Schindler, but most had been sent to Belzec. Some were sent to Auschwitz-Birkenau.

Birkenau was the second of three camps at the Auschwitz complex at Oswiecim, in Upper Silesia, which itself had been established in May 1940. Birkenau was built as an extermination camp, four miles from the main unit, and outfitted with Zyklon B poison gas, which was faster-acting than the carbon monoxide that had been utilised at Belzec. There were seven gas-chambers distributed across the sites, as well as three crematoria, and up to 2.5 million Jews, Gypsies and Russian POWs are thought to have been killed at the Auschwitz camps during the term of their operations. For as long as the deception could be maintained, those to be gassed were informed that they were merely about to shower, and gas-taps were fitted with shower-heads to reinforce the illusion. (In 1944, Birkenau was to become the greatest mass-murder arena of all time, with the killing of 585,000 Jews inside nine months.) At the turn of 1943, the SS was actively planning to extend the facilities at Auschwitz to slaughter Jews, prisoners and other undesirables in even greater numbers.

> *The rumours say that thirty thousand Jews are to be taken from the ghetto this week and sent east somewhere. In spite of all the secrecy, people say they know what happens then: somewhere near Lublin, buildings have been constructed with rooms that can be electrically heated by heavy current, like the electricity in a crematorium. Unfortunate people are driven into these heated rooms and burnt alive, and thousands can be killed like that in a day, saving all the trouble of shooting them, digging mass graves and then filling them in. The guillotine of the French Revolution can't compete, and even in the cellars of the Russian secret police they haven't devised such virtuoso methods of mass slaughter.*
>
> *But surely this is madness. It can't be possible. You wonder why the Jews don't defend themselves. However, many, indeed most of*

them, are so weak from starvation and misery that they couldn't
offer any resistance.

Captain Wilm Hosenfeld (diary entry), *The Pianist* (1946)

Aware that the end was near – that it could, in fact, come at any moment – Roman's parents had conducted several dry-runs in respect of their now nine-year-old son. Each time a deportation was announced, or was rumoured to be imminent, Roman had been despatched to the Wilks through a hole in the perimeter fencing. Before 1943, all these excursions had proved to be false alarms. But at the turn of the year, and with the Jews in the Ghetto reduced to a relative handful, Roman returned from his latest evacuation to be met by his father, weeping uncontrollably. His mother was gone.

The former Bula Katz, the mother whom Roman now was able to remember only through 'the sound of her voice, her elegance' and 'the precise way she drew thin lines over her plucked eyebrows' (there were no photographs), had been transported to the women's camp at Auschwitz-Birkenau, where she became one of the 105,000 Jews murdered between January and March.

On 13 March 1943, the order was given to liquidate what remained of the Krakow Ghetto. Under the personal direction of SS *Sturmbannführer* Willi Haase, the last few Jews were to be rounded up for deportation to Auschwitz or Plaszow. After the loss of his wife, Ryszard Polanski lost no time in readying his son for a final trip to the Wilks. This time, there was to be no coming back. With little by way of farewell, Roman was unceremoniously bundled through the hole in the fence at Plac Zgody. The next day, in his guise as 'Roman Wilk', the befuddled boy was able to watch from a distance as his father was frog-marched to a cattle-train destined for the forced-labour camp at Plaszow. 'Being without food or clothing, being cold – these things are all immaterial to a child,' he later recalled. 'Being separated from your parents is intolerable.'

For the pseudonymously-adopted Roman, now lost and alone in a hostile world, the only escape from harsh reality was provided by the cinema. While nightmare raged in the streets beyond its walls, the latest addition to the Wilks household spent every *zloty* he could muster in the Palace of Dreams, or what passed for it in Poland in wartime: crude propaganda films projected onto the walls of public buildings. Without realising it as yet, he had borne silent witness to the greatest crime of the 20th century, maybe even the history of the world, but all he knew was the pain of loss – of a mother, father, sister and grandmother Maria, uncles and aunts, friends and former school chums. All were gone from his life, and there was no way of telling when, or if, any of them would ever be coming back.

'Only swine go to the movies'

Roman Wilk dulled that pain with celluloid. He had first become acquainted with the movies through the vocal charms of Hollywood songstress Jeanette MacDonald in Paris, in 1937, as she serenaded him in *The Firefly*. Through the medium of film – even bad German films – Roman found a way to detach himself from the cruelties of life outside the theatre walls, even if only for a few hours. When the last reel cleared the projector-gate and the house-lights came up and he was returned once more to the desolate, war-torn streets of Krakow, he could replay the adventure in his mind's eye, become part of it, mould and reshape it to his heart's desire. The cinema took him to faraway places; it sang of love and kindness and happy endings; it revealed to him the world of should-have-been and someday, maybe, could be again. To Roman, at the most impressionable age of his entire life, it was more than an entertainment: it was a friend, a parent, a benefactor. The images which flickered over his retina floated deep into his subconscious, inspiring him and holding out the promise of a better tomorrow. Without even realising it, he had stumbled inadvertently upon the love of his life. All he had to do now was to find her.

Sublimating his feelings and retreating into the dark of his imagination as a way of escaping the horrors around him was not without price, however, and the psychological armour in which Roman wrapped himself to numb the pain and protect himself from harm was eventually to leave him emotionally cold. Even before he reached adolescence, he felt that life had dealt him a bitter blow: he had been wrenched from the bosom of his family, he was an outcast among his fellows because of his creed, and he was slight of build and of smaller-than-average stature – an accident of birth which often subjected him to the ridicule of his peers. 'I was not like those around me: I inhabited a separate make-believe world of my own,' he confessed. 'There were times when the obstacles in my path were such that I needed all the fantasy I could muster, just to survive.'

In the meantime, he began to collect the ephemera of the movies – photos, posters, souvenir programmes – as a way of extending his new hobby beyond the regulation three hours spent in the dark on the average double-feature. With nothing else to distract him from the prosecution of his own survival, it soon became a ruling passion, despite the fact that implicitly he was slandered as a treacherous recidivist by the sloganeering which the Polish resistance daubed on the walls of Krakow's few remaining cinemas – *Tylko swinie siedza w kinie!* ('Only swine go to the movies'). His growing treasure-trove of memorabilia gave his life focus, kept him sane, allowed him to endure.

Soon, even the city became too dangerous for Roman's protectors and he had to be despatched further afield – to austerity in the country.

> *I was weak and cold and hungry. I had no idea what to do or where to go. My parents were still not there.*
>
> *I trembled and vomited. I had to find people. I had to go to the village.*
>
> *I limped on my bruised feet and legs, cautiously making my way over the yellowing autumn grass towards the distant village.*
>
> **Jerzy Kosinski**, *The Painted Bird* (1965)

For two long years, Roman toiled under another identity in the homes of relative strangers – first in the city, then in the bleak but wondrous countryside in the foothills of the Tatra mountains. While the poor farming folk with whom he struggled to eke out a living accepted him unquestioningly and in a spirit of Christian charity, he nevertheless was often deprived of food (as were they!), as well as the warmth of human companionship. 'I felt that no one wanted me, that there was no reason for things ever to change,' he recalled. If his situation had a saving grace, it was the knowledge that he was not alone. Indeed, many of his peers were a good deal worse off than he.

The turning-point of the war in Poland came in August 1944, in Warsaw, when the underground 'Home Army', buoyed by promises of support from the Russian military (which had been advancing on Warsaw since the start of its counter-offensive in June), staged an armed insurrection against the weak German garrisons in the city. A total of 20,000 AK (Home Army) soldiers led what came to be known as the Warsaw Rising, the most concerted effort by underground forces to resist the might of Nazi Germany in the whole of the Second World War.

Soviet premier Joseph Stalin's plans for post-war Poland differed from those of the AK, however, which supported the Polish government currently in exile in London. The Red Army temporarily halted its advance on Warsaw, the British found themselves unable to assist due, in part, to the vacillations of Roosevelt and the duplicitous stand of the US administration in general, and the brave resistance fighters of the AK were left to their fates. The Poles surrendered on 2 October, after 63 days of intense bombardment. Nine-tenths of the city of Warsaw was reduced to rubble by the victorious Germans and its remaining inhabitants were deported. But the courageous stand of the Home Army was not entirely in vain; the uprising spelled the beginning of the end for Nazi occupation. By March 1945, the last remnants of the German army were being expelled from Poland by a reinvigorated Soviet advance.

As the Red Army moved, dishevelled and disorganised, through Poland, so Roman finally was able to return to Krakow from his hiding place in the country. In May, the 11th armoured division of the United States army liberated Mauthausen forced labour camp near Linz in Austria; 15,000 bodies were discovered in mass graves, but inmate Ryszard Polanski turned out not to be one of them. In a matter of weeks, Roman was safely reunited with his father, step-sister, and numerous uncles and aunts, all of whom had managed miraculously to survive internment by the Nazis, though life for many of them would never be the same again. The next few years were a time of reconciliation and remembrance. He had lost his mother; in some ways, he had lost his father also, Ryszard having taken up with a red-head named Wanda Zajaczkowska, of whom his son could not find it in his heart to approve. The feeling was mutual and, despite the years of separation, the two sides agreed to live apart. One thing that Roman determined not to lose was his passion for cinema. 'I became more sophisticated after the war when I was 12 or 13, when I could see Russian, American and French films: I used to go every day,' he said.

Poland had now come under the yoke of its Russian liberators: theirs was a milder form of tyranny than before, though it was no less authoritarian in its advancement of Stalinist ideals. The arts, in particular, were subject to strict State controls, and cinema was viewed as a potent weapon in the propaganda war between East and West. World war may have been over, but the chill of a new 'Cold' war was about to begin.

*　　*　　*

Roman resumed formal schooling, though he was largely a dissolute pupil. His real interest, which had been awakened in him during a summer camp with the Boy Scouts, was acting. In no time, through the sheer self-confidence which had been forged in him from having to make his own way in life from an early age, he was hired to feature on radio in a children's adventure series called *The Merry*

Gang. His father having remarried, Roman was in quarters of his own and free to travel to wherever fate – and his new-found career as an actor – were to lead him. In the summer of 1949, however, while he was still only 15 years old, fate was almost deprived of the chance of leading him any further afield than Krakow.

Enticed by the black-market price of a new bicycle with which he could pursue his love of cycling, Roman fell into the hands of one Janusz Dziuba. Unknown to his trusting client, Dziuba was a thief and a murderer and, having lured the boy to an out-of-the-way place to conduct the transaction, he proceeded to beat him unconscious with a brick and steal his money and belongings. Roman managed somehow to survive this encounter, but a hairline fracture of the skull was to remind him of his brush with mortality. Dzubia was later arrested and eventually hanged for the many similar crimes which he had committed, most of whose victims experienced less fortunate outcomes. Roman had seen violence on a national scale; now he had been exposed to it on a more personal level. The scars from his near-fatal rendezvous with Dziuba were to remain with him for the rest of his life, and the impact of them would filter through into his art, as well.

Roman's Bohemian bent and talent for drawing soon had him enrolled as a pupil at Krakow's School of Fine Arts, though his acting career was to continue unabated. One audition landed him at the Film School in Lodz, some 80 miles west of Warsaw, where he happened upon 26-year-old Andrzej Wajda, presently kicking his heels as a trainee director but soon to become one of the greatest filmmakers of his day and a pioneer of the new Polish cinema. At this point in his apprenticeship, Wajda had managed a mere three shorts as a director but he had co-written a screenplay called *Three Stories* (*Trzy opowiesci*), one of whose segments required Roman to play Genek – 'The Little'. In the breaks between scenes, Wajda took the budding actor under his wing. It was to prove a fortuitous friendship; it was also to open Roman's eyes to the creative side of filmmaking.

By the summer of 1952, Roman had reached the age where he automatically would be conscripted into military service unless the excuse of 'reserved occupation' could be brought into play. Having decided instead to 'dodge' the draft (long before the concept became universally popular), he at first had thought to flee to the West – but his plans in that regard had come to nought. Just as it began to look as though there was to be no way around the call-up, fate – and his brief friendship with Wajda – intervened: a phone call came from Warsaw informing him that Wajda, now working on propaganda projects for Poland's Soviet masters, was about to embark on a new full-length feature entitled *A Generation* (*Pokolenie*), and there was to be a part in it for Roman. He packed his bags, tore up his draft-papers, and took his first real steps into the world of film.

A Generation was a tale of the Polish resistance as seen through the eyes of Stach (Tadeusz Lomnicki), an idealistic young factory worker in the Warsaw of 1942, who is inducted into the rebel underground by Sekula (Janusz Paluszkiewicz) after falling for the siren-like charms of Communist Party agitator Dorota (Urszula Modrzynska). The film is elegantly photographed and excitingly staged in authentic locations, and it was to be the first instalment of what eventually would become a trilogy for Wajda, the two other parts of which were the more celebrated *Kanal* (1957) and *Ashes and Diamonds* (*Popiol i diament*, 1958). As with similar low-budget productions in the West, austerity after the war decreed the use of out-of-date, army-surplus film stock, whose heightened contrast gave *A Generation* a stark, naturalistic look. Moody, impenetrable blacks went to show that *films noir* were not so named solely because of their subject-matter, while over-stopped, sun-bleached exteriors conversely came to symbolise the harsher light of the new, post-conflict day.

'That was my first contact with serious cinema,' Polanski told *Films and Filming*'s Gordon Gow. 'It was a group of young people; the whole crew were young people, mostly from the film school ... *A Generation* was a great picture, especially when you compare it to other Polish films made during, or before, that time. It was a tremendous step forward.'

Polanski was Mundek, the smallest and youngest of a quintet of would-be freedom fighters, whose anti-Nazi plans are confounded by the conflict between Stach and the more headstrong Jacek (Ryszard Kotas). In consequence, their planned attack against a troop contingent goes disastrously wrong, and Jacek is forced to flee from a posse of soldiers. He makes it into an apartment block with his pursuers at his heels, but as he reaches the top floor of the building, entry to the one door that remains to him is barred by a lock. He turns to face the advancing soldiers, gun in hand and suddenly cognisant of the futility of his position, and in his expression – for no more than an instant – is the realisation that he will not now see the end of a day which, until that moment, had seemed like any other. In Jacek's expression can be glimpsed a fleeting acceptance of that bitter irony, before he hurls himself down the stairwell in a final act of defiance. The power of *A Generation* comes from its ability to convey the horrors of war in microcosm, by focusing on its effects on a handful of individuals, and it contained lessons in narrative irony which its 'littlest rebel' was not to forget.

Not only was *A Generation* a prime example of modern, neo-realist filmmaking at its most human and involving, it was a breakthrough production for Poland's fledgling (albeit Party-funded) national film industry. The 83-minute feature was released in its homeland on 26 January 1955, and took up to a decade to be seen in other parts of the world – but invariably it was to critical acclamation. The review in the UK trade-paper *Daily Cinema* for June 1960 was typical of its reception abroad: 'Most films about the resistance seem trite, compared with the savagery of this picture. It achieves an almost news-like quality in its portrayal of an oppressed people fighting back. Some of the scenes – a youngster killing a Nazi with near lustful glee or a grim chase in a factory – have a terrifying, compulsive authenticity.'

Despite a new-found desire to make films as well as appear in them, Polanski never thought to sideline his budding career as an actor – now or later. He was to show up in another seven films before the end of the decade, including a return outing for Andrzej Wajda: *Innocent Sorcerers* (*Niewinni czarodzieje*, 1960). He continued to see acting as the first string on his bow, but a second, more technical string made increasing sense in a world which encouraged diversity. He decided to go back to 'school'.

In the summer of 1954, Roman Polanski was accepted for enrolment at Lodz. To a film buff with ambitions in the field, the five-year degree course at Lodz was like being given the key to Aladdin's cave. Empowered by Lenin's maxim that 'the cinema is the most important of all art forms,' Poland's National Film School wanted for nothing. At a time of severe deprivation in all other aspects of daily life, it was 'lavishly equipped,' according to its newest recruit, and featured 'two projection rooms, photographic labs, cutting rooms, sound recording facilities, a library, lecture rooms, a canteen, and, last but not least, a bar.' There were student dormitories in addition, as well as facilities for social gatherings, and the whole was situated in a 19th century mansion which sat amid extensive grounds and which had been commandeered by the state in 1948 to fulfil its crucial role in Lenin's personal manifesto.

'Lodz was a dump,' Polanski opined about the heavily-industrialised location of the school, but Lodz was the only Polish town of substance which had managed to survive the war relatively unscathed. It already was home to the Film Polski studios, so it was a natural choice to serve as home to the Film School – an essential tool of the totalitarian state. Despite the fact that the school was established as a propagandist mouthpiece for Marxist-Leninist philosophy, a new mood was abroad in artistic circles the world over and the Lodz school, with its doctrinaire belief in the value of film as art, its unfettered access to (strictly 35mm) equipment and its permissive social regime, became a hotbed of creative diversity and pro-Western ideals.

As though to exemplify Jung's theory about the collective
unconscious, filmmakers across the globe were tapping into a new
wave of artistic energy; Italy had Fellini and De Sica, France had
Godard and Resnais, Sweden had Bergman. England, too, was
about to abandon its imperial Ealing past and join the revolution
in cinéma vérité. In the Film School at Lodz, in 1955, Poland was
nurturing its own sons of celluloid. Principal among them was
Andrzej Wajda.

Wajda's films, of which *A Generation* was the front-runner,
helped to establish the tradition of a new and vibrant European
cinema born out of necessity and the ravages of war – one which
was politically aware, psychologically mature and wholly devoid
of Hollywood heroics. Over the next two decades, Wajda protégé
Roman Polanski would take that cinema to the very heart of
Hollywood itself.

EXPERiMENTS iN CiNEMA

While we were making A Generation, *Polanski suddenly found himself amongst the people he wanted to be amongst – those he wanted to make himself known. He wanted desperately to show us who he was, and here I must add: Polanski was particularly well-prepared for the directing profession...*

Andrzej Wajda, *'A Ticket to the West'* (2003)

O nce Polanski settled into the National Film School at Lodz, his world became a richer and more amenable place. Apart from the fact that he was working in the profession which he now had decided to make his career, there were parties and there were girls – while the propensity for youthful anarchy among the students at large was every bit the equal of their counterparts in the West, despite the hard-line Communist regime under which the school had been founded.

Since the 5 March 1953 death (allegedly by poisoning) of long-serving Russian Communist Party Chairman Josef Stalin, there had been a relaxation in the Soviet grip on Poland and its peoples felt themselves able to breathe more easily. Western culture was still frowned upon with respect to the masses, but access to it was not prohibited for intellectuals; the well-stocked film library at Lodz was a case in point. 'Films were our meat and drink,' Polanski said of his first years at the school. 'We gorged ourselves on the great classics, which were shown again and again, discussing, analysing, criticising them ad infinitum. We used to see films that nobody else in Poland could see at that time, and we admired them secretly.'

There also was a less savoury side to the young Polanski, which was characterised in an interview by Jerzy Kosinski, Polish author of *The Painted Bird* and *Being There*, as 'a gift for arrogance'. Henryk Kluba, a friend from Lodz who later was to feature in several of Polanski's student films, went further with biographer John Parker: 'As a person, [he] was unbearable. First of all, he would talk very loudly; it was part of his character. He always had to be number one ... He had this need to excel in everything. He was very sure of himself. But that constant quest to be top of the class didn't win him any friends, rather the opposite. Many people couldn't stand him ... he was always involved in fights.'

Their imaginations nourished on the works of cinema greats like Orson Welles and Luis Buñuel, the students at Lodz were soon afforded the opportunity to embark upon film projects of their own. The standard advice offered to budding writers is to draw on experience. When Polanski first came to script a film with a view to directing it himself (albeit one which he initiated without authority), he chose as his subject his encounter with the murderer Janusc Dziuba. Entitled *The Bicycle* (*Rower*), this unfinished short was intended to be photographed in colour. Due to a mix-up at the Film Polski developing lab in Warsaw, only part of the footage that Polanski shot for *The Bicycle* ever saw the light of day – that, too, has since been lost. It was an inauspicious start to his directorial career, but as *The Bicycle* was initiated as an extracurricular activity, his progress towards a diploma was unaffected by its ultimate disappearance.

Polanski's next two films were 'set' subjects. *Murder* (*Morderstwo*) and *The Smile* (*Vsmiechze biczmy*) lasted all of one and two minutes respectively. The first bowed to Hitchcock in its idiosyncratic employment of a protagonist with a walking-stick:

A door opens slowly, and a dark figure enters the room and crosses to where a man lies asleep on a bed; he unclasps a pen-knife and positions it over the man's chest; with the palm of his free hand, he pushes the knife home. The sleeper writhes in agony but his screams are stilled by a hand placed over his mouth; blood trickles down the man's arm as the assassin returns the way that he came... The point of *Murder* was simple: it set out to shock – as Luis Buñuel's surreal masterpiece *Un Chien andalou* had set out to shock in 1929, with its shot of a razor slicing through a woman's eye (in reality, the eye of a pig). In terms of filmmaking technique, it is crude and perfunctory, flatly lit and jarringly edited, but its brief moment of violence is sufficiently visceral to counter any shortcomings in craft.

The Smile is technically more adept, as well as representing a more unified whole: a well-dressed gentleman (Nikola Todorow, a student cameraman at Lodz) descends the stairs of an apartment block. Through an open window, he spies a woman undressing in her bathroom. His momentary gloating is interrupted when her husband appears at the door; he turns to go. When the man retreats into the apartment, he steals back to the window. But his gaze falls instead upon the husband, who is now engaged in cleaning his teeth. The crestfallen voyeur slinks away.

After Soviet premier Kruschev's denunciation of Stalin as an 'enemy of the people' in 1956, a further thaw in relations with Poland brought about an easing of restrictions which now enabled Poles who had relatives abroad to apply for passports in order to visit them. Polanski's sister Annette was resident with her husband in Paris; accordingly, he was granted permission to see her there. Polanski made sure that his trip coincided with the Cannes Film Festival and, in March 1957, he turned up unannounced at the Hôtel Martinez and asked for Andrzej Wajda, whose second film, *Kanal*, was being shown in competition. Wajda added to his young visitor's growing film education by inviting him to a screening of Ingmar Bergman's *The Seventh Seal*. By the time he returned to Lodz, Polanski had also been exposed to the 'Method' acting style of Marlon Brando and the recently deceased James Dean, neither of whose films had yet been released in his homeland.

Invigorated by his first taste of foreign travel, and brimming with ideas inspired by the French trend for cinéma vérité, Polanski's next cinematic endeavour was *Breaking Up the Party* (*Rozbijemy zabawe*) – a more ambitious eight-minute featurette which he shot in the summer of 1957, with most of his school-year drafted in to help. As an example of documentary, *Breaking Up the Party* – in which a dance is disrupted by gatecrashers – was an abject failure, partly because Polanski contrived the events which his camera was meant to be witnessing for real, and because the 'staged' scenes were let down by the undisciplined montage of the footage that he captured ad hoc. He had hired a gang of local hooligans to disrupt the proceedings as they saw fit, with unpredicted results: 'No sooner were they over the wall than they started throwing punches, wrenching girls away from their partners, pushing students into the pond,' he recalled. 'My single camera crew struggled to shoot as much of this concentrated action as they could, barely managing to get enough footage before the dance turned into a shambles.'

An experimental short followed: *Two Men and a Wardrobe* (*Dwaj iudzie z szafa*) was a more ambitious blend of surrealism and satire, in which two men surface from the sea carrying the titular item of furniture. The allegory is one of alienation, and the landscape through which the men wander for the next 14 minutes is one of disinterest and deceit. Moments of Keatonesque humour alternate with random acts of violence, such as when a gang of youths (Polanski among them) stone a kitten to death; beatings follow, including those of the two men. As they return to the sea, they pass a small boy building an infinite number of castles in the sand. *Two Men and a Wardrobe* begins on a jocular note but the bleakness of its overall vision, and the constant intrusion of violence, ultimately makes for uneasy viewing. The film had an added advantage in that Polanski managed to persuade eminent Polish jazz pianist and composer Krzysztof Komeda to furnish it with a musical score. It was the first, but it would not be the last that Komeda was to provide for the diminutive director.

Polanski's demanding nature as an auteur was evident from the start, and it took its toll on the most compliant of (unpaid) performers. Even for a production as small-scale as *Two Men and a Wardrobe*, Polanski managed to stretch a ten-day shooting schedule to more than three weeks: 'At first, the atmosphere hummed with enthusiasm. Little by little, however, my principals got sick of toting a wardrobe around. Both had other commitments and were eager to get away.' The men in question were Kuba Goldberg and the aforementioned Henryk Kluba, and filming was at Sopot, a fashionable resort near Gdansk.

Despite the problems, *Two Men and a Wardrobe* won a bronze medal for Polanski at the 1958 Brussels World Fair. 'I was listening to the radio when the news came through,' he said. 'The gold medal had gone to an animation film made by two Polish graphic artists. The bronze, said the announcer, "has been awarded to R Polanski, a student at Lodz Film School."' In consequence, it became the first 'school short' to be commercially released in Poland.

In the meantime, Polanski had been given a leave of absence from Lodz to travel to Brussels to collect his award for *Two Men and a Wardrobe*. He organised the trip to include a detour to Paris, where a mutual friend introduced him to a 17-year-old Polish actress named Barbara Kwiatkowska. 'Basia', as she preferred to be called, had just appeared in her first starring role in a film called *Eve Wants to Sleep* (*Ewa chce spac*). Eighteen months later, on 9 September 1959, she was to become Polanski's wife. At that time, he would be 26 and she 19. But as 1958 drew to a close, two more shorts were required of him to bring his technical course to an end.

His next student film – *The Lamp* – was another failure, to the extent that Polanski declines to mention it in his autobiography. *The Lamp* is an exercise in irony, in which a Gepetto-like doll-maker swaps his trusty oil-lamp for a new-fangled electric light and burns his shop to the ground. But there are some interesting ideas in play, such as the clash between hi-tech modernism and the romantic tradition. The final scene, in which the camera tracks back from the shop-front as passers-by (including Polanski) go about their business oblivious to the inferno raging within, is so Hitchcockian in concept that the maestro was to use it himself in *Frenzy* (1971).

While there is a lot going on in *The Lamp*, it is technically inept and its ambition is betrayed by poor execution. Polanski's mind was elsewhere when he was making the film, and its interminable shots of dolls lying idly on shelves revealed a weakness in his cinematic abilities: he had a strong visual sense, but he was sorely in need of an editor and a writing partner with whom he could collaborate more effectively on a narrative level. His tutors at Lodz arrived at a similar conclusion. *The Lamp* was quickly glossed over and he turned his attention instead to his final 'diploma' film.

When Angels Fall (*Gdy spadaja anioly*) was a much more professional production, complete with costumes, special effects, location shooting, an intricate studio set and a cast of ... dozens. At 21 minutes, or three times the length of *The Lamp*, it focuses on the last hours of an old woman whose job is that of attendant in a public lavatory. She sits in her subterranean world as 'customers' come and go, and feet walk to and fro on the skylight overhead, in shades of Hitchcock's *The Lodger*. As the woman recollects in flashback the incidents of her tragic life, the film switches to colour, like *The Wizard of Oz*. At length, an angel in the form of her dead son descends from the grating above, to spirit her off to Heaven as snowflakes fall gently around them.

'In need of an elaborate Art Deco set, I approached a Krakow Academy student, Kazimierz Wisniak, whose work I knew and admired. Together we designed the public lavatory for *When Angels Fall*, moulded its fin de siècle ceramic urinals in plaster, and assembled it on the school's sound stage,' Polanski explained. 'Modelled on a lavatory in one of Krakow's historic squares, it had a roof of frosted glass tiles, set flush with the sidewalk, through which those inside could glimpse the tide of humanity flowing overhead, the shadows of anonymous feet coming and going.'

New love Barbara Kwiatkowska played the old woman as a young girl, and others in Polanski's unofficial stock company also put in an appearance: Andrzej Kostenko, a gang-leader in *Two Men and a Wardrobe*, is an importuning homosexual, Goldberg a meter-reader and Kluba a soldier, while Polanski himself plays the old woman in long shot and middle age, his face hidden beneath a head-hugging shawl (though his nose remains recognisable!). He is also a soldier whose legs are blown off by an artillery shell in a sequence that offers an early example of his more theatrical approach to filmmaking, which he would come to express by staging complex scenes in continuous takes. After he is shown lying on the ground, his legs bloody stumps as a result of the bombing, the camera tilts upwards and two more explosions rock the landscape beyond. Rather than cut away to a separate shot of the blasts, Polanski chooses to include them in the take. Such bravura flourishes were to become a stylistic trademark – as would sudden acts of violence, which also seemed to figure strongly in his psyche.

When Angels Fall is somewhat unevenly paced and dramatically unbalanced, with its best scenes taking place in the controlled environment of the studio set – the latrine. But the concept of an old woman whose memories are more vivid and real to her than the environment which she inhabits is a mature one, and the transitions between present and past events are handled with considerable dexterity. The film is quite a little gem, elegantly conceived and elegiac in effect, and aided immeasurably by Komeda's tender and compassionate score.

The six shorts which he made at Lodz between 1955 and 1959 contained most of the elements with which the later films of Roman Polanski would concern themselves: violence, lust, psychological manipulation, interludes of surrealism, irony and tragedy, oppression and claustrophobia. They also showed a predilection for longeurs – holding onto a scene beyond its natural length, to disturb the equilibrium and generate a sense of unease. It was part of Polanski's natural rhythm as a filmmaker, and it would strike a pleasing note when exposed to the critical sensibilities of the West. That he was now a fully fledged filmmaker was not in doubt – all the rough edges had been smoothed out, and a natural command of the language of film was there for all to see, especially the exam board at Lodz.

Passing out required students to write a thesis on some of the more esoteric aspects of filmmaking, however, and when it came time for Polanski to put pen to paper, not only could he not be bothered with what he considered to be theoretical navel-gazing but he already had made sufficient contacts outside of the school to find himself work in the domestic industry. Consequently, he flunked his final exam and 'dropped out'.

In the autumn of 1959, he was offered a job as assistant director to Andrzej Munk on a film called *Cross-eyed* – or simply *Bad – Luck* (*Zezowate szczescie*). The company mounting the production was Kamera, one of eight operational film units in Poland. Making the most of the opportunity, Polanski took a small role in the film (as a prisoner), in addition to directing the scenes which featured his wife – whom he had nominated for the part of Jola.

His stint with Munk encouraged him to try to develop a feature film of his own, but he had at last realised that he needed the help of a professional writer. (All six of his short films had effectively been silent, bar musical accompaniment and occasional sound effects.) Kuba Goldberg, who was still enjoying the brief taste of fame which *Two Men and a Wardrobe* had brought him from being touted around the festival circuit, was drafted in to help pen the script for a nominal thriller which its director envisaged would strand two men and a woman aboard a yacht as the sexual tensions between them climbed to boiling-point. Polanski set his story in the Mazury lakes district of north-west Poland, where he had spent the summer of 1954 sailing – and falling in love – with an art student named Kika Lelicinska.

Goldberg proved an unproductive collaborator, however, and Polanski was forced to turn to first-year Lodz student Jerzy Skolimowski for creative input. The 21-year-old Skolimowski was a friend of composer Komeda, and his contribution to the screenplay that Polanski eventually christened *Knife in the Water* (*Noz w wodzie*) was substantial. The vetting board at the Ministry of Culture nevertheless declined to advance the film any production monies, due to the fact that it 'lacked social commitment'. This was a setback for Polanski's directorial ambitions, as the Polish government represented the only source of funds for filmmaking inside the country.

By the end of 1959, Polanski was also a married man – not that his newly acquired domestic status was allowed to interfere with his habitual philandering. He had come to sexual awareness relatively late in life but, since then, he had been intent on making up for lost time at every available opportunity. He could see no reason to alter this pattern of behaviour now that he had tied the knot with Kwiatkowska: 'The frustration of remaining faithful at all times led, I still felt, to subconscious resentment. From my own point of view, these brief affairs didn't impair our relationship in the least,' he considered.

With *Knife in the Water* on the back burner for the time being, Polanski returned to the medium of the short film and set off for Meudon, near Paris, to realise a whimsical idea, similar in style to that which had brought him his best notices to date, *Two Men and a Wardrobe*. *The Fat and the Lean* is a surreal study of the relationship between master and servant, and how dependency decrees the balance of power. As before, the allegory is laboured and there is a sadistic undercurrent to the humiliations which each man has to endure. 'The Fat' was played by Andrzej Katelbach, a Polish businessman who was resident in France, while Polanski took on the role of 'the Lean'. The film reveals in its director a prodigious talent for mime, but the longer his servitude goes on (and it seems to go on for a very long time, despite the film's mere

15-minute duration), the more redundant the notion becomes.

There are iconic moments: 'the Lean' staring off towards the French capital in the distance mirrors Polanski's innate desire to become part of its cosmopolitan artistic elite, while the recurring motif at the close, in which he plants a field of plastic tulips then prostrates himself before them, is reminiscent of the array of sandcastles in *Two Men and a Wardrobe*. It is almost as though Polanski were constructing his own iconography, to show that five years in film school had taught him certain things which were likely to remain with him forever. Or perhaps it was because Katelbach owned a factory that manufactured plastic flowers.

Jacques Brunet, the French-Canadian producer of *The Fat and the Lean*, vanished in a sea of bouncing cheques while the film was still being shot, and Polanski managed to complete it only with the indulgence of the owner of the small studio which he had hired to house its production.

> *I heard something that sounded like a chuckle in the whistling wind. I shivered at the thought that the Devil himself was testing me by leading me around in circles, waiting for the moment when I would accept his offer.*
>
> **Jerzy Kosinski**, *The Painted Bird* (1965)

In contrast to Polanski's stuttering career, his wife's was moving effortlessly into a higher gear as she went from domestic features to pan-European ones. At the beginning of 1960, Basia was appearing in a horror-comedy set in Warsaw called *Beware of the Yeti* (*Ostroznie yeti* – in which her husband and Henryk Kluba were also offered parts by director Andrzej Czekalski). But by year's end, she was playing opposite Alain Delon in René Clément's *Quelle joie de vivre*. Polanski celebrated her achievement by purchasing a red Mercedes 190 Sport.

Barbara Kwiatkowska was to become one of many nomadic actresses in the sixties whose talents would be utilised in all manner of cheap exploitation thrillers around the globe, as independent production suddenly skyrocketed with the dissolution of the old Hollywood studio system. As her career took off, so Polanski's started to stagnate. He still had no film to his name and no diploma to show for five years' work at Lodz. Since leaving the school, he had essayed minor roles in the films of other directors but made only two shorts of his own, both of which had garnered him some plaudits but little money on which to live. The couple were increasingly dependent on Kwiatkowska's earnings as an actress. Consequently, he thought to manage his wife's career while he waited for his own to blossom. He suggested that she should change her name to one which would more readily meet with approval in the West. Flicking through a dictionary, he settled on 'Lass', meaning 'young girl'. From now on, Basia Kwiatkowska was to be known as Barbara Lass, international starlet.

While Polanski finished *The Fat and the Lean* in less than ideal circumstances after the embarrassing loss of its main backer, Kwiatkowska flew to Rome to star as Barbara Lass in an Austro-Italian werewolf drama entitled *Lycanthropus*. Along for the ride were Carl Schell and Curt Löwens, who, rumour had it, had turned down a film with Visconti in order to play the monster for director Paolo Heusch (credited as Richard Benson). On release in the States, *Lycanthropus* underwent a change of title to *Werewolf in a Girl's Dormitory*, which pretty much summed up the plot, other than to say that the dormitory in question was a reform school and the titular werewolf was the governor of same. Lass acquitted herself no better or worse than other female leads of the time, who were expected merely to look perplexed as the bodies piled up, before screaming in surprise as the obvious suspect turns out to be the killer. *Lycanthropus* went unreleased in the UK until 1964, when it surfaced briefly as *I Married a Werewolf.*

While Kwiatkowska did the rounds of Italian casting-calls, the best deal that her husband was able to muster was for a ten-minute short entitled *Mammals* (*Ssaki*), which was shot at Zakopane, a mountainous ski-resort and so-called winter capital of Poland, 60 miles south of Krakow. Like its predecessor and model, *Two Men and a Wardrobe*, the film eventually brought accolades for Polanski – the Grand Prix at the eighth Festival du Tours in 1962, for one – though the honours were more than a year away.

A review of *Mammals* in the March 1963 issue of *Films and Filming* not only provided a succinct synopsis of the film but, in its enthusiasm, was typical of the response which such foreign fare invariably elicited from British critics in the early sixties: 'Two strange Pinteresque men are walking through the snow with a sledge. They alternately feign some malady in order to be able to have an excuse to jump on the sledge and be pulled by the other. Their complaints become progressively more serious – nose-bleed, sprain, internal haemorrhage, blindness. When the sledge is stolen, their helplessness seems at first to have induced a new sense of brotherhood between them: but after walking a short way together, one of them sprains his ankle and leaps on the other's back. Some very original and amusing effects are achieved by white objects, when placed against a background of snow, seeming to disappear completely.' Critic Peter Graham went on: 'Polanski's films are marked consistently by an uncompromising pessimism; but there is always the impression that perhaps he is not taking things too seriously ... Komeda's delightfully sardonic music helps to sweeten the bitter pill.'

The two were played by Kluba and Michael Zolnierkiewicz – another graduate of the menagerie of eccentrics from which, according to Polanski's reminiscences, the National Film School at Lodz had contrived its intake: 'He suffered from hallucinations brought on by an inordinate sex-drive,' the director said (though how he might have arrived at this conclusion is not explained.) '"Hey!" he'd say, pointing to a figure on the horizon. "Just look at that fantastic chick!" It was the postman, trudging towards us through the snow.'

No sooner had Polanski returned from Zakopane with his eighth (and last) short in the can than he received a call from Jerzy Bossak, who had tutored at Lodz during part of Polanski's tenure there but who had gone on to make iconoclastic documentaries as well as becoming artistic director of ZRF Kamera. Bossak informed him that although the political climate in the country had deteriorated in recent times, the situation within the industry had improved since he first tried to excite interest in *Knife in the Water* the year before, and he thought that Polanski might profit from resubmitting his script – with a memo to the effect that he had spent the intervening period making it more 'socially committed'. Polanski did as he was advised, and, in the spring of 1961, *Knife in the Water* was finally accepted for production.

```
The film opens on an empty road. It is dawn.
Over the hump of a small hill, a car approaches
on the wrong side of the road. Its headlamps
are still on as it moves at the camera. The
credits appear over the windscreen reflection of
moving clouds and tree branches.

A couple in the front seats of the car are seen
through the windscreen. The girl, KRYSTINA, is
driving with ANDRZEJ at her side...

    ANDRZEJ
    (speaking suddenly)
    Dawn, and they are already here.

Seen through the windscreen, a YOUTH is
standing in the middle of the road. He is
wearing a pullover, jeans, canvas shoes, and
carrying a rucksack on his back - everything is
well worn.
```

```
ANDRZEJ sounds the horn and presses his foot
down on the accelerator...
```

shooting script, *Knife in the Water* (1961)

Andrzej, a sporting journalist, and his wife Krystina are heading
out to the country for a weekend's sailing. En route, they give a
lift to a young hitchhiker and invite him to join them on their
yacht. As the day wears on, a battle of wits develops between the
two men: Andrzej defends his bourgeois credentials while the
hiker insists on asserting youthful independence, as embodied by
the pocket-knife with which he toys constantly. Various 'trials of
strength' result in no clear victor, but the older man's insecurity
gets the better of him when he awakens after a night at anchor to
find Krystina and the hiker on deck alone. An altercation ensues,
and the younger man's treasured knife is dropped off the side
of the yacht; he, too, falls into the water and appears to be lost
when Andrzej and Krystina dive in to search for him. Instead, he
is hiding from them by clinging to a nearby buoy. Husband and
wife row about the hiker's apparent drowning and Andrzej swims
ashore, ostensibly to fetch the police.

In the meanwhile, the hiker clambers back aboard and he and
Krystina make love. He leaves before the boat docks, with Andrzej
waiting to meet it at the quay. Andrzej has remained undecided
about whether or not to report the matter, but Krystina tells him
that the youth did not drown – that, in fact, she had made love
with him while Andrzej was absent. Andrzej thanks her for trying
to ease his guilt over the death of the hiker but says he knows that
she is not telling the truth. Or is she? Their car sits at a crossroads:
one way leads to the police station – the other to tacit acceptance
on Andrzej's part that for all his worldly wisdom, his wife has been
unfaithful to him with a younger man...

*   *   *

The end of the war having brought about the triumph of the

proletariat, *Knife in the Water* reflected the new desire for 'social realism' in films. At a time when Hollywood could barely contemplate the idea of depicting the minutiae of day-to-day living, social realism not only exhibited the mundane but positively revelled in it, devoting hours of screen-time to characters engaged in the most ordinary of activities – dressing, cooking, drinking, smoking or, as here, relaxing or going about the business of sailing a yacht. The new wave of the 1960s had much in common with the so-called 'reality' television shows of today. *Knife in the Water* was riding the crest. 'What I like is an extremely realistic setting in which there is something that does not fit with the real. That is what gives an atmosphere,' Polanski explained to *Cahiers du Cinéma* in 1966. 'In *Knife in the Water* ... everything is based on ambiguities, on little ironies, on a kind of cynicism in half-tones.'

For the first hour of the film, there is no palpable sense of tension; to the contrary, there is a sense of antagonism latent in the occasional bouts of macho competitiveness, but any notion of an eternal triangle developing between the three is largely dispelled. Only when a sudden rain-storm strands them in a reed-bed for the night do things take on a more portentous aspect, as the trio is forced for the first time to seek cover in the claustrophobic confines of the cabin. At first, the games remain playful – literally so in the case of 'jackstraws' – but the breaking point is reached when Andrzej wakes in the morning to find the young hiker and his wife already on deck. Thinking there might be something more to the coincidence of both parties being absent from their bunks at the same time than the simple truth that neither of them could sleep, he pockets the hiker's knife and makes for the deck, where he finds the two of them engaged in separate (and entirely innocent) pursuits. He commences nevertheless to bark out orders to the youth, in an attempt to reassert what he deems to be his usurped authority. Alert to the change in her husband, Krystina attempts to defuse the potential for trouble by reassuring him that nothing is amiss. He ignores her entreaties and continues to play cock-of-the-walk.

Having demeaned himself by scrubbing the deck as Andrzej has demanded, the young man realises that he no longer has possession of his knife; he asks that it be returned to him. Andrzej tosses it at the mast, but it bounces off and slides across the deck and into the water. A tussle ensues and the hiker tumbles after it; he is quickly swallowed up in the boat's wake.

The critical point has been reached, and surpassed. Now, each subsequent decision sends the situation spiralling more out of control until, finally, it is Andrzej who swims away from the yacht, apparently also to be lost at sea – until he resurfaces in a state of mental confusion at the quayside. Polanski ended his film originally with *three* shots of the car sitting motionless at its metaphorical crossroads – each at greater distance from the conundrum than the one before. Bossak suggested to him that he remove two of the three, so that the ending would be marginally less ambiguous and certainly less 'artsy-schmartsy' (Polanski's words).

For *Knife in the Water*, Polanski initiated a means of casting the principals which he would continue to employ throughout his career. He utilised his art-school training to sketch each of the characters as he imagined them, then he sought out actors whose features matched his drawings. This was a novel approach, and it would produce many original results in terms of casting in the years to come, but it was also to inspire some discordant notes in his films. *Knife in the Water* proved to be a case in point.

Andrzej was played by 37-year-old Leon Niemczyk, an experienced actor who had made his screen debut in *Celuloza* in 1954, and whom Polanski had met the following year when both had featured in Silik Sternfeld's *The Enchanted Bicycle* (*Zaczarowany rower*); more recently, he had starred in a segment of Munk's *Eroica* (1958). The other two members of the cast were novices. Zygmunt Malanowicz, as the young hitchhiker, came straight from drama school with a preference for the Stanislavsky approach to acting (which involved immersion in a role through emotional empathy), while Jolanta Umecka, as Andrzej's wife, was discovered by Polanski as he scouted for talent at a Warsaw swimming baths.

Polanski initially had intended to play the hitchhiker himself, but he had been dissuaded from doing so by Bossak. Polanski and Malanowicz did not see eye to eye about the latter's approach, but it was Umecka's performance which raised the most doubts about his unorthodox casting methods: 'What exasperated me was having to direct someone who couldn't remember her lines or where to put her feet, or when to take off her sunglasses, in the simplest of takes,' he recalled. 'More irritating still was Jolanta's utter passivity. The naturalness and artlessness that had so impressed me at first sight turned out to be manifestations of a genuinely bovine temperament.' Bovine or not, Umecka's sultry charms were used to good effect by Polanski, and he proved equally adept at disguising her shortcomings in other directions: her inability to swim was countered by a (long-distance) double.

Indicative of the prevailing mood of chauvinism and sexual inequality among those involved in *Knife in the Water* (many of whom, not least Polanski, admitted to verbally abusing Umecka to try to coax a better performance out of her) is the almost incidental fact that the posturing of the two men is less for the benefit of the woman in their midst than it is for their own egos, though the script is savvy enough to correct this in the last reel when Krystina turns the tables on her companions – using one and discarding him, and hoisting the other by his own petard. Unfairly derided as she was, considering that she had to put up with being the only woman among a crew of vodka-swigging lechers, Umecka nevertheless gifted Polanski's first feature with an additional plus: she became the first actress to strip on screen in a Polish film (a fact that gained *Knife in the Water* an X certificate when eventually it opened in Britain).

On the face of it, *Knife in the Water* is about a yachting trip which descends into a battle of wits between the boat-owner and his cocky young sailing companion. But it is also a film of its time, in that the real arena of conflict is the generation gap, and the coming battle between old ideals and new – between the forces of conservatism and the voices which were raising the cry for freedom. Krystina, the woman at the centre of the triangle, is an interesting metaphor: she is society itself, happy to engage in a fling with fair-haired youth but just as content to return to the stability of the status quo when it is over. The passivity which Polanski found so frustrating to deal with in Umecka works more effectively in this context than he could ever have foreseen.

Niemczyk, a veteran of almost two dozen Polish films, managed to turn in a highly skilled performance which required him to deliver many of his lines while conducting various bits of business around the deck. This he did with exemplary professionalism, to make it look as though sailing a yacht was second-nature to him. 'Polanski was very demanding,' he later remarked. The outcome for his co-stars was not so positive. Much of the sound from the location shooting turned out to be unusable, so Polanski took the opportunity to correct what he considered to be deficiencies in the performances of his two non-professionals. Niemczyk was brought back to post-sync his lines, but Polanski redubbed the voice of Malanowicz himself, and he hired up-and-coming actress Anna Ciepielewska, who had recently completed *Mother Joan of the Angels* (*Matka Joanna od aniolow*) for Jerzy Kawalerowicz, to re-dub Umecka. Ciepielewska complied, even though – according to its director – she thought that the project in which she had been asked to participate was 'a piece of shit'.

Understandably, in a country as restrictive as Poland now was under First Secretary Wladyslaw Gomulka, Polanski made the most of the budget that he had been allocated to make *Knife on the Water*. In addition to hiring a yacht for his well-to-do couple on a weekend break, he furnished them with a Mercedes. This caused some consternation in party circles when a disparaging article in the Polish film magazine *Ekran* accused the crew of wild extravagance at the taxpayers' expense. An official visit to the set saw to it that the Mercedes was replaced by a more egalitarian Peugeot for the exterior scenes, though all the shots of the interior of the car were left intact. Wilfully extravagant as Polanski sometimes was, *Knife in the Water*'s Mercedes had been intended to serve an artistic end – the social comment in this instance being directed against the affluence of Communist party officials, whose predilection for luxury German automobiles was seen as representative of the rise of a 'red bourgeoisie'.

> KRYSTINA: *You're just like him, only half his age and twice as dumb.*
> HITCHHIKER: *What do you know about life? Just cafés, yachts and cars. Bet you've got a four-room apartment.*
> KRYSTINA: *I suppose you live four students to a room.*
> HITCHHIKER: *Six actually.*
> KRYSTINA: *I've been through it myself. So has he. You're no better than him. He was just like you. And you want to be like him. And you will be, if you've got the guts. Six to a room. You want to sleep, they play cards. You want to study, they douse the lights. Canteen lunches, cheap smokes. Kisses in the alley – fingers so cold you can't unbutton her blouse. Did I leave anything out?*
>
> **Jolanta Umecka** and **Zygmunt Malanowicz**, *Knife in the Water* (1961)

The most striking aspect of *Knife in the Water* is the quality of the cinematography. The film consolidated Polanski's love affair with the wide-angle lens, whose long focal-length enables objects in the foreground of a shot to be placed extremely close to camera, while objects in the background remain in focus. This puts the viewer more 'in the picture' as it more accurately simulates natural sight than lenses of shorter focal length (such as the telephoto), but a disadvantage is that its use requires more elaborate camera set-ups. Polanski had been much taken at Lodz by a technical manual entitled *Eye and Brain: The Psychology of Seeing*, by Professor R L Gregory, which contained lessons about visual perception which he was never to forget. The use of wide-angle lenses by Orson Welles in *Citizen Kane* and, famously, in *The Magnificent Ambersons* had also left an impression. It was an element which set European cinema apart from the current product of Hollywood, where speed of production invariably was more important than notions of perceptual veracity.

The ritual deployment of deep focus in *Knife in the Water* places the characters in such proximity to the camera that the viewer inevitably perceives the action from their standpoint, literally and metaphorically, rather than that of some third party or neutral observer (as more conventional compositions invariably infer). This 'favouring' of one character over another is used to considerable psychological advantage by Polanski in the film, though disconcertingly, and as part of the plan, he also ensures that there is no preferential treatment overall, so that the viewer is never consciously directed to one out of the three with whom they ostensibly are intended to side, or empathise. 'In *Knife in the Water*, the young boy is just an excuse: the conflict is between the couple,' he said of the relationships in the film.

For all its deployment of deep focus, Polanski's camera remains remarkably controlled, thus it is left to the audience to gauge the relative merits of the case in hand. The film contains many 'impossible' shots which the passage of time (and, more recently, digital trickery) has made commonplace and caused largely to be hidden from view. One such is an angle down on Malanowicz from the mast-head, as he lies sunning himself in a Christ-like posture on the deck of the yacht. To achieve it, cameraman Jerzy Lipman had to be roped to the mast in facsimile of some obscure British naval punishment, complete with bulky Arriflex. Another shot, easier to obtain but no less astonishing in its pocket grandeur, shows the hiker's feet skipping along the surface of the lake as he clings to the jib and joyously pretends to be 'walking' on the water, in an image as emblematic of youthful self-assurance as any in post-war cinema.

In what was to become a mark of Polanski's directorial daring, one conceptually complex scene is captured in a single take: in long shot, we are shown the hiker hanging head-down from the bow of the yacht as he tries to paddle it into shore. At the same time, Andrzej works the tiller to turn the boat in the opposite direction; the yacht swings full-circle within the confines of the frame, and the boy remains oblivious to the fact until he is brought forcibly before the camera again, to react in close-up.

Polanski's devotion to the wide-angle lens was to slow considerably his ability to capture the amount of footage that commercial dictates were soon to demand of him – and this from a director who already was prone to spending an inordinate amount of time tending to detail within the frame. But such conflicts are always present when art and commerce clash: Pope Julius II famously tried to jolly Michelangelo Buonarroti along as he was painting the vaulted ceiling of the Vatican's Sistine Chapel, only for his pleas to be met with the retort that 'It will be done when I believe I have satisfied art.' The Pope lived to see the work completed, but only by months. Polanski's career would be marked by a similar struggle against Philistinism – the Philistines, in his case, being the bean-counters in the front-offices of Western film studios.

> *The moon ... It was a nightmare for me.*
>
> **Priscilla (Barbara Lass)**, *Lycanthropus* (1961)

Just as the wind on the lakes was inclined to alter course in the twinkling of an eye and wreak havoc on Polanski's carefully planned set-ups, so other events conspired to confound him at every turn. To add to the emotional strain, friend and mentor Andrzej Munk was killed in a car crash on the outskirts of Warsaw halfway through shooting, and Polanski was himself involved in a crash on the very day that location work ended, leaving him with a second hairline fracture at the base of his skull. He had to discharge himself from hospital after a two-week stay in order to complete the boat interiors in a Warsaw studio.

While Polanski laboured in a houseboat on the Mazury lakes with *Knife in the Water*, his wife fell prey to the amorous attentions of Italian producer Gillo Pontecorvo. Polanski had been aware of domestic tensions, but his first full-length feature since graduating from Lodz was occupying his thoughts to the exclusion of all else. For Kwiatkowska, *Lycanthropus* was followed by *Rififi in Tokyo*, a 'caper' movie capably shot on location in Japan by Jacques Deray, in which Lass starred with *Peeping Tom*'s Carl Boehm (under his real name of Karlheinz Bohm). But this latest action thriller was more than a professional assignment. By now, her marriage to Polanski was in serious trouble due to the frequent separations and his inability to come to terms with the fact that, until very recently, his wife had been more successful than he. 'The worst situation was in Italy, where no one took any notice of his genius,' Kwiatkowska told John Parker. 'It manifested itself in his hostility towards me.' While his wife frolicked in Japan with another man, Polanski had directed this 'hostility' at poor Jolanta Umecka instead.

Boehm was the catalyst to a final parting of the ways. Kwiatkowska began an affair with the German actor during the filming of *Rififi* and Polanski agreed to a divorce. She married Boehm in 1962, though it was Polanski who shouldered much of the blame for the ultimate collapse of the relationship. 'I was very much the Polish male chauvinist,' he confessed. 'Selfish and domineering...'

Polanski had lost a wife, but he had his film in compensation. Not that it offered much of that, in the event. *Knife in the Water* did not exactly preach harmony and brotherly love, so Poland's Communist authorities took an exceedingly dim view of it. Not for Polanski was the notion of collective intelligence triumphing against the odds; of solidarity, or ideas about the homogeneousness of the human spirit. His message was one of frailty and weakness, and the ultimate futility of human endeavour.

As the film primarily is concerned with ego and power, and the fragile nature of the master-servant relationship (as were several of Polanski's early shorts), it also reflected caustically on the political structure of the country in which it was made. If Polanski or Skolimowsky had injected a political dimension into their tale, it was not one of which the authorities would have approved, had they been alert enough to notice it. Andrzej reels off a litany of sailing rules to his young guest, many of which are imparted for the sole purpose of reminding the hiker who is boss, rather than to uphold any principle of yachtsmanship. 'If two men are on board, one's the skipper,' he states at the start of the voyage, as though to prepare the stage for the confrontation to come. The officials who turned up at Mazury in their own Mercedes to cast disapproving eyes over the alleged profligacy of Polanski and his crew were representative of the petty bureaucracy which the film implicitly comments upon, and it is intriguing to read the character of Andrzej as the Communist state, whose demand for unquestioning obedience and insistence on stifling the libertarian desires of the proletariat leads ultimately to its downfall.

But any such thought in the minds of the film's screenwriters in 1961 would have been wishful thinking at best; rather, it is the attitude of mind which such a state can encourage in its citizens with which *Knife in the Water* is concerned. Domination and subservience, and the balance between the two, are characteristics of behaviour with which Polanski had been familiar since childhood. His fascination with relationships based on the exercise of power had been a feature of his films from the first. *Knife in the Water* was certainly no different – merely more sophisticated at disguising the raw emotions which it set out to explore.

Party boss Gomulka, a former Polish resistance fighter who had participated in the Warsaw uprising before being elevated to the post of First Secretary in 1956 by Nikita Kruschev himself, after soviet tanks had been used to put down riots at Posnan docks, was a liberaliser in terms of his country's dealings with the West but a hard-liner when it came to matters of domestic policy. Having arranged for a private screening, he took one look at *Knife in the Water* and decried it as morally degenerate and an irrelevance. According to Polanski, Kamera production controller Jerzy Bossak put his own career on the line by declaring to reporters, 'I am concerned with the opinion of three categories of people: filmmakers, artists, and filmgoers. As I see it, Comrade Gomulka falls into none of these categories. I am, therefore, only moderately interested in his views.' Despite Bossak's sterling defence, *Knife in the Water* was denied a premiere and saw only limited release in its country of origin. For export purposes, a change of title was considered; alternatives were 'The Long Sunday' and 'The Young Lover'. Eventually, it was agreed that the film should retain the Polish original in literal translation.

For Polanski, enough was enough. He decided to defect: 'It was unthinkable to stay in Poland. Inconceivable. I moved west as soon as I could. To any Pole, it's normal to leave, to look elsewhere, because there's no future to be found at home.'

Arriving in Paris by car, with all that he owned in the boot and barely a franc to his name (his fee for *Knife in the Water* having been paid to him in unconvertible Polish zlotys), Polanski threw himself on the mercy of friends and passing acquaintances from his various jaunts to Cannes. One of these was Andrzej Katelbach, who graciously put him up in his house in Menil-montant, which already was overcrowded with the patter of tiny Katelbachs. It was a tight squeeze, but the situation sowed the seed of an idea in Polanski's mind which the coming years would nurture to maturity.

As Polanski struggled to make ends meet by any means that came his way, *Knife in the Water* opened in the UK in January 1963, having garnered a couple of prestigious awards from the Venice Film Festival at the end of the previous year. The critics were unanimous in their praise. Having reminded his readers that *Knife in the Water* 'arrives dripping with prizes from the Venice Film Festival', Felix Barker of London's *Evening News* added to

the accolades by declaring it to be 'a film of unflawed brilliance.'
The *Daily Telegraph*'s Arthur Dent thought that the film had been
'directed and acted with a dazzling intimacy', while his counterpart
on the *Daily Express* felt that the triangle situation had 'never
been so subtly and revealingly explored'. The last word was left to
Dilys Powell, cultural diva of the *Sunday Times* and doyenne of the
national critics: 'The director is Roman Polanski, a name which if
one can judge by the achievement of this, his first feature film, is
likely to become familiar.'

Nor did the tributes end there, as *Knife in the Water* installed
itself in the Academy Cinema for an extended run in London's
West End. Peter John Dyer, viewing the film from the culturally
insular world of *Sight and Sound* in the winter of 1962, positively
beamed with admiration: 'Polanski is a holy terror of intelligent
restraint – detached, ironic, playful as a cat with a mouse,
accomplishing with ease his alternations of the deathly serious
with the dead-pan comic. The final image, with the man and the
woman ... sitting in the car at the crossroads, achieves a kind of
immobile chill which it usually needs a Bergman or an Antonioni
to convey.'

As usual with highbrow critics, especially where 'foreign' films
were concerned, every nuance, gesture, composition or camera
angle was prodded and picked over for its symbolic relationship to
the larger psychological tapestry which the exciting young Polish
filmmaker had contrived to weave. No slouch in this respect
was Ivan Butler, whose 1970 book on Polanski (*The Cinema of
Roman Polanski*) found more depth to *Knife in the Water* than
even its director had envisaged: 'The truth of the matter is that
our sympathy – our fellow-feeling – is awakened ... by numerous
subtle touches directed towards this awakening – again, largely
by means of objects: the few poor bits and pieces tipped from the
boy's haversack, the underlying pathos of all Andrzej's gadgetry, the
cooking utensils and preparations which Christine handles with
the strangely touching familiarity of long custom.'

There is no doubting the care and attention to detail with which the film is wrought, or that Polanski, by this stage, both acted like and considered himself to be an auteur in relation to his chosen profession. Witness the conspicuous allusions which he tried to inject into his film school short *When Angels Fall*, as divulged to the journalists at *Cahiers*: 'I tried to ballast the flashbacks with certain references, among others to Polish naïve painting, especially that of the 19th century, Jacek Maichewski, for example ... painters who sometimes had a pre-Raphaelite side.' But to suggest, as Butler (and others) did, that every frame of film was filled to bursting with signs and symbols during a shoot on water which was fraught with difficulties of every imaginable kind is stretching the auteur theory a little far.

Having said that, and for all its limitations, *Knife in the Water* is as expertly crafted and lovingly detailed as any film can be. And it does what all great films do, no matter that it is devoid of star players, dramatic incident or even a satisfactory conclusion – it remains in the memory as vividly and subjectively as if one somehow had shared that long Sunday voyage with Andrzej and Krystina and their young companion on a more intimate level than that of mere viewer. Part of Polanski's talent for creating tension was his skill at pacing. *Knife in the Water* revealed that talent to the world, and while it would take the world a while to catch on, the fact of its existence had at least emerged from out of the stifling bureaucratic constraints of Eastern European socialism.

*   *   *

Wandering around Paris on his uppers, Polanski met up with a 35-year-old French writer of similar physical stature and emotional disposition to himself, who was in the same dire financial straits. His name was Gérard Brach (pronounced 'brash'), and their joint destitution soon threw them together in the first of many domestic venues which the two of them would share in the years to come. Their burgeoning relationship also pooled their talents, and the working partnership which blossomed as a result bore fruit in a number of minor ways, one of which was a portmanteau film for French producer Pierre Roustang.

Les plus belles escroqueries du monde – variously *The Most Beautiful Swindlers in the World*, *The World's Greatest Swindlers* or simply *Beautiful Swindlers* in English translations – was a comedy-thriller co-written by Brach, in which each of the five stories was helmed by a different director. Polanski's contribution was 'La Rivière de diamants' ('River of Diamonds'), with Nicole Karen and Arnold Gelderman, whose slight plot concerns a young girl who cons a jewellery store out of a diamond necklace – only to be conned out of it herself in return. But he found himself sharing directorial duties with new wave luminaries like Claude Chabrol and Jean-Luc Godard, a situation which might have been good for his cinematic ego but was bad for his chances of standing out from the cinéma vérité crowd.

Polanski's taste in subjects for the screen was the same as that of Brach, so the two of them decided to pen a script of their own, with a view to pitching it to all-comers as a potential movie. The bare bones of the plot which Polanski had in mind involved a pair of marital misfits, an isolated retreat and a gangster on the run. In its first incarnation, their screenplay was called *Riri*, the French equivalent of Dickie, the name of the gangster in question. But the more Polanski thought about the character of Dickie, the more he was reminded of the portly Katelbach. In the end, *Riri* was ditched in favour of *If Katelbach Comes* – a conscious allusion to the work of Irish playwright Samuel Beckett. Interest in *Katelbach* was to prove lacklustre, however, even when the growing reputation of *Knife in the Water* was given a further boost by its release in the States in October 1963.

By April 1964, *Knife in the Water* had been nominated for an Oscar in the category of Best Foreign Language Film, only to be pipped at the post by Fellini's *8½*. Polanski was not disappointed to have lost out in the Academy Award stakes to Federico Fellini, a director in whose esteemed company he was content merely to be included. Perhaps the finest compliment on his first full-length feature came much later on, and from no less a personage than Andrzej Wajda himself: 'Polanski's *Knife in the Water* was the beginning of the new Polish cinema,' Wajda pronounced.

While Polanski looked for something more substantial than a trip to Amsterdam for a meagre share of *Beautiful Swindlers*, he discovered to his surprise that somebody had actually been looking for him. The 38-year-old Polish émigré Eugene Gutowski had spent the latter half of the fifties in US television, but his latest credit was as co-producer of *Station Six-Sahara*, a steamy wartime romp which had been awarded an X certificate in the UK due to the presence in its line-up of Carol 'Baby Doll' Baker. Gutowski had little experience as a producer, but he had a firm belief about where the action, in terms of world cinema, was going to be over the next few years – and it was not Hollywood. It was good old London town, where the expatriate Pole had recently set up shop.

Gutowski persuaded Polanski to join him in London, where the director of *Knife in the Water* had been lauded as one to watch, and where they were bound to find a ready distribution partner for projects which they could pitch as part of a package-deal – he as producer and Polanski as director. They settled on Cadre Films as the flag under which they now intended to sail, and with the celebratory chink of drinking glasses ringing in his ears, Roman Polanski set his course for Calais.

INTO THE WEST

*I cannot tell you how thrilled I was to hear from you personally
that you think* Repulsion *is probably the greatest film you have
ever seen in your life and that you consider Roman Polanski to
be probably the greatest living film director. I concur with your
opinion on both counts, but it is a great fillip to our judgment
insofar as that we gave this young man the opportunity of making
his first British film.*

Michael Klinger, letter to British film censor John Trevelyan (1964)

When Polanski arrived in London in January 1964 – in a
(minor) blaze of publicity after his success at Cannes and
his Oscar nomination, and with Gutowski acting as his
representative and producing partner – he had one internationally
known film to his name, but he had suffered the humiliation of a
broken marriage and had spent the last two years in near-poverty.
His brief taste of the high life as the husband of Barbara Lass, as
exemplified by the red Mercedes, seemed in retrospect to have been
small reward for half-a-decade at Lodz learning to be a filmmaker.
He was 30 years old, and each new setback merely confirmed him
in his view that the world was a hostile place, whose moral and
social conventions had to treated with a cavalier disregard if sanity
were to be maintained.

Under the banner of their joint venture, Cadre Films,
Gutowski already had set about contacting all the film
companies that he considered might be in the running for
what he and Polanski had to offer, but interest in the Polish

filmmaker seemed in no hurry to translate into anything concrete. In a matter of weeks, Polanski and Gutowski had exhausted the obvious avenues of approach and had begun to move down the scale towards the exploitation end of the industry. By the time the duo were reduced to pitching to Hammer Films, famous for a series of highly-coloured Gothic horrors in the late fifties and early sixties but now experiencing something of an hiatus in production terms, desperation was starting to make its presence felt in previously upbeat entreaties. When no response was forthcoming from Hammer either, Gutowski fired off an imploring note to managing director James Carreras: 'The only thing I beg you, having now tied up with Roman Polanski, is a quick yes or no. He has become my financial responsibility, and it's essential that he make a film immediately,' he pleaded.

Hammer was corporately unmoved. Three years before, it had engaged another avant-garde filmmaker whose reputation among the cognoscenti was every bit as invigorating as that of Roman Polanski. His name was Joseph Losey, and he had been signed as a favour to Columbia to direct *The Damned*, a science fiction story about a secret government plan to survive atomic war. Allowed the freedom to direct after years spent in the shadow of the 'blacklist' that resulted from Senator McCarthy's HUAC hearings in the 1950s, Losey had proved troublesome and the experience had not been a happy one for Hammer. *The Damned* – and a number of other features besides – had also been held up in release and had finally opened in the UK only eight months earlier. Still smarting over the Losey affair to the degree that it had vowed never again to use a maverick of the calibre of the expatriate American, no matter how they might be considered in critical circles, Hammer's response to Gutowski's missive was terse: not interested.

In the same way that his screenplays with Brach would require to be translated from their original French – in which both men found it easier to write – so Polanski found himself at a signal disadvantage in the British capital; he could not speak the language. Gutowski had convinced him that London, at the present moment in time, was the very hub of the movie business. A command of English was not only desirable, it was essential. In Polanski's case, it would add a fifth language to his existing tally of French, Polish, Russian – and that of film. The job of teaching it fell to Gutowski's wife Judy, a former model and British national. In no time at all, 'fab', groovy', 'far out' and 'grotty' had been absorbed into his cosmopolitan consciousness, alongside *'pocaluj mnie e dupe'* ('kiss my ass').

Shaking off or at least subduing the more extreme aspects of his native origins in order to be able to communicate effectively with his new hosts on a basic level of pitching a treatment or asking a 'dolly-bird' out for a drink was one thing, but Polanski had brought a certain amount of psychological baggage with him, as well. At a height of only 5'5", and sporting a 'funny' foreign accent, he had much for which to compensate, and compensation came in the form of a brash, brusque and often overbearing personality. 'He wouldn't care who he used,' Kwiatkowska told John Parker. 'If it was not me, then it would be someone else – that's the way it was.' Even allowing for cultural difference, there was something about Polanski's bluff and combative exterior that did not endear him to many who could have furthered his ambitions more quickly than turned out to be the case. The situation had been little different in Poland, as Henryk Kluba confirmed to the same author: 'As a person, Polanski was unbearable, irritating, and he still is.' It was the kind of view which was to become an intrinsic part of his public profile. As many on the international scene were now about to find out: with Roman Polanski, there was no middle way. You either loved him or you hated him.

Two streets away from Hammer House in London's tiny Soho film community was a company called The Compton

Group. Compton had been in business for a mere four years as
the baby of a pair of East End Jewish wide-boys – accountant
Michal Klinger and ex-cinema manager Tony Tenser – who
typically had started out in distribution before moving into the
world of 'adult' cinema clubs and ultimately dipping their toes
into sexploitation features. Klinger and Tenser's experience
of film production was necessarily limited, but so was Roman
Polanski's experience of the commercial arena. Consequently,
none of them had anything to lose and a meeting was set up
between the four – which was more than Polanski or Gutowski
had managed elsewhere. Klinger was unavailable on the day,
as it happened, but Tenser listened patiently in his absence as
the émigré pair outlined to him the plot of *If Katelbach Comes.*
'I'd heard of Polanski because he had made *Knife in the Water,*
which had got excellent critical reviews,' Tenser recalled.
'What it had done at the box-office I don't know. I guessed that
if they were coming to me then they had gone to everybody
else. But Polanski was a name – a director who draws the
press.'

Polanski's *Katelbach* idea drew no more enthusiastic response
from Compton's Tony Tenser than it had from anyone else,
but, reluctant to let any possibility slip through his fingers,
Tenser suggested that if he and Gutowski could come up with
something more obviously saleable, such as a horror film,
then perhaps they could do business together after all. The
two left Tenser's office in Old Compton Street and weighed
their options: there were none. They had hawked *If Katelbach
Comes* round every prospective production house in London
and found not a single taker, whereas Tenser had offered them
a provisional deal based on their ability to come up with a
horror property which piqued his interest. It had never been
Polanski's intention to write low-budget horror films for the
British market, but the choice was either to stand firm and wait
for a better opportunity to come along – perhaps with a different

script altogether, or at least a retitled treatment of *Katelbach* – or go with what was on the table.

Polanski had spent his life grabbing hold of whatever opportunity fate deigned to cast his way and he was not about to change tack now. He promptly returned to Paris, and he and Gérard Brach settled down to pen their horror film for Compton. 'The reason ... was purely opportunistic,' Polanski recalled. 'I needed a job – and so did Gérard Brach.' Three weeks later, a package arrived on Tenser's desk containing a draft screenplay entitled *Lovelihead*.

Despite its curious title, Klinger and Tenser were suitably impressed with the new Brach-Polanski script. They had every right to be – the story revolved around a young female London hairdresser who goes quietly mad and takes to wandering around her flat in a diaphanous nightgown, suffering all manner of hallucinatory delusions and murdering anyone foolish enough to enter her increasingly chaotic world uninvited. Polanski and Gutowski were allotted a nominal fee, plus a percentage of the profits, to undertake the directing and producing chores, and Polanski flew to London and a rented apartment in Chelsea's Eaton Place to start work on his first British film – a low-budget horror which he referred to as 'a welcome pot-boiler'.

Unwilling or unable to shake off the self-indulgent, state-subsidised filmmaking ways of multiple takes, leisured pace and the freedom to pay infinite attention to detail in which he had been reared at the Lodz Film School, however, Polanski was soon to find himself at odds with the cheese-paring, barrel-scraping philosophies of the bargain-basement end of London's Wardour Street.

```
The main credit titles unfold against the
blackness of the pupil of an eye in extreme
close-up. Then the camera tracks back to
reveal CAROL's two eyes. She stares attentively
```

at something. CAROL is holding a hand –
uncomfortably, but with great care.

Close-up of an elderly woman whose face is
smeared with a thick whitish substance; in each
of her eye sockets there is a piece of cotton
wool. The woman, MRS RENDLESHAM, is stretched
out on a steel table, covered by a sheet up to
the neck. We are in a semi-private room in a
beauty parlour. It is daytime.

Annoyed by CAROL's inattention, MRS RENDLESHAM
lifts her head slightly.

    MRS RENDLESHAM
    (wiggling her hand impatiently)
    Have you fallen asleep?

shooting script, Repulsion (1965)

Carol is a Belgian manicurist living in London; she shares an
apartment in South Kensington with her sister Helen, who is
involved with Michael, a married man. She works at a local beauty
salon and has an on-off relationship with Colin, an office worker
who often finds her distant and unapproachable. Carol objects
to Michael staying the night in the flat, as she has to endure the
sounds of lovemaking which emanate from Helen's bedroom as a
result. She notices a crack in the kitchen wall... A date with Colin
ends in her fleeing in panic when he tries to kiss her; the frenzy
with which she tries to wipe all trace of the kiss from her lips hints
that something is seriously wrong. Carol's obsession with cracks
– in walls, on pavements – becomes marked. She stares at her
distorted features in the polished surface a kettle... When Helen
and Michael leave for a holiday in Italy, she is left in the apartment
by herself.

Carol's behaviour becomes increasingly erratic. Unable to concentrate on her work, she is sent home from the salon. As she wanders distractedly around the empty rooms of the flat, she receives two phone calls: one from the landlord about the outstanding rent and one from a woman who screams abuse at her. She responds to neither. In the mirror of a wardrobe, she thinks that she sees the dark figure of a man; at night, as she tries to sleep, the same man bursts into her room and brutally ravages her... Or so she imagines. Night turns to day, day to night. The bath fills to overflowing. A discarded potato on a work-top goes to seed; a skinned rabbit on the kitchen table turns rancid. Carol remains in her nightdress throughout, lost in her own, aimless thoughts... Someone bangs at the door: it is Colin, concerned that she has failed to respond to his calls. When she refuses to let him in, he forces entry. Annoyed with himself for his uncouth behaviour, he starts to apologise – but when he turns away, Carol smashes him over the head with a heavy candlestick, killing him instantly. She drags the body to the bathtub and submerges it in the water.

No sooner has she rid herself of one irritant than another arrives, in the form of the irate landlord. He also demands entry; Carol complies and hands him the unpaid rent. The gesture takes the wind out of his sails and he calms down and becomes more accommodating, except that he now expects Carol to do the same. When he makes advances to her, she produces a cut-throat razor from behind her back and slashes his neck. He stares at her incredulously, and she launches into a frontal attack which leaves him bloodied and dead upon the floor. She covers his corpse with the sofa and takes to her bed...where her phantom assailant attacks her, over and over, as she lapses into the nightmare world of the completely insane.

Helen and Michael return to find a scene of chaos in the apartment and Carol lying prostrate under a bed. Michael summons help and himself carries the catatonic Carol to a waiting ambulance. The camera tracks around the room, coming to rest on a photo of a family group, behind which stands Carol as a child... a strange look in her eyes...

*   *   *

Lovelihead is as much about its creator's feelings of being a 'stranger in a strange land' as it is about mental illness. No real reason is offered up as to why Carol descends so rapidly into madness and murder, and the close-up of the photograph of her at the close gives the impression of having been tacked on in afterthought to imply that the seed of her insanity was always within her. By his own admission, Polanski completed the script of the film (with co-writer Brach) in a mere 17 days, which afforded little time for any analytical research of the subject in question.

Not that such was ever the intent. 'The plot ... included bloodcurdling scenes that verged on horror film clichés,' Polanski explained. 'The screenplay had to be unmistakably horrific; they [Klinger and Tenser] were uninterested in any other kind of film.' He went on to outline the modus that he and Brach employed to generate the necessary dramatic tension, almost none of it inspired by Freud. 'Having a good idea of the kind of fear we wished to convey, we sought inspiration from situations familiar to us. Most people, at one time or another, have experienced an irrational dread of some sinister unseen presence in their home. An unremembered rearrangement of furniture, a creaking floorboard, a picture falling off the wall – anything can trigger this situation.' An old, dark Gothic house then, but set in the milieu of modern London, and with an occupant not a million miles removed from the pulp-fiction lunatic of Robert Bloch's *Psycho*. In fact, Carol was based on a former girlfriend of a mutual friend of Polanski and Brach's: 'He told us strange stories about her – how she was simultaneously attracted to and repelled by sex as well as prone to sudden, unpredictable bouts of violence,' Polanski recalled.

Having spent almost the whole of his adult life in Communist Poland, Polanski was more than familiar with the concept of state censorship. He was now in the 'free' West, but his choice of subject for Compton was to bring him into contact with another form of censorship, one which he barely had thought to consider as his gaze turned towards the setting sun during his days at Lodz: censorship of works of art on grounds of 'taste and decency'.

In the UK, this aspect of the cinematic arts was handled by the British Board of Film Censors (BBFC), an industry body which regulated the content and certification of films for public consumption on a voluntary basis, and which presently was in the charge of Lord Harlech as its President and John Trevelyan as its Secretary and Chief Examiner. The BBFC may have been 'voluntary' in legal terms, but its word was law from a practical standpoint. Wise producers submitted their scripts to the Board for instruction and advice before committing a frame to film. The less-wise shot first and asked permissions afterwards, which often resulted in large chunks of precious footage ending up on the cutting-room floor at 3 Soho Square, the censor's London habitat.

Polanski's *Lovelihead* was chock-full of the very ingredients which normally sent the volunteer examiners at the BBFC into fits of apoplexy and Tenser, after run-ins with the Board over sexploitation titles like *Naked – As Nature Intended* and *That Kind of Girl*, opted to put on his wise hat and submit the script of *Lovlihead* in advance (which now had been retitled 'Edge of Darkness').

At the end of June, the first Reader's Report gave the proposed film a resounding thumbs-down: 'I should have thought there was a strong possibility of it sending some uneasily poised personality right round the bend,' the Examiner noted, 'and this seems to be a high price to pay for the right to show and to see the ultimate in degradation and beastliness. There may be some way of showing this sort of diseased mind which will not convey the impression of being in itself a diseased work of art: all I can say is that I don't think these people have brought it off.'

Appended to the damning report was a recommendation that the script should be passed to the BBFC's pet psychiatrist, Dr

Stephen Black. Two weeks later, Black reported his findings to
the Board: he, conversely, thought it a brilliant script and very
accurate in psychiatric terms – but a potentially dangerous film to
psychotics. His own recommendation was merely for its makers
to ensure that the protagonist is not seen to derive pleasure from
her violent activities and to signal in the story that were she to have
sought medical help at an earlier stage, all might have turned out
differently. The Secretary nodded approvingly.

Unlike his predecessors in the post of Secretary, John Trevelyan
was a fan both of films and their makers, and having previously
come across *Knife in the Water*, he already considered Polanski
to be 'one of the few really great directors in the world.' He
subsequently amended this view to incorporate the word 'genius',
and expressed his delight to producer Gutowski for his having
gifted Polanski the opportunity to make a film in Britain. With
Trevelyan so emphatically on his side, 'Edge of Darkness' was
now in pole position on the starting-grid – even if Gutowski did
manage to 'queer the pitch' a little by allowing Polanski to reveal to
the *Sunday Telegraph* that the Board was in the habit of consulting
a psychiatrist. 'I would prefer all our negotiations to be kept
confidential,' Trevelyan admonished him.

Consciously ignoring the meagre budget of £45,000 which
had been allocated by Klinger, Polanski set his sights on some
formidable talent. For his cinematographer, he persuaded
Compton to hire Gilbert Taylor, an industry veteran and the man
responsible for the luminous monochrome imagery of Stanley
Kubrick's *Dr Strangelove* and Dick Lester's *A Hard Day's Night* – the
first feature-film outing for the Beatles, which was in editing at the
same Twickenham Studios where 'Edge of Darkness' was about
to be shot. For his leading lady, Polanski chose French ingenue
Catherine Deneuve, whom he'd narrowly missed directing in
Beautiful Swindlers and whom he felt would bring a touch of exotica
to the role, over and above that which might have been supplied by
the likes of Francesca Annis, who was Klinger and Tenser's choice,

for no reason other than economy and the fact that she had starred in Compton's *The Pleasure Girls*.

Other parts were filled from *Spotlight*, the British casting directory, and fell to John Fraser (as Colin), TV heavyweights Ian Hendry and Patrick Wymark (as Michael and the landlord respectively) and Yvonne Furneaux (as Carol's sister Helen), who insisted that she be credited as a 'guest star', due to the relatively minor nature of her role.

With 'Edge of Darkness' in pre-production, Polanski took time out to explore his new surroundings. As a minor celebrity in his own right, he was quickly inducted into Brian Morris' Ad Lib club in Leicester Square – a London hot-spot which introduced him to many new friends among the cream of British and American showbusiness society. One who would feature prominently in his affairs in subsequent years was Victor Lownes, the flamboyant British head of Hugh Hefner's *Playboy* empire.

Tenser still felt that the new title was not strong enough. Realising that *Homicidal, Maniac, Paranoiac, Nightmare, Hysteria* and numerous others inferring psychological collapse had already been utilised (mostly by Hammer) in a slew of psycho-thrillers in the wake of *Psycho*, he shuffled the cards that remained. An alternative of 'Revulsion' was soon superseded by *Repulsion*, which seemed suitably to categorise the behavioural disorder exhibited by the film's protagonist and accordingly was met with widespread approval; to the wily Tenser, the implication of something 'repellent' in the storyline was more commercially saleable than before. (When Compton eventually produced its theatrical trailer, clips from the film were accompanied by the incomprehensible tag-line, 'Fact and fantasy are fused in a frantic fury of ... *Repulsion!*') With that issue resolved, Roman Polanski's first British feature moved into production at Twickenham Studios on 24 August 1964.

No other film has ever shown with such intense reality the terrifying journey into madness...

trailer, *Repulsion* (1965)

If Klinger and Tenser had thought that their young Eastern European discovery would show his gratitude at being offered the opportunity to direct a film in the West by meekly falling into line with the cheap and cheerful Compton way of doing things, they were soon disabused of the idea. In no time, it was clear to all concerned that Polanski had his own way of going about the business of film direction, and cutting corners formed no part of it. His fastidiousness and constant quest for aesthetic perfection soon put him at odds with his producers. Within a week, he had fallen behind on the rigorous schedule which Compton had set him – a situation exacerbated by the experienced Taylor's own measured approach to his craft.

Polanski's painstaking attention to detail and Taylor's precise way with lighting were luxuries which Compton could ill afford and, in no time at all, the budget had begun to climb, taking Klinger and Tenser's blood-pressures along with it. 'Crisis meetings, lectures and recriminations became more and more frequent as shooting proceeded,' Polanski complained. 'They wore me down to such an extent that I told Gene I was ready to quit. As someone whose worldly possessions could be packed in a single suitcase, what did I have to lose?' Tenser saw things differently. 'When we had difficulties with the directing of the film, Gutowski would act as a go-between to get it right. Sometimes it worked in our favour but more often it worked in Polanski's,' he noted wryly.

The script for *Repulsion* had been contrived to require a minimum of dialogue, due to the relative unfamiliarity of both of its writers with the language in which it was to be filmed; what dialogue there was could as easily have been ad-libbed. The fortuitous outcome of this was that conversations between Carol and Colin (Fraser) which appear to be stilted on screen (especially as many of them had to be post-synched over location footage) were considered to work to the film's advantage in terms of Carol's inability to relate to members of the opposite sex. A line of Colin's, in which he decries Carol's choice of meal with 'You can't eat muck like this', had, in addition, to be overdubbed at the request of the restaurateur in whose premises – Dino's in Pelham Street – the crew had graciously been granted permission to shoot, so that the word 'muck' could be replaced by the less offensive 'stuff'!

Myriad other advantages sprang from the cross-cultural détente which effectively dictated that *Repulsion* was conceived as something of a 'silent movie' – at least until Polanski completed his linguistic education. An early sequence in which Carol is alone in the apartment after Helen and Michael go out for dinner is succinct in capturing the essence of loneliness. She watches as an old lady walks her dog before returning to her own flat; a solitary nun wanders through the courtyard below her window; she puts a record on as daylight gradually darkens into twilight; she slouches indolently around, wondering how else to fill her time. *Repulsion* is as much a study of isolation as of sexual repression, as Polanski's camera oves over shelves laden with the detritus of a life, echoing the scenes in the doll-maker's shop in *The Lamp*.

The more Carol loses touch with reality, the more Polanski is called upon to convey her plight through visual invention. His stylised treatment is thoroughgoing and skilful: 'I must get this crack mended,' she says of a small fracture in the kitchen wall, then she stops on her way to a date with Colin to stare fixedly at a second crack in the pavement – returning to the apartment, a new crack appears next to an air-vent. She lets her bath-water overflow, takes to wandering aimlessly in the streets, and fantasises about being subjected to anal rape. Meanwhile, a rabbit which was intended for the pot begins to rot, potatoes start to sprout, and the rooms of the apartment appear to distort before her eyes, stretching into infinity and harbouring dark shadows where molesters dwell. In such an environment, walls not only have 'ears', they have arms and hands as well, as even the inanimate decor begins to grope at her lasciviously.

Then there is the phantom rapist. 'Hello darling, how about a bit of the other then?' Mike Pratt's sleazy workman inquires of

Carol as she passes him in the street. Before long, he is haunting her dreams, breaking into her bedroom, forcing himself upon her – his head appearing on her pillow just when she least expects it. Unfortunately, the almost subliminal handling of the 'dream-rapes' obscured the connection between Pratt and the rapist for all but the most attentive of viewers.

Carol is at the beck and call of everyone in her life, including the clients whom she is paid to pamper – an aspect of the scenario which recalls Polanski's own cavortings to amuse Katelbach in *The Fat and the Lean*. She is very much put-upon, at work, in her relationship with her sister and Michael ('Comment ça va?' he asks her patronisingly, tweaking her cheek and stopping only slightly short of slapping her on the behind), and also with Colin, who is forever trying to force his attentions on her, albeit for the most altruistic of reasons. Consequently, his fate is sealed as soon as he persists in intruding on her private space.

It is a kiss that sets her off: she sprints out of his sports car, wipes her mouth in the lift, cleans her teeth. The scene is reminiscent of the climax of Jacques Tourneur's *Cat People* (1942), when an equally unwelcome kiss from Tom Conway unleashes the demon within Simone Simon. Colin makes the mistake of barging in at the front door, which reminds her of the phantom rapist forcing his way into her bedroom; he winds up in the bathtub. The landlord follows suit, but in a more oily and ingratiating way; he ends up slashed to death and unceremoniously bundled under an upturned sofa. Both murders are suitably shocking, but the iciest chill is felt in the expression of terror that imprints itself on the landlord's face as Carol takes a surreptitious swipe at the nape of his neck with an open razor and his trembling fingers alight on his own blood.

Chico Hamilton's jazz score descends into a few well-chosen notes on a bassoon as the walls finally close in. Carol takes to ironing Michael's vest with an unplugged iron; she smears lipstick on herself, in automaton mimicry of the dating game, and succumbs to nightly repeats of the nightmare of rape before lying prostrate on her bed and quietly going mad... Sister and lover return from their Italian holiday to find blood and mess, anarchy and insanity. The film ends as it began, with Polanski's camera probing into the deep, dark depths of a mind at the end of its tether. *Repulsion* was completed over-time and over-budget, at a cost of £95,000 – almost twice the original estimate.

Are you all right? You look... well, I don't know – you look sort of funny.

Colin (John Fraser), *Repulsion* (1965)

The pressure of having to finish the film according to Compton's accounting edicts is exhibited in the number of rough edges to the piece, not all of them due to Polanski's unfamiliarity with either the language or his new environment. The final 'wall of arms' effect is crude, with replastering for retakes clearly in evidence, while the montage of chattering heads after Carol has been discovered under the bed goes on too long. We are asked to observe Carol's distracted behaviour in the beauty salon just once too often, and her relationship with Colin remains underdeveloped; it is entirely unclear in their first scene together whether he is attempting to pick her up or has already dated and formed a relationship with her. Attitudes that reflect the more mature sensibilities of the film's European writers jar somewhat when imposed on what amount ostensibly to stereotypically English gents of the period: 'Are you trying to play hard to get?' Colin asks of Carol after she stands him up due to self-absorption, while Michael's response to finding Helen hysterical in the flat at the climax is to slap her twice across the face.

Nevertheless, and originating from a self-declared chauvinist, *Repulsion* is remarkably unsympathetic in its depiction of the males in the film: be they landlords, lovers or mere boyfriends, all of them lie. Michael's motivation appears to derive solely from sex,

as does that of Colin's work colleagues, John (James Villiers) and
Reggie (Hugh Futcher), when they are not merely propping up
a bar. Colin himself exhibits a practised sense of decency, but he
ends up paying the price for the egotistical behaviour of the rest of
his sex.

(The pub scenes were filmed at The Hoop & Toy in Thurloe
Place; they had to be shot during closing hours, which meant that
neither cast nor crew were legally allowed to drink alcohol! The
film also fell foul of antiquated British by-laws over the filming
of the aftermath of a car crash; Polanski tried to 'steal' the scene
without acquiring the requisite permit but reckoned without the
sense of civic duty felt by disgruntled South Kensington residents,
who promptly phoned the police; production manager Bob Sterne
found himself arrested as a result.)

The film's view of London life is not so much shabby and
degenerate (apart from Wymark's Rachman-like landlord) – as was
inferred by some critics – as superficial and hedonistic, though
on the whole, *Repulsion* depicts London as it was in the fifties and
early sixties, before the idea of a 'swinging' city had really begun
to chime with the populace at large. Twelve months later and the
social scene in Kensington would take on a quite different aspect,
which the mise-en-scène of the film might have reflected as a
milieu of bistros and discotheques, rather than restaurants and
public bars. By that time, Polanski had himself become a part of
the Swinging London 'set'. 'London was a village in the sixties
– a village full of joy, and the great expectations of all the young
filmmakers, musicians (in particular) and, above all, fashion
photographers,' he noted. 'People knew each other; they would
see each other in clubs and restaurants; they were more friendly
to each other than any other place I ever remember, at any other
time.'

Catherine Denueve strikes exactly the right note of vacancy and
vulnerability in her portrayal of Carol; *Repulsion* was only her third
film, but she and her director formed an instant rapport – 'like

dancing a tango,' Polanski said. 'I think he has a lot of charm but on the set, he can be difficult – not for me, because I was very young and I needed to be directed,' Deneuve recalled. 'I had complete confidence in him ... He's very strong in his direction and he's very passionate about it.'

The problem with the film is that it often tends to appear like *Psycho* shot from the point of view of Norman Bates. Polanski's unflinching focus on Carol, and his ability to place you inside her head by observing most of the action from her viewpoint, may have swayed the censor in terms of integrity of approach but it leaves *Repulsion* without a centre of empathy. In another echo of *Psycho*, the most sympathetic character is killed off in the second act, and while one is required to identify with Carol, no reason or even hint of a reason is offered to explain her tragedy. This deprives the audience of its innate desire to invest the tale with an emotional response, and the film devolves into a case study on almost a documentary level. *Repulsion*, like Carol herself, is an object of voyeuristic fascination that one can admire from afar for its technical perfection and the cool, austere beauty of its surface glaze, but not actually *like* – and certainly never take to one's heart.

There's no need to be frightened of me, you know. I could be a very good friend to you – you know that? You look after me and you can forget about the rent...

landlord (Patrick Wymark), *Repulsion* (1965)

At the British Board of Film Censors, Secretary John Trevelyan was won over by the veneer of realism which Polanski had managed to attach to his film, a feat no doubt aided by Gilbert Taylor's grainy monochrome cinematography. 'It was a brilliant film,' Trevelyan enthused, 'and the psychiatrist whose advice I had sought told me that it was completely accurate and that he himself had learned from it. We discussed the film with Polanski, and I asked my adviser whether, if the film were seen by someone on the edge of insanity, it could be really harmful. He said that it might be in some individual case or cases, but that he could not advise me to refuse the film since people who saw it could learn something of value about mental illness and have more compassion for people who suffered from it. On this advice we took the risk and passed the film.'

After the BBFC's screening of *Repulsion*, Dr Stephen Black, Trevelyan's psychiatrist-in-residence, asked its director how he and Brach came to have such an intimate knowledge of the effects of schizophrenia. Polanski squirmed with embarrassment. 'We used our imaginations,' he informed him.

Polanski's emotional detachment from the subjects of his films also worked to his advantage with the censor when it came to the set-piece murder of Patrick Wymark at the climax. 'There was one scene in which the girl killed her landlord by slashing him repeatedly with a razor ... Although this was possibly the most horrific killing I had ever seen in a film, none of us found it sadistic,' Trevelyan wrote. 'We felt that Polanski was saying "Isn't this horrible?" and not "Isn't this enjoyable?"' Trevelyan's reaction is an indication of just how subjective his judgments could be in matters of this kind, rather than being guided by a clear set of rules and principles. Many of his thoughts and feelings with respect to the films over which he presided in the public interest (as delineated in his 1973 reminiscence of his time at Soho Square, *What the Censor Saw*) resonate uncomfortably of the words of the prosecuting counsel in the Old Bailey trial of *Lady Chatterley's Lover*, when he inquired of the jury if they thought it a book which they would wish their wives or servants to read. Trevelyan's musings have a similar ring, as unconsciously he adopts a pious tone of self-justification – 'Sadism has never appealed to me, but there are people for whom it is an attraction,' being one example.

Repulsion was submitted for certification on 15 January 1965, when it was granted the obligatory X. That Polanski's film left the BBFC with its original running time of 107 minutes intact was no mean achievement at a time when Trevelyan and his Board were still cutting significant chunks out of conventional horror films like *The Face of Fu Manchu* and *Dracula Prince of Darkness* (and likewise with Compton's subsequent *A Study in Terror*). 'The sequence of Carol lying in bed with the noises of lovemaking of her sister and boyfriend in the other room was quite unprecedented at that time and we were afraid that John Trevelyan might give us trouble, but it somehow passed without much problem,' Polanski wrote. The news that the film had escaped the censor's scissors was a key factor in assuring its box-office success when it went on limited general release in the UK in June.

Polanski's own verdict on the result of his endeavours was typically uncompromising: 'Of all my films, *Repulsion* is the shoddiest – technically well below the standard I try to achieve.' Maybe so, but its daring way with a controversial subject had got its director noticed, which had been the point of the exercise from the beginning.

At this stage of his career, Polanski was keen to comply with the censor's demands and, during the editing of *Repulsion*, the scene in which Carol is mauled by the hands in the wall was purposely darkened to obscure the image, with a fade-out applied to the very moment when one of them cups her breast. He shortened the footage of the razor-attack on the landlord, and he removed a third murder in its entirety: after the bludgeoning of Colin, the character of Michael's wife also turned up unexpectedly at the flat, convinced that she would find her errant husband in flagrante with Helen, and clutching an unlikely bottle of vitriol with which to wreak the appropriate revenge. Realising her mistake at the last moment, she accidentally spills some acid on herself and has to run to the bathroom to try to wash it off. She comes upon the body of Colin in the tub and Carol has to kill her also, by holding her head under the bloodied water until she drowns (a scene in which Polanski, in blonde wig, had himself stood in for the reluctant actress). Carol then leaves both bodies in the bath.

Polanski had shown this cut of the film to Polish ex-pat Bronislau Kaper, veteran composer of *Butterfield 8* (1960) and *Mutiny on the Bounty* (1962) and currently in London to work on Richard Brooks' adaptation of Joseph Conrad's *Lord Jim*, whom he had met in LA while attending the 1963 Academy Awards ceremony. Kaper suggested that the murder of Michael's wife, which effectively was undertaken to prevent her from going to the police, was too rational a crime for Carol to commit in her confused state.

Respecting Kaper's judgment, and aware that the BBFC already had raised a number of concerns about the sequence in question, Polanski consented to remove it; all that remains of the 'jealous' wife is a shot of her standing in the street and staring up at the flat, and a voice on the phone after the murder of Colin, when she exclaims, 'Do you think I don't know he's with you? You think you're clever but you're not that clever, you filthy – ' before being cut off. So oblique are the allusions to Michael's adultery in the release print that it is possible to read the call as yet another figment of Carol's fevered imagination. Notwithstanding this last-minute change in the schematic, editor Alistair McIntyre could still sense the magic that he felt was in the air: 'There are very few occasions when I've been conscious all the time that I was working on a bloody good film, and *Repulsion* was one of them,' he enthused.

While Compton waited for a UK release date for its mini-masterpiece, it showed the film out-of-competition at Cannes and *in* competition at Berlin, where it picked up the Silver Bear (second prize) and a deal of insider 'buzz'. In order to capitalise as much as possible on the reputation that Polanski had gained from *Knife in the Water*, Tenser had awarded him the accolade of a 'possessory credit'. 'Roman Polanski's *Repulsion*', the posters read – something that only Hitchcock had been in the habit of receiving on a regular basis. *Repulsion* finally opened in London's West End at the Rialto, Coventry Street, in the second week of June, with trade magazine

Kinematograph Weekly heralding it at the premiere as 'one of the most vibrant and daring films ever made'.

```
Finally the camera pans to the framed family
photograph. It moves closer, isolating CAROL,
then framing her face. Still closer, it shows
her beautiful and proud, implacably vague
child's eye, where madness had already gained
the day.
```

shooting script, *Repulsion* (1965)

The critics were as impressed as the censor with the technical brilliance of the film, but they were not a little disturbed by its clinical approach to its subject and its lack of emotional resonance. Alexander Walker of the London *Evening Standard* was the first to lead the charge in its defence: 'Be warned: death is made to look nasty and brutish – which it seldom is in many an 'entertainment' film. But, as I reported from the Cannes Film Festival, this is precisely why the British censor, after calling in a psychologist to check the film's honesty, passed it uncut. And also why our two film circuits are only giving *Repulsion* a limited showing. They think it is just too laceratingly realistic for their patrons. Even I, who am fairly case-hardened, found it one of the most terrifying films I have ever seen.' But he added a rider. 'I cannot easily defend this film against the charge that it lacks humanity, pity, sympathy ... *Repulsion* may not be the stuff of 'entertainment', as defined weekly at the local Odeon or ABC, but it is the stuff of which films are made.'

Dilys Powell, who previously had predicted great things for Polanski, now seemed to express some reservation. 'There is no pity for the girl, no human regard. I am aware of no rule insisting that art must feel for its characters; permissible, though, to expect from a work of imagination an attitude towards them not wholly detached. I think it is the absence of such an attitude which makes me wary of this brilliant film.' Isabel Quigley of the *Spectator* was blunter still: 'Polanski is still visually brilliant, but ... it seems woolly stuff compared with the cold certainty of his earlier film, woolly in concept as well as in effect. All kinds of small questionable details of taste and dialogue add up to a feeling that it is all taking place in a country Polanski hasn't really come to terms with, and I don't mean just London, but the very girlish, subjective world of sisterliness, virginity, jealousy and sexual fear.'

Kenneth Tynan, writing in the *Observer*, was more impressed by the novel aesthetic on display: 'Although [Polanski] is clearly a Hitchcock fan, he goes deeper than *Psycho* by presenting a double murder from the killer's, instead of the victim's, point of view. The result is very nearly as shocking and far more clinically intimate, despite the fact that Polanski (unlike Hitchcock) offers no psychiatric explanation for the ghastly exploits of his protagonist.'

While Tynan sought to detect some authorial innuendo, Polanski was forever at pains to deny that there were hidden meanings in his work, as though refusing point-blank to face up to the reality of his own subconscious urges. Yet the siting of a convent next door to Carol's apartment block in a film about sexual repression could have been no accident – nor was it merely to provide a glimpse of the exterior world, as he suggested at the time: 'The nuns playing across the yard was something that we remembered from the apartment when we were writing the script – we had nuns just across the courtyard; they were playing handball. I thought it was a great element to give the feeling of isolation later on in the picture ... I needed some signs of the world outside that could not be just an occasional siren or bird; I needed something alive. So I used on one side – on the courtyard side – those nuns, and on the street side, I used the street musicians.' (The three buskers in question, of whom Polanski became one when their number was reduced to a discontinuity of *two*, echo of the *Two Men* and their wardrobe, wandering through a similarly self-obsessed world of callousness and casual violence. *Repulsion* is full of similar examples of psychological shading and Freudian suggestion, not all of which are satisfied by glib statements from its director about acting on his instincts as a filmmaker. It is a film about effects, not causes, but it plays as though it were conceived by one who knows well the line between sanity and madness – even as it resists the temptation to let the rest of us in on the secret.

Denying the existence of subliminal meaning in his films left Polanski free to let his subconscious run away with him, which invariably it did – at least in the first half of his career. The second half was to be less imaginatively unfettered and more consciously reflective, and it would be set in train by an event of such unimaginable horror that no one – not even Polanski himself, with his childhood memories of the nightmare terrors of the Krakow Ghetto – could have seen it coming.

*   *   *

The Paris that Polanski had known from 1961 to 1963 was that of French directors like Marcel Carné, Jacques Becker and Jean Delannoy, all of them iconic figures from the thirties and forties whose time was fading fast (in fact, Becker died the year before Polanski first arrived in the city). Conversely, the London in which he found himself at the turn of 1965 was a London of Carnaby Street and cat-walks; of Annabel's and the Scotch of St James's, Biba and Bond and David Bailey, Caine and Conran, Shrimpton and Stamp, Pinter and Peter Blake; of mini-skirts and Mini Coopers, Finney and Fame (and his Blue Flames), and of Centre Point and the soon-to-be-opened Playboy Club in Park Lane. It was a London which was about to embrace the Beatles and all who went with them, as it already had embraced a reinvention of British film thanks to directors like Tony Richardson, John Schlesinger and Lindsay Anderson; which was now about to become the style capital of the world, in a country which currently was experiencing its very own *Belle Epoque*. It was London at the start of the Swinging Sixties.

To Roman Polanski, it was like another world, and it was a world which welcomed him with open arms and treated him like one of its own. On the strength of *Knife in the Water* – eagerly promoted among cinéastes as representing the crème de la crème of the new cinema of Eastern Europe – and the fact that he had shot a film on the streets of the capital, with an eclectic cast which ranged from French actress Catherine Deneuve (future wife of the aforementioned David Bailey) to ex-*Avenger* Ian Hendry, Polanski was free to feed off the fruit of all that London had to offer, which was a very great deal indeed. He partied with stars, made love to starlets, and made the kind of contacts which were to assure him of some stability in his profession in the medium-term, the contretemps with Compton notwithstanding.

Repulsion opened in the US on 2 October, to a more muted though equally positive reception among New York cinephiles. Sensing the pitfalls of trying to play an art-film to an audience spoon-fed on Hollywood sugar-candy, Polanski had persuaded Deneuve to undertake a glossy photo-shoot to promote them both, which he had placed in *Playboy* thanks to his burgeoning friendship with Victor Lownes. Against her better judgment, Deneuve complied with the request, though she would maintain that the episode was a sleazy and unnecessary distraction, despite the tasteful nature of the shoot itself and the fact that she later consented to marry the photographer (Bailey).

Despite its notional subject matter of mental illness, *Repulsion* still had managed to include the voyeuristic elements which Compton's directors required to keep their traditional punters happy (Deneuve parading around in a skimpy nightdress). Polanski had delivered as agreed and, with a couple of reservations, Michael Klinger was eager to offer him a follow-up film. On this occasion, *If Katelbach Comes* was looked upon more favourably but, again, there was a question mark over the title.

The plot of *If Katelbach Comes* involved two gangsters who, after an unsuccessful heist, were forced to hole up at the isolated

retreat of a retired businessman and his mistress while awaiting
rescue by their unseen boss – the mysterious Katelbach of the
title. The bare bones of this narrative had much in common with
the kind of noir thriller in which Polanski had steeped himself at
Lodz, in particular Archie Mayo's *The Petrified Forest* (1936), John
Huston's *Key Largo* (1948) and William Wyler's *The Desperate Hours*
(1955), all with Humphrey Bogart. But Polanski had envisaged
this spartan set-up, with its inbuilt relationship dynamic and
psychological explorations, as a kind of *Knife in the Water* on land
– more Samuel Beckett out of Luis Buñuel. The fact that Beckett's
Waiting for Godot was his model for the situation in which the
gangsters found themselves was made plain by the title of the piece
– a simple hypothetical variant, which effectively confirmed that
'Waiting for Katelbach' would have been a mite too slavish in its
acknowledgment of the film's inspirational source.

But by the time David Bailey got around to proposing to
Deneuve, production was well-advanced on what Tony Tenser
contentedly had begun to refer to as Compton's next 'Rembrandt',
the now-retitled *Cul-de-Sac*.

```
The film opens with an exterior shot of a huge
deserted beach. It is daytime. The low tide
has left the sand quite flat. From the distance
a small car can be seen moving very slowly,
following the lines of a chain of telephone
poles.

A board on the roof of the car has the words:
School of Motoring. Credits appear over this
scene...

    RICHARD
    Hang on Albie, I'll be back.
```

> Richard moves forward with a harassed gait,
> following the line of the telephone poles. He
> winds his way through the sand dunes, uphill.
> Suddenly he sees a sort of castle with a number
> of turrets, an unexpected and absurd sight in
> this deserted place...
>
> **shooting script**, *Cul-de-Sac* (1966)

Dickie (Lionel Stander) and Albie (Jack McGowran) are two gangsters on the run. What makes their plight more urgent is that their stolen car has broken down and both have been shot, Albie seriously. Dickie pushes the car along a deserted coastal highway with Albie inside; he spies a fortress in the distance – an isolated outpost on a remote crag. Leaving his partner in the car, he sets out to find help. The castle is owned by George (Donald Pleasence) and Teresa (Françoise Dorléac), ten-months-married but an odd couple nonetheless: as Dickie nears the castle, he spots Teresa enjoying a passionate interlude among the sand dunes with Christopher (Iain Quarrier). Dickie secretes himself in the building and tries to phone his boss, a man named Katelbach; George and Teresa come upon him in the kitchen and he makes the position plain: 'You'd both better help me if you want to stay healthy,' he advises.

As he settles down to await rescue by Katelbach, Dickie does his best to cover his and Albie's tracks by cutting the phone line and hiding the car. During the night, Albie calls out 'I want a gin' and expires. With Teresa's help, Dickie buries his former pal. George joins them eventually and Dickie is tempted to tell him about his wife's indiscretion, but he changes his mind. As dawn breaks, a plane flies overhead and Dickie thinks that salvation is at hand – it is not. A Jaguar speeds across the sand to the castle. Again, Dickie thinks that Katelbach has come. Again, he is disappointed – it is a party of George's friends intent on paying a visit. Dickie is forced to adopt the persona of 'James', a butler, and wait at table as the guests enjoy luncheon. Among them is Cecil (William Franklyn), the driver of the Jaguar.

With their roles reversed, even if only for the sake of appearances, the natural order is temporarily restored and George and Teresa treat Dickie as though he were a menial. The subterfuge passes off relatively unnoticed by their visitors, but the meal is brought to an abrupt end when the son of two of the guests accidentally smashes a stained-glass window with a blast from Cecil's shotgun. George is incensed, and he demands that all of them leave the castle immediately. Thinking that they still have the upper hand even after the guests have departed, Teresa plays a practical joke on Dickie which ends with him beating her with his belt in retaliation. He then takes a phone call from Katelbach which informs him, in effect, that rescue will not be forthcoming; he is to be left to his fate.

While Dickie is otherwise engaged, Teresa persuades George to steal the gun that he keeps in his jacket pocket. Dickie, meantime, has decided that there is nothing for it but to leave. He orders George and Teresa into the cellar, but George refuses to go. He looks for his gun, only to find that the pair have relieved him of it. He demands it back, his attitude menacing. George warns him off and then shoots him, three times. Mortally wounded, Dickie staggers to his car and returns with a Tommy gun. Before he can fire, he collapses and dies – and an involuntary burst of gunfire causes George's car to explode in flames. Cecil turns up again in the middle of the melée; Teresa jumps into his car and they leave together. Lost and alone, George squats on a rock in the causeway as the waves lap at his feet... Plaintively, he calls for his first wife... 'Agnes'.

*   *   *

After scouting unsuccessfully for locations for their film in Yugoslavia, Polanski and Gutowski settled on the mystical landscape of Holy Island, otherwise known by its ancient name of Lindisfarne, on the north-eastern coast of Northumberland by the Scottish borders. The island itself is situated just off mud-flats at Budle Bay and is accessible only at low tide from the village of Beal, by means of a causeway. Its is Lindisfarne castle, which sits on the highest point at Beblowe hill. The castle was built around 1550 but was converted into a private residence in 1903 by the architect Sir Edwin Lutyens; the National Trust took the building over in 1944. (Much is made in the amended screenplay to *Cul-de-Sac* of the fact that historical novelist Sir Walter Scott wrote *Rob Roy* in Lindisfarne castle – in fact, the castle is christened 'Rob Roy' in the film. Scott wrote *about* the island in poetry, but not on it. *Rob Roy* was actually penned at his stately home of Abbotsford – a mere three miles distant, in Melrose – and, in part at least, on the premises of a second claimant for the honour, The Rose and Thistle Inn in Morpeth.)

George and Teresa were to be played by Donald Pleasence and Françoise Dorléac. Dorléac was an older sister of Catherine Deneuve and she had consented to take on the role of Teresa at the last minute, after French-Canadian actress Alexandra Stewart was forced to pull out of the film and Polanski failed to secure a suitable replacement; she looked the part of a 'tart' whose sex-kittenish wiles had seduced George away from his first wife and she was happy to undertake the nude shots required, but Polanski was unimpressed by her performance. Nor could she swim, so an extraordinary single take which involved Stander and Pleasence debating on a beach while waiting for a single-engined Cessna to fly overhead on cue, as Dorléac frolicked in the surf, caused her to faint from the cold on the third take. What Polanski thought of Dorléac was later confided to Tom Hibbert in *Empire*: 'Françoise was unhappy and neurotic and difficult. She was not a bad person but her body language was not right and she knew this and she was angry. Françoise was physically more interesting than her sister ... but she was not as good an actress as Catherine.'

Cul-de-Sac afforded Polanski the opportunity to indulge his peculiarly Polish taste for 'Pinteresque' misfits which had been denied him in his first two films. As exercises in social realism, *Knife in the Water* and *Repulsion* were deprived of the kind of human grotesques which Zolnierkiewicz and (the real) Katelbach had brought to *Mammals* and *The Fat and the Lean*, but the characters in *Cul-de-Sac* were a veritable showcase of foible and eccentricity. When it came to the casting, none came more eccentric than the actor whom Polanski had picked for the role of George, in place of Compton's original choice of Donald Houston. With his unblinking, psychopathic stare, pallid complexion and pinched, heart-shaped mouth, hinting at sexual deviancy, Nottinghamshire-born Pleasence had specialised in playing degenerate and devious characters on television and in film; most appositely, he had received rave reviews from London's theatre critics for his performance in the title role of Harold Pinter's *The Caretaker* (a role which he then repeated on film).

Pleasence, however, was not as cold-hearted as his screen image made him appear, and he was keen to intimate in his performance that there was (or, at least, had been) a genuine affection between George and his wife. He already had shaved his head for the role without first obtaining permission, which had upset the equilibrium of his director in terms of how he had seen (and sketched) the character, and Polanski disagreed with his psychoanalytical reading as well. 'He was absolutely adamant that she did not find George attractive in any way,' Pleasence told Ivan Butler. 'This was the only thing that bothered me, at least as far as the development of character was concerned. As far as Teresa was concerned, I felt it was more interesting to think that she was really rather fond of George – that in fact on occasions they had quite a good time in bed together.'

The actor stuck to his guns, insisting that certain scenes – such as that in which Teresa applies make-up to George – were explicable only if a bond of love had once existed between them: 'This was a very difficult scene indeed to motivate. Why does he let her do it? He does so because they used to enjoy considerable love and sex games together – kinky games ... In actual fact, both at the end of this scene and at the end of the one in the kitchen, she and George went into a genuinely loving embrace, but these were cut ... Even so, I think this feeling comes out, with or without directorial permission!'

Polanski failed to see the need for such depth, and the two remained at loggerheads over this and other issues throughout the shooting of the film. 'Teresa is not just a girl who marries a man for her money and then gets bored and fed up,' Pleasence went on. 'This was another area of disagreement. Of course she *is* bored, but Françoise wanted the character to be more two-dimensional, whereas Roman wanted her to be simply sluttish. I don't think he ever really liked her performance very much, though I myself thought it was great.'

Surrounded by these combatants, Jack MacGowran adopted a different tack. MacGowran's film appearances had been relatively few; he was more familiar to viewers from television or the stage, where he largely confined himself to the plays of Beckett, to which his physique and demeanour made him eminently suited. The Beckett-like Albie held a familiar resonance for MacGowran, and he was supremely comfortable in the role, happy to allow himself to be upstaged by his fellow actors and pliant and uncomplaining in the hands of his director. MacGowran's co-operative attitude won him Polanski's undying admiration.

Less endearing to some in the crew was Iain Quarrier, whom Polanski had cast in the role of Teresa's lover; cinematographer Gil Taylor, for one, failed to understand Polanski's attachment to a London swinger whom he thought of as a 'layabout' and on whom he was forced to land a right hook when Quarrier's sarcastic asides became too much for Taylor to bear.

A tragic footnote to the casting of *Cul-de-Sac* came two years to the week after the film commenced production: Françoise Dorléac was driving to Nice airport when her Renault crashed on the Esterel-Côte d'Azur auto-route and burst into flames. She was

burned to death in the vehicle. At the time, she had just finished
Les Demoiselles de Rochefort in which she starred with her sister, and
she was due to fly to London for a final week's work on the Ken
Russell spy thriller *Billion Dollar Brain*; she was 25 years old.

> GEORGE: *The castle. Impossible to heat in the winter... Not*
> *practical. And then... draughts... Peculiar.*
> DICKIE: *Peculiar? – Like peculiar noises?*
> GEORGE: *No, no, no. It's something... inexpressible... Something*
> *unpleasant...*
>
> **Donald Pleasence and Lionel Stander**, *Cul-de-Sac* (1966)

To show their appreciation for the returns from *Repulsion*,
Klinger and Tenser had increased the budget on *Cul-de-Sac* to a
princely £120,000, which included a much-improved director's
fee of £10,000, and the shooting of the film commenced at
Twickenham Studios on 20 June 1965. By early July, cast and crew
were occupying every spare room in the village of Beal on the
Northumbrian coast.

'We changed the title to *Cul-de-Sac* because the theme of the
story was that the gangsters get themselves into a hole – into
a 'cul-de-sac' through their actions,' Tenser said. Not only the
gangsters. As can be imagined of a film which installed up to 12
actors and a couple of dozen crew-members on a remote outcrop of
Northumberland, the making of *Cul-de-Sac* was rife with anecdote.
Everyone involved in the production returned from the shoot with a
story to tell, all of them bad. Burly, Bronx-born Lionel Stander, who
had been cast as Dickie, bore the brunt of the criticism. With the
extremes of weather on the exposed north-east coastline (including
snow at one point), a great deal had to be crammed into the short,
seven-week shooting schedule whenever light and the conditions
allowed, and it was not long before Stander began to object to
Polanski's rigorous 12-hour days. He protested the number of takes
per scene, one of which had required him to down a pint of milk

in a single gulp, and he made it plain that he thought that he was being driven too hard.

To the technicians on *Cul-de-Sac*, the silk-suited, cravat-sporting Stander was an arrogant Yank who did protest too much, but there was a reason for his concern. Before signing up for the film, which represented a rare opportunity for yet another of the industry's faithful retainers who had been forced to leave America because of his political views during the McCarthy black-listings in the 1950s, Stander had failed to disclose a heart problem. By the time shooting was underway on Holy Island, it was too late to do anything about a replacement and Polanski was forced to show at least token consideration for the delicate state of Stander's health. He solved the problem by devious means: Gérard Brach was briefed to inform Stander surreptitiously that he was writing another film especially for him, but to add that Polanski was beginning to have second thoughts because of his unwillingness to co-operate. This fabrication had the desired effect and Stander became noticeably compliant again thereafter. Unfortunately for him, the film that Brach was writing was for his co-star Jack MacGowran, not for Stander.

As the weeks went by and the weather worsened, the tensions increased – between Stander and the crew, between Polanski and Compton. 'As soon as he saw money-men, an allergy would develop,' actor William Franklyn quipped. Polanski eventually was left isolated during the filming on Lindisfarne as, one by one, his cast and crew (with the exception of Jack MacGowran) abandoned their support for his time-consuming and autocratic methods. 'There were days when the whole crew was against me; when I felt totally solitary in my work,' he said. 'Even with Gil, it was difficult on Holy Island; it was not the same Gil I had on *Repulsion*. I was a bit sad about it. I don't think they followed me in the same way that they did on *Repulsion*; I don't think they understood the originality of the film; I don't think they understood the concept of it.'

Michael Klinger understood only the concept of a budget and a schedule, neither of which figured highly on Polanski's list of priorities. After trying and failing to rein in his director's bent for multiple takes and obsessive quest for perfection in every aspect of production bar the bottom-line, Klinger was eventually forced to close down the expensive shoot on the island and return the film to the studio for a hastier completion. 'He had no idea about money at all; it was a means to an end for him,' Tenser said of Polanski. 'All our problems came over the budget. We used Polanski's own producer, Gutowski, as the go-between and that may have been a source of friction. We had no quarrel with Gene, of course, but he had to stick up for his partner and we simply didn't want to go over budget ... We couldn't afford it.' The final sequence in which George shoots Dickie was shot at Twickenham without Taylor, as can be evidenced from differences in the lighting.

> *He just wanted to bother me... He tried to kiss me. He said dreadful things – that I needed a real man... Like him.*
> **Teresa (Françoise Dorléac)**, *Cul-de-Sac* (1966)

So what exactly did Klinger and Tenser's Compton Group get for its money? Not horror, not comedy, not drama or social commentary, but an uneasy conflation of all four. *Cul-de-Sac* is a Knickerbocker Glory of a film, in which all the favourite themes of its director have been rolled into a single outpouring inspired by years of devotion to the medium. 'When we were writing this script, we simply wanted to create a movie that would reflect our taste in cinema,' Polanski recalled. 'What was important was the atmosphere of the film, and the characters.' It is as though Polanski had thought to himself that if he were never to make another feature – a situation which was by no means impossible, given the fact that his relations with Compton were deteriorating by the day – then this was the film that he felt compelled to create before walking away.

It is not so much what *Cul-de-Sac* is about – its plot of two fugitives holed up in an isolated retreat is a staple of the thriller genre – that makes the film unique, as what it is *not* about: its director's love affair with the art of cinema. Every shot is composed with an affectionate eye, every set-up is arranged with the craftsmanship of a master. Delight springs from watching the consummate care which the 32-year-old Polanski evidently took in structuring every frame, despite the arduous conditions under which everyone laboured during the shoot. What comes across in *Cul-de-Sac* is the invigorating magic of celluloid, as filtered through the sensibility of a young man to whom filmmaking had become the foremost passion of his life and who had just been granted the freedom to indulge that passion to the best of his ability, as Welles had been in 1941 with *Citizen Kane*. And this at the very moment when the original beauty of British films, as expressed in the productions of the Archers or those from Ealing Studios, was being homogenised out of existence by the majors in their quest to ratchet up the box-office take via a new and more affluent youth audience.

Cul-de-Sac is art for art's sake, and were it to have arrived in theatres having been originated in France or Yugoslavia, as was originally planned, and in a dubbed version with non-English-speaking actors, it would doubtless have been hailed as a masterpiece of European cinema. As it was, it was simply too idiosyncratic, obscure and indulgent for British and American tastes. The fault was not entirely that of the cinema-going peasantry: in his desire to play with all the tones in the cinematic palette, Polanski had forgotten to invest his film with a gripping, or even tangentially interesting, narrative. What had begun as a power-struggle between two sets of people with alternative agendas and individual strengths and weaknesses, in a locale in which they are cut off from the rest of humanity, was transformed into something entirely different by the time a castle came to substitute for the simple house of the original draft. An unintentional element of surrealism was added to the mix by the Lindisfarne location, which is exaggerated by anachronisms such as Dickie's outmoded twenties' gangster slang ('Do you want me to bump you off?') and the fact that he apparently has conducted a robbery of some kind using a Tommy gun – the Prohibition mobster's weapon of choice – despite which he had managed to get both himself and Albie shot by an *unarmed* British police force.

Of course, the Tommy gun and Albie's wound might have been the result of a gang feud and not the outcome of some abortive heist (despite Compton's synopses to the contrary), but they nevertheless appear anomalous, especially as no explanation for either is forthcoming in the film itself. Presented with what they naturally took to be intentional stratagems, critics found themselves bending over backwards to make sense of the fundamentally nonsensical. 'George and Teresa take the incongruously named Richard and Albert for gangsters (as we do), but what was it *really* that they were up to, and that led them to disaster?' Ivan Butler inquired. 'Albie is surely an odd sort of gunman, and Richard almost too obvious to be true.'

As both are nearer to the kind of fanciful thug that Bertolt Brecht deploys in *Arturo Ui* than they are to real-life contemporaries like the Krays or the Richardsons, Butler's subsequent attempt to postulate the film as political parable might be more pertinent than it first seems: 'There is the hero's name – George – patron-saint and frequently used to personify a once influential country: this George, an erstwhile military man, now immured in his island fortress (with a French girl-wife), threatened by a violent bully from across the water, attempting abject appeasement for as long as possible, driven at last to destroy the menace, thereby causing a holocaust and ending up worse than ever, sitting alone on a rock, bereft of everything, deserted by his French bit, weeping for his past.'

The reality is less esoteric, however: *Cul-de-Sac* was Polanski's variant on *Odd Man Out*, Carol Reed's classic British film noir from 1947, in which James Mason's Johnny McQueen, a local

IRA commander, goes on the run from the law in Belfast after
a bungled wages snatch and with a bullet in his shoulder.
McQueen's personal odyssey, as slowly he shuffles off this mortal
coil, confronts him with a number of eccentric characters in an
increasingly surreal environment as fate, in the juggernaut form
of the RUC (Royal Ulster Constabulary), draws ever nearer. The
similarities with *Cul-de-Sac* will immediately be obvious: *Odd Man
Out* was a film which Polanski first saw as a teenager and never
forgot, because McQueen's situation in the story mirrored his own
as a child in so many ways: on the run from a largely unseen but
all-powerful enemy; shunted from house to house and individual to
individual, never knowing if one was friend or foe. Being a sucker
for genre clichés, Polanski's desire to recreate the iconography of
the film therefore resulted in a machine gun-toting outlaw and an
apparent armed response to attempted robbery, both of which had
been acceptable in the circumstance of the 'Troubles' in Northern
Ireland but plainly were out-of-kilter with criminal activity in
Northumberland. 'That film has an atmosphere that somehow
remains in every movie I've made,' Polanski said later of *Odd Man
Out*, the ineradicable memory which had transported him into
the realm of the senses and inspired in him an undying love for
cinema.

   Odd Man Out was based on a novel by F L Green, and in Green,
R C Sherriff and Carol Reed's memorable adaptation can also be
glimpsed the genesis of the cinema of Roman Polanski, now and
in the future: the first-person narrative which invokes images from
the landscape of the mind; the eccentric cast of characters, all of
whom have a life – and an agenda – of their own, independent of
the thrust of the plot; the protagonist who is as much used and
abused by others as he is instrumental in driving the dynamic;
the tragic, downbeat or merely inconclusive finale. The waters of
the novel's moral debate over whether or not the tale's participants
should tend to or turn in the wounded McQueen were muddied
in the transference of media by some latterday philosophical

musing on the part of screenwriter Sheriff, but the intensity of the playing, the prolific William Alwyn's powerful and unforgettable score and the heart-rending climax, more than made up for any shortcomings in the telling. *Odd Man Out* was another triumph for post-war British cinema and in the young and, as yet, uncommitted Polanski, seeing it had induced in him an almost religious fervour for the art of film. At the susceptible age of 15, one religion – that of his forefathers – irrevocably was replaced by another.

Given the stylistic anomalies which it inherited from *Odd Man Out*, *Cul-de-Sac* is a strange fusion of forties' British neo-realism and sixties' New Wave liberalism. Many critics took this cultural collision to be an example of absurdist high art – but the faintly unreal, wholly unnatural feel that permeates the piece is as much the product of its Tower of Babel composition as it was the intention of its creators: American, French and English actors were being directed by a Pole from a script translated into English from its native French, the idea of which had been drawn from a film that was itself about the Irish conflict – no wonder much of the original script was abandoned in favour of ad-libbed alternatives during shooting!

On top of these, there are the curious visitors with whom George once notionally worked, the metaphor of the kite-flying in which he habitually indulges (the detritus of which hangs in tatters from surrounding telegraph lines) and the sexual hang-ups with which Polanski and Brach seem personally obsessed: George's latent transvestism and a mysoginistic view of women as shallow and sluttish. Nor are the proceedings helped by Polanski's now-obligatory inconclusive ending. Thinking that Dickie has attempted to rape Teresa, George is persuaded to take a more defiant stand against him, at first refusing to go meekly to imprisonment in the castle cellar, and then using Dickie's own gun to shoot him dead. In Polanski's inverted universe, however, this does not make him more of a man in the eyes of Teresa (who earlier had berated him in those very terms: 'If you were a man, you wouldn't let this big creep insult me') but *less* of one, and she promptly leaves him for Cecil's superficial playboy charms while he is left stranded on the barren rock of his own impetuous creation.

This undercutting of expectation is typical of Polanski, but it offers the viewer no foothold on the thinking behind it. What *Cul-de-Sac* signally failed to share with contemporaries like Lewis Gilbert's *Alfie* or Antonioni's *Blow-up* was identifiable characters, a real sense of dramatic tension and emotional depth. Such criticism would follow Polanski to the bitter end; his second British feature had more in common with Karel Reisz's similarly quirky *Morgan: A Suitable Case for Treatment*. Enriching, instructive or merely entertaining cinema, *Cul-de-Sac* was not. But a miniature work of art it most certainly was, in the way of a Gainsborough painting: fastidiously detailed, precisely crafted, immaculately presented – but distant and somehow uninvolving.

When Klinger pulled the plug on the location shoot before the whole of the climax was in the can, one can sense the desolation and panic in Polanski in the closing scenes of *Cul-de-Sac* in which George runs frenziedly through the rising tide to a meditative rock, on which he squats, foetus-like, before crying the name of his first wife – Basia... Or rather, Agnes. 'I really felt by that time very lonely, if it doesn't sound too pathetic,' he confided to Gordon Gow. It is the most emotive moment in the film, for within the image also resides the notion of the artist trying desperately to communicate (George is an amateur painter) but hearing only the echo of his own voice in response.

How much longer are you going to stay here waiting for your Katelbach?

George (Donald Pleasence), *Cul-de-Sac* (1966)

Cul-de-Sac was submitted to the BBFC for certification during the first week of February 1966, along with the script for Polanski's proposed next feature, a parody of Gothic horror films with the title of *The Vampire Killers*, which was now looking for a new home after the bitter wrangling with Compton over *Cul-de-Sac*. In the opinion of the Examiner, the Board had been presented with a film of 'considerable artistic merit' which was 'very much off the beaten track'.

The Board had received the script of the film, under the simple title of 'Katelbach', in January the previous year, and Trevelyan reported that he had read it 'with interest but without complete comprehension'. At the time, the main point of discussion had been whether or not the film might be suitable for the more lenient A certificate, though scenes of nudity and instances of swearing seemed to be steering it towards the X. As things turned out, *Cul-de-Sac* was granted an X with no cuts and with only two small alterations required in the dialogue: the word 'bugger' became 'beggar' and the whispered expletive 'shit!' was muffled on the soundtrack so as to be unintelligible.

Klinger and Tenser were less than pleased with the film that had been presented to them at the turn of 1966. 'The film itself wasn't much of a story but we thought we could rely on the director to put some pep into it,' Tenser reflected. 'By the time we saw the finished copy I knew that we had made a mistake.' (The extent of his incomprehension was made clear by Compton's trailer, which unusually was devoid of come-hither sloganeering and merely comprised a variety of clips, picked at random and pasted end to end.) The partners already had decided that their brief association with Polanski had come to its natural end, and the release of *Cul-de-Sac* in July was not graced with the same level of razzmatazz which had accompanied *Repulsion*. The film was entered in competition, as had been its predecessor, but it managed only to pick up a 'Golden Bear' at Berlin. Press reviews mirrored the bemusement with which many viewers, from Tenser down, greeted Polanski's second Western feature.

Ian Christie of the *Daily Express* gave *Cul-de-Sac* the kind of review which helped to bestow on Polanski the beginnings of his reputation for violent sexual excess: 'The film has its humorous moments ... But it is a strange and fundamentally pointless piece of work, containing gratuitous scenes of violence and mental aberration without any obvious dramatic purpose.' After only three films, the critics already were splitting into two distinct camps – those for Polanski, and those who now lined up against him. The *Observer*'s Philip French remained of the former persuasion: 'Polanski directs with the sort of unobtrusive skill and economy we associate with Renoir and Hitchcock. It is not a pleasant world Polanski creates, the images are intense and disturbing, but it is compellingly presented with a personal, obsessive undercurrent,' he wrote.

In the case of *Cul-de-Sac*, French was to find himself in the minority. 'Slow, unreal, 'arty' in the worst, most self-conscious sense, the film's main interest lies in Mlle Dorléac's habit of taking off all her clothes. Fortunately she does this frequently,' Felix Barker gloated in the *Evening News*. Isabel Quigley of the *Spectator* continued to drive home the knife of disappointment which she had sharpened on *Repulsion*: 'There was seldom such a shooting star as Roman Polanski, whose name, made overnight, now seems firmly wedged in the morning after. *Cul-de-Sac* isn't just worthless, it is pretentiously worthless, which is worse.' It was a view shared by the critic of the *Financial Times*: 'Any unvoiced misgivings one might have had about Roman Polanski after *Repulsion* are confirmed by *Cul-de-Sac*.'

If Polanski's star had gone swiftly into the ascendant after *Knife in the Water*, it fell back to Earth with as resounding a bump less than four years later – at least in terms of critical opinion. Fortunately for the fledgling director, he no longer had need of the critics; the deal for *The Vampire Killers* had been signed and sealed before the ladies and gentlemen of the press were able to uncork their own brand of vitriol.

Three months after the opening of *Cul-de-Sac*, Klinger and Tenser finally parted company; they may have shared the same commercial vision, but they no longer saw eye to eye in artistic terms. Tenser remained in the horror/exploitation market and went on to form Tigon Films, his finest hour as a producer coming in 1968 when he released *Witchfinder General*, which won acclaim for another young director named Michael Reeves. Michael Klinger also continued as an independent, and in 1971 he found himself in charge of a second film about British gangsters – *Get Carter*, arguably one of the best of its kind ever made.

Ladies and gentlemen, we take considerable pride and pleasure in bringing you the founder and president of the international society for the prevention, detection and extermination of... vampires! – Professor Cecil Havelock-Montague, PhD, LLV, BAT – technical adviser on the forthcoming motion picture, The Fearless Vampire Killers, or: Pardon me, But Your Teeth are in My Neck...!

American trailer, *The Fearless Vampire Killers* (1967)

Even before filming was completed on *Cul-de-Sac*, Polanski had found himself courted by Martin Ransohoff, one of two directors (with John Calley) of Filmways, a US independent which served as a production arm for the mighty M-G-M. Among the numerous parties to which Polanski was forever being invited was one thrown by Filmways at the Dorchester to celebrate Ransohoff's arrival in the UK. Ransohoff had ingratiated himself with the director by virtue of the fact that he had snapped up the US distribution rights to *Cul-de-Sac*, even though Polanski's current girlfriend, actress Jill St John, considered him 'a phoney'. His association with Klinger and Tenser having come effectively to an end due to an irreversible breakdown of trust in the course of filming *Cul-de-Sac*, Polanski was on the lookout for a new benefactor; he decided to attend.

In the course of the evening, Ransohoff agreed to finance Polanski's next project with a distribution deal through M-G-M

– but with a proviso. Ransohoff had personally been nurturing the career of a young Texan-born starlet on the side, and he now suggested to Polanski that she should play the female lead in the film as part of the package. As said female lead had been written in the script as a Jewess with 'long red hair', Polanski was incredulous at the prospect of Sarah Chagal being played by a honey-blonde Texan Catholic. He had St John in mind for the role. But Ransohoff was not one to take no for an answer, and he invited Polanski to defer his decision until at least he had met the actress in question, whom he had 'discovered' on the set of *The Beverly Hillbillies*. The two of them had something in common, after all, he suggested – she was about to star alongside Donald Pleasence in *Eye of the Devil*, and Polanski had just finished directing him in *Cul-de-Sac*. Polanski capitulated, and a date was arranged between himself and 23-year-old Sharon Marie Tate.

As in all good fairy tales, Tate eventually was cast, and Polanski's reward was a $2 million budget and all the resources that M-G-M could put at his disposal.

```
EXT. NIGHT ROAD TO THE VILLAGE

Cold moonlight illuminates the snow. In long
shot a sledge dashes along drawn by two horses,
their nostrils steaming. Behind the driver, two
figures sit absolutely motionless. A harsh and
frightening voice intones:

    NARRATOR
    That night, penetrating deep into the heart of
    Transylvania, PROFESSOR ABRONSIUS was unaware
    that he was on the point of reaching the
    goal of his mysterious investigations in the
    course of which he had journeyed throughout
    central Europe for many years accompanied by
```

```
his one and only faithful disciple ALFRED.
A scholar and scientist whose genius was
unappreciated ABRONSIUS had given up all to
devote himself body and soul to what was to
him a sacred mission. He had even lost his
chair at Koenigsberg University where for a
long time his colleagues used to refer to him
as... The Nut.
```

screenplay, *The Vampire Killers* (1967)

The Vampire Killers was conceived in part as a vehicle for Jack MacGowran. MacGowran was an easy-going Dubliner and virtually the only one of the cast and crew of *Cul-de-Sac* who had not been fazed by Polanski's high-handed manner and perfectionist ways. To the contrary, he had grown rather fond of his martinet director and had remained on Holy Island with his wife Gloria for the whole of the shoot – even after his relatively brief role as Albie was completed. Polanski had seen in MacGowran's permanently quizzical features the Irish equivalent of Lodz comrade Henryk Kluba, and the ideal mix of innocence and guile that he and Brach had in mind for Professor Abronsius, the Van Helsing-like character around whom the plot of their film was intended to revolve. Polanski was a collector of characters on screen and off, as Kluba confirmed – 'He always saw people as potential actors or characters for his films' – and MacGowran was nothing if not a character. Polanski rewarded what he felt had been MacGowran's loyalty by casting him in the leading role of his new horror spoof, with himself as Abronsius's equally naïve assistant, Alfred.

It is clear from the screenplay that much mirth was meant to be extracted from the mechanics of dealing with vampires – such as garlands of garlic and stakes through the heart – as though the intended audience for the film were as ignorant of the rules of folklore as most of the characters in the story. But the formulae by which vampire films played had been established by Hammer and others long before Polanski came on the same, and his lack of exposure in childhood to a cinematic sub-genre with which Western audiences were now all too familiar was made painfully clear in the laborious attempts to extract some juvenile slapstick from various characters' inability to comprehend exactly how to dispatch a vampire by means of a wooden stake. Quite apart from a century-and-a-half of literature on the subject and half-a-century of movies, the film is set in Transylvania, spiritual home of the very creatures of which everyone in the cast tiresomely feigns no knowledge.

Taking on the role of Alfred in *The Vampire Killers* meant more to Polanski than 'doing a Hitchcock', where the Master of Suspense would make a covert appearance in the first reel of his films as a kind of good luck charm. Acting – playing the fool for an audience – remained Polanski's first love, and *The Vampire Killers* offered him his first opportunity in a feature film to refresh his skills in that direction.

Polanski's physical appearance allocated him the role of bit-part player at best, though this was not, unsurprisingly, how he saw himself (as self-portraiture testifies). Which is not to say that Polanski was unattractive; he had great personal charm and he exuded considerable appeal, particularly for members of the opposite sex, but the camera exaggerated his aquiline features and denied him the faintly rakish air which he had in life. All was well when he confined himself to smaller roles, but Alfred is effectively the protagonist in *The Vampire Killers*, which leaves the film with an unsympathetic presence driving its narrative. Jerzy Bossak, his old tutor at Lodz, had advised him against playing the young hitcher in *Knife in the Water*; international acclaim for the film had been the result. Such words to the wise had not been a feature of his career since leaving Poland for the West. No matter how adroit his thespian sensibility, one is moved to wonder if *Knife in the Water* would have had the same impact on audiences were

Polanski to have shoehorned himself into the role occupied by the authentically guileless Malanowicz.

Is there by any chance a castle in the district?
Professor Abronsius (Jack MacGowran), *Dance of the Vampires* (1967)

Professor Abronsius and his assistant Alfred are travelling through Transylvania on a mission to search out the truth about vampires. They arrive at a small inn, where hanging garlands of garlic lead Abronsius to the conclusion that there is a castle in the area. After various episodes of sexual misadventure at the inn, Count von Krolock arrives by sled. He kidnaps the daughter of the innkeeper, who goes in search of her and is murdered. Abronsius has then to persuade the innkeeper's wife that a stake through the heart is the only way to prevent him from becoming a vampire. Their efforts fail, a chase ensues, and the innkeeper leads them to Krolock's castle.

The Count welcomes them; he professes to share Abronsius's interest in bats – 'I'm a night bird. I'm not much good in the daytime,' he remarks. Krolock invites them to stay the night and they are introduced to his son Herbert. The following day, they discover the vampire's lair. Albert finds Sarah captive in the castle but loses the bag of implements with which they are to dispatch the vampires. After eluding the clutches of Krolock's son, Albert and Abronsius watch from the battlements as the dead rise from the castle's graveyard to participate in the Count's annual midnight ball; Krolock appears and reveals to them that their fate is to join the ever-growing ranks of the undead.

As the vampires dance a minuet, Abronsius and Albert join them in disguise. The subterfuge is uncovered when they alone cast a reflection in a mirror. They grab hold of Sarah and flee the castle, but the Count sends Koukol, his hunchbacked servant, after them. Koukol pursues them through the valley in his coffin-cum-toboggan, till he misjudges a slope and plunges to his death.

They seem to be safe, but Sarah shows her fangs and bites Albert. Abronsius drives on, oblivious to the truth. 'That night, fleeing from Transylvania, Professor Abronsius never guessed that he was carrying away with him the very evil he had wished to destroy. Thanks to him, this evil will at last be able to spread across the world...'

*　　*　　*

The Vampire Killers is a misguided assemblage of Polanski's current 'Swinging Sixties' obsessions: sex, skiing and Sharon Tate. It is one long, laborious hymn to the adolescent mentality, full of elaborate practical jokes and furtive sexual innuendo, and burdened by camp cameo roles devised specifically for the amusement of Polanski's new-found friends from the London celebrity circuit, like *Cul-de-Sac's* Iain Quarrier (who plays a particularly repellent homosexual vampire) and ex-middleweight boxer and part-time television guest star Terry Downes. Tate herself is accorded some huge, devotional close-ups, which are exceeded in size only by a moody shot of a malevolent Krolock, and her acting here is on a par with her star status in general. She is a pretty girl with an almost impressionistic daub of auburn hair (a radiant red wig), but she lacks charisma and the all-seeing eye of the camera does her angular features little long-term favour. Tate may be lovely to look at in an airbrushed, *Vogue*-cover kind of way, but she is stolidly soulless throughout, having been given little more to do by the prurient script than scream, run or disrobe by turns.

Polanski shows off his native iconoclasm by questioning the traditional motifs of the genre and pointing up its inherent paradoxes, such as the efficacy or otherwise of Christian crucifixes and the homoerotic implications of male-on-male vampire activity. But whereas a less-bludgeoning sensibility behind the lens might have broached these aspects with a lightness of comedic touch, Polanski exhausts the joke, if ever there was one, by repetition and heavy-handedness

No one involved in *The Vampire Killers* appeared to be cognisant of the adage that horror is a notoriously difficult genre to satirise, much of it being close to farce to begin with, and M-G-M's desire to work with Polanski blinded its executives to the precedent set by all the so-called horror-comedies which previously had sunk without trace. On top of that, there was a cultural divide for audiences to negotiate: the humour in the Brach/Polanski script is strictly of the European variety, in which Feydeau-like chases around Wilfrid Shingleton's expansive sets alternate with pratfalls, eccentric characters and much mugging to camera. The film was markedly unsophisticated by western European standards of the time, particularly the standards which were being set by advances in surreal comedy in the mid-sixties. (Among others, the inimitable Norman Wisdom had been doing similar slapstick routines so much better for more than ten years.) The one notable moment of wit comes when television's Alfie Bass (formerly 'Boots' Bisley of *Bootsie and Snudge* fame), as a Jewish vampire, is confronted by Alfred wielding the obligatory crucifix. 'Oy-oy...' he exclaims. 'Hev you got the *wronk* vampire!' So isolated was this verbal gag that it became the one joke which was quoted in every editorial review to indicate that the film was indeed to be laughed at (or perhaps *along with*).

Where *The Vampire Killers* does score unmistakably is in the exquisiteness of Douglas Slocombe's cinematography and the grandeur of Shingleton's Gothic halls. It is a film of ravishing pictorial beauty and opulent design, with the snow-capped Dolomites at Valgardena standing in for the mountains of Transylvania, while the sound-stages of three studios – Borehamwood, Elstree and Pinewood – furnished the baroque elegance of Krolock's castle, the climactic ball being shot at Elstree. The highly saturated colours on display – a trademark of M-G-M since the thirties – even manage to out-Hammer Hammer's then-infamous predilection for redolent primary hues.

In theme and plotting, however, Polanski's fourth major international feature had more in common with the Universal horrors of the 1940s than with the Hammer horrors which were shooting concurrently. Its stylistic affinity lies with *Abbott and Costello Meet Frankenstein* rather than with any notional pastiche of *Dracula-Prince of Darkness* (though Polanski's Alfred looks to have been cloned from Hütter in 1922's *Nosferatu*), and while its comic inadequacies may be explained away by its director's restricted access to more decadent fare during his sojourn at Lodz, he and MacGowran nevertheless make poor substitutes for Bud and Lou.

Ferdy Mayne, a minor villain in many a British 'B' movie (including several of Hammer's own), makes a creditable stab at the creakily named Count von Krolock, but he pales in the long (and at the time still vampirically-active) shadow of Christopher Lee. Like his Hammer counterparts, he is shorn of the ability to transform himself into a bat, despite his many references to the creatures in the script. He arrives at the inn by sled, like some dystopian Santa Claus, and has to clamber feet-first through a skylight in order to claim his first (and only) victim. Later, when the succulent human morsels that he has garnered for the delectation of his undead guests decide to jump from the frying pan towards the fire, he and his kind are held at bay by the simple ruse of laying two decorative swords on the ground in the form of a cross. Any tension implicit in the prospect of a chase is thus quickly dissipated, and the viewer is left with the impression that even the likes of *Abbott and Costello Meet Frankenstein* might seem unbearably exciting by comparison.

Apart from the film's two principals, most screen time is given over to Alfie Bass's Jewish vampire-innkeeper Chagal, but the character is completely undeveloped beyond the expected idiosyncrasies of racial stereotyping. Even with a swimming pool full of M-G-M money, Brach and Polanski apparently felt no need to employ the services of an English-speaking scriptwriter to inject

he cast and crew of *Knife in the Water*
n board the 'Christine'

Polanski directs a struggle between Niemczyk
and Malanowicz in *Knife in the Water*

Catherine Deneuve as Carole Ledoux (*Repulsion*, 1965)

Catherine Deneuve and Yvonne Furneaux in *Repulsion*

'...The rooms of the apartment appear to distort before her eyes,
stretching into infinity and harbouring dark shadows...' (*Repulsion*, 1965)

William Franklyn and Françoise Dorléac in *Cul-de-Sac*

Françoise Dorléac, Lionel Stander and Roman Polanski share a joke on the set of *Cul-de-Sac*

Sarah (Sharon Tate) and Alfred (Roman Polanski) share a kiss in *The Vampire Killers*

Polanski hams it up with Jack MacGowran in *The Vampire Killers*

Rosemary (Mia Farrow) and Guy (John Cassavetes) settle into their apartment in the Bramford in *Rosemary's Baby*

Rosemary (Mia Farrow) awakens from a nightmare of rape (*Rosemary's Baby*, 1968)

Left: Roman Polanski and Sharon Tate, shortly before their marriage in 1969

Above: Polanski directs Francesca Annis on the set of *Macbeth*

Below: 'Is this a dagger which I see before me?' – Jon Finch (*Macbeth*, 1971)

COLUMBIA FILMS présente
une PRODUCTION PLAYBOY
Un film de ROMAN POLANSKI
MACBETH
Visa ministériel n° 4535

Sydne Rome receives some unwanted attention in *What?*

Private eye Jake Gittes (Jack Nicholson) spies trouble brewing in *Chinatown*

Gittes (Nicholson) confronts the 'real' Evelyn Mulwray (Faye Dunaway) in *Chinatown*

Polanski ponders a suggestion from Nicholson on the set of *Chinatown*

a few punning or easily explicable jokes into the proceedings, so all the comic interludes are accompanied by unintelligible mutterings instead. While some of the script's cleverer notions, such as having the vampires' ball attended by personages from the pages of European history (an idea borrowed from Mikhail Bulgakov's *The Master and Margarita*, which had seen its first publication in English the same year) are lost in too subtle a transition to the screen: only the character of Richard Crookback is easily – if incongruously – identifiable to a lay audience.

Beyond its luminous cinematography and richly bilious production design, there is little of merit in *The Vampire Killers*. It is a tedious exercise in self-indulgence, whose few curious strands of Eastern European humour appear to depend for their effect on time and money being spent in disproportionate degree to the quality of the resultant joke. A scene in which Albert flees from a befanged Herbert, only to end up once more face-to-face with his pursuer, required the construction of a medieval banqueting hall complete with minstrel's gallery, so that Polanski could capture the episode in a single take, as he had with the turning of the boat in *Knife in the Water*. As the placement of the camera enables the onlooker to see the punch line coming before Albert does, one is moved to wonder how funny such a set-up was imagined to be in the planning.

Not only the subject matter was funereal; the pace was also. Polanski confounded the expectations of his intended audience by turning out what was advertised as a zany slapstick comedy that paradoxically unfolded with deadly earnestness over a tortuous 108 minutes. M-G-M had indulged him during the shooting of the film to the extent of constructing an elaborate Gothic castle, the like of which Hammer would have given its eye-teeth for, but that was as far as it went; Polanski was now in the real world of commercial filmmaking, not being pandered to in the company of Chabrol or Godard for *Les plus belles escroqueries du monde*, or pulling the wool over the eyes of a pair of amateurs like Klinger and Tenser, and

Ransohoff not surprisingly sought to pare the film down by a whole reel, to meet the less tolerant demands of the American market. Polanski was incensed, but he had no contractual control over the final cut in the US.

The Vampire Killers was released in the US in a 98-minute abridgement entitled *The Fearless Vampire Killers, or: Pardon me, But Your Teeth are in My Neck,* and later in the UK in its full-length version, as *Dance of the Vampires.* For its 13 November opening on his home turf, Ransohoff tried further to salvage the situation by having a featurette shot for the trailer in which music-hall legend Max Wall delivered a lengthy lecture on the ways of the vampire as 'Cecil Havelock-Montague', telegraphing the film's only decent joke in the process. Wall's day had been over for some years before 1967, and Ransohoff was as ill-advised in his promotional pursuits as had been Polanski in his wish to parody the Gothic horror film. *The Vampire Killers,* in either of its titular guises, drew a blank at the box-office on both sides of the pond.

> *As brooks flow into streams, streams into rivers, and rivers into the sea, so our adepts flow back to us and swell our ranks. Soon, we shall be victorious and triumphant. We shall then hold sway over this Earth, which awaits our coming as autumn awaits winter...*
>
> **Count von Krolock (Ferdy Mayne)**, *Dance of the Vampires* (1967)

The reaction of the Examiner at the British Board of Film Censors when the script was originally submitted for appraisal in February 1966 had been one of dismay: 'This is neither comedy nor farce; it is an awkward medley, and since it contains so much 'straight' vampirism, it must be judged by the same standards as an ordinary Dracula story.' The entire concept had been marked down as 'tasteless' and the filmmakers' attention had been drawn to sexual innuendoes in the dialogue and the combination of blood and sex, even when the subject was to be treated in a lighthearted way. 'In these films we are normally concerned about vampirism mixed up with sex, which brings in an element of sexual perversion; and scenes which go beyond the horrific into disgust,' Trevelyan had advised. Nevertheless, he was prepared to cast something of a blind eye over the script's notional shortcomings and he had given Polanski a tacit nod of approval: 'This should be very entertaining in a 'Charles Addams' kind of way, and I am sure that with your touch it will be a most unusual comedy,' he wrote.

When the completed film arrived for certification the following March, the Board took exception to a mere three scenes, all involving blood smeared over the mouths of vampires and two of them in the same sequence, when Krolock attacks Sarah in her bath; the third came after Shagal had assaulted a maid. Furthermore, it professed itself happy to pass the film as an A, provided that cuts were made in all of the above scenes. It was agreed that the bath sequence could be modified and the final shot of Krolock's face (as seen through the keyhole by Alfred), could be shortened. But Gene Gutowski protested that the shot of Shagal was 'almost impossible' to cut. Trevelyan studied the scene again and decided that he could let it pass also, *and* under an A certificate.

Trevelyan's query with regard to the nature of the shot in a so-called comedy had set Polanski thinking, though, and he decided contrarily that the shot could be removed without harming the film – *should* be, in fact. 'Although you very kindly agreed to pass the close-up of Shagal with blood around his mouth, on the second viewing I must admit that I felt a little uneasy myself and came to understand your original objection,' he told Trevelyan. 'I have, therefore, cut out this close-up entirely.' The amicable spirit of co-operation which is exhibited in this exchange would be notable by its absence on the next occasion that Polanski had to deal with the British censor.

By July 1967, the absence from cinemas of Polanski's latest opus was the cause of some consternation in the press. The critics may have become divided over the merits of Polanski's films to date, but his work remained a source of intrigue. A report in the *Times*, which began by inquiring 'What has happened to Roman Polanski's latest film *The Fearless Vampire Killers*?', hinted at the friction between its director and M-G-M by disclosing that Polanski had refused to enter the film in the 1967 Berlin Film Festival, as originally promised, because of Ransohoff's continued tampering. The letter that Polanski wrote to Festival director Dr Alfred Bauer, informing him of his decision to withdraw the film, made no bones about the discontent that he felt over his treatment by M-G-M: 'Although my final cut prevails outside the US, Mr Ransohoff put forth a suggestion that his version, and not mine, should be presented at the Berlin Festival. Alternatively, the suggestion was made that in return for my version being shown in Berlin, I should agree to Mr Ransohoff's cut to be shown world-wide. I hope you understand that I could not agree to either one of these suggestions.'

The best part of another four months elapsed before *The Vampire Killers* opened in the US in the emasculated form that was finally approved by Martin Ransohoff. When the gentlemen of the American press belatedly caught sight of it, they could hardly contain the laughter that bubbled under as they contrived ever more elaborate ways to lampoon the lampoon in their columns; as a result, many of the reviews turned out funnier than the film itself. Joseph Morgenstern in *Newsweek* set the tone: '"Shtick it vhere?" asks a funny fat lady in *The Fearless Vampire Killers, or Pardon Me, But Your Teeth Are In My Neck*, a stake in her fist and her mouth stuffed with umlauts. Vhere? Vhere? Shtraight into the producer's heart, shtupid! Fix him good for this witless travesty, this bloody bore of a take-off on vampire movies by some apprentice gagsters who will never be half the half-man Dracula was. The film gets some laughs, maybe one per reel.'

Hollis Alpert, in the American *Saturday Review*, was even less forgiving: 'It has been a long time since I have encountered such heavy-handed whimsicality, and the blame for the whole misguided effort must be placed on Mr Polanski, for, in addition to his directorial duties, he is the co-author of the screenplay and plays a leading role.' In the days when auteur theory held sway, it was par-for-the-course that the director of a film should shoulder most of the blame. 'That was one of the most disgraceful experiences I ever went through,' Polanski recalled. 'After I finished *Vampire Killers*, [Ransohoff] took it away from me and cut 20 minutes out of it and redubbed it and changed the music. When he was through, no one could understand it any more, so he added a little cartoon to explain what it was about ... That's how it was presented in America.' Given that Polanski had himself referred to *The Vampire Killers* as a 'cartoon with people', Ransohoff's intervention does not seem to have been *that* wide of the mark.

This famous '20 minutes' of Polanski's has since become enshrined in legend. When a print of the film was submitted to the BBFC for classification on 23 March 1967, its running time was given as 108 minutes 16 seconds (before cuts). US release prints were subsequently quoted as having a running-time of 98 minutes, the difference between the two being ten minutes, therefore, and not the 20 which Polanski had exaggerated for effect. American commentators compounded the error by taking the US running time and adding back Polanski's 20 minutes, to arrive at an 'original' time of 118 minutes for the pre-Ransohoff edit.

When the film eventually surfaced in the UK in November 1967, as *Dance of the Vampires*, British critics were marginally more impressed by Polanski's version than had been their peers in the US by Ransohoff's – though it mostly was a matter of degree. 'If from time to time the film is tedious, it is at least never predictable,' David Robinson opined in the *Financial Times*. Allen Eyles in *Films and Filming* chose also to point out some virtues: 'A cannibalistic movie, feeding off the established genre, *Dance of the Vampires* lacks the psychological subtleties of characterisation found in *Knife in the Water* and *Cul-de-Sac*; but it matches them in the impeccable evocation of setting and atmosphere.' The BFI's

Monthly Film Bulletin was more damning. 'There is no horror in the film, therefore no suspense and inevitably some stretches of tedium.'

The shambolic marketing of *The Vampire Killers* did little to advance the stop-start career of the ex-'Miss Autorama', the beautiful Sharon Tate, for whom big things had been predicted by Ransohoff for the past two years. But in Tate's eyes, it was Marty who was now a thing of the past; the new man in her life was her director on *The Vampire Killers*, with whom she had formed a closer relationship almost from the first day of filming. Polanski was no slouch when it came to bedding his leading ladies – not for nothing had he been christened the 'Playboy' director by the tabloids – but his affair with Tate was different: mutual respect and casual sex had turned to love and domestic serendipity. They had become an 'item' in the Dolomites while shooting on location for *The Vampire Killers*; by the time the film was released, they were living together with a view to making their relationship a permanent one.

'When we were on location, I asked her, "Would you like to make love with me?"' Polanski later recalled. 'And she said, very sweetly, "Yes." And then for the first time I was somewhat touched by her ... And we started sleeping regularly together. And she was so sweet and so lovely that I didn't believe it, you know. I'd had bad experiences and I didn't believe that people like that existed ... She was fantastic. She loved me."

By all accounts, including his own, Polanski was besotted with Tate – though they were an eccentric couple even by sixties' standards: they dropped acid together, and both of them had more than their fair share of weird and whacked-out misfits for friends. One of these was Jay Sebring, a celebrity hairstylist and known pusher who also happened to be Tate's former lover. Ever on the fringes of Hollywood's smart set are the pimps and pushers, hustlers and hangers-on, without whom life in LA and London would lose its sordid edge; Sebring fell into this peripheral bracket.

Polanski's growing reputation as a filmmaker to watch was somehow undented by the critical and commercial failure of *The Vampire Killers* on both sides of the Atlantic, or by the confused messages about the nature of his talent which had been sent out by *Cul-de-sac*. Memories of *Repulsion* were strong, and Hollywood studios had continued to express interest in the young Pole, even though he was now seen to have been instrumental in supplying M-G-M with a $2 million disaster.

In the wake of *The Vampire Killers*, critical noses had detected a whiff of hubris in the desire of the Polish enfant terrible to prove that he was master of all aspects of his trade, including comedy, but while their owners hinted darkly of an imminent fall from grace, Polanski already was hard at work on a screenplay for his next – and first wholly American – feature.

Some months earlier, the best-selling-book list of the *New York Times* had been dominated by a popular novel in a similar vein. The innocent-sounding *Rosemary's Baby* went on to sell more than five million copies world-wide. Before it had even hit the bookshops, however, Polanski had been approached by Paramount to direct a film version.

Author Ira Levin was the son of a successful toy manufacturer. From an early age, he had exhibited a taste for conjuring, wordplay and all things theatrical (the latter two would come to feature heavily in *Rosemary's Baby*); he even took the name of the story's 'Tannis'-root vitamin drink from Tannen's Magic Shop in Times Square. His gimmick in *Rosemary's Baby* was to tack the mythical but much-predicted birth of the Antichrist onto a recognisable urban setting of mundane normality. Rosemary and Guy are young, aspiring New Yorkers, settling into a new apartment in the stately (though reassuringly Gothic) Bramford building to await the birth of their first child. But as in all good pulp-plots, the Bramford has a history – of witchcraft and Satanism – which the Woodhouses, needless to say, laugh off with easy, postmodern disdain. As the term of Rosemary's pregnancy lengthens, seemingly ordinary events conspire to convince her of the devilish noose that is tightening around herself and her baby...

Levin's *Rosemary's Baby* was little different to Robert Bloch's *Psycho* (1959) – both were essentially 'penny dreadful' potboilers, but both featured a central conceit which caught the imagination as well as the mood of the moment. In the case of *Psycho*, a brilliant script (by Joe Stefano) and equally brilliant direction (by Alfred Hitchcock) turned what should have been an eminently disposable B-movie into a high-class A feature and one of the greatest horror films ever made.

The self-same thing was now about to happen to *Rosemary's Baby*.

SYMPATHY FOR THE DEVIL

'There's no such thing as the devil!' Ivan Nikolayich burst out,
hopelessly muddled by all this dumb show, ruining all Berlioz's
plans by shouting: 'And stop playing the amateur psychologist!'

At this the lunatic gave such a laugh that it startled the sparrows
out of the trees above them.

'Well now, that is interesting,' said the professor, quaking
with laughter. 'Whatever I ask you about, it doesn't exist!' He
suddenly stopped laughing and with a typical madman reaction
he immediately went to the other extreme, shouting angrily and
harshly: 'So you think the devil doesn't exist?'

Mikhail Bulgakov, *The Master and Margarita* (1967)

I t was not the most promising of titles. To the casual ear,
Rosemary's Baby sounded as though it were more of a self-help
guide to pregnancy than a supernatural horror-thriller. Nor did
it originate with a recognisable source of such material: Bronx-
born author Ira Levin had written only one other novel, and that
had been 14 years earlier, in 1953 – *A Kiss Before Dying*. Word from
Levin's New York publisher Random House had it that *Rosemary's
Baby was* a horror-thriller, however – and a highly original one, at
that.

The novel's plot was straightforward enough: Rosemary and Guy
Woodhouse are a young married couple in search of an apartment
to rent in New York City; he, an actor – she, a curiously career-lite
socialite from the Midwest. They settle on the Bramford, an ornate
Gothic pile situated near Central Park with the predictably morbid

history. Hutch, an old and learned friend of Rosemary's, fills them in on the details:

> 'I don't know whether or not you know it,' he said, buttering a roll. 'But the Bramford had rather an unpleasant reputation early in the century.' He looked up, saw that they didn't know and went on...
>
> 'Along with the Isadora Duncans and Theodore Dreisers,' he said, 'the Bramford has housed a considerable number of less attractive personages. It's where the Trench sisters performed their little dietary experiments, and where Keith Kennedy held his parties. Adrian Marcato lived there too; and so did Pearl Ames.'
>
> 'Who were the Trench sisters?' Guy asked, and Rosemary asked, 'Who was Adrian Marcato?'
>
> 'The Trench sisters,' Hutch said, 'were two proper Victorian ladies who were occasional cannibals. They cooked and ate several young children, including a niece.'
>
> 'Lovely,' Guy said.
>
> Hutch turned to Rosemary. 'Adrian Marcato practised witchcraft,' he said. 'He made quite a splash in the eighteen-nineties by announcing that he had succeeded in conjuring up the living Satan. He showed off a handful of hair and some claw-parings, and apparently people believed him; enough of them, at least, to form a mob that attacked and nearly killed him in the Bramford lobby.'
>
> **Ira Levin**, *Rosemary's Baby* (1967)

During their tour of the property, a note of discord is struck by an old dresser which has been moved to block the entrance to a hall cupboard; anomalous as it may be, this is hardly the stuff of nightmares and the Woodhouses agree the lease. Once installed in their new home, they are soon befriended by Minnie and Roman Castevet, an aged but ostensibly well-meaning couple who live in the apartment through the wall. While Guy becomes inordinately attached to the Castevets, and Roman's theatrical reminiscences in particular, Rosemary is less enamoured of the matriarchal Minnie's interferences in her daily routine. Nevertheless, they indulge the old couple for the sake of maintaining a 'good neighbour' policy.

Rosemary's lack of career is explained by the fact that she and Guy are trying for a baby. In her anticipatory state, an accumulation of incidents begins to give her cause for concern – among them is the sudden death of a young woman named Terri to whom the Castevets had given room and board and who fell – or was thrown? – from a window in their apartment. A soirée to which the Woodhouses are invited along with other friends of the Castevets ends with Rosemary being taken ill after eating chocolate mousse. She is put to bed by Guy, where she finds herself in the throes of a vivid dream: the dream alternates oddly between the deck of a yacht manned by a deceased President Kennedy and the Castevets' apartment – to which she has been returned via a secret doorway and in which she is tied to a bed before being raped by a scaly monster while the erstwhile assemblage of house-guests looks on. When she wakes the next day, Rosemary notices scratch-marks on her body; Guy confesses to having made love to her while she slept:

> "'I dreamed someone was – raping me," she said. "I don't know who. Someone – unhuman."
>
> "Thanks a lot," Guy said.
>
> "You were there, and Minnie and Roman, other people... It was some kind of ceremony."'

Rosemary now learns that she is pregnant.

Things are on the up for the Woodhouses – Rosemary is expecting the baby that she and Guy had wanted all along and Guy has been offered what could be a breakthrough role in a new play (albeit at the expense of the first-choice actor who inexplicably went blind after the audition). Minnie Castevet recommends Rosemary to Dr Sapirstein, one of the leading gynaecologists in New York. With Minnie's gift of an amulet of 'Tannis root' around her neck,

Rosemary settles into a second month of pregnancy as Part One of the novel comes to a close.

Part Two finds Rosemary content in her condition and ministered to by Minnie with a morning pick-me-up... Then the pains come, intense and incessant, and inexorably she starts to lose rather than gain weight as the months go by... Dr Sapirstein, the Castevets, Guy even – no one appears to be worried by the sudden turn of events. Only Rosemary is less than convinced that she is experiencing a normal pregnancy – until Hutch begins to share her concerns. Finding Rosemary alone in the apartment, he questions her about the pick-me-up, the amulet and the Castevets in general, his sage inscrutability sensing a pattern of sorts. Before he can delve deeper, Guy returns unexpectedly and interrupts their tête-à-tête. Hutch takes his leave of them; the following day, Rosemary is shocked to discover that he has been taken to hospital in a coma. In days, he is dead.

As though privy to a premonition of calamity, Hutch has had the foresight to leave Rosemary a book called *All Of Them Witches*, which contains a chapter on Adrian Marcato, the Bramford's famous 19th century wizard, and his son Steven. Rosemary wonders if there is some hidden significance in the names; acting on a hunch, she utilises Scrabble letters to ascertain that Roman Castevet is an anagram of Steven Marcato! In her paranoid imagination, the strands of the conspiracy now start to come together: Roman Castevet is Adrian Marcato's son; Marcato was a witch, as is Castevet; he, Minnie, and their curious friends form a Satanic coven which has designs on her unborn baby – they mean to sacrifice it to the Devil! And husband Guy is the Judas who has promised it to them in return for career success...

Rosemary attempts to escape the collective clutches of the coven but her suspicions are proved correct when she is cornered, forcibly sedated, and effectively incarcerated to await the delivery. She gives birth to 'Andrew', as she has christened the child in her mind, but subsequently is told that it was a stillbirth – the baby is dead. She is returned to her apartment and a guard is placed by her bed.

As she drifts in and out of a drugged sleep, Rosemary thinks that she hears the sound of a baby crying at the Castevets'; could it be Andrew, she wonders? – Not dead, but captive... She slips her minder a 'Mickey', grabs hold of a kitchen knife, and heads for the cupboard in the hall which was revealed in her dream to conceal an entrance to the apartment next door. Finding the secret opening, she follows the sound of crying to the living room – where a bassinet draped in black holds centre-stage.

Circling around the bassinet are the Castevets, their eccentric entourage – and Guy. Rosemary approaches it, knife in hand, and stares at the restless child within. She reels back in shock:

"*"What have you done to his eyes?"*

They stirred and looked to Roman.

"He has His Father's eyes," he said.

She looked at him, looked at Guy – whose eyes were hidden behind a hand – looked at Roman again. "What are you talking about?" she said. "Guy's eyes are brown, they're normal! What have you done to him, you maniacs?" She moved from the bassinet, ready to kill them.

"Satan is His Father, not Guy," Roman said. "Satan is His Father, who came up from Hell and begat a son of mortal woman..."'

The truth dawns. Infant sacrifice was never part of the plan. Rosemary *was* raped by the Devil; she has given birth to the Antichrist. 'Hail Satan!' the coven cries in unison. 'God is dead and Satan lives,' Roman Castevet rejoins. 'The year is One, the first year of our Lord.' But if her baby is half-Devil, Rosemary reasons, he is also half *her*... With love, good may still triumph.

Rosemary sidles up to the bassinet and starts to rock it gently to and fro...

*   *   *

Aware that it had a potential best-seller on its hands and wholly intent on making it so, Random House had placed a copy of Levin's manuscript with literary agent Marvin Birdt, whose job was to interest the movers and shakers of Hollywood. What Birdt had to offer was a suspense-thriller with supernatural overtones and he set about contacting the usual suspects. One of the first in the running was independent exploitation producer William Castle.

Castle had been in the film business since 1939, when he started out as a trainee at Columbia Pictures (under legendary studio boss Harry Cohn) after trying and failing to become an actor. His speciality was the dreaming up of elaborate promotional stunts to aid ticket sales, a penchant which had taken root during a brief period spent backstage with a touring production of *Dracula*. After years of labouring as a house-producer of programme-fillers for Columbia, he had put his flair for showmanship to better use by turning independent. His first feature, a sub-Hitchcock thriller called *Macabre* (1958), caught the attention of the trades through its ploy of offering to insure patrons against death by fright during screenings of the film. Castle had followed *Macabre* with *House on Haunted Hill* and *The Tingler*, both starring 'Master of the Macabre' Vincent Price. *The Tingler* was topped by *13 Ghosts* (1960) – without Vincent Price, but with 'Illusion-O' in his place – and, the following year, *Homicidal* had also got along without star names by cashing in on Hitchcock's *Psycho* and upping the gore quotient. But parting company with Price had lost Castle the best asset that he was ever likely to find.

After more years of second-feature fare like *Mr Sardonicus* (1961), *Zotz* (1962) and *I Saw What You Did* (1965), Castle had reached a crossroads. His best film had been *The Night Walker*, made in 1964 from a script by Robert Bloch, but in addition to functioning as a swan-song for Robert Taylor and Barbara Stanwyck, it effectively had represented the end of the gimmick-laden and increasingly imitative horror-fests for which its producer had become renowned. Times were changing, and the horror film had been changing with them. Psychological horror had come to the fore in the meanwhile, and narratively-inventive thrillers like

What Ever Happened to Baby Jane? had spearheaded the trend for a more contemporary version of American Gothic.

According to Castle, Levin's novel was sent to him in galley-proofs; also according to Castle, it had previously been offered to Alfred Hitchcock. (Hitchcock was in search of a project to follow *Torn Curtain*, but mention of his name may just have been a bait that Birdt used to hook Castle's interest.) At Birdt's prompting, Castle snapped up the screen rights and secured a deal with Paramount to make the film. The budget was set at $3.2 million, with Castle receiving $250,000 as producer plus 50 per cent of the proceeds. At this stage, he was also intent on directing *Rosemary's Baby*, as he had every film in which he had been involved since 1943. He could picture the campaign: black-draped push-chairs sited outside theatres; 'dummies' with bite-marks, strung up in foyers like garlands of garlic; a free diaper with every pair of tickets...

Paramount's new head of production, Robert Evans (a former 'B' movie actor who was best known for his portrayal of a psychotic killer in 1958's *The Fiend Who Walked the West*), saw things differently. Evans had been appointed on a whim by Paramount's new owners, Gulf & Western, in an attempt to save the ailing studio from bankruptcy, and he had a different director in mind.

Roman Polanski received his copy of *Rosemary's Baby* from Evans, after first having been approached by Paramount to direct a film about championship skiing that was to feature Robert Redford. This project eventually lensed in 1968 as *Downhill Racer*, but it was directed by Michael Ritchie instead. '*Downhill Racer* was just the pretext to get you here,' Evans told Polanski when they met, before handing him the proof of Levin's novel; being smarter than the average studio head, he had done his research and knew all about Polanski's love of the slopes. 'Before you read anything else, I'd like you to look at this,' he urged. Polanski did as he was bid and was duly impressed. 'Want to do it?' Evans inquired of him.

Polanski could hardly contain his desire to embark on his first Hollywood feature, but Evans advised him that there could be no producer role for Gene Gutowski, given that the rights to the property were owned by Castle and that he had contracted to produce the film himself. Furthermore, the politics of the situation required Polanski to meet with Castle first, to confirm his suitability both to write and direct the film in his producer's eyes and to ensure that the two of them could work together amicably. With actors like Redford and Tuesday Weld already in the running for the roles of Guy and Rosemary Woodhouse, Evans saw *Rosemary's Baby* as a prestige production to which Castle's perfunctory style was deemed too crude, but the cigar-chewing showman had to be eased out of the director's chair with some discretion.

As Castle tells it, his initial encounter with Polanski was somewhat frosty – due, in part, to the director's obvious reluctance to present himself for approval as he already had secured the backing of Evans. 'I took an instant dislike to him,' Castle wrote in his autobiography. 'A short, stocky man, dressed in the Carnaby Street fashion of the time, he seemed cocky and vain, continually glancing into the mirror in my office ... I asked him to sit down, which he declined. He insolently faced me, legs spread apart. It was useless trying to make small conversation with him, so I decided to make the meeting brief and get rid of him.' 'He'd wanted to direct the picture himself,' Polanski said of Castle. 'But Bob Evans had put his foot down, insisting that it was a director's film and Bill wasn't quite up to it.'

A thaw set in once Polanski dropped his imperious manner and, in no time, he convinced Castle that he was the man for the job. 'Somehow he seemed a different person now – warm, friendly, and enthusiastic,' Castle went on, in sharp contradiction of his earlier impression: 'Suddenly I found *myself* glancing into the mirror and the image there I didn't like. "Roman, if you had the choice of anybody in the world to write the screenplay, who would you pick?"

Without hesitation he answered my question. "Me, of course."
"Why you?" I asked.
"Because I stick right to book."'
Castle gave his assent to Evans' choice and on the strength of
a provisional deal for two more projects with Paramount, both of
which were to involve Gutowski, Polanski signed up to write and
direct *Rosemary's Baby*.

```
EXT. BRAMFORD - (DAY) - 1 AUGUST 1965


Panoramic of New York from a high building,
finishing on the Bramford.


GUY and ROSEMARY WOODHOUSE enter the main
gate...
```

screenplay, *Rosemary's Baby* (1967)

Sticking 'right to book' was exactly what Polanski did when it
came to writing the screenplay for *Rosemary's Baby* – so much
so, that Levin himself should have received co-credit for the final
draft. Aside from the deletion of a few minor incidents, the novel
was transcribed from the page virtually intact, not only in terms
of dialogue but in its descriptions as well. The exception was a
passage towards the close, in which Levin summarises the story so
far for the benefit of Dr Hill, a consultant whom Rosemary hopes
will save her baby from a death worse than fate: 'They went into his
consulting room, which was a quarter the size of Dr Sapirstein's,
and there Rosemary told him her story. She sat with her hands
on the chair-arms and her ankles crossed and spoke quietly and
calmly, knowing that any suggestion of hysteria would make him
disbelieve her and think her mad. She told him about Adrian
Marcato and Minnie and Roman; about the months of pain she
had suffered and the herbal drinks and the little white cakes; about
Hutch and *All Of Them Witches* and the *Fantasticks* tickets and

black candles and Donald Baumgart's necktie. She tried to keep everything coherent and in sequence but she couldn't. She got it all out without getting hysterical though; Dr Shand's recorder and Guy throwing away the book and Miss Lark's final unwitting revelation.'

Polanski took the opportunity to literalise this passage of indirect speech in such a way as to explain the plot to anyone in the audience who had still to cotton on, prior to the story's 'turnaround' climax: 'Much of the narrative in the second part of the book concerns itself with Rosemary's gradual conviction that she is being manipulated by evil forces,' he said. 'I had to convey this to the audience through action and dialogue.'

```
INT. DR HILL'S OFFICE - CONSULTING ROOM - (DAY)


Rosemary sits in an armchair. Dr Hill sits
beside the desk.

     ROSEMARY
     You see, he lied to you. He said we were
     going to Hollywood. The worst thing of all,
     he is involved with them as well. He sleeps
     in pyjamas now. He never used to before. He's
     probably hiding a mark... You know, they
     give you a mark when you join. All sorts of
     rituals. They hold Sabbaths there. You could
     hear them singing through the wall. Guy, my
     husband, said it was Dr Shand, one of these
     people, playing a recorder. Now, how did he
     know it was Dr Shand unless he was there
     with them? They're very clever. They planned
     everything from the beginning. I suppose
     they made some sort of a deal with Guy. They
     gave him success and he promised them a baby.
     To use in their rituals. I know this sounds
```

```
crazy, but I've got books here. I'll show
them to you.
```

screenplay, *Rosemary's Baby* (1967)

That left the final revelation itself – that *Rosemary's Baby* was not about a coven of Satanists who wished to sacrifice a child as part of their hideous rites, as the reader has been led to believe, but about the impregnation of a mortal woman by the Devil as the prelude to the birth of the Antichrist. This unambiguously supernatural twist to Levin's tale stuck in Polanski's ideological throat. He could not accept the premise on which it was based: to him, evil was not a force of fundamentalist dogma, it was a state of mind. An element of ambiguity had therefore to be introduced into the script to make it palatable to its director. 'One aspect of *Rosemary's Baby* bothered me ... Being an agnostic, I no more believed in Satan as evil incarnate than I believed in a personal god; the whole idea conflicted with my rational view of the world. For credibility's sake, I decided that there would have to be a loophole...'

Polanski's loophole was easy enough to come by, and it was a principle as old as the horror stories for which it was devised: leave the appearance of the baby to the imagination of the audience. That way, the rationale for all that occurs could be a delusion in the mind of the beholder. In other words, there *is* no Devil-baby; Rosemary has been in the grip of paranoia all along. '*Rosemary's Baby* was an adaptation of a book which is serious about the Devil, but I had a hard time to be serious about it,' Polanski reflected. 'That's why in *Rosemary's Baby* I never gave any supernatural hints – it could be all interpreted, in the final analysis, as some kind of a neurosis on Rosemary's part: a figment of the imagination of a pregnant woman.'

Polanski completed his script on 24 July 1967, by which time production designer Richard Sylbert had found a suitable location in New York to stand in for the novel's fictitious Bramford building. Levin reputedly based the Bramford on the Alwyn Court apartment block on West 58th Street (a notion inspired by the graphic on Paul Bacon's cover-design for the hardback edition of the novel). Alwyn Court is a 12-storey, Harde & Short-designed renaissance mansion dating from 1909, whose ornamental façade is liberally encrusted with terracotta skulls, seraphim and fire-breathing salamanders, but Sylbert felt that the nine-storey Dakota building of architect Henry Hardenbergh, on West 72nd Street near Central Park, had a more subtle Gothic appeal. (Among the Dakota's occupants at the time was that grand-daddy of cinematic horror, Boris Karloff.)

Next up was the casting. Previously in the running for the role of Guy Woodhouse was a young actor named Jack Nicholson, who had worked in low-budget horror films for producer Roger Corman in the early sixties (including *The Raven* and *The Terror*, both with Karloff) but who had done little of note since. Nicholson was tested but rejected on the grounds that he was too sinister-looking to begin with. Ever the perfectionist, Polanski had made a number of thumbnail sketches depicting how he imagined the characters in the story to look: Guy turned out to look like Warren Beatty or Robert Redford, but the former passed and the latter was locked in litigation with the very Paramount Studios that were producing the film. While the casting department tried to match more real actors to Polanski's drawings, Bill Castle was approached by John Cassavetes, a devotee of the Method school and an avant-garde filmmaker in his own right (*Shadows*, 1959), who had read about the production in the trades and wished to put himself forward. Cassavetes had a reputation in the industry as an intense and often difficult performer, but at his introductory meeting with Polanski, he was sweetness and light itself. The director was impressed and Cassavetes was given the role of Guy.

The role of Rosemary was always going to be the more difficult of the two to cast, requiring as it did an air of childlike innocence bordering on naïveté, but with a reserve of inner strength that proves implacable in the end. The studio-prepared list of possible candidates included Jane Fonda, but she was too feisty and all-American by half, as her next role in *Barbarella* was to show (and despite her increasingly voluble opposition to the current war in Vietnam). Polanski had wanted Tuesday Weld, but at Evans's suggestion his attention had been drawn to the waif-like, almost androgynous persona of 22-year-old Mia Farrow (daughter of Maureen O'Sullivan – Jane to Johnny Weissmuller's Tarzan – and director John Farrow), who recently had risen to small-screen prominence as Alison MacKenzie in the TV soap opera *Peyton Place*. Farrow had found herself even more in the media spotlight after becoming hitched to one Francis Albert Sinatra – 'Ol' Blue Eyes' himself – who was 29 years her senior.

The Sinatra-Farrow coupling was as unlikely a match as Tinseltown had ever seen and the gossip columnists were working overtime, but Farrow appeared devoted to the new man in her life. Her elfin charms went without saying, but her obvious resilience in the face of all the media pressure bore witness to a steeliness of character that was just what Polanski was looking for. Farrow was offered, and accepted, the role – but her participation required that shooting be completed according to the stated ten-week schedule; she already had a prior commitment to star alongside her husband in a Fox thriller for director Gordon Douglas called *The Detective*, which was due to commence filming in November 1967. Unaware of Polanski's cavalier disregard for the niceties of shooting schedules, Farrow set about preparing for her first starring role in a motion picture as the put-upon mother of *Rosemary's Baby*.

Despite William Castle's shortcomings as a director and his downmarket approach to drumming up box-office, his purchase of the rights to *Rosemary's Baby* had been an astute move. By the time the film adaptation went into production in August, sales of Levin's novel stood at 2.3 million copies and rising.

They promised me you wouldn't be hurt – and you haven't been, really. I mean, supposing you had the baby and you lost it, wouldn't that be the same...? And we're getting so much in return, Ro –

Guy Woodhouse (John Cassavetes), *Rosemary's Baby* (1968)

'The only way to seduce people into believing you – whether they want to or not – is to take painstaking care with the details of your film, to make it accurate,' Polanski has been quoted as saying. The philosophy is especially evident in *Rosemary's Baby*, in which a great deal of screen-time is expended on establishing the young couple in their newly rented apartment as they paint, decorate and otherwise personalise to their own youthful taste the formerly musty habitat of an hermitic old lady. Polanski helps to undercut the Gothic clichés in Levin's tale – and in the Bramford's exterior façade – by shooting everything in the over-saturated tones of a sweltering summer heat-wave and the brightly optimistic hues of Rosemary and Guy's newly-revamped life: moss greens, golden yellows, pastel pinks and oranges – the whole spectrum of the hippie palette to which flower-child Farrow, now a disciple of the Maharishi alongside the Beatles, fell prey as shooting of the film progressed.

Polanski kept faith with the dating in the novel, which had set the action in 1966, rather than updating his script to approximate the time of release. This allowed the film to feature newsreel footage of the Pope's historic visit to New York, as well as the infamous *Time* magazine cover which asked of its readers, 'Is God Dead?' – both of which added to the film's carefully orchestrated sense of verisimilitude.

Producer Bill Castle managed to contrive his usual Hitchcock-style cameo as a man who turns to face Rosemary as she tries to communicate her concerns to her original obstetrician from a phone booth; he is not, however, the man who previously has been seen standing with his back to her, as Ralph Bellamy had to stand in for his own 'double' in the shot, so as to fool the audience more successfully. 'Bellamy walked the few steps out of camera range,

I walked in, timing my movements exactly with his... I stood with my back to the phone booth for several seconds. Then I turned and Rosemary, with relief, exited the phone booth,' he wrote in *Step Right Up! I'm Gonna Scare the Pants Off America*. 'It was only me – nice, gentle, grey-haired, and chomping on my perennial cigar. I said my one line ... entered the telephone booth, inserted a dime and began dialling.' Castle initially had wanted to go further than his usual cameo and himself play the role of Dr Sapirstein, the sinister obstetrician who attends Rosemary throughout, but Polanski talked him into casting veteran character actor Bellamy instead.

The seduction of Guy – who begins the tale as something of a wise-ass New Yorker ever-ready to mimic everyone around him – through a simple appeal to his vanity as an actor is also well-handled, and neither Cassavetes's playing nor Polanski's direction put a foot wrong in recording his fall from grace after signing the Faustian pact which the Castevets evidently had laid before him; the scene in which Rosemary spits in his face on discovering his duplicity is the most shocking in the film.

The dream sequence is unique in the history of horror and looks almost LSD-inspired – devoid, as it is, of smoke, distorted imagery or other vaseline-smeared effects. As Rosemary is partially awake during the rape (having eaten only half of the prescribed drugged mousse), her impression of the experience alternates between the quasi-reality of non-human assault and the daydreaming fancies of a lapsed Catholic. So acid, in fact, is the film's attitude towards the Catholic Church that the award of a 'C' for Condemned rating from the National Catholic Office for Motion Pictures (formerly the Legion of Decency) on its release in the US on 12 June 1968, might have had more to do with sanctimonious taking of offence than the given reason of 'the perverted use which the film makes of fundamental Christian beliefs, especially in the events surrounding the birth of Jesus Christ, and its mockery of religious persons and practices.' 'I don't see what grounds they had for condemnation,'

Mia Farrow told Jeffrey Blyth of the *Daily Mail*. 'It was the Catholic Church which invented the Satan figure, not I. They're the ones who are trying to hold masses of people together by the fright of Hell.'

It is hard to imagine otherwise how a film intrinsically as innocuous as *Rosemary's Baby* could have caused an outcry over its supposedly sacrilegious theme. Admittedly, such a revisionist view of the proceedings comes with the benefit of hindsight, but no more decorous or circumspect an adaptation of Levin's thriller could possibly have been envisaged than the one that Polanski supplied. Yet only 40 years ago, censors on both sides of the Atlantic still felt that the greatest threat to mankind was represented by that old serpent, the Devil. 'This is no dream – this is really happening!' Rosemary cries as her husband lowers himself upon her, having assumed the familiar form of the Tempter of Eden.

Polanski bows only rarely to horror-film convention, but one occasion comes when his camera pans to the dividing wall between the apartments of the Woodhouses and the Castevets as Rosemary and Guy become aware of what sounds like ritual chanting from next door. This error of judgment in confirming the obvious about the weird old couple after Hutch (Maurice Evans) has spilled the beans on the Bramford's horrible history recalls the naïveté that Polanski exhibited in *Dance of the Vampires* with regard to the level of sophistication of the average horror audience – but it is an isolated lapse and the suspense, for the most part, is well maintained throughout.

For a Jewish author, Levin's depiction of Satan in *Rosemary's Baby* is remarkably Old Testament, almost Catholic in its medievalist view of the Prince of Lies. Rosemary is ravaged by a beast with a 'leathery body', 'yellow furnace-eyes' and 'sharp-nailed' hands, who smells of sulphur and wields an enormous phallus (a pagan trait which was carried over with more vigour into John Hough's *Incubus* [1981], which coincidentally also featured John Cassavetes).

So affiliated is he to the 'great dragon' in the Book of Revelation that Roman Castevet's reference to these attributes in offspring form nearly topples the tale into farce at the climax: '"*What are his hands like?" she asked, rocking him. "They're very nice," Roman said. "He has claws, but they're very tiny and pearly. The mitts are only so He doesn't scratch Himself..."*'

One cannot help but think that Levin must have had his tongue planted firmly in his cheek by this point in the narrative, when the preposterous nature of his central conceit finally hits home – where is this child with pearly claws and eyes of golden-yellow 'with vertical black-slit pupils' going to be *schooled*? Is the notion of infiltrating oneself surreptitiously into the ranks of men not just a tad undermined if one grows up to look like *The Monster from Piedras Blancas*? The novel's affinity to the short-story fictions of Bloch or Bradbury comes fatally to the fore in its final chapter – its rightful place in the *Twilight Zone* school of literature is painfully revealed.

It is to Levin's credit, however, that the crassness of this denouement does little to detract from the power of what has gone before. *Rosemary's Baby* is an exceptionally well-written book, whose spare prose and precise plotting provide the perfect conduit for Rosemary's plight to resonate realistically with the reader: 'A darkly brilliant tale of modern deviltry,' fellow author Truman Capote opined in review. 'I believed it and was altogether enthralled.' It is this aspect of the novel which also impressed Polanski, rather than Capote's 'deviltry', and he wisely chose to side-step the crude mechanics of Levin's climax so that the answer to Rosemary's plaintive 'What have you done to his eyes?' rests ultimately in the imagination of the viewer. (Despite his professed distaste for overt manifestations of supernatural phenomena, Polanski did succumb to showing the Devil in several brief shots during the rape – and exactly as Levin describes him in the novel – but that pantomimic rendition could simply be construed as part of the same allusive imagery as the rest of Rosemary's 'dream'.)

You know how actors are – they've always been self-centred.
I'll bet even Laurence Olivier was vain and self-centred. It's
difficult for him – he's got to work with crutches, so naturally he's
preoccupied...

Rosemary Woodhouse (Mia Farrow), *Rosemary's Baby* (1968)

While Farrow was supposed to be giving birth to the spawn of
Satan in *Rosemary's Baby*, hubbie Frank Sinatra was having kittens.
By the time November and shooting of *The Detective* rolled around,
it was clear that Farrow remained enmeshed in Polanski's web of
supernatural intrigue. According to Castle, Sinatra put in an urgent
call to his office. 'Mia's supposed to start in my picture on Monday,'
he reminded him. 'Will she be finished by then?' Castle made what
excuses he could, but Farrow was going to be tied up – literally
– for a further three weeks. 'Then I'm pulling her off your picture,'
Sinatra retorted. 'That'll mean shutting us down, Frank,' Castle
pleaded, to no avail. 'Sorry to have to do that to you, Bill, but there's
no other choice.' (What Castle recalled for his autobiography as
Sinatra's response to the impasse was clearly the version with
expletives deleted!) Polanski was told of developments, but the
fate of the film and all who sailed in her lay in the hands of Mia
Farrow. The following morning, she let it be known that it was to
be business as usual; she would finish *Rosemary's Baby* and Sinatra
would have to walk the streets of New York as *The Detective* without
her. As a result, Farrow was replaced by *Cul-de-Sac* bit-part player
Jackie (Jacqueline) Bisset.

Sinatra sent one of his legal flunkies to the *Rosemary's Baby* set
just as Farrow was preparing to film the scene in which Rosemary
breaks down at the party that she has thrown for her peer-group.
She was handed papers suing for an immediate divorce. Farrow was
heartbroken – she was genuinely in love with Ol' Blue Eyes. He not
so much with her, apparently. She reconciled herself to the situation
and, after a break, she told Polanski that she was ready to carry on.
The tears in the scene are real, only the reason for them was feigned.

In depicting Rosemary's plight, the film attains a sustained pitch of anxiety as it hurtles to its inevitable biological climax and beyond, fully justifying the admonition of the critics that *Rosemary's Baby* was not a tale to be told to expectant mothers. But no finer compliment could be paid to a film which, in Polanski's hands, purported to be as much a psychological study of pre-natal delusion as it was an outright horror movie.

Despite the story's origin in the pulps, Polanski's film of *Rosemary's Baby* was markedly devoid of sexual titillation and graphic violence. This was movie-making of the highest quality, notwithstanding its theme and mildly contentious attitude towards sex and religion. In his own opinion, no one could reasonably be offended by the premise of an occult thriller which even its director had found hard to swallow. But Polanski reckoned without the highly attuned moral sensibilities of the BBFC.

When the film was submitted for certification in Britain in November 1968, all eyes focused on what was referred to as the 'ritual rape' in Reel Three. The nominated Examiner concluded that the film's 'unpleasantness was largely concentrated in the scene in which Rosemary is raped by the 'Satan' figure', that it 'should be reduced to the minimum necessary to establish what has happened', and that any cuts required 'should certainly include the tying down of the girl's legs.'

Unlike *Repulsion*, which at least had the authentic feel of a psychiatric case-study and was therefore able to pass Trevelyan's test for 'serious intent', *Rosemary's Baby* was mass-market entertainment adapted from a popular horror novel – its producer was William Castle, no less! Trevelyan reverted to type and asked for a cut in the sequence involving the Devil-rape; the scene in which Rosemary's legs are prised apart and tied to either side of the bedstead was required to be removed.

Conscious of whom he was dealing with, the fact that the film was playing wholly uncensored in other territories, and that it was an adaptation of a novel which had featured on the best-seller listings for some time past, Trevelyan felt obliged to back up his Board's request for cuts in the sequence with an argument weighted by an unusual line in social responsibility: 'This is obviously a tricky scene from our point of view since it contains those elements of kinky sex which are, I believe, associated with black magic ... *It is not generally known that there is quite a lot of activity of this kind in this country.*' Trevelyan also asked for the shots of Rosemary's body being caressed by a scaly hand and adorned with red paint to be shortened or deleted, as 'there are recognisable elements of pornography in the way in which this is done', as well as the removal of the line, 'It was kind of fun in a necrophile sort of way' – Guy's response to her query about him making love to her while she slept.

As the problems that he experienced with the BBFC over *Cul-de-Sac* were mostly concerned with the use of mild expletives in the dialogue, and Martin Ransohoff had caused him more trouble over *The Vampire Killers* than had John Trevelyan, Polanski was wholly unprepared for the run-in that he was now to have with the Board over *Rosemary's Baby*. Feeling infinitely more secure in his position as an international filmmaker of repute, Polanski was righteously affronted by this latest assault on his standing as an artist. He refused the cuts, telegraphing his annoyance to the Board from his holiday villa in Cortina, Italy: 'I have no interest in pornography or corrupting cinema audiences. The scene which caused you so much concern is vital to the integrity of the film ... I feel that it is also essential to my integrity as a director that the film be shown in its original form in Britain as it has been shown everywhere else in the world.'

Realising that his regulation wish-list of deletions had not been received by the film's director in the spirit of compromise in which it was intended, Trevelyan tried conciliation. He suggested to Polanski that he would place his earnestly-felt desire to see the film pass uncut before the President of the Board. A further concession was agreed upon, and the BBFC's final offer involved the removal of a mere 15 seconds of film, most of which was taken up by the tying-down of Rosemary's legs. Still Polanski stood his ground.

The cuts went ahead – but the prickly Pole had one more trick up his sleeve.

Reasoning that Trevelyan was not about to budge on a point of honour, and with the might of Paramount behind him, Polanski took the unprecedented step of arranging a screening of the film in its uncut form for the national press. The effect was twofold: it pointed up the essential silliness of the BBFC's stand by allowing the press to see – and lovingly detail – the very shot which the censor had sought to keep from the eyes of the public, thus negating much of its impact were it to have been left intact, and it turned the film into something of a cause célèbre in the eyes of those to whom the censoring of films designed for adult viewing was becoming increasingly contentious in itself.

In addition to arranging an unprecedented screening of an uncensored film for the nation's leading critics, Polanski took every opportunity that was offered him to sound off against the cuts in the press. To the *Observer*'s Edward Mace, he railed, 'I spent four months editing that film, carefully, minutely, frame by frame, days and nights together sometimes, and then he comes along with shears. There's been no trouble in any other country. But I can't use that argument with Trevelyan. He'd say, "This is England, we know what's good for people," or some words like that.' To the *Guardian*'s Derek Malcolm he protested, 'Your censorship just makes you look foolish. I hate obscenity. When someone thinks he's found it in my work, it's like spitting in my face.'

'Trevelyan knows well enough that I am a serious filmmaker,' Polanski told Victor Davis of the *Daily Express*. 'My aim is not the corruption of audiences ... It is essential to my integrity that the same version of my picture being shown all over the world is also shown in Britain. If I had allowed him to make all the cuts he first suggested, the film would have made no sense at all.' At other times, he used the terms 'deplorable', 'barbarous', 'an assault on people's liberty' and 'Spanish Inquisition'. To add insult to injury, Polanski persuaded Paramount to screen the film uncut both for the critics *and* for the first-night audience at the premiere at the Paramount Theatre on 25 January 1969. The company also released a press statement, which had the effect of holding the inner workings of the Board up to even greater scrutiny – and derision.

'At public screenings of *Rosemary's Baby*,' it read, 'fifteen seconds will be cut from the film at the request of the censor who, subject to this cut, has given the film an X certificate. The cut involves a shot of Rosemary's legs being tied by two men in hospital gowns in the nightmare scene and includes the lines of dialogue:

'A Lady: You'd better have your legs tied down...in case of convulsions.

'Rosemary: Yes, I suppose so.

'At Mr Polanski's request, the uncut version was shown to the press and was also screened for the film's premiere. But this sets the record straight for students of censorship and those of you who saw the film on general release. Now you know what you're missing,' it added cheekily.

Polanski's one-man crusade against the cuts imposed by the censor paid dividends in the press. The response of the critic from the communist *Morning Star* was typical: 'I can only conclude that the censor, who is notoriously public-spirited, wanted to draw attention to the futility of his job so that he could follow the Lord Chancellor [*actually the Lord Chamberlain, whose office had presided over theatrical censorship until the Theatres Act of 1968 and which post was abolished while* Rosemary's Baby *was being edited*] into decent obscurity.' The *Observer*'s Penelope Mortimer was in no mood to try to understand the mind of the censor, either: 'Surely in this case the censor has lost all dignity and justification and become no more than a myopic and properly resented old nanny?' The *Sunday Telegraph*'s Margaret Hinxman was similarly nonplussed: 'Of the notorious 15-second cut in the rape-dream scene, I can understand it worrying the censor on its own, but within the context of the sequence it's surely no more deserving of attention than anything else in the film.'

In the *Illustrated London News*, Michael Billington went so far as to suggest that the BBFC might have been better employed in wielding its scissors against the gratuitous violence in the concurrently-released *Where Eagles Dare* than the supposed iniquities of *Rosemary's Baby*. Trevelyan, in one of many attempts at damage-limitation during the crisis, invited Billington for a drink to explain his 'absurd and illogical decision.'

Polanski's diatribes were not confined to the ways of the censor, however. He also weighed in against the two main UK circuit chains, Rank and ABC (neither *Repulsion* nor *Cul-de-Sac* had been granted a general release in Britain), and the ever-belligerent British film union (ACTT), making it plain that he and his new wife were now ready to up sticks from their mews home in Chelsea and resettle themselves in Los Angeles, where 'the money-men don't control the creative people any more [and] the unions let you get on with making good pictures.'

As tantrums go, it was major-league, and it worked a treat. Not only was Polanski given more column inches than at any time in his career so far, but *Rosemary's Baby* went on to become one of the biggest grossers of the year in the UK, adding to its already substantial tally in the US and raking in a cool $15 million for Paramount all told. It also helped to hammer the first nail into the coffin of Trevelyan's autocratic hold over what was and was not permissible on British screens. The cuts which the BBFC had demanded were not rescinded for the film's general release, but the episode had been a humiliating one for Trevelyan, who had been forced onto the defensive and who was inclined to adopt a less sanctimonious posture from here on. By the end of 1970, the entire classification system for the exhibition of films in Britain had been overhauled to better reflect the changes which were occurring on screen in terms of sex and violence, and the way was finally cleared for the maverick cinematic extremes of Sam Peckinpah's *Straw Dogs*, Ken Russell's *The Devils* and Stanley Kubrick's *A Clockwork Orange*, all of which would have been banned outright only a few years earlier.

> *Rosemary...Guy...The Bramford...the girl...the dead girl...the neighbours...the friend...the dead friend...the nightmare...the doctor...the vicious nightmare...the other doctor...the truth...the baby...poor baby...whose baby?...pray for Rosemary's Baby!*
>
> **advertising blurb**, *Rosemary's Baby* (1968)

Reviews were much as expected for a film which the Saturday matinée crowd was falling over itself to see and which would end up taking more than five times its $3.2 million budget. 'A highly serious lapsed-Catholic fable, going on the assumption that God is dead to imagine a Nativity for the dark powers,' Renata Adler wrote in the *New York Times*. The British critics were infected with a similar sense of ghoulish satisfaction. 'Steep yourself in the shuddering horror of this incomparable shocker,' Margaret Hinxman encouraged in the *Sunday Telegraph*, while Penelope Mortimer was more impressed by its reticent approach to its subject matter in the *Observer*: 'Polanski's genius for horror is, unlike Hitchcock's, sly, sneaky, subversive. On the face of it, everything appears fine. There are no thunderclaps, creaking doors, warning crescendos in the score. One just knows that everything is, or will be by the end of the picture, stark raving mad'. Clive Hirschorn of the *Sunday Express* thought it a 'macabre excursion into sophisticated horror,' and Cecil Wilson of the *Daily Mail* also spoke of 'Polanski's unique flair for the macabre.'

Only Gordon Gow, writing in *Films and Filming*, chose to express some disappointment: 'The galvanising quality of Levin's novel was its ability to keep us guessing until the final pages. My reservations about Polanski's film are that he relinquishes from time to time that compulsive suspense...' Polanski's emotionless style was also subject to scrutiny, although Gow conceded it to be mostly a plus in the case of *Rosemary's Baby*: 'From the director of *Repulsion*, one had somehow anticipated that this present exercise would prompt the occasional shock-thrill of *Psycho*-strength, which would have been justified on the grounds that, unlike *Psycho*, *Rosemary's Baby* is no black joke at heart but rather a knowing nod in the direction of eternal uncertainties. Shocks are absent.'

> *Asleep and sweet, so small and rosy-faced, Andy lay wrapped in a snug black blanket with little black mitts ribbon-tied around his wrists. Orange-red hair he had, a surprising amount of it, silky-clean and brushed. Andy! Oh, Andy! She reached out to him, her knife turning away; his lips pouted and he opened his eyes and looked at her. His eyes were golden-yellow, with neither white nor irises; all golden-yellow, with vertical black-slit pupils.*
>
> *She looked at him.*
>
> *He looked at her, golden-yellowly, and then at the swaying upside-down crucifix.*
>
> **Ira Levin**, *Rosemary's Baby* (1967)

The image of a Devil-baby in a cradle was the gimmick of *Rosemary's Baby*, and it was what appealed to William Castle in the first instance; it is also what Polanski opted to discard. On such fine judgments are the distinctions between art and artifice drawn. Levin's pulp-fiction plot remains the same in either case but, like Hitchcock's *Psycho*, it was able to pass more readily for the former if its idiosyncrasies were prevented from looking the audience straight in the eyes, all 'golden-yellowly'.

*   *   *

In the wake of *Rosemary's Baby*, Polanski's roster was filling up with potential projects: a second Ira Levin novel – *A Perfect Day* – but in an SF vein; a life of Russian violinist Paganini (who was said

to have sold his soul to the Devil in return for violin virtuosity);
a Western, notionally to star Lee Marvin, about a wagon-train
of immigrants who become snowbound in the Sierra Nevada
mountains and have to resort to cannibalism to survive, entitled
The Donner Party. In the event, all these ideas were sidelined in
favour of an adaptation of Robert Merle's novel *The Day of the
Dolphin* for United Artists. Tate's career was also on the up. She
had appeared, uncredited, in *Rosemary's Baby*, in the party scene
that Mia Farrow had to shoot after receiving the news of her
impending divorce from Sinatra, but she had followed this with
more significant input into *Valley of the Dolls*, from the best-selling
novel by Jacqueline Susanne, as well as a co-starring role alongside
Bruce Lee in *The Wrecking Crew*, the third of Dean Martin's Matt
Helm spy spoofs.

In his own richly-detailed reminiscences of the Swinging
Sixties' period, from the release of *Repulsion* to the era of 'peace
and love', Polanski made much of the fact that it was a time when
anything seemed possible. Whether it was clubbing in London,
partying by the pool in LA, or standing by bemused as a kaftan-
clad Peter Sellers chased moonbeams in the Mojave desert with
new love Britt Ekland, there was magic in the moment – as though
normal life had somehow been suspended and replaced by a
relentless pursuit of pleasure, and of ever more daring experiences.
Put simply, these were crazy days. Exactly how crazy was now about
to be made clear.

The signs of the coming madness were already there. No
sooner had composer Krszysztof Komeda completed his score
for *Rosemary Baby* than he collapsed and died from a brain
haemorrhage, as a result of a fall suffered during a drunken night
out. Komeda had been about to start work on a prison-break
drama for Bill Castle, entitled *The Riot* – which was exactly what
Paris descended into during the first months of 1968, as workers
protested their rights and students protested against the Vietnam
War. The unrest spilled over into the usually untroubled waters of

the Cannes Festival, where Polanski had been invited to serve on the jury. The Festival ended in shambles and uproar.

After *Rosemary's Baby* was released in the US, Castle's desk was inundated with hate mail: 'You have unleashed evil on the world', '*Rosemary's Baby* is filth and YOU will die as a result' and 'Worshiper at the Shrine of Satanism. My prediction is that you will slowly rot during a long and painful illness which you have brought upon yourself' were a few examples of the kind of diatribe which he was now required to read on a daily basis, according to the producer's autobiography. When Castle was rushed to hospital to undergo an emergency operation for the removal of kidney stones as he was about to produce *The Out-of-Towners*, from the play by Neil Simon, his natural level-headedness began to desert him. 'All my life I had yearned for the applause, approval and recognition from my peers; and when the awards were being passed out [*a total of two Oscar nominations and one win, for Ruth Gordon as Best Supporting Actress*], I no longer cared. I was at home, very frightened of *Rosemary's Baby*, and still very ill,' he wrote.

Polanski took a different line. 'If anything caused Bill Castle's illness, it was having too much success with the picture,' he told the *New York Times* (though he also had received hate mail in the wake of the film's release). Such a subject had almost been bound to invite the attentions of the lunatic fringe. There were even some who thought that Polanski had himself chosen to invoke the Dark One to ensure the film of success... Be that as it may, a shadow undeniably had fallen over the land.

Dogging the sandaled footsteps of hippiedom was a darker aspect to the Californian quest for mystic enlightenment. The general upsurge of interest in alternative religions which had been legitimised by the devotions of John, Paul, George and Ringo to the teachings of the Maharishi Mayesh Yogi proved to be a little too all-inclusive, and the coven of witches in *Rosemary's Baby* turned out not to be an isolated example of the breed, much less a writer's fancy. Censor John Trevelyan appeared to have been aware of this more noxious element of pop culture in the reason that he advanced to Polanski for wanting to cut his film in Britain: 'It is not generally known that there is quite a lot of activity of this kind in this country...'

While the Beatles sought solace in the sybaritic philosophies of the Maharishi on one hand, on the other, the proselytising Black Magic novels of jingoistic British author Dennis Wheatley were more popular than ever, and resurgent interest among the youth of the day in all aspects of the occult encouraged publishers to reissue paperback versions of a number of allegedly-learned treatises on the Black Arts by the likes of Richard Cavendish and Rollo Ahmed. But nowhere was this sudden Luciferian streak more thoroughly embraced than in the field of pop music.

If the Beatles were the Jedi knights of the sixties music scene, then the Rolling Stones of Jagger, Richards, Jones and Watts were the dark side of the Force. While Lennon and McCartney seemed content to romance 'Lovely Rita' or document teen angst in songs like 'She's Leaving Home', Jagger and Richards were parading their chauvinism in 'Under My Thumb' or unashamedly extolling the virtues of free love in the face of airplay bans, with 'Let's Spend the Night Together'. On 8 December 1967, Jagger and Co had released their much-anticipated response to the Beatles' psychedelic 'Sgt Pepper's' album; in a typically dystopian gesture, it was entitled 'Their Satanic Majesties Request'. Other bands who had thought to use the novelty of obscure Celtic legend or esoteric fringe religions to make a name for themselves (and sell records) were the Heavy Metal outfits Black Sabbath and Led Zeppelin. Zeppelin guitarist Jimmy Page went one step further and even purchased Boleskine Lodge near Foyers on the south bank of Loch Ness, which had been the home of 'Great Beast' and self-proclaimed magical adept Aleister Crowley from 1899 to 1914.

If Castle managed to talk himself into believing in the Devil after his experiences on *Rosemary's Baby*, it was not a view shared by the film's director. 'I tried to make the film in such a way that it could be interpreted two ways,' he claimed. 'You can just assume that it's all her imagination...' Many of those confronted with Polanski's film could make no such assumption, however – they took things literally. Polanski may have been able to adopt a more detached and pragmatic stance in relation to the subject matter of Levin's novel but, away from New York and Hollywood, in the middle-American home of religious fundamentalism, there were plenty who found nothing to question in the idea of a living Devil. (The filmmakers' perceived association with practitioners of the Black Arts was not assuaged by the assertion of Anton Sandor LaVey, founder of the San Francisco-based Church of Satan, that *he* had been cast in the role of the Devil for the rape sequence. The part was actually taken by Clay Tanner in a costume barely big enough to fit a 'small woman' – John Cassavetes himself donned the contact lenses for the close-up.)

As though to typify the 'sentimental mediocrity' of which Polanski had complained to Gordon Gow, even venerated fantasy writer Ray Bradbury, the author of *Something Wicked This Way Comes* and other homespun supernatural yarns along similar lines, rushed into print with what he felt would have been a more appropriate ending for the film, in which Rosemary pleads with God to take her child back to his bosom as a way of finally forgiving Lucifer for his sin of pride, all those billions of aeons before.

'Rosemary runs into a nearby cathedral,' Bradbury elaborated. 'She runs down the main aisle to the altar, holds her baby up, and says, "Lord God, take back your son." Now, there's the end of your film! If this is Lucifer's child, here's a chance to heal the wound between Heaven and Earth that occurred billions of years ago. The Devil was on the side of God, but through a sin of hubris, was cast out of Heaven and down into Hell ... I've been running in circles around religious themes for a long time. But you have to have an image, a metaphor. That's what prayer is all about. It's the power

that helps you get through terrible moments. We don't know how it
works, but it does.'

> *...And finally, then, does not God forgive? And dark-hooved child*
> *brought by blameless and sore-tried mother onto a cathedral altar*
> *on rainy night: could God refuse such needful prayers? Would not*
> *the Lord take back his ancient enemy and make of him once more*
> *a Son upon the right hand of the Throne?*
>
> *There is my script, my new and inevitable FINIS. Film it in*
> *your mind. Screen it on your eyelids tonight.*
>
> *Then turn and walk out of the cinema, the cathedral, with me.*
>
> *Leaving Rosemary there, with her sad child, waiting for answers*
> *which* must *come.*
>
> **Ray Bradbury**, 'A New Ending for *Rosemary's Baby*' (1969)

If Bradbury believed that you could hold a dialogue with the
Devil, he, too, was about to be hauled up short.

By the summer of 1968, militant counter-culturalist Jerry Rubin,
self-styled leader of America's 'Yippies', had declared the hippie
movement to be at an end. The good guys had opted to bow out
at a time of their own choosing, which left the bad alone upon
the stage. Sensing an opportunity to reclaim territory which had
been lost to them in the recent fad for floribunda, rock 'n' roll bad
boys the Rolling Stones decreed that their next concert, a 'free'
gig at Altamont Speedway in California's Alameda County, would
be policed by a local chapter of the Hell's Angels motorcycling
fraternity.

Violence was on the march. In the last week of August, clashes
between attendees at the Democractic Party Convention in Chicago
and those at a concurrent 'Festival of Love' (or 'Festival of Blood', as
Rubin christened it) reached a pitch of civil war.

The previous year had seen the first publication in English
of Mikhail Bulgakov's *The Master and Margarita*, a pseudo-
philosophical satire which also employed the Devil as literary

device, as did *Rosemary's Baby*. Bulgakov's Devil is the professorial Woland, however, a 'foreigner' of indeterminate race, who sports a jaunty grey beret, a poodle-headed cane, and whose eyes are different colours: one black and the other 'for some reason' green; Woland is a peculiarly Russian Devil – petrifying when he chooses to be, but mostly playful and perverse and prone to bouts of empathetic understanding.

The book's satirical sideswipes at the oppression and hypocrisy of Communist rule are more relevant to the time of its authorship (1938) than they were in the 1960s, but its haunting and authentic portrait of Pontius Pilate's encounters with Christ (renamed Yeshua Ha-Notsri) remain powerful and compelling. The novel quickly became a cult, read by rock stars and movie directors alike. Roman Polanski toyed with the notion of adapting it for the screen, after plucking out its climactic scene for use in *The Vampire Killers*; Mick Jagger plundered it for the lyrics to a song.

On 5 December, the Stones released their latest album – *Beggar's Banquet*, the first track of which shot straight to the top of the singles charts. Its title was 'Sympathy for the Devil' and it was inspired by Bulgakov's *The Master and Margarita*. The next day, the band's Altamont concert turned into a rout, with 850 people injured, three dead as a result of accidents, and a young black named Meredith Hunter murdered by a Hell's Angel while Jagger tried to perform 'Under My Thumb' (not 'Sympathy for the Devil', as is sometimes claimed). The Grateful Dead's Jerry Garcia later referred to the occasion as 'a nice day in Hell'.

The Swinging Sixties were giving way to the 'Satanic' Seventies, but the decade of Flower-Power and Jesus Freakery was not yet at an end. On 20 January 1969, Polanski married Sharon Tate at the Chelsea Registry Office in the King's Road; the new Mrs Polanski became pregnant almost immediately, the baby due some time around the end of August. On 12 February, in preparation for the happy event, the couple signed a lease on a house in the affluent Bel Air district to the north of Los Angeles, in the Hollywood Hills.

Cielo Drive, off Benedict Canyon Road, was a narrow street fringed with eucalyptus trees, where Joseph Stefano had written the screenplay for *Psycho*. Number 10050 had previously been rented by Candice Bergen and Terry Melcher, the record-producer son of actress and singer Doris Day, but they had vacated the premises after separating. Owner Rudi Altobelli was only too pleased to quickly re-let the house to a high-profile pair of celebrity newlyweds.

Having set up their home in readiness for the new arrival, the Polanskis jetted off to London, leaving 10050 Cielo Drive in the charge of Polish ex-pat Wojtek Frykowski and his girlfriend, a wealthy socialite named Abigail 'Gibby' Folger. Frykowski was a 'man of leisure', thanks to his father's business interests, and he had been a friend and colleague of Polanski's since he helped to finance his 1960 short *Mammals*, in which he had played the role of the sausage salesman who steals the sled from the protagonists; in consequence, Polanski chose to shrug off the fact that Frykowski and Folger were both habitual drug-users. 'Wojtek', he would state ungraciously, 'was a man of little talent but immense charm.' Polanski also now chose to shrug off his long-standing friendship with Victor Lownes in a fit of pique, despite the fact that *Playboy*'s UK Head of Operations had organised both his stag night and his wedding reception.

As she neared the ninth month of her pregnancy, Sharon Tate Polanski had to leave her husband in London to return to Los Angeles. Polanski saw her off at Southampton docks on the cruise-liner QE2, promising to join her as soon as possible – certainly in time for his 36th birthday on 18 August. In the meanwhile, she had Folger and Frykowski for company, as well as Prudence, her Yorkshire terrier, and ex-boyfriend Jay Sebring could always be relied upon to provide a helping hand. While Polanski continued to work on the script of *The Day of the Dolphin* (in addition to turning in another of his uncredited cameo performances, this time in Joe McGrath's *The Magic Christian* alongside Sellers and Beatles drummer Ringo Starr), he was entirely oblivious to the dark figure who hovered in the unpredictable shadows which had been cast by *Rosemary's Baby*.

Satan chuckled quietly to himself. He was biding his time, waiting in the wings.

The Magic Christian, like *Dr Strangelove* before it, was another opus derived from a novel by Terry Southern, which additionally took advantage of the current fad for having numerous guest stars appear in minor and mostly unrewarding cameos to pep up what, in this instance, was a fatuous social satire about capitalist corruption. Sellers was at that stage in his career where he thought that he could coast through a role simply by adopting an upper-crust accent and looking faintly bemused; Polanski, on the other hand, was required conversely to look thoroughly embarrassed as he was serenaded by Yul Brynner in drag, crooning 'Mad About the Boy'. Elements of late-period goonery wedded to embryo Python buffoonery (two of the film's writers were John Cleese and Graham Chapman) proved insufficient to salvage an acid-laced and typically indulgent venture by all concerned.

While the puerile philosophising of *The Magic Christian* exemplified the fact that 'flower power' effectively had retired exhausted from the fray, there were other aspects of the counter-cultural explosion which appeared less willing to go quietly.

At a deserted ranch in an out-of-the-way stretch of the San Fernando Valley, an ill-assorted commune of disenfranchised hippies known collectively as The Family was preaching racial Armageddon and plotting bloody revenge against the society that had rejected it. Like many of his peers, its self-anointed leader was a fan of the Beatles, and the violent escapade which he was now to instruct his followers to commit was, he claimed, inspired by one of the songs on the band's recently released 'white' album: *Helter Skelter*. 'Charlie' was himself a frustrated rock musician – a one-time friend of Beach Boy Dennis Wilson – and he had been known by a number of aliases during his 37-year life of crime and penal correction, although the latest nickname by which his acolytes were encouraged to refer to him was singularly inappropriate – 'Jesus'.

The Family's spiritual fountainhead and born-again 'guru' of the Apocalypse had actually been christened Charles Milles Maddox – the son of a prostitute – but criminal history chooses to remember him through his adoptive use of his father's surname.

As Charles Manson.

5
DEATH AND THE MAIDEN

ROSS: *Your castle is surprised; your wife and babes*
  Savagely slaughter'd: to relate the manner,
  Were, on the quarry of these murder'd deer,
  To add the death of you.
MALCOLM: *Merciful heaven!*
  What, man! ne'er pull your hat upon your brows;
  Give sorrow words: the grief that does not speak
  Whispers the o'er-fraught heart and bids it break.
MACDUFF: *My children too?*
ROSS: *Wife, children, servants, all*
  That could be found.
MACDUFF: *And I must be from thence!*
  My wife kill'd too?
ROSS: *I have said.*

William Shakespeare, *Macbeth* Act IV, Scene III (1606)

There is a human dynamic. Events can be set in motion whose longer-term effects are then impossible to detect, let alone halt. In the distance, on the wind, a voice could be heard: *'In my mind's eye, my thoughts light fires in your cities...'*

Before appearing in Polanski's *Dance of the Vampires*, Sharon Tate's main claim to fame was having been whipped by David Niven in J Lee Thompson's *Eye of the Devil* – a sequence thought to be so erotically charged by the British Board of Film Censors that it was excised from the film on its (belated) UK release.

Eye of the Devil had been bedevilled by trouble from the start. Starring Hollywood veterans David Niven and Deborah Kerr, and

adapted from the novel *Day of the Arrow* by Philip Lorraine, it was
a turgid tale of pagan rites in rural France in which the new
Marquis, Philippe de Montfauçon (Niven), has ultimately to
sacrifice his life to protect the livelihoods of his tenant-farmers, a
theme later developed to perfection by Anthony Shaffer and Robin
Hardy in *The Wicker Man* (1973). No sooner had it settled into
M-G-M's Borehamwood studios in October 1965, as the unwisely
titled *13* after weeks of location work in the Dordogne, than Kim
Novak injured her back and had to pull out of the production,
leaving Thompson to start over again with substitute Kerr. Original
screenwriter Terry Southern (of *Dr Strangelove* and *The Magic
Christian* fame) was replaced by Robin Estridge and Dennis
Murphy, and the film was re-shot from scratch and retitled *Eye of
the Devil*.

Confusingly scripted, ineptly directed by journeyman
Thompson, clumsily edited, and heavily re-cut in post-production
by the unsympathetic Martin Ransohoff, *Eye of the Devil* turned
out to be a huge mistake for all concerned, like so many of the
cross-fertilised productions which were the product of Hollywood's
imperial influence over British studios in the early 1960s. The
BBFC took fright at the sequence in which Niven takes a bullwhip
to a prostrate Tate for attempting to entice his wife to fling herself
from the battlements of their château, sensing a sado-masochistic
undertone in Tate's smirks of delight at the experience, and the
film was awarded only an A certificate as a result of the deletion. It
eventually saw release on the lower half of a double-bill. Tate's turn
as a Gallic witch was little helped by the fact that she was dubbed
throughout.

Shot evocatively in monochrome at a time when every other
major production was moving over to glorious Technicolor, the
resultant film was an uneasy clash of cultures and styles, with the
Hollywood old guard of Niven and Kerr faced off against bright
young things Tate and ex-child actor David Hemmings, while
creepy Donald Pleasence skulked moodily in the background as a

parish priest (still sporting his contentious bald pate); Hemmings was subsequently to be spotted by Michelangelo Antonioni and given the role for which he will always be best remembered, as the Baileyesque photographer Thomas in *Blow-up* (1966), while Ransohoff discovery Tate was shoehorned into *The Vampire Killers*. If it achieved nothing else, *Eye of the Devil* had launched Sharon Tate as the latest 'new face' of sixties cinema, but the film's spotty release ensured that few people noticed – not even Polanski, who had neither seen nor heard of her before being introduced. Had he done so, he might have come upon *Eye of the Devil* and been more alert to Ransohoff's proclivity for re-cutting and re-titling films that their directors had already completed to their own satisfaction.

> *Tell me, do you believe in magic?*
>
> **Odile de Caray (Sharon Tate)**, *Eye of the Devil* (1966)

By Saturday 9 August 1969, Polanski had all but resolved his problems with the screenplay of *The Day of the Dolphin*. His birthday was a little over a week away and he was keen to spend it in Los Angeles with his wife; by the end of the month, there could even be a new addition to the family. He had been ready to fly out of London that very weekend, but a problem with his visa had put off any prospect of a return to LA till the following week. He now planned to leave on Monday 11 August – or Tuesday at the latest.

Before setting off for a meal with Victor Lownes (at Gene Gutowski's instigation and in an attempt to bury the hatchet), Polanski had called a meeting with producer Andrew Braunsberg and writer Michael Braun to consolidate their approach to *The Day of the Dolphin*. As they talked, the phone rang; it was 7.00 pm London time, but still mid-morning in LA. Polanski picked up the receiver.

The voice on the other end of the line was that of Bill Tennant, his American agent. There was barely even an exchange of the usual pleasantries before Tennant suddenly blurted out, 'There's been a disaster at the house.'

At first, Polanski failed to comprehend the significance of the remark, but Tennant qualified it regardless: 'Sharon's dead. Wojtek's dead, too, and Gibby and Jay. They're all dead.'

In Polanski's absence, 10050 Cielo Drive had become a scene of mass-murder.

The House on the Hill

The dead were all those in occupancy at the property – Folger, Frykowski, Sebring and, of course, Tate herself – as well as a friend of the resident caretaker, named Steven Parent, who just happened to be in the wrong place at the wrong time.

The killings had taken place some time very soon after midnight on Friday 8 August, which made the official date of the murders 9 August. Folger had been stabbed 28 times, while Frykowski had been shot twice, bludgeoned 13 times with a blunt object and had suffered a total of 51 stab wounds – both victims had quantities of drugs in their systems at time of death. Sebring had been stabbed seven times and shot once – any one of three of the stab wounds, or the gunshot wound, would have proved fatal by itself. Sharon Tate had been stabbed 16 times – five of which wounds, all penetrating heart, lungs or liver, would also have proved fatal by themselves. Steven Earl Parent, meanwhile, had been shot four times.

Parent had been found at the wheel of a car; Frykowski had also been found in the grounds of the house, in a position which indicated that he had tried to flee the scene of the carnage but never made it. Despite being clad incongruously in a nightdress, Abigail Folger was lying nearby. The remaining victims had both been found in the lounge. A length of nylon rope had been looped around Tate's neck, thrown over a beam in the ceiling, and looped in a similar manner around the throat of Jay Sebring, who was lying less than four feet away. The word 'pig' was daubed on the front door of the house, in what later proved to be Sharon Tate's blood.

For the confused and panicked LA police, this was no 'ordinary' murder – it was a massacre. And it had occurred in a secure celebrity property in one of the most exclusive parts of Bel Air, home of the stars, fortified haunt of the rich and famous. 'The scene could hardly have been more bizarre had it appeared in one of Polish director Roman Polanski's own peculiarly nightmarish motion pictures,' *Newsweek* was to advise its readers. All Hell consequently was let loose.

> *A cloud of fright hung over southern California more dense than its smog. It would not dissipate for months. As late as the following March, William Kloman would write in* Esquire: *"In the great houses of Bel Air, terror sends people flying to their telephones when a branch falls from a tree outside."*
>
> **Vincent Bugliosi and Curt Gentry**, *Helter Skelter* (1974)

It was a murder spree that shocked the world, in the way that the assassination of US President John F Kennedy had shocked the world – or that of John Lennon (outside the Dakota apartment block of *Rosemary's Baby* fame) would subsequently. But it shocked the closed community of LA superstardom even more. Years later, director Bob Rafelson told journalist Jill Robinson of the irrational fear that surfaced in its wake: 'If someone said, "Guess which house this took place in," and if you had to sit down and think, first you would have thought of Polanski. Because something was associated with his name that made people feel uncomfortable. Something he had done had tempted the Fates...'

Every generation has its share of anxieties, but few of them equal the threat of deportation and death – or potential loss of parent or loved one without warning – with which the young Polanski had to contend on a daily basis, and before he was able even to comprehend what was happening to him. To think that such childhood trauma might have left him unscarred is to fly in the face of all reason. For years, many of those who worked with Polanski were kept completely in the dark about what he had suffered; he chose to abandon his past, as his father had abandoned his name, and to detach himself from a range of emotions which most of those around him might take for granted. He had lost his mother when he was nine; now, at 36, he had also lost his wife and unborn child.

Once again, God seemed to have abandoned him. 'Why?' was all he could find to say in response to the tragedy. 'Why...?'

The press – local at first, but soon international – used the opportunity presented by the murders to let its collective imagination run riot about what *really* went on behind the closed doors of the LA movie community. According to the increasingly hysterical reports, a large number of pornographic magazines, photographs and films were found at the house, as well as bondage equipment and copious amounts of recreational drugs, while the Polanski 'clan' indulged in all manner of sex orgies, including three-in-a-bed romps. None of it was true, except the part about the photos and the drugs – the former consisting mostly of publicity shots of Sharon Tate (in addition to an album of portraits of her wedding to Polanski), and the latter consisting of several ashtrays containing the remnants of marijuana cigarettes, or joints. On the American West Coast in 1969, it would have been surprising if something of the sort had *not* been found.

The world's press nevertheless had a field day. Never ones to let facts stand in the way of a good story, the tabloids went further, not only dragging up supposedly sordid details from Polanski's past but from those of the victims also – who no longer were in any position to defend themselves. Then, most damning of all, was the connection to *Rosemary's Baby*. Had Roman Polanski somehow tempted fate by directing the film and invoking the living Devil to send his emissaries on a mission of murder against all that he held dear?

To the superstitious and gullible, it represented a tantalising prospect. But then, why Polanski? Why not Castle (despite the fact that he claimed he *had* been singled out for some satanic tomfoolery in his autobiography), or Farrow, or Cassavetes? More pertinently, why not Ira Levin, the man who had created the story in the first place and who currently was enjoying renewed success with his latest novel, *The Stepford Wives*? But such was the hold that the atrocity exerted on the imagination that conjecture of the kind not only was inevitable but understandable in attempting to comprehend how such an arbitrary act of evil-doing could have been born out of a time when the whole world had seemed devoted to the twin precepts of 'peace and love'.

On Sunday 10 August, a second murder scene was uncovered some ten miles from the first. At their home at 3301 Waverly Drive, near Griffith Park in the Los Feliz hills, Rosemary and Leno LaBianca were found butchered. Within 24 hours of the discovery of the bodies, the LAPD detectives already investigating the murders at Cielo Drive were of the opinion that there was no connection between the two crimes, even though both sets of victims had suffered multiple stab-wounds, cords had been tied around necks at both scenes-of-crime, and words had been scrawled on doors or walls at both premises in the victims' own blood; at Waverly Drive, the phrase 'Healter Skelter' (misspelled, as here) had been daubed on the door of the refrigerator.

By Tuesday of the following week, *Valley of the Dolls* was re-released nationally by 20th Century Fox to cash in on Sharon Tate's sudden notoriety; for this outing, she was given top billing. *Valley of the Dolls* was quickly succeeded by *The Fearless Vampire Killers* and others in which she had appeared. Who says Hollywood shows no respect for the dead?

Polanski found himself sharing the LAPD's view about the lack of any connection between the Tate and LaBianca slayings, though he was as much at a loss for answers as everyone else. In the immediate aftermath of the murders, he became an unofficial part of the inquiry team, and he began to follow suspects, search for clues and generally view former friends and acquaintances with new and suspicious eyes. Even *he* had appeared on the police's provisional list of suspects, never mind the fact that he had been 6000 miles from the scene of the outrage at the time of its occurrence. A polygraph (lie-detector) test had absolved him of any responsibility in the affair as far as those investigating the case were concerned, and movie-inspired motives such as the director having arranged a long-distance 'hit' on his wife and friends were laid to rest in favour of a more prosaic solution: the Cielo Drive caretaker, a 19-year-old named William Garretson, was brought in on suspicion. Not quite 'the butler did it' but close. During several days in custody, he, too, underwent the obligatory polygraph test; Garretson passed and was released without charge.

After Garretson, the next suspects were a clutch of drug-dealers who had frequented the Cielo Drive premises to supply Folger and Frykowski; that lead went nowhere also. Having ruled out a connection with the murder of the LaBiancas, as well as the killing, on 31 July, of a music teacher named Gary Hinman (who had been stabbed to death in a similar fashion and the words 'political piggy' smeared on the wall of his living room in blood), the police remained convinced that the murders were somehow drug-related. At this stage, none of the investigating detectives thought to follow up the fact that a suspect who had been arrested on 6 August for the murder of Hinman had been living at a ranch in the LA suburb of Chatsworth, along with a number of hippie-types whose self-styled leader, a man known only as 'Charlie', appeared to suffer from the delusion that he was Jesus Christ.

The outrage at Cielo Drive forced Polanski to reflect upon his past behaviour, to ascertain whether or not he might have encountered (or inadvertently encouraged) the murderer (or murderers) of his wife and child. Examining his personal list of potential suspects, the finger of suspicion soon began to point at John Phillips, leader of the recently disbanded West Coast pop group The Mamas and the Papas, with whose wife, Michelle, Polanski had enjoyed a brief fling. Michelle Phillips had been prone to such extramarital liaisons, and her husband was known for his violent temper.

Despite the fact that Phillips was in possession of an alibi to account for his movements at the time of the murders, the increasingly paranoid Polanski became convinced that he had both the motive and the psychological make-up to commit such a crime (even though this was the man who had penned 'San Francisco', the unofficial anthem of 1967's Summer of Love). To advance his efforts at amateur detection, Polanski broke into Phillips' garage, where he examined his E-type Jaguar for bloodstains; he found none. But a passing LAPD patrol car found him making his exit in the wee small hours of the morning. Recognising who he was, the officer accepted his tale of misplaced personal property and sent him on his way.

Undeterred by a brush with the law which could have faced him with a charge of burglary and trespass, Polanski continued to pursue his own line of enquiry with regard to Phillips. A further opportunity arose whereby he was enabled to conduct a search of Phillips' Rolls-Royce convertible. This produced a diary whose entries, to Polanski's eyes, appeared remarkably similar in terms of writing style to the word 'pig' which had been scrawled on the door of 10050 Cielo Drive in Sharon Tate's blood. He submitted a sample of the entries to a handwriting expert, along with a photo of the graffito at the murder scene, but the results proved inconclusive.

(Polanski was not alone in his single-minded pursuit of the mysterious assailant[s] in the wake of the Tate-LaBianca slayings. Paul Tate, Sharon's father, had also taken to donning a disguise and haunting the seedier parts of LA in search of clues. In the event, neither man turned up anything of substance.)

On 17 August, Polanski visited his former home with a photographer from *Life* and a psychic named Peter Hurkos. Hurkos decreed that the killings had been the result of a black magic ritual, the attendees of which became 'frenzied homicidal maniacs' incited by massive doses of LSD. It is understandable that Polanski should wish personally to witness the scene of his wife's last hours on earth, but less explicable was his decision to have a psychic and a member of the press corps accompany him there and to sanction publication of photos of the event, one of which showed him sitting on the step of 10050, with the word 'pig' inscribed on the door adjacent to him in his own wife's blood. It was an error of judgment which would return to haunt him as an apparent example of publicity-seeking insensitivity – nor was it to be the last such error that Polanski would make.

Others were genuinely adroit at making the most of the opportunity for publicity which now presented itself. Serial fantasist Jerzy Kosinski, discredited author of *The Painted Bird*, claimed to have missed being slain at Cielo Drive only by having misplaced the ticket which he had bought in response to Frykowski inviting him to join him there – Kosinski having acted as matchmaker between he and Folger. As ever with Kosinki, no evidence was offered to substantiate the tale.

REWARD
$25,000

Roman Polanski and friends of the Polanski family offer to pay a $25,000 reward to the person or persons who furnish information leading to the arrest and conviction of the murderer or murderers of Sharon Tate, her unborn child, and the other four victims...

newspaper advertisement, 10 September 1969

In the meantime, Polanski had abandoned any thought of directing *The Day of the Dolphin*. The project eventually was turned over to Avco-Embassy and filmed by Mike Nichols in 1972. Early in the investigation, Polanski had posted a personal reward of $25,000 for information which might lead to an arrest. Two months after the murders, the police were no further forward in their investigations, despite the fact that within a week of the crime, they had had all but one of the killers in custody without even realising it. In November, however, Polanski's financial incentive finally bore some fruit.

A 15 October progress report by the police into the LaBianca killings listed 11 suspects, the last of whom was named as 'Manson, Charles'. Twice in the preceding five weeks, the 34-year-old itinerant ex-convict and other members of his 'Family' had been arrested in raids on outlying ranches in Los Angeles county; most were in the process of being charged on counts of felony, ranging from car theft to arson.

A Manson Family acolyte named Susan Denise Atkins (or 'Crazy Sadie', as she would come to be known) was further charged as an accessory in the murder of musician Gary Hinman, along with original suspect Bobby Beausoleil. While awaiting trial in an LA detention centre in November, Atkins confided to fellow cell-mates Virginia Graham and Veronica Howard that it was she and three others, two girls and a man, who had carried out the Tate-LaBianca killings on the orders of Charles Manson. 'I felt so elated,' Atkins enthused about her part in the bloodshed. 'Tired, but at peace with myself. I knew this was just the beginning of helter skelter. Now the world would listen.' Graham and Howard informed the police.

At the end of 1969, Atkins, Leslie Van Houten, Patricia Krenwinkel and Charles 'Tex' Watson were each indicted to stand trial, along with Manson, for the murders of Tate, Folger, Frykowski, Sebring, Parent and Rosemary and Leno LaBianca. The first trial commenced in June 1970, with 35-year-old Los Angeles Deputy District Attorney Vincent T Bugliosi acting for the prosecution. Verdicts were not returned until January the following year. (Van Houten was complicit only in the murders of the LaBiancas; a fourth person present at the Cielo Drive crime scene but who was not directly involved in the killings – Linda Kasabian – had turned state's evidence and been offered immunity from prosecution.) Watson was tried separately from the others, in August 1971; the verdict on him came on 12 October. All five defendants were found guilty of murder and conspiracy to murder. A sentence of death in each case was commuted to life imprisonment when the State of California repealed the death penalty. Graham and Howard each received $12,000 of the $25,000 on offer. The remaining $1000 went to a young boy named Steven Weiss, who had found one of the murder weapons.

In interviews given in the run-up to the trial, Manson cited the influences which had inspired his unique vision of Apocalypse. Chief among them was the music of the Beatles and the 'white' album in particular, which he thought had 'spoken' to him personally and whose tracks chimed with so many elements of the atrocity that was perpetrated inside 10050 Cielo Drive during the early hours of 9 August 1969: 'Sexy Sadie', 'Revolution', 'Piggies' and, of course, 'Helter Skelter'.

The real reason was probably more mundane. A wannabe pop star, Manson had reconnoitred the house in March while looking for Terry Melcher, not long after the Polanskis took up residence. He had been chased off the property by Sharon Tate's personal photographer, but not before his innocent victim had laid eyes on the man who was to order her destruction five months later; even then, Tate had thought him a 'creepy-looking guy'.

Before joining the Manson 'Family', Susan Atkins had been a member of Anton LaVey's First Church of Satan, erroneously alleged to have been founded on 30 April 1966, a date which the media-savvy LaVey designated retrospectively as 'Year One', Anno Satanas, while trying to capitalise on his alleged appearance as the Evil One in *Rosemary's Baby*. According to Atkins' own testimony, when 'Tex' Watson surprised a sleeping Wojtek Frykowski at Cielo Drive by thrusting a revolver under his nose, he introduced himself with the words, 'I am the Devil and I'm here to do the Devil's business...'

On 26 September 1970, a series of wildfires swept through Southern California, destroying more than 100,000 acres of land. Among the outlying buildings razed to the ground in the conflagration was the Spahn ranch, where Charles Manson and his cult of death had plotted their 'Battle of Armageddon'.

*   *   *

The puzzle was solved, the mystery at an end. The chastened Polanski could return to his work, though nothing would ever be quite the same again. For one thing, he had lost the abundant self-confidence which had made him friends and enemies in almost equal measure, and which had brought him to where he was today. The unmitigated joy which, by his own admission, he had found with Sharon Tate was now a thing of the past, and in its place was a permanent sense of melancholy: 'I not only developed a closer physical resemblance to my father after Sharon's death but began to take on some of his traits: his ingrained pessimism, his eternal dissatisfaction with life, his profoundly Judaic sense of guilt, and his conviction that every joyous experience has its price,' he wrote.

Sharon Marie Tate Polanski was laid to rest in the Catholic Holy Cross cemetery in Culver City, California, on Wednesday 13 August 1969, along with the boy-child who never was – Paul Richard Polanki as would have been, named after the two grandfathers whom he was never destined to see.

Some two weeks later, Polanski found himself in Elaine's famous Italian-American restaurant at 1703 Second Avenue in New York City, in the company of Sharon Tate's sister Debra and Mia Farrow. As they entered the premises, Farrow was hailed by rising journalistic star Lewis H Lapham, formerly of the *Herald Tribune*. Lapham was dining with Wall Street investment banker Edward Perlberg and Perlberg's current girlfriend, a 23-year-old Norwegian fashion model named Beatte Telle, and he asked Farrow and her friends to join them; Polanski pulled up a chair and seated himself between Telle and Perlberg. Few words were exchanged; according to Farrow, Polanski was in no fit state to converse (in fact, he and Farrow subsequently left the restaurant without eating their meals). But during the short time that he spent in Telle's company, the distraught director stared at her so fixedly that it made her uncomfortable enough to ask Perlberg to take her elsewhere. Whether Polanski recognised something in Telle's expression or appearance only he could say, but this incident would also return to haunt him – though in a quite different and unexpected way.

Polanski gave his own eloquent tribute to Tate in his 1984 autobiography: 'There are little things, like packing a suitcase or getting my hair cut, or dialling the 213 code for California or the 396 code for Rome, that invariably steer my thoughts back to Sharon. Even after so many years I find myself unable to watch a spectacular sunset, or visit a lovely old house, or experience visual pleasure of any kind, without instinctively telling myself how she would have loved it all.'

With Manson in custody, Polanski headed out of California, first for Paris and then to Gstaad in Switzerland, where he spent a winter rediscovering the pleasures of the flesh with the inmates of a nearby finishing school, as though it were a scene from his first wife's Italian horror-romp *Lycanthropus* come to life. 'The death of Sharon and the whole tragedy was a measurable shock to me,' he later recalled. 'And at such moments some people turn to drugs, others to alcohol, some go to a monastery. But for me, it was sex. I looked for solace and tried to forget.'

'Pecunia non olet'

When eventually his thoughts turned back to films, Polanski attempted to float an adaptation of Henri Charrière's novel *Papillon* with Warren Beatty in the lead. As with *The Day of the Dolphin*, this idea came to nought, and the film was made instead in 1972 with Dustin Hoffman and Steve McQueen, directed by Franklin Schaffner. In its tale of two escapees from the French penal colony of Devil's Island, *Papillon* was a tale of triumph in adversity; the project which Polanski finally settled upon after an afternoon on the ski slopes with Andy Braunsberg was, conversely, a tale of triumph turned into disaster. Out of the blue, he decided to make a film of Shakespeare's *Macbeth*. He and Braunsberg promptly set off for the airport to find themselves a backer.

Polanski had long wanted to film a play of Shakespeare's. Ironically, the one that he chose was considered by many in theatrical circles to be an omen of bad luck. The last director to tackle *Macbeth* on screen was Orson Welles, in 1948 (leaving aside Akira Kurosawa's samurai version, *Kumonosu jô* [*Throne of Blood*] in 1957). The original Welles version ran for 107 minutes, complete with full-on Scottish accents, but a disastrous opening in the US encouraged makers Republic to re-dub the film in its entirety and cut it to 89 minutes, hacking out many of the play's most famous lines in the process.

Is this a dagger which I see before me,
The handle toward my hand? Come, let me clutch thee.

Macbeth, William Shakespeare (1606)

Having tried and failed to strike a deal for *Macbeth* in Hollywood, with Universal and Allied Artists among others, Polanski turned to Victor Lownes, whose sway within the mirrored halls of the newly initiated Playboy Productions was second only to that of head honcho Hugh Hefner himself. With Lownes agreeing to stand as guarantor for the project, Hefner gave it the go-ahead from his seat at the gaming tables of Marbella and the budget for the film was set at $2.5 million, with Playboy stumping up $1.5 and distributor Columbia the remaining $1 million. Polanski replaced the now-defunct Cadre Films which he had formed with Gutowski with a

new operation, appropriately christened Caliban (after the character
in Shakespeare's *The Tempest*), in partnership with Braumberg.
True to ostentatious form, the duo acquired a Rolls-Royce Phantom
6 as their company car, despite the fact that Polanski could barely
see over the steering wheel.

To invest the project with as much artistic integrity as possible,
Lownes required a literary talent to pen the script who would
be perceived to be on a par with the Bard himself. To this end,
he chose as Shakespeare's interpreter for the occasion one of
the foremost critics of the day (and Polanski admirer), Kenneth
Tynan – a man who had been accorded the highest honours of
his profession but who maintained what might be regarded as a
Playboy sensibility. He had been the first person to utter the word
'fuck' on national television and he was presently engaged in
putting together a bare-arsed theatrical revue entitled *Oh! Calcutta!*,
which was intended to push the envelope of sexual permissiveness
right off the edge of the desk.

In the true spirit of the sixties, Italian director Franco Zeffirelli
had made youthful, exuberant and irreverent versions of *The
Taming of the Shrew* and *Romeo and Juliet* in 1967 and '68
respectively, so it followed that in line with the times, a Roman
Polanski adaptation of *Macbeth* was bound to be iconoclastic. That
notion was compounded by the fact that the film was to emanate
from the *Playboy* stable (which many in the press thought of as
Polanski's personal fiefdom) and have a script penned by the
licentious Tynan – one of a breed of writer, like Anthony Burgess
or Bernard Levin, who invariably gave the impression that they
thought the Bard their intellectual inferior. Tynan was acid in his
opinion of Polanski personally, as he made plain in several pieces
that he penned during their time together: 'We are driving along in
his Rolls and stop at a red light and there is a pretty girl standing
on the corner. Without hesitation, Polanski rolls down the window
and leans out: "Hey, miss, excuse me, you have a beaudiful arse.
Where are you going??" And the girl ends up in the car.'

The lower orders at Shepperton Studios were equally acid about Tynan, the standard joke in respect of the production being a variant on the theme of why a film version of *Macbeth* required a screenwriter in the first place. The idea of a writer of Tynan's ego turning up at the studio each day in his Bentley, with its notional *Playboy* Bunny bumper-sticker, in order to carry out script revisions to one of the greatest works of drama in the language was simply too much for them to bear.

The film was perceived from the start as a massive vanity project for Polanski, for Hugh Hefner and Victor Lownes, and for Tynan himself – and reports from the set of a young Lady Macbeth wandering naked as nature intended in the 'sleepwalking scene' in Act V did little to reassure critical commentators that they were in for anything more cerebral than a blood-spattered soft-porn romp through the Welsh valleys (Polanski's location of choice), by a director whose command of the language of Shakespeare was faltering to say the least. None of this was helped by the fact that the *Playboy* opus was said to be even bloodier than Hammer's yet-to-be-released *Countess Dracula*. Given that the play from which it was adapted is the granddaddy of Gothic horror, with its spectral visitations, witchcraft, dreams and portents, madness and mass murder, this was hardly surprising, but implicit in the criticism was the fact that the Bard's work was being used merely as a titillating exercise in exploitation and as a sop to several extra-large egos.

Polanski made much in interviews of the fact that he thought previous adapters had been too quick to lay the weight of guilt on Macbeth's shoulders: 'We were determined to cut across the long-established theatrical clichés,' he insisted. 'Macbeth and his wife are young and good-looking, not middle-aged and doom-laden.' Yet John Gielgud had played the role on stage at the age of 26, and Laurence Olivier at 30. Even Welles was only 33 when he mounted his own film version in 1948. Nevertheless, the idea took hold and the role of the Thane was offered to Jon Finch, who was not exactly a spring-chicken at 29, but who came fresh from an introductory stint with Hammer Films (*The Vampire Lovers, The Horror of Frankenstein*), still the repertory company of choice for many a budding British actor in 1970. When it came to Lady Macbeth, Polanski had had more than six years to reconsider Francesca Annis (originally mooted for *Repulsion*), whom he now felt had matured from a Compton glamour girl into a competent – and confident – young actress.

The changes that Tynan made to the text were mostly those of abridgement, which allowed Polanski to imbue the tale with a more cinematic dynamic. The plot unfolds at a lively clip, highlighted by the depiction of dramatic incidents which the Bard chose to keep off-stage (such as the execution of Cawdor and the murder of Duncan and his guards, as well as the death of Macbeth himself) and unencumbered by the weight of the long discourses which made the Welles version too heavy-going for many. Polanski treats the film as historical epic: the fact that the dialogue is Shakespeare's rather than, say, Robert Bolt's, is largely inconsequential to the overall design of the piece, and the longest speech left intact by Tynan – Act I, scene VI's 'If it were done when 'tis done, then 'twere well It were done quickly' – is delivered across *three* separate scenes in the film, thus ensuring that there is always something of interest to hold the attention, over and above the prose. To the same end, other scenes are transposed – Act V, scene III with Act IV, scene III for example – and minor characters are omitted. But Tynan only *rewrites* the Bard inasmuch as such change is necessitated by compression of the text or similar, and only by a word or two even then.

In the interval between *Rosemary's Baby* and *Macbeth*, relations between Polanski and the BBFC's John Trevelyan had returned to their previously cordial state after the contretemps between the two over the cutting of the former. No one with any sense of compassion could hold a grudge against Polanski after the terrible events of August 1969, and Trevelyan was nothing if not a compassionate man: 'I have often thought what a tragic irony of fate it was that [Polanski's] own wife, a lovely girl, was killed in a similar way,' he would write, in reference to the razor murder in *Repulsion*. Consequently, he took it resolutely on the chin when, in June 1970, and with his tongue firmly in his cheek, the director wrote to inform him that he was intending to film *The Tragedy of Macbeth*. 'It cannot be denied that this is an extremely gory subject, involving a large number of brutal killings, most of them committed by members of the upper classes,' Polanski chided. 'It is up to you to decide whether there is any artistic justification for bloodshed on this scale and at this social level.'

Accordingly, the Secretary replied in kind: '[Shakespeare's] books, like those of Mickey Spillane, who has I believe a nearly comparable circulation, exploit every form of violence, brutality and horror, together with sexual deviation, and are clearly unsuitable as screen material even for the most mature adults.' He then told Polanski that he planned to have his letter framed and mounted on his office wall. Trevelyan had decided to adopt a less partisan approach to Polanski's latest opus, but there was also another, more personal reason for the untypical tone of self-mockery: he was actively contemplating hanging up his censor's scissors.

Trevelyan had always been alert to shifts in the public mood; during his time at the BBFC, he had rarely been caught off-guard by the media (*Rosemary's Baby* being one of the few exceptions), but he could sense trouble ahead. A new breed of iconoclastic director was virtually baiting the Board by pushing the concept of 'taste and decency' to its absolute limits. Foremost among these was one-time amateur filmmaker and BBC documentarist Ken Russell, whose public pronouncements in defence of his films were to drown out the measured responses of the more cultured Trevelyan by their sheer din.

In the knowledge that he was unlikely to see the completed item, therefore, Trevelyan picked up Tynan's script for *Macbeth* with an eye to mediation. He had been left with no choice: the assessment of the Examiner nominated to report on it had been candid to the point of contemptuousness. 'I have the uncanny conviction that it was written by the Hammer boys with delusions of grandeur and for export to the USA and Japan,' he noted. 'The old gimmicks and clichés are there in very strong measure ... This is classic horror-comic stuff and reeks of the Sharon Tate shambles ... Ever since Tynan broke the 'fuck barrier' on TV, he has succeeded in becoming one of the world's most tedious enfants terribles.'

Trevelyan met with Tynan and Polanski and tried to persuade them to tone down the scenes of violence and nudity. Tynan weighed in with Shakespearean authority on the text, and he left Trevelyan in no doubt that neither of them was for turning – though Polanski did concede that he was unlikely to have Macbeth 'decapitated visually', as this would only make the resultant film look like standard horror fare. (In the event, Macbeth's full-frontal beheading became one of the main talking points of the piece.) In light of the filmmakers' unwillingness to compromise, Trevelyan advised them that *Macbeth* most probably would end up with an X.

> *Hear it not, Duncan, for it is a knell that summons thee to heaven or to hell.*

Macbeth (Jon Finch), *The Tragedy of Macbeth* (1971)

Shakespeare had been commissioned to write the play in 1606, for the new King James I of England (James VI of Scotland). Given the nationality of his monarchical audience, he calculated that an intrinsically Scottish subject might best fit the bill for this latest 'Tragedy', and a trawl through Raphael Holinshed's *Chronicles of England, Scotland and Ireland* (1577) turned up the story of Macbeth, an 11th century Scottish nobleman who usurped the throne of Scone by assassinating the incumbent, Duncan, and who subsequently was defeated in battle by Malcolm Campbell, Duncan's eldest son. The version of events in the *Chronicles* was not Holinshed's, however, but that of Hector Boece, another scholar, whose *Scotorum Historiae* had been incorporated into the whole. Polanski duly defended his decision to up the traditional number of witches in *Macbeth* from three to 13 on the grounds that Shakespeare probably settled on a lower figure due to space restrictions on the Elizabethan stage; in point of fact, it was Boece who gave the number of 'weird sisters' as three, long before the story was even considered for adaptation in the theatre.

Shakespeare embellished his *Macbeth* with details from the history of King Duffe, as well as larding it with the kind of supernatural blood and thunder which he previously had employed in *Hamlet*. This was par for the course for a royalist playwright keen to ingratiate himself with his Sovereign. James' interest in the occult was well known: in 1597, he had published his *Daemonologie*, which he followed in 1598 by a treatise on morality entitled *Basilicon Doron* – the latter of which influenced Shakespeare in the writing of *Macbeth*. James was also reputed to be a direct descendant of Banquo, one of the alleged historical figures represented in the play.

As told by Shakespeare, the brave warrior Macbeth is seduced into assassinating King Duncan during the latter's stay at his castle in Inverness by a witches' prophesy (which promises the throne of Scotland) and the wiles of an ambitious wife. Despite his misgivings, Macbeth carries through the murderous scheme, blaming it on the King's retainers. Duncan's sons – Malcolm and Donalbain – smell a rat, however, and they flee to England with loyal lieutenant Macduff, there to raise an army with which to overthrow the usurper. Blood demands more blood, as others who stand in the way of Macbeth's successful succession to the throne are mercilessly disposed of: his onetime friend and ally Banquo, as well as Macduff's entire family.

As Macbeth feels more secure in his position, his wife conversely becomes wracked by guilt and descends inexorably into madness. The witches who predicted Macbeth's rise to power also foretold of his fall; until that time, he is assured that he need fear no man 'born of woman'. As Malcolm's forces march on Dunsinane castle, they camouflage themselves with branches cut from the trees in Birnam wood, thus fulfilling the witches' fateful prophesy ('Macbeth shall never vanquish'd be until/Great Birnam wood to high Dunsinane hill/Shall come against him.') In the battle that follows, Macbeth is confronted by Macduff, who reveals that he was 'untimely ripp'd' from his mother's womb (birthed by Caesarian section). Macbeth's fate is sealed; he is killed by Macduff, and Malcolm is crowned King in his stead. The real Macbeth was defeated in battle at Dunsinane, near Dundee, on 27 July 1054, but he was not killed by Macduff until three years later, in 1057.

*   *   *

Filming began in November 1970 and was spread over six months, with the unit based at Shepperton. Location shooting commenced on the North Wales peninsula of Portmeirion, famously the setting of the cult 1960s' television series *The Prisoner*, before moving on to the north of England. The experience of *Cul-de-Sac* did not prevent Polanski on this occasion from returning a second unit to Lindisfarne, whose castle stands in for Macbeth's Inverness retreat in the first half of the film, while Bamburgh on the Northumbrian mainland took on the role of Dunsinane for the second half (though imposing by themselves, both structures were further embellished by the art department). The rest of the location work was conducted in the Welsh National Park of Snowdonia, as evidenced by the interminable rain.

The vagaries of the British weather, Polanski's notorious perfectionism and the sheer scale on which the film had been envisaged soon sent *Macbeth* a half-million dollars over its allotted budget. Relations between Polanski and Lownes became strained as a result, with Lownes torn between affection for his friend and loyalty to his lord and master at the Playboy Mansion in Chicago. Film Finances, *Macbeth*'s nominal insurers, prosecuted for a change of director in the face of the overruns; to hedge its bets, Columbia placed Peter Collinson, the British director of *The Italian Job* (1968), on standby at the studio. Eventually, Hefner flew to London to adjudicate and accepted Polanski's version of events – that with the problems entailed in the production, shooting was progressing as fast as humanly possible. 'Hef' reached for his *Playboy* pen and wrote out a cheque for the extra half-million bucks. Polanski and his crew were now free to complete the picture as planned and *Macbeth* wrapped on schedule, and in time to meet its December 1971 premiere engagement.

Polanski supplied his own epitaph for his *Playboy* experience. 'Billy Wilder once said, "Did you ever hear of someone saying, 'Let's go to the Roxy, they're playing a movie that was made within its schedule'?" – The Polish proverb is, "The better you make your bed, the longer you sleep",' he clarified. 'There's something in my character that appears to all my financiers as something bad – which is that I care. Whereas some other directors, the ones who give up and yield to these attacks, do not care.'

The film originally had been scheduled to open in London, but Hef was keen for it to inaugurate the newly opened *Playboy* Theatre on West 57th Street in New York. In unwise contravention of accepted industry practice, the film's premiere was deferred to January in the US – a bad time for openings, even in the Big Apple. The New York critics, who were not particularly disposed to Shakespeare to begin with, lambasted the film. The basic humourlessness of all the strutting chauvinists involved in the production quite failed to spot the obvious pratfalls in store for them; the titles, for instance, open with the words 'A Playboy Production' – a legend which elicited sniggering in the audience before the film proper had even begun. Hefner was made to look foolish in his presumption that Shakespeare could have been made to climb into bed with a copy of *Playboy*, and Lownes lost considerable face with his previously-tolerant boss. There had been more than a career at stake for Lownes: there was an entire lifestyle. Someone had to take the blame, and Lownes decided that that someone should be Roman Polanski.

The crunch came when Polanski agreed to an interview to promote *Macbeth* which was to be conducted in *Playboy*'s own premises in Park Lane. When asked why he had chosen to join forces with such an organisation for such a serious project, his habitual forthrightness got the better of him, and he replied – in mimicry of the Latin inscription on the door of Hef's Mansion ('Si non oscillas, noli tintinnare' or, 'If you don't swing, don't ring') – 'Pecunia non olet', which translates as 'Money doesn't smell.' When he read the piece, Lownes was incensed. It was the final straw. Years before, Polanski had presented him with a statuette of an erect penis, which he had specially commissioned as an in-joke between the two of them. Lownes now returned this 'golden prick' to its donor, with a note which this time sealed the end of their friendship for good: 'In view of recent developments,' he wrote, 'I no longer want to have this full-length, life-size portrait of you around the house. You'll have no difficulty in finding some 'friend' you can shove it up.'

> *I have almost forgot the taste of fears;*
> *The time has been, my senses would have cool'd*
> *To hear a night-shriek; and my fell of hair*
> *Would at a dismal treatise rouse and stir*
> *As life were in't: I have supp'd full with horrors...*
>
> **Macbeth (Jon Finch)**, *The Tragedy of Macbeth* (1971)

Macbeth is full-blooded Gothic horror, long before the term was coined officially – a delirious descent into a whirlpool of treachery and deceit, blood and madness – yet Polanski's version is somehow constrained by its own potential for excess. Macbeth flies into a mock rage at the discovery of Duncan's murder and hacks the two guards who have been posted outside the King's bedchamber (and whom Lady Macbeth has lined up to take the fall) quite literally to pieces, but he is a model of composure immediately afterwards; Milady takes her own climactic fall off-camera, a few brief glimpses of her grotesquely distorted corpse being all that bear witness to the shocking nature of the act. In his efforts to avoid cliché and melodrama, Polanski had strayed too far onto the side of naturalism. He has his characters behave in a more studiedly realistic way towards the horrors with which Shakespeare surrounds them, but the net result is that the scheming couple in *Macbeth* are simply too normal, and their sudden lurch into insanity strains credulity. Jon Finch does well by the brooding and the self-doubt, but less well in the wild-eyed, paranoid and self-deluding stakes; Francesca Annis does the opposite.

Orson Welles accurately sought to set his 1948 *Macbeth* in the Dark Ages; Tynan and Polanski opted to move their film more towards the medieval period of Bruce and Wallace. The result is a curious clash of styles, with a pseudo-Norman castle perched atop a highland crag and barely a single Scot among the cast of National Theatre players, which only makes Shakespeare's Elizabethan prose stand out all the more against a backdrop of alleged authenticity. Even with a scholarly scribe like Tynan at his side, Polanski bit off more than he could chew in his attempt to film *Macbeth*. Too many sequences veer dangerously close to caricature, and its director's propensity for casting quirks produces the kind of Macduff in Terence Bayler who is more suited to a satirical sketch than the real thing, although he turns in an able performance. Finch is effectively conflicted, but the transition from conscience-stricken regicide to expedient killer of any who stand in his way is frankly incredible, while the assemblage of naked hags who cast their unholy ingredients into a too-literally bubbling cauldron is almost a cartoon rendering of the geriatric coven in *Rosemary's Baby*.

Cleverly, some of the more famous speeches are conveyed as voice-overs, rather than declamations, which keeps attention focused on the visuals: the 'ghostly' dagger of Macbeth's mind is an inspirational highlight (if a little too much like a sequence in a video game). One or two of the violent episodes also manage to capture something of the shocking impact of the murders in *Repulsion* – the coup de grâce, when Macbeth thrusts his blade into Duncan's throat as he lies on the floor of his room, mortally wounded; the similar slaughter of Young Siward at the climax. The sighting of Banquo's ghost is equally impressive. Macbeth is encouraged by his kinsmen to occupy an 'empty' place at table in which the dead Banquo is already seated, back to camera; it takes a moment for the anomaly to register, and the realisation that the solid-seeming figure is actually Banquo's shade dawns on the viewer at the same time as it does on Macbeth. It is one of the most chilling scenes of supernatural terror ever committed to film. Polanski's taste for the difficult-to-achieve shot is catered for by the famous incident in which Birnam Wood comes against Dunsinane, which is captured in a single take as Macbeth stares out at the distant hills from the battlements of his castle and, seeing nothing, turns away, only to turn back a moment later as the soldiers of the opposing army mount the hilltop enshrouded by striplings.

The film strives hard for authenticity. In the duel between Macbeth and Macduff at the climax, their heavy armour hinders movement and contributes to an ungainly tussle as they tumble awkwardly about. But as though to counter the plodding nature of such arduous combat, Polanski under-cranks the scene to speed up the action, which creates an incongruously comic effect, reminiscent of such intentional antics in his early shorts and in *The Vampire Killers*. Macbeth eventually takes a sword-thrust diagonally through the torso, keeping faith with the fact that breast and back-plate inhibit his being pierced anywhere else, and before he has time to contemplate the imminent loss of his throne, his head is lopped from his shoulders in another graphic nod to Hammer Horror.

In a highly original interlude, Polanski bows briefly to the notion (enshrined in myth from observation of the victims of

Revolutionary guillotining) that consciousness remains for some moments following decapitation: he offers a glimpse of Malcolm's triumph from the point-of-view of Macbeth's severed head, at which the victors laugh in silence as it is hoist to the battlements atop a pole. This is a stunning directorial flourish, of a kind which only Polanski has the brio to conjure up. But a smattering of original moments do not make up for some fundamental weaknesses.

Less successful are the changes that Tynan makes to Shakespeare's plotting, based on his own peculiar interpretation of authorial intent. When the character of Ross, in response to an enquiry from Macduff, states that the latter's wife and children are well, only to reverse his stance moments later and reveal that all have been murdered on Macbeth's orders, Tynan chose to read more into this volte-face than mere diplomacy. He saw in Ross' hesitancy a duplicitous nature, reasoning that Macbeth's lieutenant changed his mind about revealing the truth of what happened to Macduff's retinue only after observing the strength of the opposing army and being faced with the prospect of certain defeat. This revisionist reading consequently required the character of Ross to be changed throughout, and Tynan substitutes him for Shakespeare's anonymous '3rd Murderer' during the assault on Banquo and his son Fleance, as well as creating additional acts of subversion for him to commit in silence: he oversees the disposal of Banquo's murderers (a foolish notion which requires that new murderers be recruited straight afterwards to deal with the kin of Macduff!) and he arranges for the doors to Macduff's castle to be left open, so as to allow entry to the hired assassins.

All of this only adds psychological clutter to a story already mired in moral quandary. As Shakespeare did not provide one, Ross is accorded no comeuppance for his various betrayals in Tynan's take on events – beyond having the helmet knocked off his head by an axe hurled pointedly towards him by Macbeth. Given that he has been complicit in the murder of Macduff's wife and child, the lack of suitable retribution in a play about crime and retribution looks like a sin of omission on the part of the Bard; instead, it is Tynan trying too hard to be clever. The error is compounded by the casting of John Stride, a naturally sympathetic actor whose poise exudes honesty and integrity, not deceit and treachery.

Cinematographer Gil Taylor does much with the varied lights of dawn and sunset, but the film as a whole is too over-lit for its subject, let alone its period in history. For all of its pretty painting with sky, sea and landscape, and its yellow-clad soldiers trudging over rust-coloured earth in preparation for their assault on Dunsinane, the battle scenes smack a little too much of Italian epics from a decade before. What the film so clearly lacks is the sheer intensity that Welles brought to the role of writer, director and star in 1948 – the *fire* in the blood, not just the blood by itself.

Too many of the cast in Polanski's version are merely poor players, strutting and fretting their hours upon the stage, to be heard (of) no more. (Finch went from here into Hitchcock's *Frenzy* [1971], though he is probably best remembered for Robert Fuest's cult rendering of Michael Moorcock's *The Final Programme* two years later, in which he played Jerry Cornelius; after that, his career went into the doldrums.) Even Tynan's tagged-on epilogue, in which Malcolm's brother Donalbain also comes upon the witches on their blasted heath, seems more of an afterthought than a genuine attempt to rework the play. According to Polanski's *Macbeth*, the cycle of violence and death is implicitly set to continue, which not only flies in the face of the facts of Scottish history but encouraged critics in their assertions that its director's bleak and downbeat view of the world had hardened significantly since the death of his wife.

Polanski's *Macbeth* – or *The Tragedy of Macbeth*, to give it its full title – is a film of rain and drizzle, and sea-mists and sunsets, and overcast skies; it is a meteorologist's *Macbeth* – a weather man's view of Shakespeare – in which the climate is as much of an actor in the drama as its human participants. Weather by itself is not

atmosphere, alas, and its employment in the film is no substitute
for the real thing, which has to be created by the interplay of
characters, rather than the soddenness of their surroundings. For
all its studied avoidance of traditional histrionics, this is a dour
and sombre retelling, as though the damp and miserable weather
which is so much a feature of the proceedings had seeped into the
spirit of the piece and sapped it of its macabre vitality.

*   *   *

When *Macbeth* was finally submitted to the BBFC in October 1971,
after a year in production, much had changed. John Trevelyan had
resigned his position as Secretary in June (though he remained in
situ till the end of July), and his place had been taken by Stephen
Murphy; the system of certification had also been revised, with
the age for the X being raised to 18, while that of the 'old' X was
lowered to 14 and the certificate reclassified as AA. On condition
that Polanski reduce the bloodshed in two of the murders (those of
Duncan in the first act and Siward at the close), Murphy felt that
the film was suitable for the AA and had it categorised accordingly.
Polanski was grateful for the concession. Others were less
impressed with Murphy's magnanimity.

One of Trevelyan's last acts in office had been to pass Ken
Russell's bawdy film of *The Devils* as an X (after cuts); among
Murphy's first acts in the job was to oversee the classification of
Sam Peckinpah's *Straw Dogs* and Stanley Kubrick's ultraviolent
A Clockwork Orange, both of which were also passed X. All three
rebounded on the new censor, whose more liberal approach was
met with a concerted campaign of personal vilification in the
national press. The backlash had begun, and Murphy's tenure at
the Board would last a mere three years.

The film opened in America on 20 January 1972, and in Britain
on 2 February. The *Chicago Sun-Times*'s Roger Ebert led the charge
to associate the blood-and-thunder of *The Tragedy of Macbeth*
with the tragedy which had befallen its director in his personal

life: 'I might as well be honest and say it is impossible to watch certain scenes without thinking of the Charles Manson case. It is impossible to watch a film directed by Roman Polanski and not react on more than one level to such images as a baby being "untimely ripped from his mother's womb..." Polanski's characters resemble Charles Manson: They are anti-intellectual, witless, and driven by deep, shameful wells of lust and violence ... This is certainly one of the most pessimistic films ever made, and there seems little doubt that Polanski intended his film to be full of sound and fury – which it is, to the brim – and to signify nothing.'

Time magazine was reticent to draw any direct parallels – 'Polanski is most at home dealing with black magic. His affection for the supernatural is so unrestrained that many of the movie's straight scenes have an almost cursory air' – but other critics were less circumspect in their employment of cod-psychology. *Newsweek* found the theme to be 'a rationalisation of a psychic compulsion' on Polanski's part, adding that 'No chance to revel in gore is passed up. We watch bodies crushed and mutilated by spiked clubs, limbs severed, hands bathed in crimson, necks broken, heads lopped off...' and suggesting that if such scenes were indispensable to the telling of the famous tale, then the film was 'a work of art – in the grand manner of Buchenwald, Ludice, and, yes, the Manson murders'.

American predisposition towards Freudian theory saw to it that the consensus of opinion found a link between the often-overwrought violence of the Scottish play and the slaughter which had taken place only two years earlier at Cielo Drive – as though some strange form of catharsis was being acted out before the collective critical gaze. Polanski had hit upon the idea of filming Shakespeare partly as a way of avoiding the 'knowing' criticism which he felt instinctively would have come his way had he chosen another genre, such as comedy or horror; the American reviews proved him wrong.

British critics made much of *Macbeth*'s affinity to Hammer horror, which critics of the day tended to do with any film which employed more than a droplet of blood in a fight scene. On the whole, their attitude to the film was more constructive, though, *and* more discriminating – any insinuations about subtext were made in terms of its link to *Playboy*, rather than the Manson case. Nevertheless, they split into two camps when it came to a debate about merit. The *Evening Standard*'s Alexander Walker protested the bastardising of Shakespeare's text: 'The real charge against this film is that continually the eyes have it against the claims of poetry, so that time and again some of the most magnificent dramatic language ever written is thrown away in a mutter or mumble. The images smother the words, and in the process is lost all the drama's sense of pace.' Nor could he resist the obvious jibe against the production company: 'Miss Annis is made to play the sleepwalking scene in the nude, and looks very fetching, but Lady Macbeth was not Highland Playmate of the Month.'

Derek Malcolm supplied a timely rejoinder to Walker's narrow classicist view in the *Guardian*. 'Kurosawa's *Throne of Blood* was better, but then, as Peter Hall has said, it had hardly any words and none of them by Shakespeare. This stopped anyone in their tracks who complained about the lack of poetry, which everyone always does when they can't think of anything else to say about a production of *Macbeth*.' Then he ended by coming down firmly on the side of the revisionists. 'It is, for the most part, a straight and freshly imagined version of the play with the emphasis on sight rather than sound, so that the final clanking duel between Macbeth and Macduff gains enormously by its awkwardness.'

For all its faults, Polanski's *Macbeth* is a film that rewards repeated viewings. It lacks the maniacal edge and noir intensity of the Welles, but at a time when the demographic of the cinema audience was devolving to a single age-group – that of 18-30 – here was a *Macbeth* which was tailored to appeal to the corresponding change in taste. Finch gives quite a remarkable performance in only his third film role, and Polanski's intricate staging is never less than interesting to observe, savour and often wonder over. But the film as a whole is too squeaky-clean, too medievally pristine to warrant serious consideration alongside the Shakespearian endeavours of the likes of Welles or Olivier.

The adverse critical reception which was accorded to *The Tragedy of Macbeth* sent Polanski scurrying for cover again, and he next surfaced in Italy with a more frivolous idea in tow, after the amateur Freudians in the press had him expiating his grief in the blood of one of the world's great tragedies. With that in mind, the public opted to leave him to his tears and the film failed to recover its final cost of $3.5 million.

* * *

Whatever virtue once was implied by the writing partnership of Brach and Polanski looked in some danger of being exposed as an illusion by their next project. *What?* was typical of the kind of inane sex-comedy that started to proliferate in the late sixties and early seventies as figures for cinema attendance began to nose-dive. It owed its madcap antics – and abbreviated title – to Clive Donner's *What's New Pussycat?* (1966) and its sexual licence to former pop star Mike Sarne's *Myra Breckinridge* (1969), to which it nods and winks in its final reel (Sarne was a friend of Polanski's). Its humourless and self-congratulatory plod around the sexual peccadilloes of the nouveau riche is entirely the product of its two creators, however, and their talent looked to have become flaccid and flatulent on the shores of Amalfi.

Polanski and Brach now had no one to please but themselves, and they had become bloated in the belief that whatever they did would automatically be construed as art by the cognoscenti – either that, or they were too self-indulgent to care. Ten years before, they had toyed with the notion of writing an erotic, live-action version of *Snow White and the Seven Dwarfs*; on this occasion, they thought to film an erotic, live-action version of *Alice's Adventures in Wonderland.* With Italian producer Carlo Ponti's Neapolitan villa at their disposal, they indulged themselves in a menopausal sex-comedy with little rhyme or reason, and certainly no potential for enjoyment for anyone outside the magic circle of friends with whom Polanski had again surrounded himself.

> *I must confess that I feel utterly overwhelmed with pessimism. For some time now, none of my plans – even the most modest ones – have worked out properly.*
>
> **Joseph Noblart (Hugh Griffith)**, *What?* (1972)

Having narrowly avoided a gang-bang at the hands of a trio of louts with whom she naïvely hitched a lift, Nancy (Sydne Rome) finds refuge in the villa of eccentric ex-pimp Alex Noblart (Marcello Mastroianni). Among the odd characters she encounters in this oddest of households are a priest, a piano-player and an annoying little buzz-fly of a man named Mosquito (Polanski). Tea-parties are held, Ping-Pong is played by a pair of neighbours who resemble Tweedledum and Tweedledee, exotic masquerades are undertaken prior to bouts of sexual congress, frescoes are delivered, any semblance of sense is systematically abandoned by all and sundry in favour of some insane logic that must have been driven by drugs or drink until, at last, Noblart's father (Hugh Griffith) decides that the time has come for him to shuffle off this mortal coil and, in so doing, to provide the increasingly incoherent storyline with a different sort of climax. He asks Nancy to stand astride the bed on which he lies. 'What splendour – hallelujah!' he cries, after spying her mons veneris. His eyes close in bliss and he duly expires, a glass ball tumbling from his dead hand like the snow-shaker in *Citizen Kane.*

Such is the extent of the original thinking in *What?*, though it might have been appropriate in context if he also had uttered the word 'Rosebud...' The actors even acknowledge that they are in a film at the close, in a slick, postmodern touch. 'We're in a movie, aren't we?' Nancy calls to Alex as she hitches a ride to the surface. 'What movie?' he asks. 'That's right... *What?* – That's the name of the movie!' she replies.

*   *   *

Polanski's sabbatical in Italy was fast developing into permanent exile as a plan for a creative 'commune' began to take root, the initial fruit of which was *What?* But in what is little more than a pseudo-arty soft-porn exercise, all that he and Brach proved by abandoning the strictures of commercial discipline was that the result of any artistic endeavour was likely to be of limited appeal beyond the shores of the Meditterranean. Twenty-year-old Ohio-born Sydne Rome is endearingly unaffected by the states of partial or full-frontal nudity in which she has to spend much of the film. Rome is bright-eyed and beautiful, and she must have thought that her big break had come after auditioning for – but failing to be cast as – Terry Southern's *Candy* four years before. (Her screen career thereafter was an eclectic one of Eurotosh fillers, but she has worked consistently.) Polanski wanders the periphery of what narrative there is as 'Mosquito', another of his self-deprecating cameos (he is referred to as a 'vicious dwarf'), and Mastroianni's Mad Hatter ('What would be nice, you see, would be if we could get together quietly some time – to have tea, for example, round five o'clock, today or tomorrow. All right?') and his own March Hare make for a watchable double-act.

What? is Polanski in surrealist mode, and all the elements of surrealist fantasy are present and correct – the Buñuelian dinner-party (an echo of *Cul-de-Sac*); the resident priest; the cast of eccentrics; idiosyncratic pursuits, such as the game of Ping-Pong in the adjacent villa or the piano-player obsessed with his arthritic hands. But all these are seconded to the needs of cinematic sexual fantasy, as Rome is shorn of what garments she can find to wear at every opportunity, and to the accompaniment of Mozart's Piano Sonata in F Major – which itself is utilised to give the titillation an air of respectability, in the same way that *Playboy* would publish fiction by well-known authors alongside the colour photos of its reclining nudes.

Despite Ponti's backing, *What?* went unreleased in many territories for more than two years, eventually showing up in the UK at the Curzon Mayfair in April 1974. The critics were united in condemnation. Christopher Hudson of the *Spectator* delivered a particularly pithy appraisal: '*What?* – a tiresome rhetorical question to which the only proper response is Why?' 'The dialogue is as limp as the reactions of its audience are likely to be,' he continued. 'The only mystery is why an immensely talented filmmaker like Polanski should have turned his finger to it.' The *Guardian*'s Hugh Herbert shared Hudson's sense of bewilderment: 'What is nearly incomprehensible is that a director of Polanski's potential should churn out a dismal, amorphous, tired and tasteless mess like this.' In the *Sunday Telegraph*, Margaret Hinxman felt likewise: 'If I thought hard about it I might be able to find some hidden, even serious meaning in Roman Polanski's lunatic comedy, *What?* But the exercise is not worth the effort.' Even Dilys Powell could find nothing of virtue in the film: 'Perhaps one ought to call the farce and the sexual clowning not so much desperate as despairing,' she wrote in the *Sunday Times*. The *Observer*'s Russell Davies simply wrote it off as 'an unholy mess'.

If *What?* was intended to be a comedy, only Italians and Poles were able to see the joke. There is simply no amusement to be had in a feeble yarn whose origins must have lain in one bottle of Chianti too many. The name of Mastroianni's character – Noblart – is a none-too-subtle pun: after his adventures in Gstaad and on the Italian Riviera, one can imagine which 'noble art' Polanski might have been preoccupied with at this point in time. With *What?*, however, he chose to do it to the viewer.

By the time *What?* saw release in the US under the more obviously exploitable title of *Diary of Forbidden Dreams*, not even the usually reliable crowd of voyeuristic sado-masochists could be bothered to turn out to see it. Ponti had sunk $1.2 million of his own money into *What?* On its completion, Polanski and crew found themselves on the lookout for a new villa.

> *Maybe you can buy us some wine...?*
>
> **man in tavern (Roman Polanski)**, *Blood for Dracula* (1973)

If the shooting of *What?* achieved little of artistic or commercial value, it inspired in Polanski a brief infatuation with all things Italian. He and his entourage of producer Andrew Braunsberg, writer Brach and general factotum Hercules Bellville decided to make Rome their new base of operations. The quartet rented a house on the Via Appia Antica, and there they were to remain for another three years. It was not long before *la dolce vita* attracted other existentialist refugees from the sixties art-house scene, and to help pay the $3000-dollar-per-month rental to villa owner the Countess of Warwick, Polanski soon found himself appearing in a horror film executive-produced by – of all people – pop artist extraordinaire Andy Warhol.

Warhol's latest experiment in mass-market pop culture was to be a brace of horror films shot back-to-back in the summer of 1973 and glorying in the decades-old wonder of 3-Dimension. Both would feature the classic Gothic monsters on which Hammer Films had built its name and reputation, and both would feature Euro-wacko Udo Kier and Warhol's regular penis-flaunter and star of *Flesh* (1968) and *Trash* (1970), Joe Dallesandro – thus a punning title for *Flesh for Frankenstein*, but a more generically derivative one for its stablemate, *Blood for Dracula*. There was only one 'director' of sorts in the Warhol stable, so the pair were allotted to 33-year-old Paul Morrissey, who had cut his cinematic teeth on any number of curious Factory shorts. (By the time Morrissey turned his attention to *The Hound of the Baskervilles* [1977], with comic duo Peter Cook and Dudley Moore as Holmes and Watson, it had become obvious to all that directorial talent at The Factory was in short supply.)

As the creative juices in the Polanski camp began to dry up in
the Italian sun, Braunsberg offered to co-produce the two Warhol
horrors at Rome's Cinecittà Studios; Polanski's weakness for
'people from the demi-monde', as his ex-wife Basia would put it,
encouraged him to volunteer for a cameo in the second of them.

If *Flesh for Frankenstein* was farce by another name, *Blood for
Dracula* attempted to infuse its prep-school plot with a certain
Gothic poetry, not least by the inclusion of a plaintive piano score
by Claudio Gizzi. How else can one account for the participation
of the great post-war director Vittorio de Sica as a foppish Italian
Count, complete with an accent so thick that no knife could cut it?
Polanski's turn as a corduroy cap-wearing, moustachioed drunk, in
a tavern where peasant women exclaim that they 'just dropped in
for a quick one', is more easily explicable: he felt no shame about
how he earned his money or whose name was on a cheque – as
witness the recent contretemps with Victor Lownes – and he had
always had something of a connoisseur's taste for insufferable
artistic bores like Warhol and Morrissey. Both films gained
theatrical release on the novelty value of Warhol's name; were it
not for that, the decidedly amateur nature of writing, directing and
acting would surely have consigned them to oblivion immediately
upon their completion.

How much of the idea behind *Flesh for Frankenstein* and *Blood
for Dracula* was Warhol's and how much Polanski's is a point in
question. After the murder of his wife, Polanski had contacted
Eye and Brain's Richard Gregory with a view to having him act as
technical consultant on a '3-D horror film' that he was intending
to make. The two men experimented with various applications
of the process before the idea was dropped for lack of industry
interest; some months later, Polanski consented to appear in
Blood for Dracula. His fascination with the technology might
explain his otherwise inexplicable participation in a piece of utter
dross – though, as it turned out, the film, unlike its Frankenstein
predecessor, was *not* shot in 3-D.

What? had been one exercise in collective therapy too far for
Brach and Polanski, and the latter's appearance in the Morrissey
film merely added to the sense of outrage that was felt by those
who had predicted great things for him. The wave of sympathy
which had come Polanski's way in the wake of the events of four
years earlier seemed suddenly to be in danger of draining away.

As his luck would have it, however, the delay in releasing
What? meant that Polanski's next feature was already in the can
and awaiting only the late addition of a new musical score before
unveiling itself to the world. Instead of sexual shenanigans on the
Med, it was a crime caper on Main Street USA, and it had reunited
him with Paramount's Bob Evans, with whom he had shared the
triumph of *Rosemary's Baby.*

The title of their latest joint venture was *Chinatown.*

PARADISE LOST

I don't blame myself. You see, Mr Gittes, most people never have to face the fact that at the right time and the right place, they're capable of ... anything.

Noah Cross (John Huston), *Chinatown* (1974)

Life in Rome had proved altogether too pleasant for Roman Polanski, and a prolonged period of inactivity after the completion of *What?* had been broken only by two phone calls from LA – the first from actor Jack Nicholson, the second from *Rosemary's Baby* producer Bob Evans. Both were on the subject of a screenplay called *Chinatown* by a young writer named Robert Towne, whom Nicholson had known from the days when he and Towne were protégés of producer-director Roger Corman. In Towne's case, he had scripted *The Tomb of Ligeia*, the seventh and last of Corman's Edgar Allan Poe adaptations for American International Pictures.

Evans originally had approached Towne to pen an adaptation of F Scott Fitzgerald's *The Great Gatsby* for him, but Towne had passed on that (and the accompanying $100,000 pay cheque) to concentrate on the embryonic *Chinatown* instead. *Chinatown* was a *noir* thriller in the mould of Dashiell Hammet and Raymond Chandler, in which the archetypal world-weary private eye finds himself investigating a corruption scandal whose ramifications lead to the very heart and soul of the City of Angels. Nicholson was committed to the role of the iconically named P-I, J J 'Jake' Gittes, and Evans had chosen to produce the film himself while remaining uniquely in his executive position as Vice President of Paramount Pictures. Both men also wanted Polanski as their director, though, in Evans's case, only after Peter Bogdanovich had turned him down.

Given the level of inducements on offer (which included a percentage share of the profits for the first time in his career), Polanski was in no position to refuse. His sojourn in Rome was taking him nowhere fast, bills were mounting up and the coffers were running dry, as usual. Not that he had a mind to refuse: he was every bit as enthused by Towne's screenplay as were Nicholson and Evans, only thinking it a little long and somewhat over-complex, in the first instance. Polanski flew to Los Angeles, agreed terms and set up shop in a palatial studio-rented house at Sierra Mar to work on tidying up the script with Towne.

Two months of rewrites produced a more coherent version of *Chinatown*, but neither man could agree upon a suitable ending with respect to the fate of villain Noah Cross and his daughter Evelyn. 'Originally, I had Evelyn kill her father and I had the detective try and stop her,' Towne recalled. 'In the first and second drafts he got the daughter out of the country. It also ended in a funny way: you knew that Evelyn was going to have to stand trial and you knew that she wasn't going to be able to tell why she did it. But it was bittersweet in the sense that one person, at least, wasn't tainted – the child.' But Polanski had the final say and decided to do it his way, and *Chinatown* commenced production in October 1973. 'Roman is nothing if not contentious. It was good. I still think it was probably the best working relationship I ever had with a director,' Towne conceded.

Los Angeles, 1937. There are lots of guys like J J Gittes, they're easy to find... if you want to find them.

trailer, *Chinatown* (1974)

The first thing to be said about *Chinatown* is that Polanski's second

American film is over-rated. Its director later admitted as much himself. 'I missed some opportunity for visual inventiveness,' he said. 'I felt sometimes as if I were doing some kind of TV show. I thought I had always been an able, inventive, creative director and there I was putting two people at a table and letting them talk. When I tried to make it look original, I saw it start to become pretentious, so I concentrated on the performances and kept an ordinary look.'

For all its painstaking recreation of 1937 Los Angeles, with its white-sidewalled sedans, pastel-coloured zoot suits and heavily rouged 'broads', the film's noir-thriller plot of dark familial secrets, civic corruption and land-grabs was novel only because it was set in a milieu which had been all-but absent from the screen for more than two decades. The Chinatown of the title is the immigrant sector of LA where Gittes used to work the beat as a police officer before going into business for himself ('We worked Chinatown together,' he says in the script of his relationship with Lieutenant Escobar), but Towne employs the term in a figurative sense, to suggest that the *whole* of LA is 'Chinatown', a hotbed of vice and corruption.

'The title had come from a Hungarian vice cop,' Towne recalled. 'He had said that he worked vice in Chinatown and I asked him what he did, and he said "As little as possible". And I said, well, what kind of law enforcement is that? And he said, "Hey, man, when you're down there with the Tongs, and the different dialects, you can't tell who's doing what to who and you can't tell whether you're being asked to help prevent a crime or you're inadvertently lending the colour of the law to help commit a crime. So we decided that the best thing to do when you're in Chinatown is as little as possible".' That was altogether too obtuse a rationale for Polanski, who insisted that the location had to feature in reality: '*Chinatown* was a great title, but unless we set at least one scene in LA's real-life Chinatown, we'd be cheating – pulling in the public under false pretences,' he protested.

Towne had written specifically for Jack Nicholson before, in the previous year's *The Last Detail*, and he had followed that up by acting as script doctor on the Warren Beatty vehicle *The Parallax View*, another thriller about political corruption which also happened to feature John Huston; both Nicholson and Huston were now cast in *Chinatown*. Rumour had it that Bob Evans had wanted his actress wife Ali MacGraw for the role of Evelyn Mulwray, but she recently had left him for actor Steve McQueen, and the prospect of several more roles at Paramount had vacated the marital bed with her – including that in *Chinatown*.

Not that Polanski was likely to have considered her; MacGraw had a strictly 1970s look, whereas Dunaway had famously played Bonnie Parker in Arthur Penn's *Bonnie and Clyde* in 1967, which had been set in the Depression Era of the early 1930s. Polanski had Dunaway made up to look like the mother that he remembered from his childhood days in Paris and Krakow, with plucked eyebrows and 'cupid' lips, though the resemblance ended there. 'She was neurotic and argumentative ... irritable and unprepared,' Polanski said of her. 'Faye was the very worst to work with.'

'There's no one quite like him,' Evans, conversely, said of Polanski, after their film together struck box-office gold. 'I never thought it was a masterpiece, but I thought it could have been a failure,' he noted. In reality, it was neither of those things. It was instead perceived as an original and inventive thriller for the post-Watergate age, which made an A-list star of Nicholson and proved a return to form for the man who had given world cinema a string of original and inventive works, from *Knife in the Water* to *Rosemary's Baby*. After the foolhardiness of *Macbeth* and the misfire of *What?*, Polanski was back in Hollywood and back on top.

Gentlemen, today, you can walk out that door, turn right, hop a streetcar, and within 25 minutes end up slap in the Pacific Ocean. Now you can swim in it and you can fish in it, but you can't drink it – and you can't irrigate an orange-grove with it. Now remember, we live next door to the ocean, but we also live on the edge of a desert; Los Angeles is a desert community. Beneath this building – beneath our streets – is a desert. And without water, the dust will rise up and cover us as though we never existed.

Mayor Bagby (Roy Roberts), *Chinatown* (1974)

Ex-cop-turned-private eye Jake Gittes (Nicholson) is hired by a Mrs Evelyn Mulwray to investigate her husband Hollis, chief engineer of the LA Water and Power company, whom she suspects of having an affair. Gittes follows Hollis Mulwray as he checks out water outlets and reservoirs, but he strikes gold when he manages to photograph him with a young woman. The shots hit the papers, Mulwray is discredited, and Gittes is about to move on to his next infidelity case when the *real* Evelyn Mulwray (Dunaway) appears in his office to serve him with a writ for defamation. Figuring that Mulwray and he were set up, he asks Evelyn where he might find him; she suggests that he try the Stone Canyon reservoir – Gittes arrives there just as the police drag Mulwray's body out of the water. 'Isn't this something? – Middle of a drought and the water commissioner drowns! Only in LA,' the police surgeon declares.

Sensing a web of civic corruption in relation to the building of a dam which Mulwray opposed, Gittes returns to the reservoir, where he is confronted by two thugs – the smaller of whom (Polanski himself) slits his nose open with a knife to warn him off. Gittes is now convinced that Hollis Mulwray was murdered because he discovered that thousands of gallons of water from the city's supply were being 'dumped' to simulate a drought and encourage support for a new reservoir and dam.

Evelyn's father is a land-baron named Noah Cross (John Huston), who once owned the water supply in partnership with Mulwray, until the two of them had a falling-out. Gittes meets with Cross, who curiously hires him to discover the whereabouts of the mysterious girl whom Mulwray was alleged to have been seeing. Slowly, Gittes puts the pieces together: Cross and his cronies have been buying up the drought-hit land in the northwest valley under assumed names and at knockdown prices; when reservoir and dam are built, the area will become fertile again and the price of land will rise. He and his cohorts stand to make a killing. Of the killings that they have made already, one is now that of the woman who initially pretended to be Evelyn, which brings Gittes into conflict with an LAPD out to arrest him as an accessory. None of this explains Evelyn's part in the conspiracy, however, until Gittes questions her about the girlfriend. Evelyn finally comes clean – the girl is her daughter, from an incestuous relationship with her father, from whom she was being hidden by Mulwray.

Convinced that Cross is the real villain of the piece, Gittes arranges for Evelyn to flee to Mexico with the daughter. Cross forces him to reveal Evelyn's whereabouts at gunpoint, and Cross, Gittes and the police all arrive in Chinatown just as Evelyn is about to make her escape. Cross entreats her to let him see his 'other' daughter; instead, she draws a gun and shoots him, wounding him in the arm. As she attempts to flee the scene, a police officer opens fire and she is shot in the head. Cross takes charge of the daughter. Gittes is dragged away by his associates, one of whom delivers his own pertinent epitaph to the tragic turn of events: 'Forget it, Jake – It's Chinatown.'

*　　*　　*

Towne had taken his inspiration for *Chinatown* from the scandal that accompanied the expansion of Los Angeles at the turn of the 20th century. The continued growth of the 50-year-old desert city was suddenly threatened by a shortage of water. In 1904, mayor Fred Eaton convinced city engineer William Mulholland that a river in the agricultural community of Owens Valley, 200 miles north of LA in the Sierra Nevada Mountains, could be diverted by means of an aqueduct to provide the much-needed supply. Eaton began surreptitiously to buy land in the Owens Valley and, in 1908, with the approval of the House of Representatives, work began on the aqueduct. By November 1913, LA had a new source of water, but the Owens Valley farmers voted to fight to prevent the sole means of irrigation for their crops from being diverted to LA; this fight went so far as the attempted dynamiting of the aqueduct in 1924. The city fathers purchased more land in the valley, mounted guard-patrols culled from the ranks of war veterans and eventually forced the remaining farmers out of business. Towne acknowledged his debt to the so-called 'rape' of the Owens Valley in his script, recalling the participants in the names of his characters, such as Hollis Mulwray for William Mulholland.

Corrupt dealings from 60 years before were all very well, but what made Towne's script more timely was the fact that America as a whole was presently embroiled in a new political scandal: as *Chinatown* moved into preproduction, the nation was riveted by the Watergate hearings, which were being televised throughout the summer of 1973 to investigate the circumstances of a break-in at the Watergate Building in Washington, headquarters of the Democratic National Committee. It transpired that the burglary had been authorised by White House staff, as part of a 'dirty tricks' campaign intended to ensure a Republican victory in the 1972 Presidential election. It had achieved that aim, but the name of Watergate thereafter became synonymous with corruption at the very heart of government and led directly to the resignation, under threat of impeachment, of President Richard Milhous Nixon in August 1974, less than two months after the US premiere of Polanski's film.

While Polanski did much in the redrafting of Towne's script to straighten out the general air of confusion in *Chinatown*, the plot remains oblique by the standards of the average thriller. The reason for this is that the script has two narrative threads, each of which is often indistinguishable from the other. This is not in itself unusual in detective thrillers, which thrive on multiple storylines. In *Chinatown* however, neither is allowed to take precedence over the other – even at the climax.

Superficially, the plot is one of political corruption: multimillionaire land-baron Noah Cross (Huston) has been utilising water (or lack of it) to force farmers out of the San Fernando Valley, north of Los Angeles, so that he can buy the vacated land cheaply and by proxy, the plan being to construct a dam which will irrigate said land and increase its value many times over. The dam ostensibly is to provide an additional source of water for the drought-hit city, but Cross has a more financially rewarding purpose in mind, and city officials and the police department on his payroll to ensure compliance. Cross's scheme is long-term and megalomaniacal: the valley land that he plans to own will eventually be subsumed into Greater Los Angeles and give him a significant say in the development of the city for the foreseeable future.

As thriller plots go, that of *Chinatown* is fairly routine stuff, although Towne's fastidiousness at carving his premise out of the real history of LA is to be admired. But a second, more caustic thread runs alongside this conspiracy, and in line with the prevailing mood of post-'60s cynicism, it involves a family tragedy whose ramifications threaten to disrupt Cross's intricate plans for land-grab. It transpires that Cross had an incestuous relationship with his own daughter, which in turn resulted in another child. Evelyn and her husband had hidden the child from him along with the truth, but he is determined to acquaint himself with this second daughter and will go to any lengths to discover her whereabouts.

These two threads are interwoven through the intervention of Gittes, who initially is hired on a pretext in order to discredit the husband. The crossover is arrived at when the characters in one plot begin to play a major role in the other: Evelyn Cross's husband, Hollis Mulwray, not only has helped his wife to hide her daughter from her father for 15 years, but as chief engineer of the water company, he is also suspicious of the motives behind the building of the dam; the murder of Mulwray is the catalyst for things to start unravelling in both directions – with a little help from Jake. *Chinatown* is an elaborate Chinese puzzle, therefore, which mostly lives up to the insidious promise in its title, though some of the changes which Polanski insisted upon with Towne were not obviously to its advantage.

What Towne had done with *Chinatown* was to take all of the expected elements of the genre – the hard-boiled private eye, the femme fatale, the deep-rooted and wide ranging conspiracy – and turn them on their heads. Jake Gittes is not so much hard-boiled as opportunistic and ultimately naïve, Evelyn Mulwray may deploy hot-shot lawyers on a seductive whim but her motive is not self-aggrandisement, and the conspiracy involves a public utility and civic jurisprudence rather than gold statuettes or insurance swindles. Consequently, Gittes turns up fewer facts relating to the unravelling of the mystery than might seem to be the case from the way in which the plot is developed, surmises others and stumbles upon the remainder.

As the viewer has also to witness the action unfold from Polanski's favoured subjective viewpoint (in this case, that of Gittes), some of the pieces which are required to solve the puzzle are never actually forthcoming (early in the film, Gittes tells Evelyn that the girl with whom her husband was supposedly having an affair has 'disappeared', but nothing more is offered as to how he happened upon this nugget of information). Omissions, such as Evelyn explaining to Gittes the circumstances under which she fell into bed with her own father, are down to Polanski and his need to impose a more rigorous dynamic on Towne's languorous and convoluted original, but they leave gaps in the narrative which are not satisfactorily filled by the substitution of the director's predilection for extended takes of characters coming and going between the various locations in the story.

Despite scything Towne's screenplay down by a third and losing several important plot details in the process, Polanski still managed to turn out a mystery-thriller lasting a full 125 minutes, but in his

hands, *Chinatown* is less of a mystery than it is a sleazy slice of LA
life, which happens to incorporate an incident of domestic unrest
and a hint of political corruption.

> EVELYN
> (almost screaming it)
> She's my sister *and* my daughter!
> (continuing)
> — my father and I, understand, or is it too
> tough for you?

Gittes doesn't answer.

> EVELYN
> (continuing)
> ...he had a breakdown...the dam broke...
> my mother died...he became a little boy...
> I was fifteen...he'd ask me what to eat for
> breakfast, what clothes to wear! It happened,
> then I ran away...

> GITTES
> ...to Mexico...

> EVELYN
> ...Hollis came and took...care of me...after she
> was born...he said...he took care of her...I
> couldn't see her...I wanted to but I couldn't...
> I just want to see once in a while...take care
> of her...that's all...but I don't want her to
> know...I don't want her to know...

> GITTES
> ...so that's why you hate him...

```
Evelyn slowly looks up at Gittes.

    EVELYN
    – no ...for turning his back on me after it
    happened! He couldn't face it.
    (weeping)
    I hate him.
```

screenplay (revised during shooting), *Chinatown* (1974)

(Given the events which were later to overtake Polanski, it is the more surprising that, during shooting, he reduced the above exchange to a simple query on Gittes' behalf: 'He raped you...?' – to which Evelyn half-shakes her head in reply.)

In the end, some of the mystery aspects of the story are better thought through than others, as are some of the set-piece scenes. The verbal trick of having the Mulwrays' Chinese gardener mention to a disinterested Gittes that some unspecified thing is 'bad for *glass*' while tending to an ornamental pond produces a genuine moment of frisson when the real meaning behind the remark finally dawns on him: 'Salt water ... *velly* bad for glass.' (The pond is full of salt water, and is thus revealed to have been the scene of Mulwray's drowning before his body was dumped in the reservoir.) A similar play on words occurs over the Albacore Club, which is the front for Cross's illegal activities in relation to the swindle; one of Gittes' associates tells of a conversation between Cross and Mulwray in which the words 'apple core' figured. This second is less successful, as the club itself has only a tangential relationship to the plot, its profile in Towne's original draft of *Chinatown* having been whittled down to relative non-existence by the time the film went before the cameras.

A similar unevenness affects the structural dynamic of the piece. For a private eye thriller, *Chinatown* is noticeably lacking in dramatic highs and lows. Genre convention is followed in the scene at the Stone Canyon reservoir, when Gittes asks to speak with

Mulwray; 'There he is,' Lieutenant Escobar (Perry Lopez) replies, pointing off-camera. Polanski cuts to a long-shot of something being dragged along a sluice channel, then he cuts again to a close-up as Mulwray's pop-eyed corpse is hauled into frame.

The initial confrontation between Gittes and the two 'heavies' is equally effective: 'Hold it there, kitty-cat,' Polanski's hyperactive gunzel calls to him out of the darkness as he is about to make his escape from the same reservoir. 'You are a very nosy fellow, kitty-cat. You know what happens to nosy fellows... ? Huh? No? – Wanna guess?' Gittes soon finds out, as the knife-wielding psycho slits his nostril open with a deft flick of the blade, in a scene which is staged in the identical manner to that in which the younger Polanski beat up one of the *Two Men and a Wardrobe* back in 1958. (Polanski used a real blade with a blood-tube and a simple hinged tip for this trick – a full-frontal effect which had audiences gasping.) A later confrontation with the same heavies is somewhat muffed, however, as is the scene in which Gittes finds a broken pair of glasses in the pool in Mulwray's garden, leading him to the conclusion that he has discovered the murder scene: the glasses are later revealed to belong to Cross, not Mulwray. As it is obvious by then that Cross is behind everything in any event, the viewer has ceased to care about further twists in the slender plotting.

Therein lies the root of *Chinatown*'s success and failure. In pure thriller terms, it is no more memorable than most and a good deal less redolent of the genre than classics like *Double Indemnity* (1944) or *Dead Reckoning* (1947). Where it scores is in ambience – its sense of good things gone bad, its fin de siècle recreation of a sun-bleached time and place that was soon to vanish forever, due to pressures from within and without. Most of this is down to Polanski, with his devotion to detail and his willingness to linger over sights and situations, in order to soak up atmosphere or share more intimately in emotional interplay. But that is not to forget the acting powerhouse that is Jack Nicholson, and just to watch the scene in which he tells a shaggy-Chinaman story to his two partners while Evelyn stands behind him unobserved is to see a previously edgy but undistinctive actor glide effortlessly onto the path of superstardom.

The climax of the film is cursory, almost derisory in its contrived assemblage of all the participants for a showdown on the streets of Chinatown – one of two scenes which Polanski insisted on adding to Towne's original, the other being a love scene between Gittes and Evelyn. 'I wrote each of these two scenes the night before they were actually shot,' he said, and it shows. Evelyn and her daughter are in the process of making their getaway. Enter Cross, followed by the police. Gittes tries to explain the conspiracy to Escobar. Evelyn pulls out a gun and shoots Cross; she drives away, and is shot in turn. Cross exits with his daughter, Gittes with his partners. Evil triumphs; good lies dead in the gutter. 'It's Chinatown,' Gittes is informed. Unsatisfactory? Indeed, it is – like life, a common theme in the films of Roman Polanski. 'To satisfy is an unpleasant way for me,' he told Gordon Gow. 'Satisfaction is a most unpleasant feeling.'

Chinatown is not so much a *noir* thriller as a nocturne, a mood-piece, a tone-poem set in the not-quite-so-mean streets of a city where Bogart walked and Bacall whistled. Towne intended his screenplay to be the first part of a trilogy, whose second and third instalments were *The Two Jakes* and *Cloverleaf* (the second was about corruption in the power industry and the last about that in construction; 'Cloverleaf' is the name of a famous downtown interchange in LA). The final part has not yet been filmed, but Nicholson directed *The Two Jakes* himself, in 1990, after circumstances prohibited Polanski from becoming involved. That *The Two Jakes* is virtually forgotten today while *Chinatown* not only is fondly remembered but regularly championed as one of the greatest films ever made says much about Polanski's contribution to American cinema.

GITTES: *He passed away two weeks ago.*
EVELYN: *Well, is that unusual?*

GITTES: *He passed away two weeks ago and one week ago, he bought the land... That's unusual.*

Jack Nicholson and Faye Dunaway, *Chinatown* (1974)

If the atmosphere of *Chinatown* evokes a certain loss of innocence – an unspecified yearning for simpler times – the reason for it is not hard to find. In an interview in the *Sunday Times* some 20 years later, Polanski reflected upon his feelings about finding himself back in the city where his wife was murdered during the making of the film: 'Everything about the place reminded me of her, the streets, the hills, the evenings. I remembered how happy we had been there when we first met and began to live together. I was so close to that terrible house all the time, and the very atmosphere of the city terrified me. So, as I always do when I feel like this, I buried myself in the work. And it was good work.'

It was, according to the critics, very good work indeed.

Chinatown opened in the US in June 1974, and in the UK at the Empire Leicester Square during the first week of August. Enthusiasm was largely undiluted, as witness the opinion of Margaret Hinxman in the *Sunday Telegraph*: 'If ever a film had 'success' written all over it, *Chinatown* is that film. It is so handsomely constructed, so sure of itself, so certain of its principal actors,' she gushed. 'The film comes as close to being a great thriller as makes no difference.' As if to redress the misgivings that he had expressed over *Macbeth*, Alexander Walker in the *Standard* waxed positively lyrical: 'It is a rare experience in the cinema these days – to see a film succeed so completely in its aim of turning a new buck out of past nostalgia without depreciating the private eye currency in the process. But care, love and skill – the residual qualities still to be found in the once great and still considerable Hollywood studios – have done it in *Chinatown*.'

'It is satisfying as a period piece, intriguing as a thriller and highly provocative as social comment,' Richard Barclay declared in the *Sunday Express*. The *Spectator*'s Duncan Fallowell was won over in equal measure: 'A very advanced entertainment. Polanski has not filled the screen with superb examples of the enamelled Art Deco cocktail trolley, the cars are mostly cars rather than museums on wheels, we are not force-fed with a self-conscious simulacrum of the past by parody of its most obvious stylistic mannerisms. The period is an assumption and consequently completely credible, a natural working mood from which to begin.' Fallowell added that he thought the nose-slitting scene was 'the most wince-making moment ever filmed.'

The thing that the critics found shocking about the violence in Polanski's films was not the extent of it but the level of realism employed in its depiction: the spurting blood during the razor attack in *Repulsion*, the spreading pool of gore beneath the body of the girl who has fallen, or been thrown, from the Bramford in *Rosemary's Baby*. While such graphic imagery is commonplace nowadays, it was startling and unsettling in its time. Unlike most filmmakers, Polanski had witnessed in person the kind of violence that he was often called upon to visualise – or had indirect experience of it, as Kenneth Tynan was reminded when he queried the amount of blood that the director felt should result from the stabbing of Macduff's son in *Macbeth*: 'You didn't see my house last summer,' Polanski is alleged to have told him. 'I know about bleeding.'

Towne had wanted Evelyn to shoot Cross to death, thereby protecting her daughter from his malign influence and implicitly exposing the conspiracy at the same time – the proverbial 'happy ending', which to Polanski was anathema. The latter insisted, oddly, that Evelyn should be the one to die, and that Cross and his nefarious schemes should survive. The script was amended accordingly and Towne matched the dialogue to the remainder. For those seeking evidence of the psychological impact of Sharon Tate's murder on Roman Polanski's art, it is to be found in *Chinatown* rather than *Macbeth*. The strange resonance of the film lies in its last act – its irritating lack of conclusion, its lack of apposite justice, and its casual climactic doing-away with the innocent are surer signs of a more pessimistic Polanski in the wake of the Cielo Drive tragedy than any of the supposedly cathartic scenes of violence in the more proximitous *Macbeth*.

Whether the film's eventual reputation was made by Polanski's decision to go for a downbeat ending or by something less esoteric, like the singular playing of Nicholson or the famous nose-slitting sequence, is for the individual to judge. But like so many of Polanski's films, *Chinatown*'s power lies in its unemotional and unsentimental view of the world which it is at pains to portray, where deceit is par for the course, corruption is king, money is the moral currency and purity ends up dead in the water, to no more purpose than to furnish the next day's tabloid headlines.

Chinatown was nominated for a total of 11 Oscars, including those of Best Picture, Actor, Actress and Director; the rest were for Cinematography, Art Direction, Sound, Score, Editing, Costume Design and Original Screenplay. Faced with the competition from its own studio of Francis Ford Coppola's *The Godfather Part II*, it won only in its last nominated category – that of Best Screenplay for Robert Towne.

During the production of *Chinatown*, Bob Evans had called Polanski's judgment into question on three separate occasions. The first two were over his choice of cinematographer and leading lady: Polanski had wanted Orson Welles' ex-cameraman Stanley Cortez to shoot the movie, but Cortez had not worked behind the lens in years and after ten slow days in the saddle, Polanski was left with little choice but to replace him with John Alonzo. Faye Dunaway proved even more difficult to cope with than Evans had predicted, but bringing in another actress at the point when things came to a head with the irascible Ms Dunaway was not an option – Polanski had to bite the bullet and carry on regardless.

The third occasion involved the music score for the film. Polanski was much taken by the work of a young, untried composer named Philip Lambro, but his completed score was generally felt to be under par. Evans delayed the opening of the film and hastily had it re-scored by veteran Jerry Goldsmith (which also accounts for the several long periods of musical 'silence' in *Chinatown*). No penalty was levied against Polanski as a result of the delay, but Evans said in an interview that, in his opinion, the director of *Chinatown* liked to surround himself with sycophants and that, when he did, 'his films turn out badly'.

Years later, Polanski conceded that Evans had been right on all three counts, but he took bitter exception to his friend's intemperate remarks in the press. Despite the huge critical and commercial success of the two films that he and Evans had made as a team, they were never to work together again.

* * *

Having paid the piper in Hollywood, Polanski once again found himself with the film director's equivalent of 'writer's block'. Nothing much appealed to him, and what offers were coming his way were variations on formulae which had succeeded in the past but which he had no wish to repeat. Left to his own devices, he liked to genre-hop; his ambition had always been to make at least one film in all of the genres which he had watched and loved as a child. It was a personal game-plan which helped to account for the sometimes inexplicably long gaps between films. While producers pursued him to repeat a previously successful performance, he, contrarily, preferred to go about things the hard way, trying to rustle up interest in ideas which were untried and untested, and for which no precedent existed to show his aptitude.

To studio bean-counters, Polanski was a director of horror-thrillers. *Chinatown* had changed that perception somewhat, but not by much. The genre which now interested Polanski was that of the seafaring adventure or 'pirate' yarn, with nary a private eye in sight, and a quick tout round possible partners in Hollywood soon drew the predictable blank.

The main reason was the lack of commitment by Jack Nicholson. Polanski had conceived his homage to the era of *Captain Blood* (1935), *The Sea Hawk* (1940), *Treasure Island* (1950) and *The Crimson Pirate* (1952) as a starring vehicle for Nicholson, and he and Brach had written it accordingly. But Nicholson knew his worth after *Chinatown* and the ceiling had been lifted off his fee. Whenever Polanski inquired of Nicholson's agent how much the actor might require in order to participate in the project, the reply was always the same succinct intangible: *more*. With Nicholson choosing to maroon himself on an island of self-importance while awaiting a higher bidder, Paramount's interest waned. Polanski was forced to take the finished script for what now was entitled *Pirates* to a succession of other majors, but to no more positive results.

Polanski and Brach were still based in their creative 'commune' in Rome, despite retaining an office in London. But Caliban Films had started to implode due to inactivity, a lack of funds and the intrusion into its collective consciousness of some unwelcome truths, such as the fact that during the year that Polanski had spent on *Chinatown*, several of its number had become more interested in their next heroin fix than their next production deal. With *Pirates* moored in dry-dock due to budget estimates which had escalated from an original $8 million to a more prohibitive $14 million and still were largely dependent on whatever figure Nicholson had a mind to settle for (which currently included a bonus of $50,000 per day for each day that the proposed film went over schedule), Polanski turned his attention instead to a book to which Paramount already owned the rights, the nature of whose story would allow him to call a halt to proceedings in Rome and set up shop again in his native Paris.

The Brach-Polanski screenplay for *Pirates* had featured two protagonists, the bluff and blustering 'Captain Red', scourge of the high seas and mainstay of movie myth in respect of the Spanish Main, and 'The Frog', his permanently put-upon sidekick;

both had been based on the characters played by Katelbach and
Polanski in *The Fat and the Lean*. As with his short, Polanski
had devised The Frog as a role for himself, playing opposite
Nicholson, but prospective producers already wary of the subject
were doubly unsettled by the thought of Polanski as one of the
leads. Determined to prove that his credentials as an actor were
as substantial as those of director, he saw the opportunity for
an alternative role in the Paris project – that of star of the film!
Given the comparatively modest budget involved, new Paramount
Head of Production Barry Diller shrugged his shoulders and
provided additional American support in the form of Shelley
Winters, Melvyn Douglas and Jo Van Fleet, and *The Tenant* took up
residence in Paris's Epinay Studio in September 1975.

> *'The tenant who used to live here threw herself out of the window,'*
> *the concierge said, seeming suddenly to have become more friendly.*
> *'Look, you can see where she fell.'*
>   *She led Trelkovsky through a jumbled labyrinth of furniture to*
> *the window, and gestured triumphantly towards the wreckage of a*
> *glass roofing over the courtyard, three stories below.*
>   *'She's not dead,' she said, 'but she might just as well be. She's at*
> *the Saint-Antoine hospital.'*
>   *'And what if she recovers,' Trelkovsky murmured.*
>   *'There's no danger of that,' the odious woman laughed.*
>
> **Roland Topor**, Le Locataire chimérique (1966)

The book which had been cluttering up the Paramount shelves
was *Le Locataire chimérique* (which figuratively translates as 'The
Imaginary Tenant') by French actor, illustrator, songwriter and
surrealist Roland Topor. Best known outside the confines of French
television and puppet-show *Télechat* for his designs for René
Laloux's animated SF film *Fantastic Planet* (*La Planète sauvage*;
1973), Topor also was an occasional author and had published
his novel in 1966. Three years after the release of Polanski's

The Tenant, Topor himself was to be seen as Renfield in Werner Herzog's *Nosferatu the Vampyre*; Isabelle Adjani – Stella in the film – also joined the cast of *Nosferatu* as Lucy Harker.

Brach and Polanski dropped the difficult-to-define adjective and simply entitled their adaptation *The Tenant*. On the face of it, Topor's story was conventional: a mild-mannered clerk named Trelkovsky rents the apartment of a recent suicide and finds himself intimidated by the antics of his elderly neighbours, to the point where he contemplates suicide himself. But scratch the surface and the more illusory elements of the piece come startlingly to the fore, like the mythical 'chimera' to which the original French title alludes.

Vanity was not the only consideration when it came to Polanski taking on the role of Trelkovsky; speed was another. Given that the character is centre stage for most of the action, it was quicker for the director to also be his own actor. Polanski's legendary perfectionism was more easily mollified by a personal rendition of Topor's character than by trying to induce such a rendition out of another. It was potentially less fractious simply to play the part himself, in other words – especially in a film which depends so much for its success or failure on a single virtuoso performance as does *The Tenant*. 'I don't do it to satisfy my ego, but for practical reasons,' Polanski explained. 'Sometimes it's very handy to be an actor, rather than look for somebody who could do what you want him to do exactly the way you want it. It's just simpler to do it yourself.'

The Brach-Polanski adaptation of Topor's novel was as faithful to its source as was Polanski's script for *Rosemary's Baby*. Unlike most screenwriters – even Tynan, when it came to *Macbeth* – neither Brach nor Polanski felt any compunction to reinvent scenes in their own image. To the contrary, all their adaptations from literature are as true to their originals as any purist has a right to expect, with only the merest of concessions made to meet the needs of transference of medium, such as narrative compression or dispensing with minor characters. The two invariably exhibited great respect for the material which was placed in their hands for translation to film, and no distinction was made between a classic work and something like *Rosemary's Baby*.

The Tenant was adapted almost word-for-word from the page, and any criticism of the film must therefore be levelled as much at the novelist as at the filmmaker. Few critics appeared to be aware of this, and much discussion of *The Tenant* equated it with Polanski's own life and obsessions, past and present. While affinity with the material might have supplied part of the reason that he found the project attractive, there is little in reality to suggest that its studied catalogue of neuroses are those of Polanski, rather than the character of Trelkovsky – or even Topor himself. Such musing might make the work more interesting, but those who viewed *The Tenant* as a mirror to Polanski's soul would have been well-advised to read the novel before they rushed to the open window of hasty psychological misjudgment.

A coincidence with slightly more meat on the bone in terms of its curiosity value is the fact that *Le Locataire chimérique* was written at roughly the same time as *Rosemary's Baby*. Both novels involved the taking up of a tenancy in an apartment building with a strange history, and unusual and inquisitive neighbours; both had their protagonists subject to persecution or delusion, depending on preference, and both climaxed with a theoretical conspiracy played out to its logical conclusion. Which came first, the tenant or the egg in Rosemary's womb? – And was either one an influence on the other, or were both merely another example of Jung's 'collective unconscious' in action?

> TRELKOVSKY: *You know ... there's something odd going on in my building. We quite often see people in the toilets, on the other side of the courtyard.*
> SIMON: *What are you, a peeping tom now?*
> SCOPE: *You mean people together in the shit-house? Like an orgy?*

Trelkovsky: *No, no, they just ... stand there for hours, you know. Absolutely dead still.*

Roman Polanski, Romain Bouteille and Bernard Fresson, *The Tenant* (1976)

A timid clerk named Trelkovsky (Polanski) rents an apartment in a seedy building in Paris; he learns from the concierge that the previous tenant, a woman named Simone Choule, threw herself out of the window and is presently hospitalised and in a coma. Trelkovsky pays her a visit and finds her awakened from her coma but bandaged from head to foot, with only her eyes and mouth visible. One of her front teeth is missing. She lets out a shrill scream in his presence and dies later the same day.

Trelkovsky moves into the vacant apartment, but no sooner is he installed than he begins to endure the complaints of his elderly neighbours: firstly, because of the noise from a 'housewarming' party that Trelkovsky throws for his work colleagues, then, increasingly, over other noises that he is not aware of having made – or for no reason at all. Trelkovsky also begins to experience some curious fancies. The communal toilet is situated in a building on the opposite side of the courtyard from his apartment and, from time to time, its occupants appear to do little more than stand there and stare at him. He drops some items on the stairs while carrying his rubbish to the bins, but when he returns to clear them up, someone else appears to have done it for him. He moves a heavy armoire in the apartment and, tucked into a hole in the wall behind it, he finds a tooth wrapped in cotton wool.

All these anomalies and more lead him eventually to the possibly paranoid conclusion that his neighbours are engaged in a conspiracy to turn him somehow into the apartment's previous tenant. A sudden compulsion to don the makeup and floral-print dress that he earlier uncovered during a search of the premises adds to the illusion that sinister forces are afoot.

Events reach a crescendo when he is led to believe that Stella (Isabelle Adjani), a friend of Simone's in whom he had begun to confide, is also part of the elaborate plan. Employing the logic of the insane, he decides to deny the occupants of the building the pleasure of watching him torture himself any longer: he climbs onto his balcony and hurls himself into the courtyard. As the neighbours crowd around his prostrate form, he berates them for their malicious cunning before crawling his way agonisingly back to his apartment and flinging himself out of the window a second time. As Trelkovsky lies in his hospital bed, swathed in bandages from head to foot, he fancies that he sees himself and Stella standing by his bedside – as they did beside the bed of Simone Choule. He opens his mouth and emits a long, tortuous scream...

*   *   *

As a study of paranoia, *The Tenant* is without peer. Polanski's languid and closely observed study of alienation and mental disintegration is the culmination of what he and Brach began in *Repulsion*. Indeed, *The Tenant* is a companion piece to that film – a continuation of it, in effect, as Trelkovsky could as easily have been renting the apartment of Carol Ledoux, from *Repulsion*, as that of Simone Choule, as here: both were vacated in circumstances shrouded in mystery, and both are situated in blocks which are infested with a motley of meddlesome neighbours. Polanski also utilises some of the same tricks that he applied to *Repulsion*. As Trelkovsky descends into madness, phantom hands clutch at him from behind the wardrobe that he has positioned to keep the outside world at bay, in the same way that Carol was forced to fend off a wall of arms; on investigating the wardrobe, Trelkovsky opens and closes a 'mirrored' door, and the viewer finds himself anticipating the sight of a figure reflected in the glass – the shock on this occasion being transmitted by the fact that it does *not* appear.

There also are unnerving illusions perpetrated by the furniture, whereas in *Repulsion*, it was the rooms themselves: Trelkovsky reaches for a bottle of water on the chair by his bed but the two become non-material to his grasp. (The effect was achieved by a life-sized 'flat' of chair and bottle; Polanski being 'old school', he retained an aversion to optical trickery and preferred old-fashioned floor-effects where possible.) On another occasion, the same chair and other items of furniture noticeably enlarge as he walks by them, as though to underline the fact that his personality is being subsumed into his claustrophobic environment. All these and more echo *Repulsion*, but where that film featured a protagonist whose psychological dysfunction was unlikely to have been shared by many in the average audience, *The Tenant* paints its madness on a more universal canvas.

Trelkovsky is Everyman – a little quieter and more subdued than most, perhaps, but clearly subject to commonly identifiable paranoid delusions. He knows from the outset that the apartment which he has rented in urban Paris was previously the domicile of a suicide, and the building subconsciously takes on a malign aspect from that moment. No surprise, then, that every sound – every curious object that he uncovers as he investigates his acquisition – resonates of the former occupant, taking on new and indiscernible form, like warning shadows, vague portents of impending doom. Polanski is masterful at engineering an insidious atmosphere of dread, and Hideo Nakata's *Dark Water* must have found some inspiration in *The Tenant*. The film's ambiguous title is itself a clue to the narrative puzzle: is Trelkovsky a tenant of the apartment, or merely of his own corporeal form?

The first half of the film is a textbook example of the psychological study of social inadequacy – of the loner in society, and his attempts simply to comprehend, let alone deal with, the malignant impulses of the human pack. But the second half takes a much darker turn, if a little too abruptly for some of its critics, who happened to include its director: 'Trelkovsky's insanity doesn't build gradually enough ... His hallucinations are too startling and unexpected,' Polanski wrote in retrospect. 'The picture labours under an unacceptable change of mood halfway through.'

The Tenant labours under a change of mood, as Polanski correctly identifies, but it is far from unacceptable. The second half of the film is Edgar Allan Poe out of director David Lynch (particularly his Gothic fable *Lost Highway*, with its allusions to the W W Jacobs short story, 'The Monkey's Paw'), while the atmosphere of creeping terror which is insinuated when Trelkovsky begins to assume the physical traits of Simone Choule owes much to the scabrous SF fantasies of H P Lovecraft. Polanski adds some references to the mysteries of Egypt, which are absent in the original and which also conjure up the shade of Lovecraft; the ancient Egyptians believed in reincarnation, in the form of transmigration of the soul, and the tale is given real supernatural bite by the revelation that Simone was a student of Egyptology.

The idea was gleaned from a mention in the novel: 'He turned out the light again. The room sprang back at him like a taut elastic band when it is suddenly released. It surrounded him like a *sarcophagus*, weighing down his chest, circling his head, crushing in against the back of his neck.' When Trelkovsky receives a letter in Simone's name containing a photograph of a sarcophagus, or imagines that he catches sight of her in the bathroom swathed in the bandages of a mummy (which she then proceeds to unwrap from around her head to reveal a toothless grin), there is a genuine sense of the paranormal in play.

A later scene in which he enters the mysterious toilet and peers towards his own apartment to see *himself* staring out from the window calls to mind Robert Altman's *Images* (1970), another tale of insanity told from the point of view of the percipient. Even an otherwise uneventful scene inside a cinema, in which Trelkovsky and Stella try unsuccessfully to grope one another, is reminiscent in its strangely disquieting effect of the similar set-up in Graham Greene's short story, 'A Little Place off the Edgware Road'. But Polanski is too adept at planting us inside Trelkovsky's mind for the film realistically to be construed as anything other than a clever depiction of the delusions of a madman, and if parts of *The Tenant* resonate of Poe, it is with the insanity of 'Berenice' (with its dental fetish), 'The Crowd' or 'The Man Who Wasn't There', rather than with the mystic antiquarianism of 'Ligeia'.

Repulsion, Rosemary's Baby and *The Tenant* form a triptych in the director's oeuvre: all three revolve around apartment dwellers who suffer breakdowns as a result of some real or imagined horror, the apartments themselves acting as visual extensions of the oppressive confines of the disturbed mind. There is a limit to how far one can extrapolate the coincidence of these three narratives with events in Polanski's life, especially when only the first of them was originated by him. But the attraction of such a dynamic to a director who was confined as a boy in similarly Gothic apartments, while evil without was enacted alongside potential betrayal within (via the activities of the Judenrat) is undeniable. Polanski is keen to deny all but the conscious elements of this aspect of his work, but *The Tenant*, in particular, betrays a deep-rooted sensibility in respect of the situation which it depicts so meticulously.

Polanski taking the central role of Trelkovsky only adds to this impression. His grimaces as he tip-toes around his abode for fear of disturbing his highly volatile neighbours have the ring of truth about them; his bemused reaction to the endless litany of complaints smacks of long-dormant memory, as well as present predicament. 'In Paris, one is always reminded of being a foreigner,' he once said. 'If you park your car wrong, it is not the fact that it's on the sidewalk that matters, but the fact that you speak with an accent.' But the most telling reference to his past is the scene in which Lila Kedrova expresses her contempt for the other tenants who have been trying to drive she and her daughter from the building by leaving dollops of excrement outside their doors – except that of Trelkovsky, whom she considers to be an ally. He, however, is moved to scoop up some of the faecal matter in her absence and deposit it on his own doorstep so as not to be seen as 'different' by his neighbours. This unsettling vignette perfectly captures the atmosphere of intimidation and fear under which Polanski's parents were forced to live in the Krakow Ghetto.

Polanski also denied any similarity between *Repulsion* and *The Tenant*, beyond the obvious one of claustrophobic confinement in an apartment block. Catherine Deneuve herself formed a different and more intriguing view: 'To me, there are very important common points between *The Tenant* and *Repulsion*. I think Roman was frustrated not to have been able to be the girl of *Repulsion* and he did *Le Locataire* as something very related to me in *Repulsion* ... He had a very heavy and difficult past as a boy – a very heavy past and a very solitary story as a child. And I suppose he feels more of a foreigner than anyone I know.'

The speed with which Polanski undertook the film left no time for visual invention to be pasteurised out of existence. Consequently, all manner of allusions abound, referencing the work of Hitchcock (*Psycho, Rear Window*), Corman (*Tales of Terror*) and even Seth Holt (*Blood from the Mummy's Tomb*). Having finished the filming within its allotted schedule, Polanski took time out to shoot a specially designed trailer, as had Hitchcock for *Psycho*.

The circular construction which had become a feature of his more personal films was never utilised better than here: Trelkovsky ends in the same hospital bed as the previous tenant, enshrouded in plaster and bandages as was she. He opens his eyes to two visitors: they are himself and Stella staring down at him, as they did at Simone in the prologue. He opens his mouth, and the agony of his soul gives vent to Poe's 'one loud, long, and final scream of despair' – as had hers. He has become her, finally, and now he must follow where she went before.

You gang of killers! I'll show you some blood ... You wanted a clean death, didn't you? It's going to be dirty ... Unforgettable. It was better last time, wasn't it? Well, I'm not Simone Choule – I'm Trelkovsky!

Trelkovsky (Roman Polanski), *The Tenant* (1976)

The Tenant is a masterful study of encroaching madness. If it is not a masterpiece to sit alongside *Repulsion* or *Rosemary's Baby*, it is not far short. Polanski spiked his commercial guns by casting himself in the lead, and his predilection for peppering the supporting cast with amateur or unknown players did little to help matters. It is a film where few concessions are made to mainstream dictates, bar the inclusion of American faces like Douglas, Winters and Van Fleet, and it suffered at the box-office as a result.

Its critical reception in the US when it opened there during the first week of July 1976 also was underwhelming, with reviewers tending to focus on the supposed similarities between the character of Trelkovsky and the actor who was playing him on screen. 'It is a serious, exact film about the ache of exile. Exile from country. Exile from gender. Exile from the person whom others recognise as the self but whom the self, at times of extreme self-questioning or torment, can find quite foreign,' Penelope Gilliatt wrote in the *New Yorker*. Well and good as a study of the artist and his relationship to his work, except that in this case, the artist was actually Roland Topor, a Parisian, and not Roman Polanski.

The *Chicago Sun-Times*'s Roger Ebert failed to find any relevance whatsoever. '*The Tenant* was the official French entry at Cannes last May, and in the riot to get into the press screening one man was thrown through a glass door and two more found themselves amid the potted palms. It's a wonder nobody was killed in the rush to get out. *The Tenant*'s not merely bad – it's an embarrassment ... [It] might have made a decent little 20-minute sketch for one of those British horror anthology films in which Christopher Lee, Peter Cushing and Vincent Price pick up a little loose change. As a film by Polanski, it's unspeakably disappointing.'

It took the British critics to see virtue in *The Tenant* when it opened in the UK two months later, although by then the damage was done. '*The Tenant* is brilliantly made: not, perhaps, the best of Polanski but the best of his horror movies – far better, for instance, than *Repulsion*,' Dilys Powell opined in the *Sunday Times*. 'What makes this more than an exercise in Grand Guignol is the feeling of a reference, beyond the merely grisly and bizarre, to a knowledge of other voices, other rooms,' Tom Hutchinson echoed in the *Sunday Telegraph*. 'Polanski's most enthralling film since *Rosemary's Baby*. And certainly his quirkiest,' was the view of the *Financial Times*'s Nigel Andrews, while the *Guardian*'s Derek Malcolm considered it, with reservations, to be 'a superior horror story'.

The *Evening Standard*'s Alexander Walker turned out to be the exception who proved the rule. His personal 'swingometer' on Polanski's oeuvre having lurched back into the negative again, Walker was singularly cool: 'The fact that Roman Polanski has not only written and directed [*The Tenant*], but has cast himself as the timid little Pole who only wants to 'belong' after a lifetime of being a displaced person, argues a fairly close relationship between the film-maker and his subject, which was only reinforced when Polanski recently took on French citizenship.' (Polanski's application for French citizenship had been granted him in July, just as *The Tenant* was being welcomed with bile in his adopted America.)

Despite the show of solidarity, *The Tenant* dropped quickly off the cinematic radar. After playing the art-house circuit, it disappeared without trace and Polanski's career looked to be following its usual path of one hit followed by one (or even two) flops, followed by another hit, another flop and so on.

While he again waited for something better to come along, Polanski took solace in his photography and the company of more young girls, including a 15-year-old actress named Nastassja Kinski, whose screen career had just been launched by Hammer in a film based on Dennis Wheatley's novel *To the Devil a Daughter*. At 43, his celebrity status and fondness for hanging out with girls of considerably less than half his age was becoming a dangerous combination, and it was now to wreak an irrevocable change in the course of his life.

Polanski had spent the best part of a decade immersed in a culture of hedonism and high-rolling. With the success of

Chinatown, he had come to the belief that everything – anything – was up for grabs by anyone who wanted it enough to go out there and take it for themselves. The world – certainly the world of Hollywood celebrity – was his very own oyster. It was a daily diet of dames and the dreaming up of ideas for the next big project. Life was to be indulged; *only swine go to the movies*.

But he was about to learn that not everything was up for grabs – not even by one of the most celebrated movie directors in the country. The Devil had not yet finished with Roman Polanski.

*   *   *

By the turn of 1977, Polanski had given up hope of ever mounting a production of *Pirates* – not one with Jack Nicholson in the cast, at any rate. He had turned his attention instead to a different project: an adaptation of a Lawrence Sanders novel entitled *The First Deadly Sin*, what in Hollywood parlance would be called a 'police procedural' about a serial killer. Columbia had agreed to finance the film, which Polanski was to write and direct. As the usual preliminaries got underway, he thought to keep himself amused by accepting an assignment from the editor of French *Vogue* to photograph an assortment of 'nymphets' in a variety of exotic locations around the globe for a special edition of *Vogue Hommes*. He had shot pictures of former love-interest Nastassja Kinski during a winter break in the Seychelles during his guest-editorship of the magazine's Christmas issue, but now he was back in California and looking to supplement his portfolio.

No sooner had Polanski begun to settle once more into the Hollywood routine than a friend of a friend put him in touch with a San Fernandan teenager named Samantha Jane Gailey, the photogenic daughter of an occasional actress, who already had one TV commercial to her name. Polanski agreed to see the girl, with a view to using her as a model for his *Vogue* spread. An afternoon's photo-shoot was arranged, the results of which turned out well enough for Polanski to suggest a second session some two weeks

later. On 10 March, he collected Gailey from her home in the Valley
and drove into the Hollywood Hills. The 13-year-old was relaxed
and voluble; according to Polanski, she told him that she had had
her first sexual experience at the age of eight.

Polanski had two venues in mind, both of them on Mulholland
Drive. The first was the home of Surrey-born actress Jacqueline
Bisset, to whom he had given her first real break in *Cul-de-Sac*
and who since had become internationally famous. Bisset had
just finished shooting *The Deep* with Robert Shaw and Nick
Nolte, and she presently was sharing her home (and her life) with
Moroccan actor, later producer, Victor Drai. The alternative was Jack
Nicholson's house. Nicholson was out of town, but new girlfriend
Anjelica Huston (daughter of John) was in residence and prepared to
allow them entry. By the time Polanski and Gailey reached the Bisset
homestead, the light had moved to Nicholson's part of Mulholland.
Polanski took several shots of Gailey by Bisset's pool before deciding
that Nicholson's place was the better bet. They returned to the rented
Mercedes and drove further along the Drive; it so happened that
Huston was out, but a neighbour let them into the house.

As a prelude to this final session of the day, Polanski cracked
open a bottle of Crystal champagne which he found in Nicholson's
fridge. Gailey barely touched her glass, but Polanski wanted it in
shot – so the more photos that were taken, the more she sipped
at the champagne. As the afternoon wore on, Polanski produced
a pep pill in the form of a Quaalude. He gave part of it to Gailey
and took the remainder himself. He now asked her to undress
and climb into Jack's Jacuzzi, which she had appeared to him to
admire. With the light fading, he fired off a last couple of shots of
the naked girl and laid the camera aside. He then undressed and
joined Gailey in the Jacuzzi; from there, they retreated to a spare
room down the hall. 'I began to kiss and caress her,' he recalled.
'After this had gone on for some time, I led her over to the couch...'

But Gailey's recollection of the incident was somewhat different.
'He reached over and he kissed me. And I was telling him "No,"

you know, "keep away." But I was kind of afraid of him because there was no one else there.'

There are times – no matter what anyone does – when events conspire. When those involved in them are swept along on a wave of inevitability. Thurday 10 March 1977 was such a time. The compliant actress and mother, the famous director, the photo-shoot for *Vogue Hommes*, the willing daughter, the movie-star pad, the drink, the drugs... The situation in general; the moment in particular...

Polanski made a mistake: opportunity presented itself and drugs, and the illusion of the invulnerability of celebrity, dulled his sense of self-preservation. He had developed something of a feral instinct from having to forage for food, water and the wherewithal to survive during the German occupation of his homeland almost 35 years before, and the hedonistic hunting ground of LA appealed to the society prowler in him in a similar way: everything was there for the taking. Just like now. Temptation was spread-eagled in front of him – young, nubile, fresh and inviting – and the Devil whispered in his ear. Before he had time to weigh the consequences, it already was too late: the Beast was in the ascendant. *Evil is not a force ... it is a state of mind.*

There was a knock at the door. It was Anjelica Huston, inquiring after his welfare. Coitus interruptus – and a last chance to think again. But this time, there was no gap in the fence, no escape plan, and Huston had never liked him anyway. Polanski sent her away, and went back to kiss his career in America goodbye...

ROMAN THE WANDERER

'Why go back?' Woland continued, quietly and persuasively. O thrice romantic master, wouldn't you like to stroll under the cherry blossom with your love in the daytime and listen to Schubert in the evening? Won't you enjoy writing by candlelight with a goose quill? Don't you want, like Faust, to sit over a retort in the hope of fashioning a new homunculus?

That's where you must go – where a house and an old servant are already waiting for you and the candles are lit – although they are soon to be put out because you will arrive at dawn. That is your way, master, that way! Farewell – I must go!

Mikhail Bulgakov, *The Master and Margarita* (1967)

Dissolve...

The front pages of several newspapers swirl once more into view. One in particular holds centre screen. The **Washington Post** *for 26 March 1977:*

'POLANSKI INDICTED ON DRUG, RAPE CHARGES

A grand jury has indicted Roman Polanski, director of *Rosemary's Baby* and other macabre movies, on six counts of drugging and raping a 13-year-old girl at actor Jack Nicholson's home. Conviction on the charges lodged Thursday could send Polanski to prison for up to 50 years. Polanski, 43, remained free on $2,000 bail and was given until Tuesday to surrender in Superior Court. Prosecutors said Polanski's attorney told them he would appear before then.'

A phone rings... Polanski picks up the receiver.

The voice on the other end is that of Douglas Dalton, his recently acquired defence attorney. *'Bad news, I'm afraid,'* Dalton says. *'Huston's been granted immunity from prosecution on the drugs charges if she takes the stand against you.'*

Dalton rings off and Polanski takes a moment to absorb this latest setback, and to reflect on his present predicament...

*   *   *

The judge in the case was to be Laurence J Rittenband, a proud, imperious panderer to tabloid sensation. The 71-year-old 'judge of the stars' had presided over the divorce proceedings of Elvis and Priscilla Presley, a custody battle involving Marlon Brando and a paternity suit against Cary Grant; he was also a respected member of Bel Air's exclusive Hillcrest Country Club. Now another high-profile case had come the way of his gavel and he was intent on making the most of it. On 9 August, the eighth anniversary of Sharon Tate's murder, Rittenband accepted a 'plea bargain' on Polanski's behalf, whereby he would plead guilty to a single charge of unlawful sexual intercourse if the remaining five counts of the indictment were dropped. Unlawful sexual intercourse was by far the least of the six charges, especially with the age of consent in California having been set at 18, and not necessarily an imprisonable offence, at that. With that in mind, Polanski held up his hands to count number three on the sheet.

In consequence, Rittenband set a sentencing date for Polanski of 19 September, but he ordered that he undergo examination by two court-appointed psychiatrists to establish whether or not he was a 'mentally disordered sex offender'. Most observers considered that a prelude to probation, but Rittenband muttered darkly about deportation, and how it made no difference that the girl had consented, as was indicated by the preliminary reports. From the way that he began to veer tantalisingly between probational salvation and the effective damnation of an indefinite prison

sentence for his famous charge, it almost seemed to Polanski that
Rittenband had assumed the appearance of the shadowy figure
who had slipped in and out of his consciousness since the events
at Cielo Drive. It also seemed to those on Polanski's defence team
that he was starting to see himself as more than judge: as jury and
executioner, as well. A very Devil of the law, in fact.

Dalton had advised Polanski to try to resume as normal a life as
possible while the legal proceedings took their course. Columbia
had dropped its planned production of *The First Deadly Sin* with
the scandal-prone director as soon as reports of his arrest hit the
news stands, but prodigious Italian producer Dino De Laurentiis
had stepped smartly into the breach and offered him the reins
of a remake of the old John Ford-Dorothy Lamour vehicle, *The
Hurricane*. Polanski was used to working under pressure, but
he had to embark on the screenplay for *The Hurricane* against a
background of speculation in the media that he could be handed
down prison-time of up to 50 years for his transgressions. Before
long, even that figure had risen during Rittenband's increasingly
regular press briefings to a period of 100 years!

Turning a deaf ear to events in Los Angeles, Polanski scouted
locations for the film in Bora-Bora and suggested to De Laurentiis
that Nastassja Kinski be offered the lead role. But a week in
advance of the scheduled September hearing, Rittenband suddenly
ruled that he was sending the errant director to Chino State
Penitentiary for a period of 90 days for psychiatric evaluation
– incarceration being deferred until 16 December, to allow time for
the completion of preproduction work on *The Hurricane*.

As a result of this seemingly arbitrary ruling, Roman Polanski
spent the Christmas of 1977 in solitary confinement in a California
correctional facility, undergoing tests to ascertain if he was
sexually deviant. After 42 of the regulation 90 days, on 27 January
1978, he was released. But five days later, on 1 February,
Rittenband was back in front of the press-pack, assuring them
that he intended Polanski to serve the full term of his evaluation

– ie, another 48 days. Not only that, but he was now thinking of jailing him for an indeterminate period, followed by deportation. 'Polanski could be on his way to prison this weekend,' he told the Los Angeles *Herald-Examiner*. The reason for the judge's quixotic behaviour was presumed by Polanski to have been the publication of a photo of the director with a bevy of beautiful girls at the Munich Oktoberfest, which he had found time to attend while conducting a casting-call for *The Hurricane*.

This latest development was conveyed to Polanski by producer Howard Koch, who had overheard Rittenband make his resentments known to anyone within earshot at the Hillcrest Club. Polanski could see no way forward. His intent to resettle permanently in the US was being thwarted at every turn, and any future which he might have contemplated in Hollywood no longer was viable. He told De Laurentiis of his plans; the flamboyant Italian pushed $1000 into his hands and assigned Swede Jan Stoller as the new director of *The Hurricane*. On 2 February, Polanski packed a couple of travelling bags, jumped into the Mercedes, and drove to LAX – Los Angeles International Airport. That same evening, he was in London. The following morning, he touched down in Paris.

Close the door when I'm gone, and forget me.

Johnny McQueen (James Mason), *Odd Man Out* (1947)

'I've been tortured by this for a year and that's enough,' Polanski told a journalist from the BBC when news of his flight from justice eventually hit the wires. Rittenband was furious; he gathered the media around him and stated his intention to sentence the fugitive in absentia. After an abortive attempt to persuade Polanski to return to the US to face the music, Dalton filed a petition to have Rittenband disqualified from sitting in judgment on the case, citing the legal equivalent of bias, prejudice and unprofessional conduct. Caught with his judicial pants down, Rittenband stepped aside voluntarily and, a year after his charge skipped the country, the State of California vs Roman Polanski was handed to the more fair-minded Judge Paul Breckinridge, who declared that it was his intention to put the case on hold until such time as the defendant came once again within American jurisdiction. That is the situation which pertains to the present day.

*   *   *

A few minutes of sheer madness had cost Roman Polanski the illustrious career which he had been so assiduous in pursuing, and it almost had cost him his liberty. He was safe, for the moment, in Paris, but his filmmaking days in America were ended, if not necessarily in the rest of the world – at least in those parts with which the US did not share any form of extradition treaty. Extradition arrangements with France did not extend to naturalised citizens, a category into which Polanski fortuitously had fallen in July 1976.

The irrepressible and hard-won air of self-assuredness had left him now; the smug, self-satisfied Polanski of old was no more. On the other side of the Atlantic, his name was mud, and it was being smeared with puritanical zeal across every tabloid headline. Polanski was made out to be a 'paedophile' in the public mind, before the term gained common currency. Worse still was the fact that his brief liaison with Gailey somehow justified the more intrusive elements of the media to trawl through the archives of the Tate-LaBianca slayings and regurgitate anew the salacious allegations of the past. This time, the hacks who wished to term him a 'dope fiend' or a 'poison dwarf', or who had sought to accuse him of weird sexual practices, adulterous affairs or the organising of drug-fuelled orgies, could do so with impunity. He was now an all-but-convicted felon and indisputably on the run from the law.

Eternity for me began one Fall day in Paris, aboard the 96 bus, which shuttles between Montparnasse and Porte des Lilas.

Oscar (Peter Coyote), *Bitter Moon* (1992)

The French showed more compassion towards Polanski than had his erstwhile pals in Hollywood, however, and within weeks of his arrival in Paris he had a new project pencilled into his diary. For some years past, he had been in discussions with producer Claude Berri over a screen adaptation of Thomas Hardy's *Tess of the d'Urbervilles* – a book which Sharon Tate had asked him to read only months before her death. Given the parlous state of his finances, the time seemed suddenly to be right and, with Berri aboard and Kinski lined up to play the lead, Polanski launched into a mere four months of frantic preproduction for a 7 August 1978 start on *Tess*.

Hardy's 1891 masterpiece was a massive novel to prepare for filming in a matter of a few months, but after his abortive association with De Laurentis on *The Hurricane*, Polanski was determined to get back into the director's chair as soon as possible, if for no reason other than to take his mind off his newly-acquired status as international fugitive from justice.

Tess of the d'Urbervilles was written originally by Hardy for serialisation (in *The Graphic*, eventually), which paid more handsomely than straightforward novel-writing. Moulding the story to meet the strict moral requirements of Victorian magazine editors proved to be an arduous task, though, and many changes had to be wrought in the text before it was considered acceptable for publication, even in a Victorian England which had been shaken to its very foundations by the activities of Jack the Ripper less than three years before. Among the illustrious organs which passed on the chance to publish the work were *Murray's* and *Macmillan's* magazines; among the changes required of the text were that Tess's seduction by Alec d'Urberville had to be rewritten as a 'bogus marriage', while all references to the illegitimate child that results were to be expunged.

The working title of Hardy's Wessex tale had been the Ross Hunter-like 'Too Late, Beloved!' This was soon changed to *Tess of the d'Urbervilles*, complete with ironic sub-head: *A Pure Woman*.

When *Tess* was published as a novel (in three volumes and unexpurgated, in November 1891), it met with a mixed reception: some critics considered it a 'coarse and disagreeable' or merely 'unpleasant' tale, while others thought it a 'tragic masterpiece'; time and enlightenment has cast the last of these as the proper evaluation. Hardy's determination to chart a humanist course through the Victorian moral maze in his writing was again in evidence four years later in *Jude the Obscure*, but the ambivalent reviews with which it too was greeted brought his career as a novelist to a premature end, after 14 books and 24 years in print.

> *'Do you mind my smoking?' he asked.*
> *'Oh, not at all, sir.'*
> *He watched her pretty and unconscious munching through the skeins of smoke that pervaded the tent, and Tess Durbeyfield did not divine, as she innocently looked down at the roses in her bosom, that there behind the blue narcotic haze was potentially the tragic mischief of her drama – one who stood fair to be the blood-red ray in the spectrum of her young life. She had an attribute which amounted to a disadvantage just now; and it was this that caused Alec d'Urberville's eyes to rivet themselves upon her. It was a luxuriance of aspect, a fullness of growth, which made her appear more of a woman than she really was. She had inherited the feature from her mother without the quality it denoted. It had troubled her mind occasionally, till her companions had said that it was a fault which time would cure.*
>
> **Thomas Hardy**, *Tess of the d'Urbervilles* (1891)

During a chance encounter with local antiquary Parson Tringham, peasant farmer Jack Durbyfield discovers that he shares a common ancestry with the wealthy family of d'Urberville, who happen to live nearby. Durbyfield sends his teenage daughter Tess to pay a social call at d'Urberville manor and inform the present occupants of their kinship, thinking that it might result in some charitable

munificence. Alec d'Urberville, the son of the house, is impressed
with the fair-skinned Tess (only notionally his 'cousin' in fact, as
the d'Urbervilles to which Alec belongs have merely purchased the
name and title), and invites her to become a poultry-maid on his
farm.

As the weeks go by, Alec's interest in Tess becomes an obsession,
and on a pretext of escorting her home from the Saturday dance,
he detours into a wood and there seduces her. In time-honoured
fashion, she becomes pregnant, but Alec is prepared to stand by
her, in his way – to the extent of setting her up as lady of the manor.
This arrangement does not meet with Tess's ideal of romantic
love, however, and she abandons her post at the d'Urbervilles and
returns home.

In the fullness of time, the child is born – but it soon dies.
Recovered from her ordeal, Tess finds work as a milkmaid at
another farm, where she meets clergyman's son Angel Clare. Love
blossoms between them under the summer sun and Tess agrees
to become Angel's wife. In due course, they marry and retire to a
rented country house to enjoy their nuptials. After dinner, Angel
tells Tess that he has a confession to make; he informs her of a
romantic interlude with an older woman, some time prior to
their own meeting, and she duly forgives him. In the spirit
of mutual soul-baring, Tess decides to tell Angel of her own
encounter with Alec and its tragic consequence – despite the fact
that her mother expressly advised her not to. Angel's reaction to
her story is not as high-minded as was that of Tess: he abandons
the honeymoon and takes himself out of Tess's life. All contact with
Angel now denied her, Tess once more is forced to look for work in
the fields.

When Tess's family are evicted from their tied cottage after
the untimely death of her drunken father, Alec d'Urberville steps
gallantly in to the breach. He houses them and offers Tess her
former position by his side. At first she spurns his advances but,
at length, she is worn down by the force of his argument against

her absent husband and his kindness towards her kin. In no time, she has exchanged her farm-hand's rags for finery and longing for expedience. Angel, meanwhile, has been in silent receipt of Tess's many letters and has decided to relent on his previous proud stance; he sets out to find his errant wife. When eventually Angel discovers the whereabouts of Tess and Alec, they are living as man and wife in a boarding house in Sandbourne. He requests an audience with Tess and makes his peace, then he takes his leave. She is reluctant to let herself be abandoned by love for a second time, however; on impulse, she stabs Alec to death with a carving knife.

She catches up with Angel and confesses her guilt, and the two take flight across country. After an interlude in a deserted house, they find themselves at Stonehenge, where they are forced to spend the night – their last, as it turns out. As dawn breaks, the henge is surrounded by mounted policemen and Tess is taken away. A screen caption proclaims that she was tried and hanged at Wintoncester for the murder of Alec d'Urberville.

*   *   *

The shooting of *Tess* was therapeutic for Polanski – not only because he had left the hot-house atmosphere of Hollywood far behind him but because it meant eight months of travelling around the idyllic French countryside with an unusually harmonious cast and crew. Due to the fact that Britain was party to extradition proceedings with the US, filming in Hardy's native Dorset was out of the question; shooting had therefore to be confined to Europe, in particular, France. Alternative locations were found in Brittany and Normandy, although the completed film suffered in the way that *The Tenant* had by being confined exclusively to foreign shores. The dubbing of some of the minor players left much to be desired and, in this instance, French châteaux did not stand in well for English country houses, any more than Catholic chapels did for Anglican churches.

In addition, there were the monetary concerns which now seemed to afflict every film of Polanski's: the disparate locations required the schedule to accommodate an inordinate amount of travelling time, which in turn inflated the budget for *Tess* to an unprecedented $12 million, making it the most expensive production ever to have been mounted in France and almost sending producer Berri bankrupt in the process. For all its financial tensions and unwieldy shooting arrangements, not to mention the stress of the charges which still hung like a Sword of Damocles over Polanski's head, the *Tess* set was a happy one. Its director's desire to disavow his recent past is reflected in the tone of the film, which is relentlessly heroic and upbeat despite the omnipresent threat of encroaching disaster.

(For all the camaraderie and joie de vivre, two months out of the nine-month shoot nevertheless were lost to strikes by French technicians; among the sequences delayed as a result was the finale at Stonehenge, because the full-scale replicas of the henge stones which had been built for erection in a field on the outskirts of Paris were locked away in a werehouse for the duration of the dispute!)

The film was not without its tragedies offset, however. Less than three months into the shooting, multi-Oscar-winning cinematographer Geoffrey Unsworth, of Kubrick's *2001: A Space Odyssey* and *The Magic Christian*, collapsed and died of a heart attack. He was 63, and had come straight to *Tess* from a lengthy schedule on *Superman* and its sequels without awarding himself a much-needed break in between. His place was taken by Ghislain Cloquet, but as most of the film's exteriors had been shot by the time of Unsworth's death, Cliquot was able to confine himself to the interior sets and any contrast in style between the two is barely noticeable. For much of *Tess*, Polanski chose to eschew directorial mannerisms in any event, preferring to let the luminous cinematography of both men add its own eloquence to the adaptation.

Nastassja Kinski is Tess personified in her first major screen role; Polanski went to great lengths to vocally 'anglicise' her, but

the Dorset accent that she attempts to adopt for Hardy's milkmaid
– as well as her pouting throughout – remind one incongruously
of Ingrid Bergman's 'mockney' barmaid in Victor Fleming's *Dr
Jekyll and Mr Hyde*. Bergman's beauty nevertheless was the abiding
memory from that film, as Kinski's is from this. 'Nasty', as she
liked to be known, celebrated her 20th birthday on the set of *Tess*,
on 24 January. Of the two male leads, it is the Devil, as ever, to
whom the best of the tunes are accorded, even though one-time
'Double Decker' Peter Firth's fickle and ineffectual Angel gets to
play an acceptably anachronistic Polish lullaby on his fiddle. Leigh
Lawson, the one-time husband of Hayley Mills and star of the 1974
sex-comedy *Percy's Progress*, was no stranger to caddish roles and
he essays Alec with aplomb, finding just the right mix of sexual
opportunism and genuine old-world charm, despite the rakish
cigar that is clutched permanently between his teeth. (Lawson
turned the film down initially, having had a bad experience as one
of the cast of the Alistair Maclean adventure *Golden Rendezvous*, in
which he starred with Richard Harris.)

> *I was your master once ... I shall be so again. If you're any man's
> wife, you're mine!*
>
> **Alec d'Urberville (Leigh Lawson)**, *Tess* (1979)

The perennial attraction of *Tess of the d'Urbervilles*, beyond its
superficial value as a romantic tear-jerker in the manner of Emily
Bronte's *Wuthering Heights*, lies in the enigma at the heart of the
tale. As soon as the pivotal misunderstanding – that of Tess's
alleged kinship to the supposedly wealthy family of d'Urberville (in
reality, Stokes) – is laid to one side, there follows the incident that
is key to the drama which subsequently unfolds: the implicit 'rape'
or otherwise of Tess by Alec d'Urberville.

Hardy's depiction of this scene in the novel is a model of
Victorian reticence and has been the source of considerable
consternation among literary critics for more than a century.

Following a cider-fuelled Saturday-night dance of near-Saturnalian intensity organised by the farm workers at Chaseborough, a row erupts between Tess and lusty Car Darch, former mistress of Alec d'Urberville. Alec rescues Tess from the fray and offers to escort her to the village on horseback, but the route he chooses is a circuitous one through The Chase – 'the oldest wood in England', he pointedly informs her. Tess protests this scurrilous tactic to delay their return to Trantridge and prolong his time in her company, but they are now in the thick of The Chase and an impenetrable mist (a favoured device of Hardy's) has closed in on them, blinding Alec to the way ahead. He wraps his coat around the weary Tess and deposits her on a bed of leaves while he goes in search of an exit; when he returns, she is fast asleep. He lies beside her, his passion inflamed by her warm breath and virgin beauty... and Hardy's narrator turns discreetly away, by means of several euphemistic passages, such as: 'Why it was that upon this beautiful feminine tissue, sensitive as gossamer, and practically blank as snow as yet, there should have been traced such a coarse pattern as it was doomed to receive; why so often the coarse appropriates the finer thus, the wrong man the woman, the wrong woman the man, many thousand years of analytical philosophy have failed to explain to our sense of order. One may, indeed, admit the possibility of a retribution lurking in the present catastrophe.'

As Hardy's original serial editors surmised (and had amended), the implication is that Alec ravishes Tess while she sleeps, vulnerable and defenceless in the bourne of nature, and all that leads on from this incident in the remainder of the novel, up to and including the death of Alec and the execution of Tess for his murder, is the inevitable result of a cruel twist of fate over which she had no control. But Hardy was too assured a novelist to offer such a stale premise – even to a popular readership hand-reared by a puritanical establishment on melodramatic moral fables about the fate of fallen women, like *East Lynne*.

For a start, Tess has shown herself to be neither vulnerable nor defenceless, and Alec has accepted her various rebuffs with relative grace. Hardy is careful to set the scene of copulation in an antediluvian grove, shrouded in mist, thus giving it primal force, and both of their bloods are up as a result of the dance and the fraças which followed it. In the days before Rohypnol, there is no suggestion in the text that Tess has slept through Alec's assault – to the contrary; she does not subsequently accuse him of rape, but of taking advantage of her in a moment of weakness. Hardy's intention here was to imply a certain complicity on Tess's behalf, and this was the way that contemporary reviewers read the passages.

The deflowering of Tess Durbeyfield is therefore not as black and white as was often assumed in 20th century interpretations of the novel, nor is what follows from Alec the behaviour of a cad and bounder. He offers to set Tess up as a lady, and when eventually she refuses his ministrations and steals away from 'The Slopes' before dawn, he makes a point of catching up with her to persist in offering her his help in the future, should she ever need or require it. Alec already has done much to compensate Tess for a momentary weakness of the flesh for which he cannot be held entirely accountable, but just as the blackly villainous Heathcliff of *Wuthering Heights* has long been held in the popular mind to be something of an anti-hero – thanks to a sympathetic portrayal by Laurence Olivier in the Selznick film version of 1938 – so Alec d'Urberville invariably is cast in the stereotypical mould of rapacious aristocrat, even when the facts of Hardy's novel mitigate against the accusation.

Perhaps because of his own circumstances at the time of the film's making, Polanski is alert to this anomaly in the telling: he neither fades out the scene, as Hardy was bound to do, nor does he offer up an unwilling Tess, who is violated as she slumbers. Instead, the heat of passion encourages Alec recklessly on, but Tess soon submits and voluntarily embraces the moment.

If Polanski's treatment of the character of Alec in *Tess* is seen as apologia in part, it is no more than is meted out to him in Hardy's novel. If Tess is wronged by Alec, he ultimately is wronged by her in greater measure, *and* after penitence and recompense. The Brach-Polanski-John Brownjohn screenplay picks up on the mention of 'scroff' in Hardy's text – the dust which the dancers at Chaseborough kick up with their feet and which country folk believed to have aphrodisiac properties once it had found its way into female undergarments! – and Tess and Alec's tussle in the undergrowth produces just such a flurry, which eventually is sufficient to screen the scene from view.

When tragedy does eventually strike in the form of Tess's stabbing to death of her erstwhile assailant while *he* sleeps, the scene is treated with even more reticence than its author had sought to display on the page. The landlady of The Herons, the sea-front boarding house at which the couple are ensconced in Hardy's Sandbourne (the town of Bournemouth, in reality), espies a red splotch on the ceiling underneath their rooms. On investigating the curious stain, she discovers it to be blood. Polanski then cuts to Tess symbolically attired in a crimson dress as she joins Angel Clare in his train carriage, thus depriving the viewer even of what small detail Hardy had seen fit to impart about the violent demise of Alec d'Urberville, as a workman is despatched by Mrs Brooks to ascertain the condition of her lodger:

'He opened the doors, entered a step or two, and came back almost instantly with a rigid face. "My good God, the gentleman in bed is dead! I think he has been hurt with a knife – a lot of blood has run down upon the floor!" The alarm was soon given, and the house which had lately been so quiet resounded with the tramp of many footsteps, a surgeon among the rest. The wound was small, but the point of the blade had touched the heart of the victim, who lay on his back, pale, fixed, dead, as if he had scarcely moved after the infliction of the blow.'

A similar reticence is evidenced in the story's famous climax at Stonehenge, when Tess and Angel are surrounded by the posse of mounted policemen and she utters the immortal line, 'I am ready', before being escorted away. Polanski jettisons Hardy's epilogue, in which Angel stands vigil outside the prison as Tess takes the eight o'clock walk, and opts instead to close on a simple screen caption: 'Tess of the d'Urbervilles was hanged in the city of Wintoncester aforetime capital of Wessex.' After a whopping 190 minutes of meticulous observation of English country life in the latter half of the 19th century, this reluctance on Polanski's part to bow to the climactic conventions of melodrama is almost wilful, as though he were wholly unwilling to break the pastoral spell which he has woven over the preceding three hours.

'It was absolutely essential to recreate the country atmosphere the way I knew and remembered it,' he said. 'When I was a child and ran away from the ghetto, I lived in the country exactly like the one in *Tess*. It was in the forties, but it was 19th century Poland, because the peasants were virtually medieval in that part of Poland. I knew all about the country life: how you sowed, how you harvested ... so I wanted to recreate this.'

But Polanski's *Tess* is not about crime and retribution any more than is Hardy's. It is a summer idyll of green grass and cloudless skies, and youth in bloom and sap on the rise; it is nostalgia and wistfulness and what-ifs and whys, and errors of judgment that ultimately cost lives; it is a summer Sunday's hymn to a time gone by – an elegy to the schemes of mice and men, all going awry. If Polanski were to have been a character in his own film, he would have been Tess, not Alec d'Urberville, destined to pay the price for a crime which he may well have committed in the eyes of the law, but for which life and circumstance, rather than malice aforethought, unwittingly had equipped him.

Brach and Polanski had sought out a new collaborator for *Tess* in the form of gifted translator John Brownjohn. Given the pains that were taken over many minor passages in the novel, it is the more surprising that all three writers chose to omit the melancholy exchange between Tess and Angel, during their last night together at Stonehenge: 'Do you think we shall meet again after we are dead?' Tess inquires, to which Angel replies with silence. 'O, Angel – I fear that means no,' she rejoins. 'And I wanted so to see you again.' Also gone is Hardy's famously grandiloquent epilogue – "Justice' was done, and the President of the Immortals, in Aeschylian phrase, had ended his sport with Tess. And the d'Urberville knights and dames slept on in their tombs unknowing.' It seems by these abstentions that Polanski was unwilling to participate in Tess's death, even if only to the extent of showing the black flag raised above Wintoncester gaol, as Hardy does. His otherwise reverential adaptation of the novel therefore differs from its source in one important respect: his is a *Tess* with no end-title.

Nevertheless, there was a finite element to Polanki's work now – a certain sense of ennui. Ten years before, he had confided to Gordon Gow that he liked his films to end with an air of anticipation: 'In *Cul-de-Sac* the man sits on a rock after the car has taken his second wife away: and he shouts the name of his first wife. And you don't know what's going to happen. Maybe the second wife will come back, maybe she won't. In *Dance of the Vampires* the professor whips up the horse and he doesn't know that he is carrying two vampires on the seat behind him: even in a comedy I still leave this window open. In *Rosemary's Baby* the girl rocks the cradle, but the film is never completed: it will never satisfy.' Tess may not hang on screen; even so, Polanski could think of no way to avoid the inevitable. He had at last acquired the sense that in art, as in life, all things must pass.

ALEC: *Why did you never say anything?*
TESS: *I had nothing to ask of you.*
ALEC: *That isn't so. You wear your ridiculous pride like a hair-shirt, and you put me even more in the wrong than I was – against my will ... I'd have done my duty by the child, on my honour I would.*
TESS: *Honour?*

ALEC: *I want to take you away from this wretched place; it's unworthy of you. What is this strange temptation misery holds for you? Come to your senses – come away with me.*

Leigh Lawson and Nastassja Kinski, *Tess* (1979)

Polanski's approach to filmmaking invariably was slow and precise and mood-building but, on *Tess*, he excelled himself. When the film was readied for its premiere engagements in Germany and France in October of 1979, it was three-and-a-half hours in length. Initial reviews were hostile, and Claude Berri blew a fuse as a result and demanded that it be cut by an hour. Polanski relented in the face of the adverse press criticism and called in Sam O'Steen, a Hollywood editor whose expertise he admired and whose contribution to *Rosemary's Baby* had been instrumental in its success.

O'Steen cut some 36 minutes out of *Tess*, but his version was summarily abandoned when *Godfather* director Francis Ford Coppola came calling with a view to releasing the film in the States through his Zoetrope company. Coppola's list of excisions for *Tess* was even more extensive than the wishful-thinking hour of deletions which Berri had demanded to begin with; rather than keep faith with the novel, as Polanski and his co-writers had done, Coppola's plan was to cut-and-paste a kind of 'Tess Redux' – a crass reinvention of the sort that he was to impose on *Bram Stoker's Dracula* a dozen years later. Polanski waved Coppola and his Zoetrope thinking goodbye and re-cut the film himself, bringing it down to a more user-friendly three hours plus.

After a year in editing in an attempt to make it acceptable for audiences who may or may not have known who Thomas Hardy was, and a moderately successful run on its home turf of France, Columbia Pictures finally picked up the gauntlet and bought *Tess* for screening in the US. The film opened on 12 December 1980, in time for the 1981 Academy Awards, and to rave reviews – the best of Polanski's entire career. '*Tess* is the best work yet of a master of the screen,' Charles Champlin wrote in the *LA Times*. 'Mr Polanski has achieved the impossible,' Janet Maslin agreed in the *New York Times*: 'A lovely, lyrical, unexpectedly delicate movie. Elegant, plausible, affecting.' The *Daily News*' Kirk Honeycutt thought much the same: 'A masterwork. Polanski's direction is the best of the year,' he opined, as did many more. The pattern was repeated when the film opened in Britain four months later, after it had become the recipient of a total of six Oscar nominations. 'One of the most faithful and satisfying film versions of a classic English novel in my memory,' claimed the *Daily Telegraph*. 'The most beautiful, sustained, honestly structured tragedy we are likely to see this year,' echoed the *Sunday Times*.

Lest anyone should think that a reformed Polanski had somehow spiked the guns of his enemies by hiding his darker instincts behind a 19th century soap opera, there were those who remained ready to put things into perspective: 'There is one vital ingredient missing from *Tess*, and that is passion,' David Castell wrote in the *Sunday Telegraph*. 'Against all expectations, Roman Polanski has given us a still life in water colours instead of a turbulent canvas in oils.' And having complained about the 'unconvincing model of Stonehenge', the romance-resistant Ian Christie of the *Daily Express* was moved to conclude, 'I haven't seen such beautifully photographed melodramatic twaddle in a long time.'

Twaddle or not, *Tess* was awarded three Oscars from its six nominations – that for Art Direction and Set Decoration (Pierre Guffroy and Jack Stephens), Costume Design (Anthony Powell) and Cinematography (Unsworth and Cloquet). Not for the first time, Polanski had himself been nominated in the category of Best Director, but that was a road too far for the Academy to travel at this early remove from criminal proceedings.

Polanski dedicated *Tess* 'to' rather than 'for' Sharon, inferring that a full ten years after the event which had claimed the life of his wife and child, she was still very much alive in his thoughts. But there was more to his desire to film *Tess of the d'Urbervilles* than the fact that Sharon Tate had passed him the book to read over a decade before: *Tess* is the tale of a young country girl whose violation at the hands of the local squire leads to her disgrace and eventual downfall. If catharsis was a part of Polanski's psychological game plan, then *Tess* could be construed as the latest example of it. Tess is a child of the Fates, as Polanski now felt himself to be.

> '"The girls became an all-encompassing thing with Roman," says another film director with whom the Pole became close friends. "When I first met him back in 1967, they were important, to be sure. But by 1975, 1976, they were all-important. By then he was into group sex, and of course he hung out with this society where girls were easy to come by and a dime a dozen – the real jet-set. I was in London with him once and it was hard to tell the regular girls from the expensive hookers. Not that he paid for sex. But all the girls he hung out with looked like they could just as easily have been hookers. With all his macho enthusiasm, Roman didn't realise it but he was beginning to degrade himself. The girl fetish was no longer amusing. He was becoming a parody of himself."'
>
> **Thomas Kiernan**, *Repulsion: The Life and Times of Roman Polanski* (1980)

Tess was the last act in a long and harrowing chapter in Polanski's life, which had begun with the death of Sharon Tate. The 18-month-long debacle over the distribution of *Tess*, and its initially poor reception, had taken its toll. He had reached a cross-roads – a crisis of confidence in his own ability and faith in his chosen profession. Two years on from there and Polanski temporarily had lost all interest in films and filmmaking. He was nearing 50, and he had reached that time in his life when suddenly it seemed relevant to reflect upon where he had been, where he was now and how he had got there. A nostalgic trip to Krakow and sight of what remained of the Ghetto and the various farms in the Polish countryside which had offered him refuge as a boy, seemed somehow imperative. He had gained much since then – more than anyone could ever have imagined – but he had lost much also: the most important thing in his life – the one thing that he prized above all else. It was a time for reflection, but he was still a relatively young man and his journey was not yet done. To lend tacit support to the newly insurgent Polish anti-Communist trades union Solidarity (Solidarnosc), he directed and starred in a well-received production of Peter Shaffer's play *Amadeus*, which later transferred to Paris with similar success.

As another element in the process of regeneration, and to redress the wrongs done him in a recent unauthorised pop-biography by American writer Thomas Kiernan, Polanski decided to take up pen and paper – not to write a script, but an autobiography: *Roman by Polanski*, a candid and self-effacing appraisal of the story so far, circa 1983.

Three writers were picked for the task of distilling the essence of almost 50 turbulent years into 461 pages, with the bulk of the work falling to *Newsweek*-staffer and author of *The Last Emperor* and others, Edward Behr, who organised the material and typed up Polanski's recorded reminiscences. Peter Gethers and *Tess*'s John Brownjohn also helped to give the manuscript the appropriate polish, and Polanski got his own hands inky in the final stages.

As in everything to do with Polanski, the published work had its supporters and its detractors. 'Edward Behr, who helped Mr Polanski, may take credit for organizing this large and vivid autobiography. But the passion and imagination of the work are clearly Mr Polanski's,' *Schindler's List* author Thomas Keneally wrote in the *New York Times*. 'The ardent gnome we encounter here, a creature of fierce but ultimately genial insights, obviously knows how to tell his own tale.' But some reviewers found it odd that it presented a different view of events from the one which they had expected of its author after years of tabloid headlines – one in which he would confess all, repent all and beg forgiveness. Others merely took issue with its ghost-written prose, seeing in it the opportunity to advance their own careers by sneering comparison.

Martin Amis, for example, pompously suggested in the *Observer* that the book was 'a tribute to the searing power of the cliché.'

Having drawn a line under the past, to his own satisfaction at least, Polanski found that he was able to look to the future again. Life had been too serious, too grim, for too long; what he needed to rekindle his passion for cinema was something lightweight and spectacular. He trawled through his back catalogue of aborted projects and alighted upon the one whose failure to reach the screen had been pronounced a source of infinite disappointment to him in the final pages of his autobiography. Fired with renewed enthusiasm, Polanski set about once and for all to find a backer for *Pirates*.

> *Devil take you, Frog – 'aven't I told you to trust me? 'aven't I proved right again? Well, you're not to forget it, you little rascal. Never lose faith in divine providence... Never!*
>
> **Captain Red (Walter Matthau)**, *Pirates* (1986)

After a self-imposed five-year absence from the director's chair, Polanski raised his megaphone on 25 November 1984 to call 'Action!' on the first shot of *Pirates*. He had persuaded Tunisian financier Tarak Ben Ammar (whose credits in production included Monty Python's *Life of Brian* and Steven Spielberg's *Raiders of the Lost Ark*) to part with an extraordinary $25 million to float the project – literally, as a third of that figure had gone on the building of a 14,000-ton Spanish galleon named 'Neptune', which also had to act as a studio-at-sea for the nine months of filming.

Taking over from where Nicholson never began as Thomas Bartholomew Red, scourge of the seven seas (when he can be bothered to do any scourging), was veteran Walter Matthau, whose best days with Jack Lemmon and playwright Neil Simon already were far behind him and who had little to lose by trying something as out-of-character as a crafty Caribbean pirate captain. Never one to make it easy for his cast, Polanski encumbered Matthau with an unlikely wooden leg and an incongruous Cockney accent, which meant him having to act with what sounds like a speech impediment for much of the film, as well as him requiring a real one-legged stand-in (no doubt part of the reason why Nicholson turned the role down).

The logistics of the exercise prohibited Polanski from taking on the servile role of The Frog as he originally planned, and who represented the same downtrodden foil that he had essayed twice before (as 'The Lean' in *The Fat and the Lean* and as Alfred in *The Vampire Killers*). Consequently, The Frog became the feature debut of unknown French actor Cris Campion. The villain of the piece is Spanish grandee Don Alfonso de la Torré, played by Egyptian-born Damien Thomas – forever remembered by Hammer aficionados as the vampire Count Karnstein in John Hough's *Twins of Evil* (1971).

The supporting cast also was drawn from the ranks of Polanski's favourite British character players: Ferdy Mayne (*The Vampire Killers*), Richard Pearson (*Macbeth, Tess*), Robert Dorning (*Cul-de-Sac*). There is a cameo by the irrepressible Roy Kinnear and walk-ons by Ian Dury and Cardew Robinson, while Maracaibo's governor is played by another Hammer alumnus, Bill Fraser of *That's Your Funeral* (1974) and the 'Snudge' half of the *Bootsie and Snudge* television series which had turned *The Vampire Killers'* Alfie Bass into a household name in Britain in the early 1960s.

Able though all of them are, none could add sufficient counterweight to Matthau's clowning. The result is a film in which the centre of gravity is a bumbling incompetent – a secondary character, in truth – and where the pitfalls into which he unfailingly plunges are supposed by themselves to hold the attention of an audience for a patience-stretching 124 minutes.

The throne carries a curse if it is removed from its rightful place; the other night I dreamt it was red with blood. If we were wise, we would hurl it overboard.

Captain Linares (Ferdy Mayne), *Pirates* (1986)

Adrift at sea on a raft, Captain Thomas Red (Matthau) and his faithful retainer The Frog (Campion) are picked up by a Spanish galleon en route to the port of Maracaibo with a cargo of Aztec treasures. When he realises that the man-of-war is harbouring a golden throne in its hold, Red attempts to inspire a mutiny among its beleaguered crew. This is easily thwarted by ship's master Don Alfonso (Thomas), and Red and Frog are force-fed with a dead rat before being led on deck to be hanged from the highest yard-arm.

As they are about to swing for their supper, Frog makes a leap for freedom and rallies his shipmates. A melée ensues – but this time the uprising is more successful and Red takes control of the ship. He claps his Spanish captives in irons and makes for an island refuge where he can trade the hostages for gold. On the island, he is reunited with his crew of cut-throats, but he finds to his chagrin that the captives are worthless. During the night, Don Alfonso manages to stage an escape and the 'Neptune' is once more wrested from Red's command, to continue on its voyage to Maracaibo with its golden prize.

With money that he was owed from trading in illicit goods, Red buys himself a brig and sets out in pursuit. The daughter of the Governor of Maracaibo is still his prisoner and, by threatening her with a fate worse than death, he persuades the governor to draw up an order turning transportation of the throne over to him. His scheme to relieve Don Alfonso of his prize also runs aground, but after another battle at sea, he and The Frog eventually acquire the throne... and lose their ship in the process. They find themselves back where they started, adrift on a raft and wondering what their next adventure will be...

*   *   *

Pirates euphemistically was termed a comedy-adventure, but it presents the unsuspecting viewer with precious little of either. The first two reels are moderately amusing; the slapstick is novel and the situations original. But after a more indulgent middle section, plot and coherence break down completely in the final half-hour as one tediously contrived incident leads inexorably to the next – but never, it seems, to the last. It also is one of those annoying films where characters are meant to be manhandling an object made of solid gold – an Aztec throne, in this case – but the ease with which it can be heaved in and out of small boats makes its origins in the prop-shop all too obvious. (Polanski's usual fastidiousness over incidental detail appears to have deserted him whenever this 'golden' throne hoves into view.) The film serves up one or two fitfully funny set-piece sequences, such as Don Alfonso forcing Red and Frog to eat half a rat apiece at the point of a sword, but Polanski's predilection for realism spoils the joke as the captain takes a mouthful of raw rat-meat and laughter turns instead to disgust.

The film's protagonist is Captain Red, a salty old sea dog with a wooden leg and a sure-fire talent for turning triumph into disaster. In other circumstances, this buffoonish buccaneer would have been a foil to the hero of the piece, his hapless antics providing the light relief, but Brach and Polanski place him centre-stage, where his foibles become more annoying than endearing and his comedic peg-leg is a clear obstruction to the potential for serious action. With Nicholson in the role, Red might just have passed muster as a comic caricature; Jack has the requisite twinkle in his eye to take the audience along with him on a satirical ride. Matthau is merely grouchy.

The physical condition of the 64-year-old actor imposed further restrictions on his ability to supply the requisite performance. Fight arranger William Hobbs, who previously had worked with Polanski on *Macbeth*, recalled the situation on-set for author John Hamilton: 'Walter had had three heart by-passes by then,' Hobbs said. 'I would be rehearsing out in Tunisia and Walter would come over and tell me about his by-pass and whisper, 'I don't want to do too much today, but don't tell Roman.' He didn't want to work too much, so I did what I could with him... The seceret is simplicity, brevity and stunt-doubles!'

Polanski's eccentric casting methods are again called into question by the inability of many of the performers in the film to rise to the intended humour of the situations. *Pirates* screams out for comic actors able to milk a scene for all it is worth, as opposed to supporting players who merely happened to approximate the character-drawings in their director's sketchbook. One key scene has Red present himself again to his former ship's company after being marooned on a desert island for four years. The expressions on their faces as they greet him in silence are meant to intimate their disappointment at the prospect of being reunited with their hapless commander, a reaction that the viewer comprehends while Red remains nonplussed – and therein lies the joke. But the lack of suitable mugging among his crew when he makes his entrance gives the scene a more sinister undercurrent, as though a conspiracy were afoot, and thus deprives it of its intended levity.

Many a dire comedy script has raised belly laughs from the most mundane situations or banal of lines through careful casting; *Pirates* is a film that would have benefited from such a sea of familiar farcical faces. As it is, the burden of bawd falls on the ample shoulders of Roy Kinnear, an ensemble player at best who found himself in this instance without an ensemble with which to play. (It is to Kinnear's role of Dutch that the script turns for its occasional shard of wit, as when he offers Red a reality-check on the economics of hostage-taking: 'A hostage isn't worth his keep nowadays,' he tells him.)

What action sequences the film contains are limp and unconvincing – a fatal flaw in Polanski's staging which was overcome in *Macbeth* only by sudden explosions of gore. No such fail-safe mechanism was available to the director on *Pirates*, which was planned as a comedy, despite the British censor's removal of some of its queasier moments in order to qualify it for a requested PG rating.

Hail, me 'earties, 'tis I. I've lost a drumstick, true, but the rest is all Captain Red. I'm half seized-over with joy at seeing your friendly

*physiognomies again ... Diddler! Still alive and kicking, you old
skunk, you? Where's Meat Hook? – Ah, there you be! Sour-faced
as ever. Bibleback, haven't grown much straighter, have you? So,
Moonhead, took me for Satan his'self out there, did you? Soiled
your linen, did you? Strike me blind, you've as much to say as a
shoal of mackerel ... Look at me! Four years and more on a poxy
desert island, yet I can still crack a smile ... What ails you all?*

Captain Red (Walter Matthau), *Pirates* (1986)

Pirates is a throwback to a bygone and more tolerant age, not only
in terms of the undemanding nature of the movie itself but also in
relation to Polanski's progress as a filmmaker. He had reverted by
more that two decades to produce a work of such simplistic excess
that even the wide-eyed thrill-seeking audiences of the 1960s would
have been hard-pressed to find anything in it to comfort them. After
an hour at sea, when it seems that events might be moving towards
a climax, its director has the temerity to bring the film to a halt and
announce in a screen caption: 'Captain Red has invested his 632
doubloons in an old brig...' The action then starts over again.

If this looks like expedience, it was; long before the shoot was
ended, Polanski had lost control of the whole bloated affair and was
keen to bring proceedings to a halt. Indulgence was not so much a
product of artistic vision in *Pirates*, it had become a way of life – a
wilful means of making up for five lost years of filmmaking. But
once he had satisfied his desire to show that anything Hollywood
could do, he could do better (and bigger), the thrill of holding sway
over an entire North African seaport, as well as a cast and crew that
numbered in the hundreds, began to pall. 'Enough of this stuff,' he
said at length to long-suffering producer Thom Mount (a former
protégé, like so many of the young Turks in Hollywood at the time,
of legendary producer-director Roger Corman). 'Let's get back to
civilisation and make a *real* movie.'

Had Polanski ever thought that he could simply throw money at
the screen, fill it with sound and fury, and still have the resultant

film receive a rapturous reception, that notion was dispelled when *Pirates* landed in American theatres on 28 February 1986. '*Pirates* proves, if nothing else, that Matthau is not an action star and that Polanski is not an action director,' Roger Ebert confirmed. '*Pirates* should never have been made, at least not by a director with no instinctive sympathy for the material, and not by an actor whose chief inspiration seems to be the desire to be a good sport.' The *New York Times*'s Walter Goodman fired another broadside: 'It's pretty much a one-pirate show, and Mr Matthau has his moments. But he is manhandled and finally left adrift by the script, on which Mr Polanski collaborated, and by the director's determination to leave no convention of the swashbuckler intact.'

Pirates opened in the UK at the beginning of September. To the British critics, the funniest thing about Polanski's film was their copy. Ian Christie's column in the *Daily Express* was typical: 'Is there no end to the comic potential of Walter Matthau? I asked myself after watching his performance in *Pirates* ... But shortly after the film got under way another question came to mind, which was: Is there no *beginning* to the comic potential of director Roman Polanski?' Not to be outdone in the humour stakes, Angela Brooks of *Today* followed suit. 'First the good news: 12 minutes have been sliced from *Pirates*, providing a merciful reprieve for a film that is about as stimulating as two Mogadons and a cup of hot cocoa. Now the bad news: 12 minutes have been sliced from *Pirates*, making it even more choppy than the original version shown at Cannes this year.'

Even serious commentators could barely refrain from lapsing into the crude language of outright dismissal. 'Not to put too fine a point on it, *Pirates* is an almost total cock-up,' Polanski admirer Derek Malcolm wrote in the *Guardian*. 'The cast flail away as best they can within the melée of comic effects, over-ripe lines and palpably samey situations.' The *FT*'s Nigel Andrews thought the same: 'A wacky regression to infantilism in which literacy, wit, structure, good taste and other hygienic unnecessaries are thrown firmly overboard.'

In 2002, long after the sound of 'raspberries' had faded, the Neptune found itself moored in the Molo Vecchia (Old Quay) marina in Genoa harbour, Italy, where it now serves as a floating museum. 'The damn boat has made more money than the movie did,' Polanski said. 'They've got it as a permanent tourist attraction someplace and it makes millions. [*Pirates*] was a disaster, there's no doubt about that, and it just wasn't funny enough. Still, if you look at it now, it's not too bad.' Yes, it is – but that is neither here nor there. While still shooting *Pirates*, Polanski and Mount came up with the idea of a film that would represent the antithesis of the one on which they were currently engaged: a small-scale, studio-bound, closely controllable thriller in the classic mould. As though to comment adjectivally on their present predicament of having to preside over a Babel-like boatload of multinational extras, they even thought up a title for the new project: *Frantic*.

Pirates sank without trace in every territory in which it played and Polanski's next genre outing, a Hitchcock-style thriller set in Paris, would go against his long-standing principle of thematic anarchy and adhere to formulaic conventions, up to and including the requisite 'happy ending'. For all its unfamiliar attributes, *Frantic* nevertheless was to turn out more of a return to form for the director than had the misfire of *Pirates*.

The Mysteries of Paris

He asked me to add an extra 'something' to each scene. I spontaneously improvised gestures, attitudes and comic touches on the set. I preferred to express myself in this way, by my body and my face, rather than by dialogue. Roman left me complete freedom. He trusted my instincts and my imagination because they went in the same direction as the character. He knows me, he knows exactly what I can do. I will always remember the shooting of the first tests: it was very moving.

Emmanuelle Seigner, talking about the filming of *Frantic* (1988)

I f proof were needed that Polanski's life and career might have taken a different course had it not been for his involvement with Samantha Gailey, it came early in 1988, when Jack Nicholson touched down at Orly airport in Paris to see if anything could be done to persuade him to return to the States and face the music. Nicholson had an agenda: he was looking for a director for *The Two Jakes*, Robert Towne's long-delayed sequel to *Chinatown*, and naturally he had thought of Polanski.

Back in 1985, Nicholson, Towne and producer Bob Evans had formed themselves into a company which they named TEN, after the initial-letters of their own surnames, for the sole purpose of making *The Two Jakes*. Towne was to have directed the film and, having resigned his position at Paramount after a series of scandals, Evans was to have returned to his days as an actor to take on the role of Jake Berman, the other of the 'two Jakes' to Nicholson's JJ Gittes. The proposed film had actually moved into production, only to move out of it again after a matter of days when Towne fired Evans and acrimony closed the project down. After much legal wrangling, TEN was dissolved and Nicholson took the project over; he and Towne never spoke to each other again, even though their friendship went back to the time that they had spent together at the Actors Workshop run by blacklisted forties' star Jeff Corey.

By 1988, the double-Oscar-winning Nicholson had fifteen years of hits behind him (including *Terms of Endearment*, for which he had won Best Supporting Actor in 1984, and most recently *Batman*, in which he had played The Joker), and he felt that the time was right to try to revive his most iconic role. Whereas *Chinatown* had been about water, *The Two Jakes* was about oil, and embroiled in the shady dealings this time out is another client suing for adultery, in the form of Gittes's namesake 'Jake' Berman. The role of Berman was eventually awarded to Harvey Keitel, after Dennis Hopper and Joe Pesci had been considered in the wake of Evans's abrupt exit, but that still left the film without a director. Enter Nicholson, new Los Angeles District Attorney Ira Reiner and Roman Polanski.

Polanski had now been in exile from the US for ten years, but his American agent had been in contact with the DA's office through a lawyer since 1986, in an attempt to hammer out a deal whereby Polanski might apologise to the court and submit to some form of community-service penalty in lieu of a prison-sentence. The thinking behind this scheme was naive at best, as Polanski no longer was in possession of a visa to visit the US and any 'return' would have had to be negotiated through the American Embassy in Paris; even then, no guarantee could be offered that he would not face the prospect of incarceration on landing, even if only until the legal necessities were dealt with. Reiner and those in Polanski's camp could arrange no route to the States between them which did not incur an amount of risk, so their absent charge declined the latest overtures on his behalf and returned to the matter in hand

– promoting the film which he had mooted to *Pirates* producer Thom Mount in Tunisia, three years before.

Polanski's Hitchcock-style thriller had been shot in Paris in the spring of 1987. By a curious coincidence, writer Robert Towne's original choice to play Jake Gittes in *The Two Jakes*, which he had set eleven years after the events in *Chinatown*, was 'Indiana Jones' action-hero Harrison Ford. It was Ford who had been enlisted by Polanski in the meantime to play Robert Walker, the everyman-hero of *Frantic*. Commenting on what many still considered to be a signal lack of contrition from a director with whom he had himself enjoyed a harmonious and trouble-free shoot, Ford said, 'He was not defiant. He was also not remorseful, and somehow you liked him better for it.'

```
INT. DEDE'S APARTMENT - NIGHT

It is a loft apartment, quite spacious and
messy: the bed is unmade and clothes lie on the
floor. A light comes from an open door at the
other end of the apartment. A cat sitting on an
armchair watches Richard as he enters.

    RICHARD
    (quietly)
    Anybody here?

There is no answer. The cat jumps off the
armchair and comes to Richard to rub against
his leg. Richard advances towards the light.

    RICHARD
    Hello? Monsieur Martin?

Richard enters into the brightly-lit kitchen.
```

On the table are the remains of breakfast:
a bowl of coffee, a piece of baguette, some
butter and the racing form, 'Paris Turf'.
Looking to the side, Richard sees a man lying
propped against the refrigerator, his throat
cut, dried blood staining the front of his
pyjamas...

Screenplay, *Frantic* (1988)

American cardiologist Richard Walker (Ford) and his wife Sondra
(Betty Buckley) are on a visit to Paris – 'City of Lights' – which is
part-medical convention, part-second honeymoon. No sooner have
they settled into their hotel-room than Sondra disappears without
trace while her husband is in the shower (immediately prior,
they had discovered that they had collected the wrong suitcase
from the airport, picking up an identical one by mistake). At first,
Walker thinks little of what he assumes to be Sondra's temporary
absence but, as time goes by, concern begins to grow. Tackling
the hotel's concierge and head of security, he finds his increasing
anxiety met initially with bemusement and typical Parisian *sang
froid* – 'Does your wife have a *friend* in Paris?' he is asked. A trip
to the local sûreté to report a missing person produces little by
way of result and he is left with no alternative but to embark on a
search himself; a round of nearby bars and night-clubs culminates
in the discovery of Sondra's identity bracelet lying discarded in
an alleyway. Convinced now that she has been kidnapped, Walker
prises open the duplicate suitcase. He ascertains that it belongs to
one Dede Martin and once again sets off in search. Tracing Martin
to his dingy apartment, Walker finds the door ajar and its occupant
slumped on the kitchen floor with his throat cut. But Martin has
a second visitor – a young girl named Michelle (Emmanuelle
Seigner) whom Walker had earlier encountered in the bar in
which he had obtained Martin's address. Michelle claims the
suitcase for her own, and it transpires that she was acting as

unwitting courier for an anonymous Middle-Eastern terrorist group who had hired Martin to smuggle a nuclear trigger into France, hidden inside a plaster model of the Statue of Liberty. One of the factions in pursuit of the missing device now reveals its hand: Sondra is being held captive as a bargaining-chip to facilitate its return. A pursuit over Parisian rooftops and an abortive exchange in a car park lead eventually to the banks of the Seine, where the rival factions shoot it out for possession of the trigger and Michelle accidentally is killed. Walker manages to grab hold of the trigger and throws it into the river, bringing the conflict to an end. The warring parties retire from the fray, and Walker is reunited with his wife.

* * *

If the plot of the film is Hitchcockian in its premise of an American innocent who becomes entangled in international intrigue abroad – as in 1956's *The Man Who Knew Too Much*, *et al*, not to mention the incorporation of a Hitchcock-like 'macguffin' into the storyline (in this case, a device to trigger an atomic bomb), then it was entirely intentional: Polanski still sought to intersperse projects of more interest to himself with *hommages* to the kinds of films which had impressed him as a boy. Thus he already had notched up his pastiche Universal-Hammer horror film in *The Vampire Killers*, his Raymond Chandler-style private-eye thriller in *Chinatown*, his Errol Flynn-Erich Wolfgang Korngold-Warner Bros buccaneering adventure in *Pirates*, and *Frantic* was his Hitchcock mystery-suspenser. The very fact that the film did *not* originate with the Master of Suspense prompted critics to resort immediately to the adjectival phrase 'sub-Hitchcock' in reference to it, as invariably they did when confronted with one of Brian de Palma's Hitchcock 'tributes', but there really is nothing sub-Hitchcock about *Frantic* – sub-Polanski, perhaps, inasmuch as the film sets out merely to entertain and amuse, in the main, but it remains every bit as expertly crafted as any of the maestro's own forays into the field of one man's struggle to comprehend the true nature of the inexplicable events in which he reluctantly has become embroiled.

Frantic features many deft Hitchcock touches through which Gérard Brach exhibits a profound comprehension of, and admiration for, the famous director's familiar *oeuvre*: the potentially-lethal misunderstanding, as when Walker is accosted by a drug-dealer in a nightclub and takes his taunts about 'the white lady' to be a reference to his wife; the sticky situation from which the hero manages to extricate himself only by quick-thinking improvisation, as when Walker frees Michelle from the clutches of a pair of heavies by pretending to be an irate lover installed in the bedroom next door; Hitchcock's fixation with heights, in everything from *Saboteur* through *Foreign Correspondent* to *Vertigo*, as when Walker finds himself dangling from a television aerial atop a Paris rooftop while the contents of his suitcase tumble towards the courtyard below (a feat of derring-do on Ford's part which was accomplished on a forced-perspective set constructed entirely in the studio).

Other references are less obvious than the plot's focus on a lady 'vanishing', albeit in Paris, or Walker and his wife taking prolonged showers in the opening reel. Walker becoming circumstantially attached to the mysterious Michelle recalls the plight of Richard Hannay in *The 39 Steps*, while the abortive 'exchange' in the underground car park revisits the cold war paranoia of *North by Northwest* in contemporary guise. The first half-hour of the film being conducted virtually in real-time to engender a genuine sense of suspense is even more subtle in its allusion to Hitchcock; the technique which Polanski employs to convey the action harks back to the master in experimental mode, as in the ten-minute takes of *Rope*, or the first-person narrative of *Rear Window*.

Polanski was unable to capitalise on the trick of setting the climax of his film on or around the very monument which was employed in miniature to disguise its macguffin, but even the Parisian location reminds one of Stanley Donen's *Charade* (1963), itself a parody of classic Hitchcock. (With more than a touch of irony, given the concurrence of the production with the latest efforts on Polanski's behalf to have his fugitive status revoked, he and Brach *did* set their climax at the Statue of Liberty, as had Hitchcock in *Saboteur* – but theirs was a *model* of the statue situated at the Pont de Grenelle, on the River Seine!)

Ford is his usual bemused self, excelling in the white-knuckle department as a man on the edge of hysteria whose ability to meet a challenge increases in direct proportion to the toughness of the spot in which his character finds himself. The Slavic-looking Seigner also impresses in her first feature-film role of substance (she previously had acted for avant garde director Jean-Luc Godard in *Détective* in 1985), though she is not quite up to the tone-changes which the script demands of her Bohemian 'junkie'. The minor players are uniformly excellent – all have the ring of authenticity about them – from the concierge (Gérard Klein) who passes his off-duty hours working-out at a local gym to the police inspector (Yves Rénier) who takes affront at Walker's suggestion that he is not moving fast enough in pursuing the inquiry: 'You are being taken perfectly seriously here, sir. As a matter of fact, you have a special treatment. Usually, we fill out this form after a week or so...'

Most of the expected Polanski trademarks are also well in evidence, beginning with the growing sense of unease which can be inspired by relatively minor incidents – what Victorian ghost story writer M R James referred to as 'the malice of inanimate objects', such as when the couple's cab suffers a puncture on the way into Paris from the airport – and ending with a typically downbeat finale which seems to be stuck halfway between anti-climax and pregnant pause. Alongside these is the attention expended on minutiae; in this instance, Polanski used the knowledge that he had gained while researching *The First Deadly Sin* to insert some fascinating scenes of investigative procedure, made all the more interesting by their everyday mundanity.

If *Frantic* disappoints – and it does, to some degree – it is in its denouement and its lack of idiosyncratic Polanski touches to offset the overtly Hitchcockian air. Polanski's favoured over-the-shoulder shots are kept to a minimum in this instance, as Hollywood star Ford is afforded his requisite quota of close-ups; nor are there any morally-dubious sexual shenanigans to be had between he and Seigner while the kidnapped cat is away. The climax is typically low key: having revealed that action spectacle is not his forte in *Pirates*, Polanski confines himself to a modest gun battle on the banks of the Seine and in sight of the Eiffel Tower. A few bullets later, and it is all over: Ford sheds a tear for the fallen Michelle in a trademark Polanski twist of fate, a là *Chinatown* (in which the innocent suffer while the guilty parties go free), and the Walkers resume their sojourn in Paris from the point at which initially it was interrupted. A melancholy accordion score by Ennio Morricone adds an elegiac quality to the closing credits.

This faintly disharmonious finale, as though Polanski could not quite bring himself to apply the expected formulaic wrap-up, tempers somewhat one's enjoyment of what has gone before. *Frantic*'s last few minutes are almost designed to deny the viewer the innocent *frissons* of the conventional thriller by offering up a 'real' victim to all of the fundamentally-fake good-guy-versus-bad-guys frolicking which has preceded them; it imparts the same air of disquiet that Polanski seems involuntarily inclined to inject into each and every one of his films, and which takes the edge off the urge to applaud them for more simplistic reasons. The easier explanation for the change of mood, and the one to which most critics succumbed, was that *Frantic* simply was not very good. The film is actually very good indeed, but if Polanski chose not to observe convention in respect of Walker's relationship with the male fantasy-figure of the leather-clad Michelle, then he was equally unlikely to furnish a happy ending in the expected manner.

Frantic fades out on Walker and his wife, reunited but clinging desperately to each other for comfort in the face of a new world of uncertainties – and in grief, at the loss of a young life for no sane reason. It is a climax that evokes a mood of sober reflection, and it shows beyond question that *Frantic* is a Roman Polanski film, not a pale shadow of one of Alfred Hitchcock.

> SHAAP: *You ever heard of Krytron before, Doctor?*
> WALKER: *No.*
> WILLIAMS: *I must admit, neither had I.*
> SHAAP: *It's... It's a... an electronic triggering device. A miniature high-performance switch, capable of withstanding severe shock and vibration.*
> WALKER: *What's it for?*
> SHAAP: *It's used in missile-separation, and for the detonation of nuclear devices...*
> WALKER: *This thing sets off atomic bombs...?*
>
> **Jimmie Ray Weeks, Harrison Ford and John Mahoney,** Frantic (1988)

Frantic opened in the US on 26 February 1988, and in the UK six months later, on September 15. After the large-scale disaster of *Pirates*, its reception in critical circles was remarkably positive, if a little more muted than might have been the case were it to have followed *Tess* or even *The Tenant*.

The *Chicago Sun-Times*'s Roger Ebert was in forgiving mood: 'Every scene of this film feels like a project from Polanski's heart – a film to prove he is still capable of generating the kind of suspense he became famous for. And every scene, on its own, seems to work. It is only the total of the scenes that is wrong... But perhaps Polanski was so happy to be back where he belonged, making a big-budget thriller with a big star, that he lost his objectivity. It's understandable... Even with its excesses, *Frantic* is a reminder of how absorbing a good thriller can be.' Desson Howe in the *Washington Post* was more conciliatory still: '*Frantic* is vintage Polanski... Is it time for the exiled maker of *Repulsion*, *Rosemary's Baby* and *Chinatown* to come home?'

On the other side of the Atlantic, a similar mood prevailed. '*Frantic* sets itself (and us) up brilliantly. Nearly 40 minutes are

teasingly consumed in reducing Ford to a state of helplessness
familiar to anyone who ever suffered fear and frustration in a
foreign land,' Alexander Walker confided in the *Standard*. 'The
drip-feed of paranoia – such as Polanski himself surely had to
submit to in his early days of self-exile – is powerfully persuasive.'
Iain Johnstone, the resident Polanski-knocker of the *Sunday Times*,
was obliged to agree: 'It's a pleasure to see Polanski returning to
form after the dreaded *Pirates* – the ship from that movie is still
berthed in the Old Port at Cannes to warn all young directors what
happens to you if you have too much money and too few ideas.
And if this story eventually gets lost in the murky metropolis
he has created, he at least has his consummate style to see him
home.' The *Sunday Telegraph*'s Richard Mayne was more succinct:
'...An edgy, elegant, well-observed thriller.' Dissenters were in
the minority, but *Today*'s Sue Heal tried hard to speak for them.
'*Frantic* exudes all the tension of a dead conger eel,' she hissed.

Frantic took a modest $17 million for Warners, a long way short
of the average for a Harrison Ford feature. The presence of Ford
in the cast, following hot on the heels of Walter Matthau in the
preceding film, did little to dissuade observers of the scene from
their view that Polanski's best days were behind him, regardless
of critical indulgence in relation to his latest opus, and that run-
of-the-mill Hollywood-style fare was all that now lay ahead. A year
after *Frantic* confirmed many in their belief that its director was
fast-becoming a spent force, Jack Nicholson embarked on *The Two
Jakes* with himself clutching the megaphone. When the film was
released, critical opinion was unanimous: *Chinatown* it plainly
was not, and regret within the American industry at the seemingly
permanent loss of Polanski was brought home all the more.

* * *

Pirates had been a 'man's' film in that the lone female in the cast
was no more than a token presence whose charms proved too
elusive even for the one eligible bachelor in the vicinity. *Frantic*

also was something of a man's film, given that the plot revolved around an American cardiologist's search for his kidnapped wife in Paris, which placed the medico centre-stage and removed his spouse from the action after a few brief scenes. But the screenplay to *Frantic* had added a secondary female character in the form of Michelle, an enigmatic *femme fatale* whose partnership with the hero brought about a solution to the mystery. Michelle was played by 20-year-old Emmanuelle Seigner, granddaughter of character actor and respected Comedie Française veteran Louis Seigner and sister of Marie-Amélie and Mathilde (now a celebrated actress in her own right), and it was not long before the sultry, statuesque and singular-looking Miss Seigner was sharing more with the director of *Frantic* than script meetings.

Seigner was 33 years Polanski's junior, but the attraction between them turned out to be more durable than the casual fling between director and starlet in which Polanski had engaged habitually over the years. On August 10, 1989, the two were married, and Roman Polanski – at nearly 56 years of age – could at last look forward to the domestic bliss which cruelly had been denied him all those years before. Another two years were to elapse before he was in a position to embark on his next film and, in the meantime, he made a detour to the heart of the Soviet Union, ostensibly to supply a cameo for a juvenile chase-thriller entitled *Back in the USSR*.

Back in the USSR is badly-dubbed, determinedly unwatchable, straight-to-video dross, in which Polanski is one of many minor villains employed to chase a precious religious icon around the tourist streets of Moscow, in obvious echo of *The Maltese Falcon*. His role in the film appears to be as unscripted as that of the rest of the cut-price cast and, while he exhibits marginally more life than his co-stars – especially in scenes where he tries to inject some *Chinatown*-style sadistic depth into the character of the hero's tormentor, the film which all of them inhabit is a poor excuse for a thriller by anyone's standards. Director Deran

Sarafian obviously learned much about shooting off-the-cuff from the improvisational style of father Richard (of *Vanishing Point* fame), but he learned nothing at all about pacing or coherence of narrative.

Polanski had other reasons for slumming it in *Back in the USSR*, however – he had thought at the same time to scout locations in the Russian capital for his long-projected film version of Bulgakov's *The Master and Margarita*. 'I was looking for material in the late eighties, and I thought of *The Master and Margarita*,' he told Mia Taylor. 'I have a very good relationship with Warner Bros [the producers of *Frantic*]. When I mentioned the book, the development department got very excited. They knew and loved it. They said yes, definitely, let's do that.'

'I thought of doing part of it in Poland and the rest in France, with some shots in Moscow,' Polanski went on. 'I went location scouting in Moscow, but there is nothing left from that period, with the exception of the Kremlin, and even the Kremlin changed a little bit. I felt it could have been done much better in a place like Krakow with some construction.' A problem which he and John Brownjohn were forced to address in the adaptation which they worked on for Warners was the fact that Polanski already had used the climax of the book in *The Vampire Killers*, twenty years earlier. 'I don't think that Satan's ball, which is so prominent in the book, matters really for what Bulgakov is trying to tell,' Polanski shrugged. 'Sometimes the most popular pieces can be removed without hurting much...'

'It was quite expensive and complex, and I suspect that Terry Semel, the head of Warners, didn't read the book himself. He knew only what was reported to him. And when it came time for him to give the so-called green light, he must have read the script for the first time and he didn't believe the picture had the commercial potential to justify the expense. I said, okay, let's forget it, and tried to set it up with some other companies, which I think was a mistake, because once the word goes around that the studio dropped the project – even if you asked them to – the word is out, and I couldn't put it together.'

Instead of *The Master and Margarita*, Polanski put together a dark, psycho-sexual thriller adapted from the novel *Lunes de Fiel*, by French philosopher Pascal Bruckner. Again, he sought Nicholson for the lead role of a crippled American writer who relives the sexual exploits of his youth by relating them to a repressed Englishman on board a cruise-liner, but again Jack was committed elsewhere. Former student activist and real-life author Peter Coyote stepped into the breach, and Polanski's wife of two years was elevated to star-status alongside him. The couple on the receiving end of the writer's erotic fantasies were to be Oxford graduate Hugh Grant and Kristin Scott Thomas, both of them two years away from the sleeper success of *Four Weddings and a Funeral* (Grant's most noteworthy appearance previously had been in 1988's *Lair of the White Worm*, for director Ken Russell). 'The fact that sexual attraction wanes, that's what fascinated me,' Polanski revealed. 'That has nothing to do with love – which can actually deepen as sex declines. It's a universal issue, is it not?' To Geoff Andrew of *Time Out* magazine, he went further in explaining his rationale for returning to thematic concerns which had more in common with *Knife in the Water* or *Repulsion* than they did with *Pirates* or *Frantic*: 'I hadn't done a movie like this for a long time,' he said, 'and I felt strongly not only that *I'd* like to do it, but that people who know my work were somehow expecting and wanting me to return to this kind of material.'

FIONA: *How far are you going?*
MIMI: *Further – much further.*
Kristin Scott Thomas and Emmanuelle Seigner, *Bitter Moon* (1992)

What is it about Polanski that makes his films different – that makes them stand out from the crowd? It is that they exhibit an originality of vision, both stylistically and thematically. Whether they are dark and morbid and psychotically-disposed, or merely frivolous and disposable, they are plainly the work of a singular intelligence, a unique psychology, a rare aesthetic. 1992's *Bitter Moon* was representative of all three. It was also Polanski's take on Billy Wilder's classic 1952 *noir* thriller *Sunset Boulevard*, the 'flashback' movie to end all flashback movies...

Bitter Moon begins with another of Polanski's devices to evoke claustrophobia: the view through a window – on this occasion, a porthole of the ship on which Nigel (Grant) and Fiona (Scott Thomas) are cruising to Istanbul over the New Year. Their marriage has reached the point of the proverbial 'seven-year itch' and, as they go their separate ways around the ship, Nigel finds himself drawn to the beautiful Mimi (Seigner). He is soon accosted by her wheelchair-bound husband Oscar (Coyote), a failed writer, who seduces him, in the manner of Scheherazade to Haroun al-Raschid, into listening to the tale of his affair with Mimi (whom, in his dime-novel prose, he refers to as a 'sorceress in white sneakers') – an affair which left him emotionally, and *physically*, crippled...

In a series of flashbacks, Oscar tells Nigel how he wooed and won Mimi – romantic love quickly giving way to the more extreme sexual fetishes, as their passion for each other intensified to the point of obsession. Nigel, trapped like an unwary fly in the web of a mysterious spider, listens reluctantly as Oscar explains how the flames of desire then burned themselves out and he tired of his once-great love. Much as he now wished her gone from his life, Mimi's feelings for him had not changed reciprocally; she begged to be allowed to stay by his side. For a time, Oscar relented, but love had turned to hate and he demeaned and humiliated her at every opportunity. Eventually, he engineered her departure and returned to his former life of sexual adventure. After one particular night on the town, however, he was hit by a truck and found himself in hospital with a broken leg. Mimi paid him a visit. His recent treatment of her finally had done the trick: she now despised him equally. But a woman scorned... Mimi pulled him from the bed on which he was strapped in traction and broke his back...

Oscar goes on to reveal that he and Mimi were married as a result, and that their previous roles were reversed: the crippled Oscar was now dependent on Mimi, so he was the one who was demeaned – to the extent of her bringing lovers home and having sex with them in his helpless presence. Nigel begins to wonder if Oscar's tale is merely part of an elaborate charade in which *he* has become a participant, but his suspicions are overridden by his desire for Oscar's wife...

Comes New Year's Eve, and Nigel finds himself on the dance-floor with Mimi. To his surprise, she spurns his advances. Oscar's scheming has orchestrated the situation so that Fiona has witnessed events; she takes to the floor with Mimi instead, and they wind up in bed together. Nigel is distraught; he goes to Mimi's stateroom where he finds Oscar voyeuristically observing the scene. Nigel tries to strangle him, but Oscar pulls a gun. He shoots Mimi dead and blows his own brains out. The game is ended.

*　　*　　*

Bitter Moon is a provocation – a rabid exploration of the destructive power of love; an antithetical assault on the ideals of romance; an antidote to happy endings. In many respects, novel and film go deeper into the darks of sexual obsession than comfortable viewing can sustain, but it is to Polanski's credit that he never tries to skirt around the hazards in his path through filmmaking 'cheats', like symbolism or inference or simple evasion by means of grammatical device – dissolve, fade and the rest. Short of shooting the film as artistic hardcore, in the style of the more contemporary *Baise-moi* (2000) or Michael Winterbottom's *Nine Songs* (2004), Polanski comes as close as he can to the raunchy and sometimes risible antics of two people whose lustful desire for each other knows no bounds – closer still, when it comes to Oscar describing their activities to the compliant Nigel: 'Steady on, old chap,' Nigel protests, as Oscar regales him in graphic detail with an intimate verbal portrait of Mimi's clitoris.

Like sex itself, the film veers dangerously between passionate intensity and comic fumbling. A first, tentative kiss between Oscar and Mimi after a long night on the town (during which he charms her by playing the parlour-game that Polanski devised for his own character in *Blood For Dracula*) is soon replaced by whip-and-leather, and Oscar in pig-mask and on his hands and knees; much later, their relationship becomes one of golden showers and sado-masochism. But the honesty of the depiction shines through, and Polanski manages to prevent premature ejaculations of laughter by making it clear in his careful (and sometimes self-mocking) presentation of events that titillation is not the primary purpose.

All four actors engage in a brave adventure, but none are braver than Seigner and Coyote, who have to run the sexual and emotional gamut before their journey is done. The film's complex flashback structure requires Coyote to alternate between handsome and hopeful, and lecherous and incorrigibly corrupt, while Seigner has to go from fresh and trusting to sophisticated and seductive; the transitions are expertly managed, with Coyote ultimately coming off worse in the 'after' section of the before-and-after stakes. Oscar's manipulation of Nigel through the recounting of unexpurgated reminiscences is less believably handled; Nigel ostensibly is attracted by Oscar's story because of the promise of what lies in store for him should he party up with Mimi, but his relationship with his own wife never seems quite that cold to begin with, despite the clichéd asides about 'marital therapy' and the two of them being an 'old married couple', thus his implicit sexual frustration is never properly established. Be that as it may, the means by which Oscar inveigles him into participating in his sexual game-playing calls to mind the seduction of Guy by the Castavets in *Rosemary's Baby*. At the end of the day, Oscar's appeal is as much to Nigel's vanity as it is to his libido. *Bitter Moon* is almost *Rosemary's Baby* presented as 'Guy's story', rather than that of his titular spouse.

Where love has gone, hate must follow. By the time Oscar in his selfish disinterest not only has sapped Mimi of her will but robbed her of the last vestiges of independent personality, the reformed misogynist in Polanski has the viewer rooting for her to take her revenge, in the manner of the ill-used wife in the Patrick Hamilton thriller *Gaslight*. The power-play between individuals which Polanski examined in whimsical fashion in *The Fat and the Lean* more than three decades before reaches its zenith in *Bitter Moon*, as Mimi is turned from menial into monster by the simple expedients of contempt and neglect. 'Every time I looked into one woman's eyes, I could see the reflection of the next,' Oscar declaims in voice-over, as he looks forward to playing the field again after freeing himself from what he sees as the shackles of Mimi and marriage by packing her off to Martinique without him (and in the process of his narrative, straining credulity in the fact that he is meant to have four *un*published novels to his name). From that point on, it is inevitable that creator and created will somehow come to destroy each other. 'What did I do wrong? – Did I ever harm you?' Mimi asks; 'You didn't do anything,' he tells her. 'You exist, that's all.'

Polanski's adroit way with the sudden shock had not diminished over the years: when Oscar is hit by a truck in an absent-minded moment, the impact on the viewer is nearly as great, while the scene in which Mimi breaks his back and kneels down beside him as he screams, to whisper, 'Asshole – did you think I'd forgotten?' is sublimely Hitchcockian in its abrupt downshifting of mood, specifically the Hitchcock of Boileau-Narcejac or perverted sexual obsession, such as in *Vertigo* or *Psycho*.

Nigel is teased into Mimi's bedroom – only to find Oscar there waiting for him, but even that ignominy proves insufficient to dampen his ardour. A final, fateful attempt to entice her between the sheets with a declaration of love has the effect of sending Fiona into her arms instead. Polanski makes good use of the musical track throughout: Peggy Lee's 'Fever' plays during Nigel's initial encounter with Mimi at the ship's bar, while Bryan Ferry's 'Slave to Love' accompanies his last. Having found as a side-issue of his sexual scheming that love is about giving, not simply about taking, Oscar shoots Mimi and then himself, while a chance to salvage their relationship still remains to Nigel and Fiona. The last word is left fittingly to Oscar, before he puts the gun to his mouth. 'We were just too greedy, baby...'

> *She came to see me when I got out of intensive care. She said there's bad news and there's good news. You're paralysed from the waist down. Okay, I said, let's have the good news. That was the good news, she said. The bad news is that from now on, I'm taking care of you.*
>
> **Oscar (Peter Coyote)**, *Bitter Moon* (1992)

Had Polanski not already fallen in love with Seigner by the time that this film was made, he would have fallen in love with her during the making of it: she had come a long way since *Frantic*, and her performance is a revelation – subtle, powerful, intense. As an actor himself, and therefore one who appreciates the craft of acting, Polanski was doubly impressed by his wife's range and ability. 'It was very difficult for her,' he told Neil Norman of the *Standard*. 'She acts it for *real*, it is not pretending. And doing that with someone you're intimate with is not easy. But there are great rewards. You share a passion, the work, expectations, and you have the consciousness of creating something together.' For many critics of the film, however, what they had created together on this occasion was controversy. *Bitter Moon* opened in Britain on October 2, 1992, but its US release was held up for almost 18 months; even when it did eventually see the light of an American day, in March 1994, the film was given only limited play-dates.

Polanski engaged in the usual round of media interviews to promote *Bitter Moon*, but he concentrated effort on the subject of imminent fatherhood: Seigner was now expecting their first child, some time in January 1993. 'I would have had a child a long time ago if circumstances had been different,' he pointedly informed Neil Norman of London's *Evening Standard*. And a note of wistfulness: 'We were lucky, were we not? Can you imagine growing up now? The sixties and seventies were a period of the greatest joy of mankind. Now it looks like they were the peak.'

The air of regret was understandable from a man whose work increasingly was seen as anti-climactic, with the best of it in the past. *Bitter Moon* was greeted with the same lukewarm praise as had been *Frantic*, with many critics pointing up the similarities to earlier successes but few claiming the present offering with the inflated hyperbole which they once had reserved for Polanski's more serious outings. Alexander Walker, Norman's critical colleague on the *Standard*, was openly contemptuous: 'Oscar Wilde, echoing an earlier writer, remarked that good Americans, when they die, go to Paris. Good filmmakers hit the same city when they die too, professionally speaking. The case of Roman Polanski supports the point. An American at heart, if not by birth [Walker forcing his analogy here], he fled the United States at the height of his commercial success and critical reputation... *Bitter Moon*... is about an American who exiles himself in Paris to be a writer, forms a claustrophobic relationship with a French girl, fails in his art and his affair and ends up a physical cripple. Polanski has warned that we shouldn't read his own fate or predilections into his fiction. So we shouldn't, in detail. But given that *Bitter Moon* reflects the dilemma of a man who is a captive of circumstances of his own making, and suffers a paralysis of the creative will, the parallel in the wider sense is arguable. I think it's apposite too.'

Today's sniping Sue Heal felt the same way: 'It has become fashionable to treat the outpourings of Roman Polanski as a few saucy giggles from an experienced old wag. But here he gives us a poorly executed, exploitative exercise in peep-hole titillation and enjoyment of cruelty.' The *Mail*'s Tom Hutchinson went further down the road of confusion with regard to the respective roles of created and creator: 'The extraordinary comeback of Roman Polanski forces me to a strange conclusion. He resents sex,' he wrote – a curiously unqualified statement, but it turned out to be one with which Philip French of *The Observer* concurred: '*Bitter Moon*...is the work of a perverse, exhausted talent narrated by a perverse, exhausted talentless writer to trap a dim-witted listener.' As did Anthony Lane, in the *Independent on Sunday*: '*Bitter Moon* makes you wince, occasionally with fear, but mostly at the sight of genius gone silly and sour.'

It is fair to assume that an intelligent filmmaker like Polanski would, from time to time, be attracted to subjects with which he felt emotional or psychological empathy – that there would, as a result, be 'points of contact' or intersections between the artist and his work, as in *Macbeth*, *Tess* or even *The Tenant* – but that is not the same as to suggest that what is depicted on screen must somehow mirror the life of the man who put it there. 'When I pick a theme for a movie, I don't think,' he was subsequently to tell French daily *Libération*. 'I go for whatever grabs me at that moment.' Other critics were not so foolhardy as to try to exercise their dubious analytical powers on each new film from the Wandering Pole. *The Spectator*'s Vanessa Letts cast aside the personal allusions and high moral tone of her more cynical compatriots and found much of the old Polanski still to be admired in his latest opus. 'It is his triumph to have given us a *Last Tango in Paris* [*Bernardo Bertolucci's controversial sex-drama of 1972, starring Marlon Brando*] for the Nineties... For anyone who has ever felt desire, or the secret hankering to be recognised as an artist, this is a film not to be missed.' Jeff Sawtell in the *Morning Star* also was won over, praising the film as a 'spellbinding tale about the bitter fruits of obsessive love.' Mark Salisbury in *Empire* trod a middle path, calling it 'deliberately provocative' while steadfastly refusing to be provoked: 'This is a film that begs not to be taken seriously, and requires a ready suspension of moral discernment for maximum

Polanski as the troubled Trelkovsky in *The Tenant*

'The room...surrounded him like a *sarcophagus*...' – Roman Polanski (*The Tenant*, 1976)

Leigh Lawson as Alec and Nastassja Kinski as Tess in *Tess*

'I would rather take it in my own hand'
– Nastassja Kinski (*Tess*, 1979)

Polanski puts his troubles behind him on the set of *Tess*

ABOVE AND BELOW: Walter Matthau as Captain
Thomas Bartholomew Red in *Pirates*
RIGHT: Polanski sets up an action scene for
Matthau (*Pirates*, 1986)

Polanski with Emmanuelle Seigner and Harrison Ford on the set of *Frantic*

Richard Walker (Ford) finds himself in a tight spot in *Frantic*

Peter Coyote and Emmanuelle Seigner find that attraction is not so mutual in *Bitter Moon*

Mimi (Seigner) casts her erotic spell (*Bitter Moon*, 1992)

Ben Kingsley and Sigourney Weaver exchange blows in *Death and the Maiden*

Dean Corso (Johnny Depp) ponders the significance of *The Ninth Gate*

Devil or angel? – Emmanuelle Seigner (*The Ninth Gate*, 1999)

Wladyslaw Szpilman (Adrien Brody) finds solace in Chopin's Nocturne in *The Pianist*

Harrison Ford presents Polanski with his Oscar for *The Pianist*
at the 29th American Film Festival in Deauville, France

Polanski directs as Oliver (Barney Clark) looks on (*Oliver Twist*, 2005)

Polanski orchestrates a chase sequence on (art director)
Allan Starski's sprawling Prague set for *Oliver Twist*

enjoyment. Go with the flow and you'll be rewarded, otherwise you might find it all rather absurd.'

Bitter Moon was a watershed for Roman Polanski: it marked the end of his 30-year writing partnership with Gérard Brach. From this point on, the two went their separate ways – Polanski to a new partnership with South African Ronald Harwood, after a brief association with noviciate Rafael Yglesias on his next project; Brach, who had penned *Jean de Florette* and *The Name of the Rose* (both 1986) without input from his former chum, to the less cerebral territory of giallo gore-master Dario Argento's abortive 1998 remake of *The Phantom of the Opera* (*Il Fantasma dell'opera*).

As he again took stock of his life in the wake of the birth of his first child, Polanski partnered another Gérard for the short term, but this was an acting assignment: *A Pure Formality* (*Una Pura Formalita*) is a Kafkaesque thriller about a writer named Onoff who is hauled before a mysterious Inspector investigating a death – or is it murder? – in his isolated and rain-swept jurisdiction. Gérard Depardieu is the writer with the curious name and Polanski the Inspector in a moody and intriguing drama, until its predictably metaphysical finale. *A Pure Formality* was a French-Italian co-production, written and directed by Giuseppe Tornatore and graced with a score by the great Ennio Morricone (who did Polanski's *Frantic*). The principals are worth watching, and Polanski more than holds his own with Depardieu, who not only is a French national institution but is twice his co-star's height and stature into the bargain. But the sub-*Twilight Zone* plot was unworthy of either man, having more in common with *Secret Window* (2003) than with anything by the author of *The Trial*. Polanski and Depardieu hold the attention for most of the way, but the outcome of their shared plight is so gloriously feeble that not even their combined talents can sustain it beyond ultimate banality.

By the end of 1993, the ever-restless Polanski had moved seamlessly into his next project before *Bitter Moon* had even found itself a US distributor, but a footnote to the affair came from an unlikely source: the news. Polanski's judicial nemesis, Laurence J Rittenband, died of cancer on December 30. Another chapter of his life had closed, but his fugitive status remained unchanged and no one – least of all he – had any idea what the next chapter might bring.

> *It's a long time ago, but I recall the press went on about*
> *breakdown... breakdown... an endless terror of the blank page, right?*
>
> **Inspector (Roman Polanski)**, *A Pure Formality* (1994)

In 1991, an Argentinian-born Jew named Ariel Dorfman had written a play called *Death and the Maiden* (*La muerte y la doncella*). Dorfman had spent his early years in the US, but his family moved back to South America in 1954, when he was 12 years old, and eventually he obtained a professorship from the University of Chile. In 1970, Dorfman exchanged the academic life for an administrative one, when he was asked to join the government of President Salvatore Allende. But when Allende was overthrown in a military coup backed by the CIA in September 1973, new Chilean dictator General Augusto Pinochet sent him into exile. Dorfman remained a staunch critic of the bloody Pinochet regime and when democracy was restored to the country in 1990, he set about writing the play which for him would typify the truth of tyranny everywhere.

Dorfman's drama revolves around a victim of state-sponsored torture inadvertently coming face-to-face with the man who systematically had raped her in her prison-cell, and to add the relevant musical connotation, he contrives to have the torturer brutalise his victim to the idiosyncratic accompaniment of Franz Schubert's 1824 string quartet in D minor – which is known as the 'Death and the Maiden' quartet, due to the use in its second movement of a song of that name which Schubert had composed seven years earlier (*Der Tod und Das Mädchen*). The play is a three-hander, the action being confined to the intrigue between Paulina Escobar, her lawyer husband Gerardo and her alleged torturer, Dr

Roberto Miranda, as the couple try to establish Miranda's guilt or innocence in the kangaroo court that Paulina finds herself in a position to institute at their isolated home.

When, in 1993, Polanski decided to adapt Dorfman's play for the screen, he chose Oscar-winning Royal Shakespeare Company player (Sir) Ben Kingsley for the difficult role of the enigmatic Dr Miranda, and one-time British television regular Stuart Wilson for that of Gerardo. The pivotal role of Paulina Escobar, née Lorca (Salas in the play), went eventually to New Yorker Sigourney Weaver, still best-remembered for her numerous outings in the *Alien* movies, as well as her 1984 appearance in *Ghost Busters*. Production company Warners had proposed Glenn Close, the *femme fatale* of *Fatal Attraction* (1977), who had played the role on Broadway during the summer of 1992 opposite Richard Dreyfuss and Gene Hackman (as Miranda), but to less than universal acclaim. Polanski had not seen that production for obvious reasons – nor a better-received one at the Royal Court Theatre in London in July 1991, which had starred Juliet Stevenson, Bill Paterson and Michael Byrne – but the poor notices for Close had been brought to his attention. At his insistence, Close's $2 million fee was increased by another $1 million and offered to Weaver instead, who was persuaded to accept the role despite the 3000-mile separation from her daughter that shooting the film in France was inevitably to necessitate. 'Doing the movie was like undergoing three months of therapy,' she told Simon Kinnersley of *The Mail on Sunday*, 'It opened up a can of worms – nothing I want to discuss – yet I felt a lot lighter when it was over.' Weaver's participation in what had been written as a chamber-piece sent the budget soaring to a whopping $12 million, or the same amount that Polanski had at his disposal 15 years earlier, for the epic *Tess*.

For *Death and the Maiden*, Polanski swapped his customary pitch at the Epinay Studios for the more historic Studios de Boulogne, also in Paris (where he had shot the interiors for *Bitter Moon*), and he decided to shoot the story chronologically, whereas most films are shot out-of-sequence to accommodate the vagaries of weather, cast and crew availability and other variables. This was a bold departure from convention, once again akin to the cinematic experiments of Hitchcock, and it was met with approval by all three of the actors in the piece. 'I think it's great to work chronologically,' Kingsley observed, 'and with such a remarkable director... What interests Roman is the visual within the room, within the people's psyches.' For the climactic scenes on the headland near the Escobar's home, Polanski chose the rocky coast of Valdoviño, in the Galician region of Northwestern Spain.

Kingsley had reason to identify more strongly than the others in the small cast with his role, and with the situation in general which they were now called upon to depict. In his days as a young actor at Stratford-upon-Avon, he had met with Chilean poet/guitarist Victor Jara and his wife. When the freely-elected government of Salvador Allende was overthrown in 1973, Jara was imprisoned along with hundreds of other pro-democracy demonstrators and summarily executed, but not before his persecutors had taunted him to try to play his guitar after they had broken both his hands.

> *I can't really remember anything about how I felt since that night. I came back, beat-up and crazy. You were half-dead; you'd taken punishment a thousand times worse than anything I could have taken and you did it to save my life. How do you think that makes me feel? I would have given them your name to save my skin; they would have broken me on the first day. So you see, I don't really remember anything about how I've felt since that night you came back. But I love you. I love you. It's been the logic of my life but I have a feeling it's going to destroy me...*
>
> **Gerardo Escobar (Stuart Wilson)**, *Death and the Maiden* (1995)

The film opens with a screen caption: *A country in South America... after the fall of the dictatorship.* Lawyer Gerardo Escobar (Wilson) is to head up a Truth Commission to prosecute those who colluded with the fascist government; he and his wife Paulina (Weaver) had belonged to the democratic underground, and she had been imprisoned under the old regime. Escobar suffers a flat tyre en route to his isolated coastal home after his audience with the new president and he is given a lift by Good Samaritan Dr Miranda (Kingsley). Escobar invites him in for a drink, and Paulina recognises him as the man who tortured and raped her when she was held in captivity, and to the strains of Schubert's 'Death and the Maiden'. As the two lapse into a drunken stupor, Paulina steals Miranda's car and pushes it off a cliff. Surprising the doctor while he sleeps, she ties him to a chair. Her husband wakes also and is bewildered by the scene which now confronts him. Paulina tells him of her suspicions with regard to Miranda, but he has difficulty in believing her due to the lack of supporting evidence; Miranda appears to have an equally good alibi for the period of Paulina's imprisonment. She persuades her husband to extract a confession from him, but this proves impossible without resorting to the same inhumane techniques that the regime had used on its victims. Faced with a stalemate, Paulina walks Miranda to the cliff-top at gunpoint with a view to ending it there. Escobar, meanwhile, seemingly has been able to corroborate Miranda's alibi. He rushes to the cliff to tell his wife, but she remains convinced that all of it is part of a prearranged set-up. Believing himself to be staring death in the face, Miranda confesses finally: he *did* torture and rape Paulina, he says, but he was corrupted by the system; circumstance and opportunity are the roots of such evil, not individual perpetrators. Paulina relents in her desire to kill him and she and Gerardo return home, leaving him on his own. The fade-out sees them sharing the auditorium at a Schubert concert, and having to live for the rest of their lives with the consequences of their collective past.

* * *

Echoing the porthole opening of *Bitter Moon*, *Death and the Maiden* begins with a figure standing behind a rain-sprayed window in another of Polanski's claustrophobic dialogues with himself. Paulina Escobar scurries around her exposed coastal home like a frightened rat, waiting for her husband. The lights flicker and instinctively she reaches for candle and gun. When Gerardo does eventually arrive, the exchanges between them are strained, as though something of import is consciously being left unsaid. All of this is classic Polanski: the unsettling air of things not *quite* right; the everyday occurrences undercut by the suspicion that this is not just an ordinary day and these are not ordinary people. If an air of high Gothic camp intrudes from time to time, it comes in the film's insistence on using the elements which were absent on stage as a fourth character in the drama – the raging sea pounding against the promontory on which stands the Escobar's home; the wind and rain which lash constantly around the house, portending doom.

The evident tension between the couple is explained by the fact that Paulina thinks that Gerardo is engaged in a whitewash, whereas he views his participation in the Truth Commission as a first tentative step on the long road to obtaining justice. As with all of Polanski's more serious work, *Death and the Maiden* concerns itself with the peeling away of the layers of civilised behaviour to reveal the raw emotions, and the real nature of the relationships which lie beneath.

Gerardo has been saved from the storm by a passing motorist, who graciously gave him a lift home when his car burst a tyre. The stranger is mild, compliant, only too willing to be of help – impressed and reverent, even, when he discovers that the stranded driver to whom he has been of service is Gerardo Escobar, chair of the Commission. Having taken his leave too quickly, he arranges to return to the Escobar house on a pretext, so that he can express more fulsomely his admiration for Gerardo; only later, do we begin to question this motive – was his reason for returning as innocent as he suggests, or did he wish conversely to discover more about the workings of the Commission and who it might have in its judicial sights?

Kingsley's performance as Miranda is engaging, meek and terrified at first, as the tables not so much are turned on him but *up*turned and he finds himself strapped into a chair with a gun pointed at his head, but cool and commanding when he is able to wrest control away from his captor – albeit temporarily – and turn them back in his favour. The ratcheting-up of tension as the burden of proof see-saws between Paulina and Miranda is brilliantly executed, as each accusation is countered by another plausible explanation and the viewer is put in the same position as Gerardo, of having to make a judgement which instinct decrees to be a correct one but which the facts, such as they are, seem diametrically to oppose. If *Death and the Maiden* fails to connect with the viewer in quite so powerful a way as it did onstage, at least in London, the fault lies with the static nature and obvious theatricality of the piece. Polanski's film is a three-hander like *Knife in the Water*, but on speed, and reminiscent of the suffocatingly-intense dramas which a young BBC Television was prone to transmit in the days of captive audiences, particularly in its dependence on what effectively is a single set.

The artificiality of the situation eventually begins to descend on the proceedings, as evidence for or against the accused cannot realistically be produced and accusation and denial appear able to go on indefinitely – or at least as long as the parties can contrive convincing explanations for their actions. Dorfman therefore imposes a deadline on the impasse by having Gerardo take a phone call from the President in which he is told that police are being sent to protect him because of death threats, and that they will reach the house by 6.00 am. This imbues the characters with a new sense of urgency and increases the force of their arguments, but it also tips the film towards melodrama. Weaver's performance is stagey, histrionic and mannered, in any event. She kicks off the proceedings at too high a pitch of antagonism towards her infinitely-patient husband (for whom she later professes undying love!) and she consequently is left with nowhere to go but into the heights of hysteria, which she leavens only by dropping into her *Alien*-baiting Ripley persona at moments of physical stress. While the two men are reduced to nervous wrecks by her psychotic determination to extract the truth from her erstwhile tormentor in the manner of a dentist to whom anaesthetic is anathema, she keeps a clear – if increasingly unbalanced head – the credibility of which posture is not sufficiently supported by the revelation that while in captivity, she was not broken by her torturer's sadistic wiles.

Although little of the circumstance in which the protagonists find themselves in *Death and the Maiden* ultimately rings true, the story exerts a powerful hold on the viewer as it unfolds. There is a physical tussle or two when Paulina has occasion to let her guard drop, but the bulk of the drama is extrapolated from the moral dilemma with which Gerardo is faced: what if Paulina is mistaken in her identification and Miranda is innocent? – And how can he pursue the judicial line without appearing to his wife to have gone over onto the side of the enemy? Gerardo is torn between a search for truth and what is seen by his wife to be a personal act of betrayal, and Polanski contrives the empathy of the viewer by pulling off an unusual casting-coup in relation to the character. Instead of matching Kingsley and Weaver to another actor of similar star-stature, or falling back on first-person-narrative camera tricks, he gave this all-important role to one-time British television regular Stuart Wilson, whose previous screen appearances had been confined to minor turns in nondescript sequels of the likes of *Lethal Weapon 3* and *Teenage Mutant Ninja Turtles 3*. Wilson is a supremely competent actor, immensely sympathetic, and he more than holds his own with the two Hollywood heavyweights in the film, but he remains relatively unknown on screen and his very anonymity engineers the audience identification with his plight which Polanski felt was critical to the piece.

Had *Death and the Maiden* been made after '9/11', the moral dilemma that it presents might have seemed more apposite in the present political climate than it was at the time of its production: when faced with barbarity, is it defensible to use the same methods to counter it – or does that imply the triumph of the very evil which is being opposed? But that is only one of the quandaries posed by Polanski's film, foremost among which is the idea that given suitable incentive, anyone is corruptible, and we can no more condemn than we can condone the flaws in our human make-up. Miranda's expiational speech at the close makes this only too clear, in its perverse logic and brutal honesty: he did it because he *could* – because the situation presented itself, and what at first was inspired by fear eventually became an end in itself. If you can't beat 'em, join 'em: the tune to which so many Nazi collaborators danced.

> PAULINA: *Don't move, Doctor. There's still a little matter pending.*
> *Brief pause.*
> *It's going to be an incredibly beautiful day. You know the only thing that's missing now, Doctor, the one thing I need to make this day really perfect?*
> *Brief Pause.*
> *To kill you. So I can listen to my Schubert without thinking that you'll also be listening to it, soiling my day and my Schubert and my country and my husband. That's what I need...*
>
> **Ariel Dorfman**, *Death and the Maiden* (1991)

Polanski's film posits a more specific outcome to events than does the play, which is odd for a director who self-confessedly takes more satisfaction from ambiguity. In the original, Paulina's interrogation of Miranda climaxes at the end of Act III, Scene 1, when implicitly she kills him after he has retracted his confession but she is convinced that she has tricked him into revealing the truth; the actors 'freeze' in their positions and the lights dim on Paulina's rhetorical summation: 'Why does it always have to be people like me who have to sacrifice, why are we always the ones who have to make concessions when something has to be conceded, why always me who has to bite her tongue, why? Well, not this time. This time I am going to think about myself, about what I need. If only to do justice in one case, just one. What do we lose? What do we lose by killing one of them?' Scene II is the epilogue at the concert; present are Paulina and Gerardo. As they engage in small-talk, Miranda appears to one side, like Banquo's ghost, and with lighting to match: 'He could be real or he could be an illusion in Paulina's head' is the stage-direction. Their eyes meet for a moment, then she turns again to the Schubert recital. The message is clear: it is retribution which has given Paulina her life back.

The film tempers this Old Testament, 'eye for an eye' resolution with ambivalence. Miranda is not killed by Paulina – he is allowed to return to his new life; the holding up of a mirror to his past misdeeds has been enough of a punishment, and a salvation, for both of them. Polanski's *Death and the Maiden* is therefore more about the abuser than the abused, and somewhere along the line, it appears to have been felt that comprehension and compassion offered a more fitting finale than cold-blooded revenge. As Ariel Dorfman wrote (or co-wrote) play *and* screenplay, it would seem that he underwent a change of heart at the prospect of the permanence of film in the years between them.

If there is evidence of introspection in Polanski's recent work, it was to be seen not so much in *Bitter Moon* as in *Death and the Maiden*. Its last reel serves as an apologia for a man who abused a position of power, having found himself in the wrong place at the wrong time – as did Polanski himself in 1977. But only up to a point. By exposing the psychopathology behind Miranda's actions, Polanski also reveals why the concept of remorse is as misplaced as those who seek it are misguided. The Fates decree the outcome of all human endeavour, and there nevertheless are consequences to be faced by Miranda, as well as his victim, even if being thrown from a cliff does not turn out to be one of them. Polanski was now

the father of a daughter, and the last shot of the film has Miranda
in the balcony of the theatre beside *his* wife and children, staring
fixedly at his victim in the auditorium below; she, on the other
hand, stares fixedly ahead. The allusion is inescapable: the past has
to remain as much of a penalty for Roman Polanski himself as it
does for Dr Miranda.

> *I was naked in the bright light and you couldn't see me. You*
> *couldn't tell me what to do — I owned you; I owned all of them. I*
> *fell in love with it. I could hurt you or I could fuck you, and you*
> *couldn't tell me not to. You had to thank me. I loved it. I was sorry*
> *it ended. I was very sorry it ended...*
>
> **Dr Roberto Miranda (Ben Kingsley)**, *Death and the Maiden* (1995)

The film's American outing over Christmas 1994 was short-lived
and uneconomic, due, as much as anything, to critiques like that of
Hal Hinson in the *Washington Post*: 'It's little more than a swanky
revenge fantasy for *Vanity Fair* liberals who like to have their anti-
fascism dressed up in garter belts and handcuffs,' he wrote. When
Death and the Maiden opened in Britain the following April, it fared
no better. Marcus Berkmann called it an 'ingenious, serpentine
psychological thriller' in the *Daily Mail*, but most of his colleagues
were less enraptured. 'There is none of the perverse edginess that
characterises earlier Polanski three-handers, such as *Knife in the
Water* or *Cul-de-Sac*... I found myself longing for the more peculiar
sloppiness of *Pirates* or *Bitter Moon*,' Anne Bilson confessed in
the *Sunday Telegraph*, while the *Independent on Sunday*'s Quentin
Curtis began his review by taking the accepted link between
artist and art to a new and novel extreme: 'The themes of Ariel
Dorfman's *Death and the Maiden* are mournfully appropriate to its
director Roman Polanski's life and work: political oppression, rape
and blind vengeance.' His readers had to work out for themselves
where the element of 'blind vengeance' came in, but *The Observer*'s
Philip French opened his piece with an equally contentious

statement. 'Though his films continue to excite great expectations and generate attendant publicity, Roman Polanski has not (with the possible exception of *Tess*) directed a work of consequence for 20 years. Sadly [*Death and the Maiden*], while competently made and moderately gripping, is a commonplace affair...'

*   *   *

While critics like French talked of a fallow period in Polanski's oeuvre between *Chinatown* and *Death and the Maiden*, all that actually had happened was that the kind of subject with which Polanski dealt most effectively had simply gone out of fashion. Small-scale human dramas of the *Bitter Moon* and *Death and the Maiden* variety were being brutally swept aside by the sudden impact of CGI – computer-generated imaging – which was showcased in 1993 by Steven Spielberg's $63 million adaptation of Michael Crichton's novel *Jurassic Park*; Spielberg's film had featured an island filled with cloned dinosaurs which, for the first time on screen, looked so realistic that one could almost smell their foetid breath as they stomped and slavered through a cod-scientific reworking of *King Kong*. Overnight, the film-going experience was changed out of all recognition as conventional dramas were elbowed aside in the rush to product whose sole purpose was to showcase the work of 'digital artists' – a new breed of film technician whose contribution to a production was now perceived to be more important than even that of a director. The cinema was returning to its early days as a visual spectacle, when audiences went to gawp and gape at a screen on which trains arrived at stations or actors kissed in close-up, simply because they could not believe what they were seeing. For years after the arrival of *Jurassic Park*, as the computer-wizards honed their alchemical skills, the narrative film took a back seat to that in which all manner of wondrous creatures descended on plots from land, sea and air. What began as a modern miracle of technology soon palled through repetition and the ridiculousness of the excesses which undisciplined directors were able to commit to celluloid in their pursuit of the next big cinematic thrill.

This automaton form of filmmaking – empty and shallow and deprived of a human scale at worst – was alien to every belief which Roman Polanski held dear in relation to the art of film, as well as every principle that he had practised since his first fumblings with a camera in 1955. He may have been out of sympathy with the latest advances but he still had his reputation as a filmmaker of importance, and that alone ensured that he remained able to mount new projects with relative ease.

Neither *Bitter Moon* nor *Death and the Maiden* had caused so much as a flicker of the needle on the box-office register, but Polanski's ability to attract big-name talent to his films remained undiminished and, in 1996, few were bigger than John Travolta. The career of the iconic star of director John Badham's 1977 disco classic *Saturday Night Fever* was undergoing something of a renaissance after his recent showings in Quentin Tarantino's cult-hit *Pulp Fiction* and Barry Sonnenfeld's *Get Shorty*, and Polanski cast him along with John Goodman and *The Tenant*'s Isabelle Adjani in a comedy-thriller called *The Double*, about an American accountant in Paris who is haunted by a doppelganger.

Prior to hiring Travolta on behalf of production companies Mandalay and Sony at an astronomical salary of $17 million, Polanski had called Tarantino discuss his choice of star. 'If you hire John, be prepared to not know what you're going to get,' Tarantino had advised him. 'He's not a predictable actor. I have no idea what choices he's going to make, and they're always different from what I expect.' In May 1996, Travolta flew over to Paris from LA just as Harrison Ford, Peter Coyote and Sigourney Weaver had before him – the difference in his case was that *he* then flew straight back again.

According to Travolta, the screenplay that was presented to him two weeks before shooting was due to commence was radically different to the one for which he had signed on in Hollywood. 'The interpretation was a broad comedy, where I had in mind more of a subtle comedy. Then it spread more into slapstick and I didn't know how to do it,' he explained to journalist Douglas Thompson. 'I had approval, and I arrived in Paris and there were changes and I didn't know how to do the movie, the new movie they wanted me to make. I love strong directors. I just think that there's only one simple point: you have to agree on the movie you're making and that's everybody's right. If you're offered A and then you're given B, you say wait a minute..'

Travolta made his excuses and left the set – the excuse being that his 4-year-old son Jett was in need of an ear operation and he wished to join his wife Kelly Preston at the boy's hospital bedside. As it happened, an operation proved unnecessary, but it quickly became clear to all concerned in the production of *The Double* that John Travolta now had no intention of returning to Paris. As lawyers from both camps began to circle, the film's producers cast comedian Steve Martin to replace their absented star at a 'reduced' salary of $12 million. Meanwhile, rumours began to surface in the press on the nature of the rift which had opened up between Travolta and Polanski – that what lay at the heart of the matter was Polanski's autocratic behaviour, or that he had required his star to do an unscripted nude scene. 'I liked Roman a lot,' Travolta corrected. 'He was a charming fellow but it wasn't about that. It was about viewpoints on a movie and it wasn't the movie I was presented with originally. It was a different one.'

When confirmation came that Travolta was not for (re)turning, Isabelle Adjani also pulled out of the film, citing as her reason the fact that she had signed to work with the star of *Saturday Night Fever*, not that of *Father of the Bride*. Seeing what could have been a good film go rapidly bad, Polanski followed suit and relinquished his director's chair. Mandalay then filed suit against Travolta alleging breach of contract; he, in turn, counter-sued that the company had reneged on its promise of a second starring-role. In the midst of the turmoil, *The Double* was shelved indefinitely. (Suit and counter-suit were not disposed of until May 2001, when an out-of-court settlement was reached which Travolta attorney Richard Posell considered to be 'to everyone's satisfaction'.)

*   *   *

After the debacle over *The Double*, Polanski's preferred two-to-three year interval between projects turned inevitably into another five-year hiatus. By 1997, two subjects had caught his attention, however – a memoir by a concert pianist about his experiences in the Warsaw Ghetto during the Nazi occupation of 1943-4, and an esoteric novel by a Spanish author named Arturo Pérez-Reverte, called *El club Dumas*.

In looking to compete with the megabucks effects epics which were proliferating in cinemas, the second of these two possible subjects seemed to Polanski to represent the better bet – especially as the story involved an element of 'black magic', reminiscent of the heady days of *Rosemary's Baby*. Nevertheless, it was typical of his nonconformist streak – even in the face of the so-called digital revolution – that his new feature would revolve around a medium in which imagery is conjured in the mind's eye, instead of on a computer-screen. When Polanski next set foot inside Epinay Studios, in the spring of 1998, it was to make a film about *books*.

> *"Who are you?"*
> *"The Devil," she said. "The Devil in love."*
> *And she laughed. The book by Cazotte was on the sideboard, next to the Memoirs of Saint-Helena and some papers. The girl looked at it but didn't touch it. Then she laid one finger on it and looked at Corso.*
> *"Do you believe in the Devil?"*
> *"I'm paid to believe in him. On this job anyway."*
>
> **Arturo Pérez-Reverte**, *El club Dumas* (1993)

Pérez-Reverte's novel is a brilliantly-realised literary puzzle, which is designed to play a clever trick on the reader's perception in the same way that its protagonist, rare book-dealer Lucas Corso, is wrong-footed by his own reading of the mysterious events to which he finds himself party in the course of the narrative. Corso is hired by one Varo Borja, the owner of a treatise on demonology called 'The Nine Doors to the Kingdom of Shadows', to seek out the other two copies of the book which are known to exist. At the same time, Corso is trying to authenticate a manuscript which purports to be a missing chapter from Alexandre Dumas' *The Three Musketeers*. The two plots become imperceptibly interwoven, to the extent that Corso imagines himself being pursued by devilish agents in the form of well-known characters from Dumas' renowned adventure-serial. But straddling these strands is a third, which involves a strange, green-eyed girl, who believes that she is one of the angels fallen from Heaven in Lucifer's battle with God; this last thread supplies the tale with its conclusion, although much of the black-magical chicanery which has preceded it is merely a blind to mask the main plot, the secret of which gives the novel its title.

Despite its evident complexity and reputation as 'difficult' novel, it was *El club Dumas* which Roman Polanski had now chosen to film as *The Ninth Gate*. 'It's all very convoluted, one of those rambling books; enjoyable and literary, with clever observations; very erudite,' he told Cynthia Fuchs. 'The problem was how to make a movie out of it, because at first glance, it really doesn't look like it's possible. We had to abandon a lot of elements, because a movie must be much more rigorous. But I had no hesitation, because I knew it would be fun to do.'

(Another attraction of Pérez-Reverte's novel for Polanski was the fact that the story took place predominately in France, Spain and Portugal, so it could be adapted to the screen without having to set foot outside Europe; notwithstanding, he set a sequence at the beginning of the film in New York [as opposed to the novel's Toledo], which he cheekily accomplished by the imperceptible employment of CGI. The tale also held out the prospect of a featured role for his wife.)

The genesis of *The Ninth Gate* dated back to 1997 and the period immediately after the collapse of *The Double*. Polanski had been sent a copy of a screenplay which had been adapted from Pérez-Reverte's novel by fellow Spaniard Enrique Urbizu. He had been intrigued enough to want to read the novel himself, and with his collaborator John Brownjohn, he had set about redrafting Urbizu's script. 'We did quite extensive work on the script,' he told Caroline Vie. 'The story was very complex and we were obliged to simplify it a lot for the screen version. Even if the avid reader in me is sorry we had to cut parts from the book, I knew as a director that it was unavoidable.'

Essentially, what Polanski and Brownjohn did was to jettison the primary narrative of the novel, that of the missing chapter from *The Three Musketeers*, and enlarge on the secondary, that of 'The Nine Doors'; they then utilised the action from the first to provide the storyline for the second. The strange girl was retained in all her ambiguous, otherworldly glory. Thus their retitled *The Ninth Gate* became a supernatural thriller, in which the rechristened *Dean Corso* is pursued across Europe by Devil-worshippers while he searches for the elusive grimoires. 'I liked the supernatural part of the book and it was one of the reasons I made the movie. The Devil is a good protagonist for films, plays, books... I'm not a believer myself and I have a hard time to talk about the Devil without humour or irony, but I must say that he's a good guy to make a film about – even if you don't see him,' Polanski reminded those in the press who sought to question his motives in making the film. But the hope was that Old Nick would elicit a quite different reaction from on an audience.

BALKAN BUILDING: COLLECTION. INT/NIGHT.

    BALKAN
    Ever heard of the 'Delomelanicon'?

```
                    CORSO
                    Heard of it, yes. A myth, isn't it? Some
                    horrific book reputed to have been written by
                    Satan himself.

                    BALKAN
                    No myth. That book existed. Torchia actually
                    acquired it.

          He returns to the window overlooking the sheer
          drop. Gazing down, he goes on:

                    BALKAN
                    (cont.)
                    The engravings you're now admiring were
                    adapted by Torchia from the 'Delomelanicon'.
                    They're a form of satanic riddle. Correctly
                    interpreted with the aid of the original text
                    and sufficient inside information, they're
                    reputed to conjure up the Prince of Darkness
                    in person.
```

Screenplay, *The Ninth Gate* (1998)

From the first, Polanski had in mind a 'look' for Corso that was more in keeping with the description of him in the novel as a world-weary soldier of fortune. 'From a hidden packet he brought out an unfiltered cigarette that was as crumpled as his old overcoat and corduroy trousers. He turned it over in his fingers, watching me through steel-rimmed glasses, set crookedly on his nose under his untidy fringe of slightly greying hair.' During his usual attendance at Cannes, Polanski had been approached by another young American actor in the Travolta mould, but one who as yet was without a *Saturday Night Fever* to his name. The 33-year-old Johnny Depp was in competition with his self-directed film *The*

Brave, and though a major hit had so far eluded him, he had shown
a willingness to experiment and to work with interesting directors,
such as Tim Burton (*Edward Scissorhands; Ed Wood*), Jim Jarmusch
(*Dead Man*) and Terry Gilliam (*Fear and Loathing in Las Vegas*).
Polanski was unconvinced by Depp's age and even more youthful
appearance, but when finally he gave him a copy of *The Ninth Gate*
to read, the young Kentuckian set out to persuade the director
that he was right for the part. 'He convinced me that age didn't
matter that much,' Polanski explained. 'I came to understand that
people like Corso tend to mature very young. Their character and
reputation are formed when they're in their thirties.'

To play the shrewd and cynical Corso, Depp adopted a guise of
goatee and glasses, as well as greying his hair a little at the temples
and functioning with a marked economy of movement; all of
Corso's agility is of the mental variety. 'Johnny has an extraordinary
and spontaneous way of giving his own rhythm to a character,'
Polanski said. 'It seems quite natural for him and you never feel
like he's making any effort whatsoever. His work was brilliant. The
Corso that you see on the screen is exactly the one I had in mind
before hiring Johnny.'

The excellent but undervalued Frank Langella was cast as
villain-in-chief Boris Balkan (who is actually the narrator in the
novel, but whose alliterative name was felt by Polanski to be more
suitable for the film than Pérez-Reverte's Varo Borja), a millionaire
dealer in antiquarian texts, who hires Corso to substantiate the
provenance of the pride of his private occult collection: an arcane
text entitled 'The Nine Gates to the Kingdom of Shadows', which
reputedly enables its owner to summon up the Devil himself.
Langella was still best-known for his performance as Count
Dracula in John Badham's 1979 remake of Universal's vampire
classic, and Polanski had nothing but good words to say about him
after seeing his performance in Adrian Lyne's *Lolita* the previous
year: 'Frank is charming and disturbing at the same time,' he said.
'He was a great sport. We almost burned him one time, when his

character was on fire. And I love his voice, which was extremely important since he exists in this movie over the telephone, for most of it.'

The role of the Devil(?) in the film, referred to only as 'The Girl' in the credits, accordingly was given to Polanski's wife, the ethereal-looking Emmanuelle Seigner. Another actress originally had auditioned for the part: Vanessa Paradis, the 25-year-old chanteuse of 1988's 'Joe le Taxi' fame, had been building a new career for herself in films, and she was presently in Paris shooting the low-budget *La Fille sur le pont* (*The Girl on the Bridge*) for director Patrice Leconte-her first since recovering from the broken leg which she had acquired in a snowmobile accident in Canada five months before. Paradis may have failed to impress Roman Polanski enough to be cast in *The Ninth Gate*, but she had the opposite effect on Johnny Depp.

As Depp and his director dined out amid the marble-and-glass opulence of the exclusive Hotel Costes K, at 81 Avenue Kleber in the heart of Paris, he saw Paradis seated nearby. Depp invited her to join them, and a passionate relationship was formed which resulted in Paradis becoming pregnant. The press-pack was quickly alerted to the news: 'He would come to work shattered sometimes, because the photographers would make his and Vanessa's life miserable,' Polanski recalled. When shooting of the film was over, Depp and Paradis set up home together in France. If *The Ninth Gate* did nothing else for Johnny Depp, it introduced him to the woman with whom he subsequently was to have two children and who shares his life to this day.

> *There have been men who have been burned alive, or disembowelled, for just a glimpse of what you are about to witness.*
> **Boris Balkan (Frank Langella)**, *The Ninth Gate* (1998)

The premise of *The Ninth Gate* is conventional enough: Balkan has tried out the invocation which he thought was contained in

his copy of 'The Nine Gates' but has failed in his efforts to raise
the Devil. Surmising something to be amiss, he hires Corso
to find and examine the other two copies, to see if there are
discrepancies between them; the singular attribute of the grimoire
is its nine elusive engravings. The story then devolves to Corso's
pan-European search for the remaining books, and the resultant
game of spot-the-difference as he finds that only *three* out of nine
illustrations in each copy are genuine, inasmuch as they are signed
LCF – Lucifer himself. But Balkan has followed close behind, and
he now steals the other two books after murdering their owners:
his plan is to combine the three sets of genuine woodcuts into an
entirety, and make the magic spell complete. His ultimate aim is
power, of a kind which only Satan can grant him.

Corso's search for the various copies of 'The Nine Gates' takes
him first to Toledo, where twin brothers named Ceniza reveal to
him the secret of how to spot the genuine engravings. However,
Liana Tellfer (Lina Olin), the leader of a satanic coven called The
Order of the Silver Serpent, is also on his tail; Tellfer originally
was the owner of Balkan's copy of 'The Nine Gates', which Corso
carries with him, and she wants it back. Throughout, Corso is
aided by a mysterious girl who seems to have supernatural powers.
Events come to a head when Balkan gatecrashes a Black Mass and
strangles Tellfer, who by this time has recovered her own copy.
With all three books finally in his possession, Balkan retreats to the
Devil's Tower, his castle in Portugal, to invoke his Dark Master. But
the elaborate spell goes awry, and after Balkan inadvertently sets
himself ablaze, Corso delivers the coup de grâce by shooting him
dead. It transpires that the ninth engraving was a fake engineered
by the Cenizas; Corso returns to their former workshop and
obtains the real one, and the Ninth Gate opens up for him..

*   *   *

Contrary to critical expectation, which seemed to be suffused with
fond memories of *Rosemary's Baby* of more than thirty years before,

The Ninth Gate is not so much a horror film as another homage to Hitchcock with supernatural overtones. The film has more in common with Polanski's Hitchcockian *Frantic* than it does with his adaptation of Ira Levin's seminal satanic novel of 1967, even though the director referred to it as a cross between that and his Oscar-winning *Chinatown*. There are other influences also, as *Se7en* cinematographer Darius Khondji recalled: 'Roman kept reminding me about *Touch of Evil* by Orson Welles. We watched that film together, and we both liked its sense of darkness; we decided that feeling was one side of *The Ninth Gate*.' The other side was exotic location-shooting in Spain, Portugal and France, where Polanski found Balkan's *tour de Diable* in the 14th century Puivert Castle at Aude, in the French Pyrennees. But not New York, because of Polanski's outstanding arrest-warrant. The scenes in the Big Apple were all created at the Epinay Studios in Paris, including that of Balkan's library aerie at the top of his personal skyscraper. As Corso examines 'The Nine Gates', Balkan stands before a window that stretches from floor to ceiling and gazes down upon the world of men from on high, as did Satan in the Old Testament. 'Don't you get dizzy standing there?' Corso asks him, in a scene that brings to mind the real-life meeting between Polanski and his LA lawyer Douglas Dalton.

Depp plays the enigmatic Corso with the imperturbability of Cary Grant, reacting to the disturbing events in which he finds himself embroiled with contained concern and a nice line in dry wit: 'I had thought about it, yes,' he says, a faintly hysterical edge to his voice, when asked by The Girl if he would like to gain entry to a house whose owner he has found dead in a fish-pond. Khondji also input into the characterisation of Corso: 'I had to take into account that Johnny was playing a character with two sides,' he said. 'We present the Dean Corso character as very ambiguous. He definitely has a dark, cold side, but at the same time there's a side of him we don't know about, so it was a simple decision to half-light him throughout.'

There is one aspect of the film which stands out uniquely in relation to the changes that were going on in the industry at the time of its making. An enormous number of process shots were required in post-production, from the early scenes in New York City through to the fiery skies which frame the 'Devil's Tower' at the climax, but *The Ninth Gate* is that rare beast of a fantasy film in that few of them are detectable, so well-integrated are they into the tapestry of the piece as a whole. The most blatant are two brief shots in which The Girl appears to 'fly', and the occasional use of demonic eyes of the now-you-see-it, now-you-don't variety. But even the fact that no less than *two* pairs of two characters in the story are played by the same actor in the same shot (one of whose voices was dubbed by Polanski himself) is likely to pass unnoticed before the eyes of the average viewer. 'I used more post-production tricks on this film than on any film before,' Polanski said.

A significant cameo is provided by Barbara Jefford OBE, as the wheelchair-bound Baroness Kessler, whose area of expertise is Old Nick. German actress Hildegard Knef originally was cast in the role but she caught pneumonia and a replacement found the lines too difficult to learn in English; Polanski called Jefford in a state of panic and persuaded her to step in at short notice, German accent and all. 'When we realised we had no actress and we couldn't change the schedule for the scene, I was quite desperate and I called Barbara; I was literally begging her to do the role.' At least Jefford did not have to lose her arm to play the Baroness – an amputee as well as a paraplegic – 'which would have been cheaper,' Polanski joked; CGI was employed in this instance also, to paint out the real limb in post-production.

The woodcuts which are seen in the film appear in the published version of *El club Dumas*, but they incorporate subtle differences. 'I kept part of the illustrations shown in *The Dumas Club*,' Polanski explained. 'But I had the characters' faces altered for some of them, to look a bit like the actors in the film.' Some of this authorial addenda was contributed late in the day, as shooting progressed, and it brings an unwelcome element of confusion to the finished piece. *Balkan* is the killer of at least three out of the story's four murder victims and he confesses as much in the original script, yet the etching that Corso is working on when he is knocked unconscious in the Baroness's library (a scene which is shot in a manner reminiscent of the murder of Colin in *Repulsion*), and which depicts the murder of Corso's bookseller buddy, shows Tellfer's albino henchman committing the deed. Whether Polanski chose consciously to muddy the waters along the way is a matter of conjecture, but his final cut differs markedly from what was intended prior to filming.

The major alteration comes at the climax. The screenplay had only the revelation that the Ceniza brothers – the old forgers who put Corso on the track of 'The Nine Gates' – had long been dead before apparently he spoke to them, and that The Girl was the Devil all along. In other words, there *was* a supernatural element to the story, but Corso only realised it in the closing scene, when the final engraving of the Whore of Babylon sitting astride the seven-headed beast is in his hands and he is startled to note her resemblance to The Girl who has helped him to obtain it. He walks away, his cynical belief-system shattered forever. 'She can be interpreted as the Devil, who takes an appearance which is more suitable for the work he has to do,' Polanski explained.

This rather feeble ending was subject to drastic revision when the film was on the floor – one which brought it more in line with the closing passages of the novel. Corso has sex with the girl as the Devil's Tower burns behind them, during which her face 'morphs' almost imperceptibly, but quite chillingly, between a demon persona and that of Liana Tellfer. The pact is thus sealed, and Corso retrieves the last engraving of the Whore from the Cenizas' workshop, which is now revealed to have been a front for agents of the Devil (the original brothers are replaced by two workmen, and all four are played by the same Jóse López Rodero, who was also production manager on the film). He returns to the castle and walks through the Ninth Gate in a white-out of light, where the Devil waits to greet him.

Few critics were to grasp the significance of this finale, which contributed towards the hostile reception which *The Ninth Gate* was subsequently to receive. A trickster to the last, Polanski had made the narrative too obtuse for its own commercial good by removing the scripted reference to Balkan's culpability for the murders (thus positing a number of suspects; there are *no* murders in the novel), and adding ambiguities which encourage an alternative reading of the plot; several scenes now invite the possibility that Corso himself is the Devil, even though this is shown to be erroneous by internal logic. But it provides for a fascinating collage of hints and allusions, all the same, and it produces an exercise in satanic game-play that turns *The Ninth Gate* into a worthy addition to the *ars diavoli*, as Boris Balkan might have put it.

To remove any doubt about who the Devil actually *is* in *The Ninth Gate*, the clue was meant to have been the book which The Girl was to have been reading in the lobby of Corso's hotel in Sintra, Portugal. Novel and original screenplay both have this as *The Devil in Love* (*Le Diable amoureux*), a Gothic fantasy by French author Jacques Cazotte, dating from 1772, in which the hero falls in love with the Devil in his *female* form, under the name of Biondetta. ('The truth is that the Devil is very cunning. The truth is that he is not always as ugly as they say.') Polanski substituted Dale Carnegie's much less obvious *How to Make Friends and Influence People* for the film. It won him few admirers.

By November 1999, more than a year after its completion, *The Ninth Gate* was still awaiting release, but advance screenings did not bode well for its chances. When it did eventually open in the US on Christmas Eve and in the UK the following June, reviews were downbeat and its performance in both territories followed the pattern which had been set by its immediate predecessors. 'Leaping Lucifer! Is it possible that Polanski, the legendary director of *Repulsion*, *Rosemary's Baby* and *Chinatown* concocted this bloodless,

soulless and airless affair?' Carrie Rickey asked in Philadelphia's
Enquirer. *The Washington Post*'s Stephen Hunter thought to
damn the film by conjuring images from the Delomelanicon:
'Polanski, generally, has fallen farther than Lucifer, and into a more
profoundly depressing hell, the hell of utter banality,' he wailed.
An example of the best that Polanski could find to give him a shred
of critical comfort came from Jami Bernard in New York's *Daily
News*, who thought the film a 'sly and elegant detective story'.
More typical was *The Observer*: 'The end is neither frightening nor
funny, pure Eurotosh,' Peter Preston wrote. 'No wonder Depp,
toiling quietly away, looks dazed and confused'. With the benefit
of a five-year interval for reflection, the most rigorous assessment
of the film has come from F X Feeney, in an excellent coffee-table
tome on Polanski which was published in 2006: '*The Ninth Gate*
is the least appreciated, most richly ambiguous and most unjustly
neglected of Polanski's best films.' More than that, it is one of the
best horror films ever made.

* * *

Unlike the last two of Polanski's films, *The Ninth Gate* eventually
went on to make $58 million against an estimated budget of $38
million – although it did better in Europe and the rest of the world
than it did in the US.

   The Ninth Gate has a nice, old-fashioned feel to it, and is none
the worse for that. The pace is measured and stately, as befitting
its subject: rare and expensive old books. 'I loved the idea of a
book being the hero of a movie.' Polanski said. 'I don't believe it's
ever been done before. That's one of the reasons why the script
appealed to me.' The plot's reverence for the mystical reputation
of the fictitious 'Nine Gates of the Kingdom of Shadows' extended
to the director's treatment of it in the film: 'I really considered the
book as a whole character,' he continued. 'I designed the pentacle
for the cover, and chose its colour and size as I would have done
for an actor.' Polanski's single-minded desire to exercise his usual

measure of control over all the elements of the production was not to everyone's taste, however – including that of Johnny Depp.

If John Travolta had refused to state publicly that he found it difficult to work with Polanski's style of director, Depp felt no such compunction. After completing his next role as a pioneering police detective in Tim Burton's film of Washington Irving's *The Legend of Sleepy Hollow*, he made no bones about their lack of rapport: 'Working with Tim Burton on *Sleepy Hollow* was like an exorcism,' he said. 'It was a cleansing from my *Ninth Gate* experience. It was not an easy film to make. Roman is pretty set in his ways. I'd heard things about his methods but I decided to see for myself,' he continued. 'He didn't tell me how to say my lines. If he had, I'd probably be in some French jail – but he's definitely out there in his own world.' At least Depp stayed the course with his demonic director, which was more than could be said for Travolta.

> CORSO: *I'm sorry, Baroness, were you in the middle of something?*
> BARONESS KESSLER: *My latest work – 'The Devil, History and Myth'. A kind of biography. It will be published early next year.*
> CORSO: *Why the Devil?*
> BARONESS KESSLER: *I saw him one day. I was 15 years old... and I saw him as plain as I see you now. It was love at first sight.*
>
> **Johnny Depp and Barbara Jefford,** *The Ninth Gate* (1998)

In the wake of the uninspiring returns from *The Ninth Gate*, Artisan Entertainment, makers of the film, filed suit in LA's District Court against Roman Polanski, claiming that he and his R P Productions had siphoned off refunds of value-added tax instead of turning them over to the completion guarantors who acted on Artisan's behalf during the shoot. Polanski was alleged to have received $619,000 in refunds, with another $577,000 on the way, and to have 'brazenly deposited the money in a private account,' refusing all requests for its return.

Two years earlier, the previously unnamed victim of the 'rape' case which changed the course of Polanski's life had gone public for the first time, under her married name of Samantha Geimer. Now a twice-married mother of three, living quietly with her sons and second husband on the Hawaiian island of Kauai, Geimer had granted an interview to syndicated US television news-show *Inside Edition*, in which she stated that she had neither been raped nor harmed by Polanski in 1977. Whether this sudden outburst was one of a genuine concern for justice to be served or merely part of another concerted attempt by Polanski's supporters in America to have his fugitive status lifted became a matter of public debate, especially when the likes of the *Daily Telegraph* fell to quoting show business lawyer Eric Weissman as saying that 'every agent in town would love to represent him. I think directors who have scored great hits and are believed to have unusual talents are always in demand...'

Whatever the truth of the revival of interest in Polanski's fortunes, the pleas of Geimer, Weissman and the rest fell on deaf ears. As the millennium dawned, Roman Polanski was no closer to resolving his conflict with the biblically-unforgiving Los Angeles court authorities than he had been 23 years before; to the contrary, a new lawsuit was about to be filed against him, adding fraud and deception to the catalogue of his crimes. On a brighter note, his wife had presented him with a son to complement their daughter who, at six years of age, already had made her screen debut in *The Ninth Gate*, playing opposite Johnny Depp.

Like that involving Mandalay and Travolta over *The Double*, Artisan's suit against Polanski was eventually to be settled amicably and out of court, but his own battle with the LA District Attorney's office was to rumble on for years. He had lost much because of it, but the greatest loss that he could suffer from his inability to set foot on American soil was still to come.

A POLISH BOY'S PROGRESS

*It's already getting more and more difficult to make an ambitious
and original film. There are less and less independent producers or
independent companies and an increasing number of corporations
who are more interested in balance sheets than in artistic
achievement. They want to make a killing each time they produce
a film. They're only interested in the lowest common denominator
because they're trying to reach the widest audience... But then,
from time to time, you have a film like* The Usual Suspects *or...
I'm trying to think of something American with some kind of
originality...* Pulp Fiction.'

Roman Polanski, talking to Taylor Montague (1996)

Reflecting on his past while playing the role of Mozart in
his 1981 stage adaptation of Peter Schaffer's *Amadeus*,
Polanski wrote, 'It dawned on me that there was a
theatrical thread running through my life, with its triumphs and
tragedies, joys and sorrows, intense love and unimagined grief.'
It was only fitting, therefore, that the drama should come full
circle and be returned to where it began, like *The Vampire Killers*
or *The Tenant* or others of his films which had adopted such a
stratagem.

Polanski's films no longer were creating the stir that once they
did. *The Ninth Gate* showed that he was directing as well as ever
– better – but his style had become passé, his ability to shock had
been superseded by that of younger directors for whom no holds
were barred, and his personal cinematic preoccupations had been

swamped by a deluge of effects-laden spectacles against which his human-centric dramas could not compete.

At the turn of the millennium, Roman Polanski was in his 66th year; he now had a young wife, a seven-year-old daughter and a son of almost two. For the first time in his life, there were more important things than films, unless a film happened to come along which was more important than anything. In many respects, the millennium represented the end of an era; it was consigning the 20th century to history; a century which would be remembered as one of great progress – in the arts; in science – and of great conflicts: the 20th century had bestowed two cataclysmic wars on the world, the second of which had taken Polanski's mother and turned him into the man that he was. It was a time to look back and remember. The invasion of Poland – the air-assault on Warsaw – the occupation of Krakow – the rounding-up of the Jews – the Ghetto – the camps... The loss of innocence on the bloodstained streets... It was all a long time ago, but it had been brought back to him with some force in an autobiographical memoir by a Polish concert pianist named Wladyslaw Szpilman, and by a play called *Taking Sides*, which was written in 1995 by Ronald Harwood and had much in common with Dorfman's *Death and the Maiden*, in that again it involved the question of guilt or innocence, but in relation to the conductor of the Berlin Philharmonic during World War II. Almost a decade before, Polanski had been offered the director's chair on the Universal production of *Schindler's List*, but he had not then felt ready to face the ghosts of his past; in 2000, through his affinity with the sights and sensations in Szpilman's book, he finally decided that the time was right to return to the Ghetto of his childhood – and to pay a tribute of his own to those who had suffered there.

Szpilman's book was entitled *The Pianist*, but it was published originally as *Death of a City* (*Smierc Miasta*), in 1946, when the period to which it refers was still fresh in its author's memory. Interest in the book in Poland was revived during the 1960s, but the country's then-Communist authorities were less than enthusiastic about Szpilman's spin on events, so further publication was thwarted. The retitled edition did not appear in the West until 1999, through Victor Gollancz, and in a translation by Anthea Bell. The narrative of *The Pianist* is an account of one man's odyssey into Danté's Ninth Circle of Hell and back again, as Jewish pianist Wladyslaw Szpilman escapes persecution by the Nazis who have invaded his Polish homeland through a combination of chance and circumstance, and by having to live for years like a hunted animal.

> *A businessman's family lived in the flat directly opposite ours; we knew them well by sight. When the light went on there too and SS men in helmets stormed into the room, machine pistols ready to fire, the people inside were sitting around their table just as we had been seated at ours a moment ago. They were frozen with horror. The NCO leading the detachment took this as a personal insult. Speecheless with indignation, he stood there in silence, stunning the people at the table. Only after a moment or so did he shout, in a towering rage, 'Stand up!'*
>
> *They rose to their feet as fast as they could, all except for the head of the family, an old man with lame legs. The NCO was seething with anger. He went up to the table, braced his arms on it, stared hard at the cripple, and growled for the second time, 'Stand up!'*
>
> *The old man gripped the arms of his chair to support himself and made desperate efforts to stand, but in vain. Before we realised what was going on, the Germans had seized the sick man, picked him up, armchair and all, carried the chair onto the balcony, and thrown it out into the street from the third floor.*
>
> **Wladyslaw Szpilman**, *The Pianist* (1999)

Polanski's choice of screenwriter for his film version of Szpilman's book had been made for him by *Taking Sides*. He contacted Ronald

Harwood, whose previous credits included *The Dresser* (1983) and *Cry the Beloved Country* (1995), and offered him the job; Harwood readily agreed. As was his practice, Polanski greeted Harwood's original draft by requesting that the two of them be locked away for a month in a chateau in the French countryside, in order to knock it into better shape; a final polish was achieved over a couple of days at the director's villa in Ibiza. This was par-for-the-course for a writer when it came to working with Polanski now – he had employed the same methodology since his days of battling with Robert Towne on *Chinatown*, back in 1972.

To play the 'pianist', Polanski initially had in mind British actor Joseph Fiennes, younger brother of Ralph, who had essayed the title-role in playwright Tom Stoppard's Oscar-winning *Shakespeare in Love* (1998) and more recently had starred as a Russian commissar alongside Jude Law in *Enemy at the Gates*. Polanski had been in touch with the real Szpilman and there were photographs of the musician from the relevant period, all of which convinced him that Fiennes was his man. But Fiennes turned the role down in favour of one of his habitual returns to the theatre and, in September 2000, Polanski held an 'open audition' in London in a new attempt to cast the lead; of the 1400 or so wannabe movie stars who turned up at the Covent Garden Actors Centre, none proved to be suitable. Rumour had it that American actor Adrien Brody had already been cast in the film in place of Fiennes and that the audition, advertisements for which had been accompanied by a picture of Fiennes and a request for someone 'sensitive, vulnerable and charismatic', was an elaborate practical joke by Polanski in response to the rebuff by his original choice.

(In one of life's tragic ironies, Wladyslaw Szpilman died on July 6, 2000, just a few months before his moving testament to endurance and the will to survive against the odds went into production. He was 88 years old. 'No other director could make this film,' he had told his son Andrzej after meeting with Polanski.)

Polanski had met Brody in Paris while the latter was working on *The Affair of the Necklace*. The New York-born Brody was actually half-Hungarian on his mother's side and Polanski thought him perfect for the role. Brody, for his part, more than justified his director's faith in him: 'I was very excited about getting this role and in an effort to be as truthful as possible, I decided to get rid of my apartment, drop my phone lines, sell my car, basically lose touch with most people that I knew aside from a few key friends and loved ones, and because the character loses so much, I wanted to kind of have a glimpse of what that loss would feel like.' If that were not enough, there was the matter of the piano-playing to contend with: 'I stopped listening to my kind of music, and I cut out television; I would have piano lessons every day because it was very important for Roman that I learned to play, so he could actually use it, and fortunately I was able to pick up a lot pretty quickly. I practised all the time, and I starved myself, because the character basically didn't eat for quite a long period of time, so I couldn't eat very much for a while and I lost about 30 pounds.'

Principal photography on the film commenced on February 19, 2001, at an outdoor set of Warsaw which had been constructed at Babelsberg Studios near Berlin; cast and crew subsequently moved on to locations in the actual city itself. The Warsaw scenes were filmed in Praga, a part of the city that already was under Russian control when the German army razed the remainder to the ground; consequently, it has survived as it was to the present day. The shots of a ruined Warsaw which appear later in the film were obtained at a former Soviet army barracks which were due for demolition – the filmmakers cut a deal with the military authorities to do the job for them. CGI could have 'painted' in this set, but Polanski typically preferred a more realistic approach. He had decided at the outset that the subject of *The Pianist* was not one which lent itself to technical trickery or any other form of *auteural* intrusion which might detract from the raw impact of the drama. 'The way it was – no more, no less,' was his concept of how the story should be told. 'There were good Poles and bad Poles, the same goes with the Jews, the same with the Germans. They are simply human. The book was like this and that is why I was attracted to it,' he explained.

The Pianist producer Gene Gutowski, with whom Polanski had renewed their working relationship after a gap of nearly 30 years to mount the film, told Marilyn Cole Lownes, wife of Victor, a personal memory of the production: 'It was during the projection of some really gruesome documentary films that the Germans had made for propaganda purposes. They had shot the film in the ghetto, showing these horrible scenes of starving people. We had to look at these films before starting our picture to assure historical accuracy. We had three days of relentless screenings of this kind of footage. I remember at one particular moment in the screening room, the lights suddenly went on and I saw that Roman was crying. He said, "Only now that I am a father, that I have my own children, do I realise fully what went on – the terrible horror of it all."

'I think Roman realises that, after all the pictures he has made, this may well be the most important film of his life – the one for which he will be most remembered.'

```
INT. WARSAW APARTMENT - NIGHT

The family are gathered around the table,
listening to FATHER reading from the newspaper.

The apartment has even less furniture now. The
paintings are gone.

     FATHER
     (reading)
     'Re: emblems for Jews in the Warsaw District.
     I hereby order that all Jews in the Warsaw
```

```
District will wear visible emblems when out
of doors. This decree will come into force
on the 1st December 1939 and applies to all
Jews over 12 years of age. The emblem will be
worn on the right sleeve and will represent a
blue Star of David on a white background. The
background must be sufficiently large for the
Star to measure 8 centimetres from point to
point. The width of the arms of the Star must
be 1 centimetre. Jews who do not respect this
decree will be severely punished. Governor of
Warsaw District, Dr Fischer.

Silence. Then:

HENRYK
I won't wear it.

REGINA
I won't wear it. I'm not going to be branded —
```

Screenplay, *The Pianist* (2002)

Wladyslaw Szpilman is a classical pianist with Polish Radio
when war breaks out in Europe in August 1939. He, his parents,
his brother Henryk and his sisters Regina and Halina all refuse
to leave their home in Warsaw in the belief that with Britain
and France declaring war on Germany, Hitler's Third Reich
will swiftly be defeated. They are proved tragically wrong when
the German army marches into Warsaw and places the Polish
capital under marshal law. Soon, the pogrom begins and Jews are
singled out for 'special' treatment: first, they are forced to wear
armbands emblazoned with the Star of David and subjected to
daily humiliations by the invading army; at length, they are herded
into a designated area of the city, which is then enclosed by a

perimeter wall to create a ghetto. Like other Jews in Warsaw, the
Szpilmans lose their belongings and apartment in this process
of 'resettlement'. It becomes clear that the ghetto is gradually to
be dismantled and its inhabitants transported to their deaths in
specially-constructed extermination camps to the East. All that
the Szpilmans can do is await their inevitable fate. Comes the
day, and they assemble in the *umschlagplaz* (place of deportation)
with hundreds of others in readiness to board the trains. At the
last minute, Szpilman is grabbed by the scruff of his neck and
thrust unceremoniously to one side; a much-disliked cousin, a
member of the ghetto police, has intervened to save him. He is
told to make himself scarce and the train, with the others of his
family aboard, departs for Treblinka. Szpilman finds work among
Jews who have been allocated duties in the city, first as a hod-
carrier and then in administration. He also finds time to help
with the supply of arms for the Resistance movement. Knowing
that the work-gangs are also to be disbanded, he secretes himself
in an empty flat with the help of the resistance and continues his
struggle to survive in isolation – broken only by occasional visits
from sympathetic supporters to supply him with food-parcels.
His presence eventually is revealed to his neighbours, who drive
him from the building. Increasingly debilitated both physically
and psychologically, he begs help from a former girlfriend,
since married to another. She and her husband find him a new
apartment in which they inveigle him for another lengthy period of
hiding. As the Resistance makes its move and the Warsaw Rising
begins, Szpilman's building is shelled by a tank. He is forced to flee
into the now-deserted ruins of the once-great city. In a bombed-out
building, he finds a can of pickled pimentos; his attempt to open it
sends it careering across the floor to land at the jackbooted feet of
a German officer. Thinking that the game is up, Szpilman awaits
the bullet that will bring his torment to an end – but it does not
come. The officer asks his occupation and when told that he is a
pianist, he orders him to play something on a piano in an adjacent

room. He is moved by Szpilman's rendition of Chopin and decides
to leave him unharmed, returning later with food and the news
that the Russian army is advancing; he tells Szpilman to hold on
for a week or two more and gifts him with provisions. Soviet troops
liberate the city and Szpilman eventually is rescued but, despite his
best efforts, he is unable to trace the German captain whose simple
act of humanity enabled him to complete the last leg of a long and
harrowing journey. (Wilm Hosenfeld, the captain in question, died
in a Soviet prison-camp in 1952.)

*   *   *

The Pianist is one of the great anti-war statements, and its strength
lies in its unflinching depiction of the brutalities of conflict at
'ground zero', through the eyes and experiences of a single victim.
The Pianist is also a story of survival – although it is not a morality
tale of triumph in adversity, for Szpilman's survival in the grand
scheme of things had little or nothing to do with him; instead, it is
a salutary lesson to all who witness his years of endurance under
the crushing jackboot of tyranny that never again should a nation
be allowed to descend to such depths of collective depravity.

Despite his professed desire to shoot the film version in more
conventional mode, Polanski nevertheless indulges in some
subtle directorial flourishes in The Pianist: prior to the invasion
of Warsaw, Szpilman is allowed a reel or so in which to conduct
a normal life for the sake of comparison, and the Technicolor
print is rendered to look like a sequence of hand-tinted black-
and-white photographs of the period; when a tank blasts a hole
in Szpilman's apartment wall, Polanski cleverly muffles the
soundtrack immediately after the explosion to better convey the
deafening impact of the blast to the viewer. He and Harwood also
add poignancy to the first act by allowing Szpilman the tender
beginnings of a fictional love affair. 'All will be well,' Szpilman's
aged father (Frank Finlay) assures his family, and the army of the
Third Reich marches into Warsaw in the very next shot.

Szpilman *père*'s first encounter with the soldiers, when they slap him for failing to acknowledge their presence and order him to walk in the gutter, is chilling in its echo of what Jewish political philosopher Hannah Arendt referred to as the 'banality of evil' in relation to the crimes of Adolf Eichmann. The horror implicit in the prospect of acts of intimidation conducted by unsophisticated German 'squaddies' who suddenly find themselves in a position to play God over a people who have been classified as less than human is well captured – as is the terrifying scene where a crippled patriarch is thrown from the balcony of his third-floor apartment to the street below by the SS, complete with wheelchair. Polanski shoots the incident in a matter-of-fact manner, as viewed by the Szpilmans across the way, all the while resisting the temptation to over-direct or stylise; its very ordinariness makes it all the more shocking. Small ironies whisper to be heard above the clamour of a seething humanity fighting desperately to stave off the day of its own extinction, such as the Jewish 'fixer' whose perennial adage of 'look on the bright side' is not enough to prevent him from ending up in the gutter along with so many other dashed hopes – a bullet in his head, and in those of his wife and children.

By the time the Szpilmans are required to assemble in the *umschlagplaz* and a screen-caption informs us of the date – August 16, 1942 – Polanski's own memory is casting picaresque variations over Harwood's script, such as the bright sunshine which forms the incongruous backdrop to the bloody embarkation of the first batch of Jews from the Ghetto. Polanski remembered it thus in Krakow when his father was marched off to the camp, and that served as his model for the sequence in the film, whereas dramatic convention might otherwise have dictated dour, overcast skies and grim, grey walls in the compound to suit the sober mood. The family share a last supper: a caramel bought from a junior black-marketeer for 20 zlotys and divided into six pieces, and by this point in the proceedings, the audience is aware – even if the participants are not – that in this confused and chaotic gathering are the first of many millions to go on their unwitting way to the gas chambers. Saved from inevitable death by a random act of benevolence, Szpilman is left to wander through a landscape composed of repetitive images, like the sand-castles in *Two Men and a Wardrobe* or the field of tulips in *The Fat and the Lean*; in this instance, the motif is supplied by the hundreds of abandoned suitcases en route to the *umschagplaz*.

```
EXT. BUILDING SITE, OUTSIDE GHETTO - DAY

Szpilman and Majorek sip gruel out of mugs.
They sit apart from the others who are also
taking a break.

    MAJOREK
    They're going to start the final resettlement
    now. We know what it means. We sent someone
    out. Zygmunt. A good man. His orders were
    to follow the trains out of Warsaw. He got
    to Sokolow. A local railwayman told him
    the tracks are divided, one branch leading
    to Treblinka. He said every day freight
    trains carrying people from Warsaw forked to
    Treblinka and returned empty. No transports
    of food are ever seen on that line. And
    civilians are forbidden to approach the
    Treblinka station. They're exterminating us.
```
Screenplay, *The Pianist* (2002)

Another poignant scene comes when Szpilman is forced into many long months of hiding out in empty apartments and having to remain as quiet as *The Tenant* did – not for fear of upsetting the neighbours but for fear of discovery. One such bolt-hole has a piano; he seats himself at it and lifts the lid – but all he can do is shadow-play to the music in his head, his fingertips dancing above the silent keys. 'Sometimes, I'm still not sure which side of the wall I'm on,' he says to the benefactor who has helped him to gain this modicum of freedom. In terms of technique, *The Pianist* is Polanski's most personal film; the story is told entirely from Szpilman's point of view, using the same first-person camera which the director has relied upon throughout his career – though rarely to more devastating effect than here, as when great events like the calamitous Warsaw Rising are only partially glimpsed from Szpilman's vantage-point behind the broken window-panes of his hiding-place 'in the heart of the lion's den'.

As Szpilman begins to run out of food, Polanski returns to the 'sprouting potato' of *Repulsion*, just as he reprises the rooftop scramble of *Frantic* when a tank-shell leaves Szpilman hanging precariously outside the building and temporarily exposed to a couple of German pot-shotters; nor is Polanksi averse to a little directorial prestidigitation in his ongoing attempts to confound audience expectation, to which end, he pulls a neat double-bluff in the scene where Szpilman is confronted by Hosenfeld, the 'German Captain' of the script: a can of pimentos falls from Szpilman's feeble grasp and rolls across the floor, coming to rest against a wooden step – whereas the knowing viewer has been led to expect that it will loll against a jackboot; Polanski holds the shot for a beat, then pans his camera up to a *second* step, whereon the anticipated jackboot actually resides.

When Hosenfeld finally arrives on the scene, Polanski changes point-of-view from Szpilman to the German. This is the first time for many reels that the viewer has been enabled to identify with someone other than Szpilman himself, and in order to maintain tension with the switch of protagonist, Harwood deleted the Captain's original response – 'I've no intention of doing anything to you' – to Szpilman's invitation, 'Do what you like to me. I'm not moving from here.' Instead, the German officer merely beckons the Jew into another room, where sits a piano, and politely orders him to play.

As Szpilman moves with trembling fingers through the first movement of Chopin's Nocturne in C minor, Hosenfeld appears increasingly affected. He slips silently into an adjacent chair and sits contemplatively, as the melody washes over him. As Szpilman continues to play, the tragedy of the circumstance through which these two polar opposites – artist and warrior – happen to have found one another writes itself on each of their faces. Hosenfeld moves nary a muscle – his lips part slightly at one point – but his gaze reveals the utter folly of war: the infinite sorrow of a loving husband and father, wrenched from the bosom of his family – the sheer stupidity of human bigotry...and the transcendent beauty of music as a more fitting monument to man's meagre achievements. The triumph of the spirit, rather than of the will. It is a startling performance by Thomas Kretschmann, who barely even blinks his eyelids but on whose features can be seen the lost dreams for the future which so many millions were forced to endure because of the megalomaniacal whims of the few. The pacific tenderness of the scene, as Hosenfeld listens impassively while Szpilman plays – his breath forming an icy mist in the freezing air, not knowing with each passing second if his next note will be his last – is quite beyond the descriptive power of mere words. Polanski shows his class in *The Pianist* by letting the music speak. There is no accompaniment; the piano solo is simply that, and the emotional register of the film is the better for it. The scene between Szpilman and Hosenfeld is one of the greatest in the history of the cinema, showing once and for all that while Polanski's vision might be pessimistic, his philosophy remains resolutely the opposite. 'I could see how much the members of the crew were moved,' he said, reflecting upon the shooting.

In the war-weary and spiritually-desolate Szpilman's encounter with a military man whose given mission is to destroy him utterly exists a great truth, which every politico should be required to study

before attempting to gain office: the things that tear men apart are
as nought compared to those which bind them together; love and
hate may be two sides of the same coin, but one is made of base
metal. A piano concerto speaks to both men in the same tongue
and enmity dissolves away, leaving only the tragedy to which they
are party. It is a triumph on the part of Polanski and his actors, not
to forget the helping hands of Fryderyk Chopin, that they manage
to extract the maximum emotional impact from the scene without
resorting to any of the jaded Hollywood tricks of orchestration
or glycerine. It is enough to see these two notional enemies find
common purpose in a 107-year-old concerto, and to rediscover their
shared humanity as a result. This scene – this film – is Roman
Polanski's finest hour.

> GERMAN CAPTAIN: Wo wohnen sie? Arbeiten sie etwa hier?
> (Do you live here? Do you work here?)
> SZPILMAN: Nein. (No.)
> GERMAN CAPTAIN: Wovon leben sie? (What do you do?)
> SZPILMAN: Ich bin... Ich war pianist. (I am... I was a pianist.)
> GERMAN CAPTAIN: Pianist..
> (motions towards the piano)
> Spielen sie mal. (Play something.)
>
> **Thomas Kretschmann and Adrien Brody**, *The Pianist* (2002)

Polanski's treatment of the encounter between Szpilman and
Hosenfeld is notable for its lack of sentimentality or the cloying
heroics of Spielberg's *Schindler's List*; the captain treats the
unkempt Jew before him as any decent human being would
another in whom he recognises misfortune and sees the need for
compassion – he is not smitten by guilt or any sudden attacks of
remorse on behalf of his Nazi masters, nor is he a closet humanist
operating clandestinely in the uniform of a Wermacht officer. He is
one man looking upon another with an acute awareness that their
fates have irrevocably become entwined, and that the unfortunate

in his sights is now ironically to be the likely victor in the present conflict. The aid offered is therefore modest, pragmatic and a product of common courtesy – no less courageous for that – but not the *grand geste* of a character who could so easily have been written to operate from a historical perspective. In such small honesties does this film's greatness truly lie.

The two re-establish their innate dignity through their love of art – specifically, music – not through the imagined collapse of some racial or ideological divide by the application of Hollywood schmaltz. Yet Polanski's treatment is even less sentimental than the reality, as depicted in Szpilman's own prosaic and sometimes melodramatic account. 'Only now did he seem to understand my real reason for hiding among the ruins. He started nervously. "You're Jewish?" He asked. "Yes." He had been standing with his arms crossed over his chest; he now unfolded them and sat down in the armchair by the piano, as if this discovery called for lengthy reflection. "Yes, well," he murmured, "in that case I see you really can't leave."' The film paints a less obviously heroic portrait of Hosenfeld, but a more gallant and realistic one:

> GERMAN CAPTAIN: *Halten sie sich hier versteckt? (Are you hiding here?) Jude? (Jew?) Wo ist ihr versteck? (Where are you hiding?)*
> SZPILMAN: *Im dachboden. (In the attic.)*
> GERMAN CAPTAIN: *Ziegen sie mir. (Show me.)*
>
> **Thomas Kretschmann and Adrien Brody**, *The Pianist* (2002)

Through the harrowing and often punitive plight of another individual with whom, like Hardy's Tess, the gods had made 'their sport' can be viewed the calamity of which countries are capable. The intent of *The Pianist* is to draw attention to that fact, not glory in sentimental nonsense about one man's imperturbable will to survive, or the ultimate triumph of right over wrong. How can any film with the Holocaust as its subject feign a pretence of good ultimately vanquishing evil when blind eyes were turned to so many who faced terror and death? No – *The Pianist* is more than a saccharine re-enactment of one of history's darkest hours; it is the testament of two men: Wladyslaw Szpilman and Roman Polanski. It shows the crucible of fire from which both of them sprang, and to which both of them owe the sensibility which conversely turned them into great artists. In Polanski's case, the greatest filmmaker of his generation.

*   *   *

After he had finished with *The Pianist*, Polanski returned once more to his roots in acting by signing on to play the role of Papkin in friend and mentor Andrzej Wajda's adaptation of Polish playwright Aleksander Fredro's popular farce *Revenge* (*Zemsta*). This comedy of manners from 1834, like *Romeo and Juliet* with laughs, concerns the intrigue between the warring neighbours of a medieval castle whose marital designs for the son of one and niece of the other are advanced by a boastful intermediary – Polanski's Papkin – who tries to be all things to all men (and women). Polanski showed by his finely-nuanced playing that he had lost none of his ability to craft complex and attractive characters, just as Wajda showed by his choice of subject that his bent for political statement could be served equally well by a comedy classic whose knockabout antics held up for inspection some of the less savoury characteristics of his Polish countrymen.

In May 2002, *The Pianist* was entered in competition at the Cannes Film Festival, the first film of Polanski's to be so for more than 30 years. 'It is probably my most personal film for the simple reason that I was able to use my own recollections of the period,' he told Nigel Reynolds of the *Daily Telegraph*. 'It was actually more painful to go through the research preparations than it was shooting. However, during the six months of production there were moments that so vividly reminded me of events that I felt very taken aback.' The critics at Cannes were equally taken aback: *The Pianist* was awarded the top prize of the coveted Palme d'Or by the Festival jury, to the chagrin of many. *The Guardian* reported that the jury's verdict was greeted with 'polite applause and some boos' – this despite calls from some quarters which had demanded a boycott of the Festival to protest about the increasing growth of anti-Semitism in France.

When the film opened theatrically in January 2003, there were no such expressions of discontent. For the first time in what Philip French and others alleged to be decades of artistic abstinence on Polanski's part, the critics were united in acclaim: 'The feeling of time and place is convincing,' French opined in his *Observer* column. 'Not only is there no triumphalist ending, but by playing down such acts of kindness and decency as Szpilman experiences, it refuses to join in any easy celebration of the human spirit. In this resides a stoic honesty.' It was a view echoed by author Norman Lebrecht, writing in the *Standard*: 'Polanski, relying on memory, revives apartment blocks that feel like prisons and streets on which no one can be trusted. His scenery is the most evocative of any filmic account of the Holocaust, convincing beyond criticism.' The *Independent on Sunday*'s Jonathan Romney agreed: '*The Pianist* is a major achievement, at least as far as realistic evocation goes... This is surely the most exhaustive, painstaking screen recreation yet of the place and period... so much so that you're grateful the story does not ask us to follow it into the camps themselves.' Romney's colleague Anthony Quinn of the *Independent Review* was also lost in admiration. 'One senses in every frame of this film a determination to fill an absence, to convey exactly the pressure and detail of an experience whose horror, even now, affronts our understanding... Whether Polanski thinks survival a miracle or a black joke isn't certain, but he has created something here that won't be forgotten.'

Amid the gush, it fell to Philip Kerr of the *New Statesman* to make the most salient points: '*The Pianist*... is possibly one of the best movies made about the Holocaust, and certainly the best movie Roman Polanski has made since *Chinatown*, almost 30 years ago,' he wrote, before rounding off his review with an eloquent plea for the welfare of the film's director: 'While being without question worth an Oscar, it remains to be seen if, in this current climate of hysteria about paedophilia, Hollywood will feel equal to the task of recognising the work of a man who put himself beyond the pale in 1979 [1978], when he fled America while awaiting sentencing on a charge of unlawful intercourse with a minor. Like me, you might think Polanski has suffered enough.'

In one of those wonderful liberating gestures in which the American industry finds itself able to indulge on occasions of moment, Hollywood did indeed feel equal to the task of recognising Polanski's work at the 75th annual Academy Awards ceremony in 2003. *The Pianist* won Oscars for Best Actor, for Brody (the youngest actor ever to be so awarded), Best Adapted Screenplay, for Harwood, and Best Director, for Polanski himself, out of a total of seven nominations, including that of Best Picture. Timing her appearance better on this occasion than she had on the last, Samantha Geimer had once again popped up on the American airwaves to grant her own form of absolution to her former abuser: 'What he did to me was wrong,' she told Larry King of CNN, 'but I wish he would return to America so the whole ordeal can be put to rest for both of us. After the publicity came out, I knew it was just as bad for him as it was for me. I'm sure if he could go back, he wouldn't do it again. He made a terrible mistake but he's paid for it.' Not according to the Los Angeles District Attorney's office, which before the awards had issued a party-pooping announcement to the effect that if Polanski were even to think of attending the ceremony, he would be arrested as soon as he put a foot on the tarmac at LAX. Consequently, *Frantic* star Harrison Ford handed him the golden statuette in Deauville, France.

One day, you'll die, Shell, but this... this picture will live...

Lukey (Robert Newton), *Odd Man Out* (1947)

With one BAFTA, seven French Césars and a clutch of other gongs following suit, *The Pianist* became the crowning achievement of Polanski's career. One is tempted to posit the possibility that in an industry which has always had more than its fair share of Jews in positions of power, filmmakers desirous of an Oscar have only to make a film about the Holocaust in order to secure one. Witness *The Diary of Anne Frank* (1959), *The Pawnbroker* (1965), *Sophie's Choice* (1982) and *Schindler's List* (1993), of which only *The Pawnbroker* failed to gain its nomination (for Rod Steiger). But whatever was the reason in the case of *The Pianist*, win it did, and Polanski found himself vindicated at last – at least in the court of his peers.

For the remainder of 2002 and beyond, it was not the court of his peers with which Polanski was to be concerned but that of the High Court, in London.

*   *   *

Like most celebrities, Polanski has had a love-hate relationship with the press. The 'hate' element was especially relevant in the wake of the Manson murders, when the opposite should realistically have been the case. Reasons for that are difficult to fathom – envy, perhaps; anti-Semitism possibly. More probably, the crime was so appalling that some simplistic belief in natural justice came inexplicably to the fore: such a thing could not have happened at random – somehow, they must have *deserved* to die. When faced with events beyond their comprehension, people tend to take refuge in the most primitive fancies. Following the Gailey affair, the American press in particular adopted the attitude that Polanski was fair game for populist displays of moral outrage at every opportunity – that any mention of his name should be accompanied by an appropriately disparaging adjectival noun, and that nothing in his prior history should be allowed to compensate for the fact that his actions in relation to Gailey had put him beyond the pale. In such a climate of collective indignation, further besmirchings of his character were not only considered free from recourse but were felt almost to be a moral duty on the part of certain sanctimonious sections of the media which like to pander to those obsessed by breaches of public decency.

The same Academy which had honoured Polanski with a Best Director Oscar had honoured Andrzej Wajda with an Oscar for Lifetime Achievement in 2000, and Wajda, in turn, gifted the statuette to the Jagiellonaian University in Krakow. Within a week of Polanski receiving his award, Jagiellonaian director Franciszek Ziejka let it be known that the University where pope John Paul II had taught theology would not be granting the same honorary doctorate to Polanski that it had to Wajda, because of the former's dubious past. 'Nobody questions his artistic achievements,' Ziejka said, 'but there is a question of moral stance here and therefore we have doubts.'

Perhaps encouraged by the news that apparently not everyone was so impressed by Polanski's Oscar win as to conveniently forget the charge of lewd behaviour which still hung over him, the July 2002 edition of Condé Nast magazine *Vanity Fair* published an article by one A E Hochner in which the same Lewis Lapham with whom Polanski had briefly shared a table at Elaine's in August 1969 alleged that on the very day of his wife's funeral, Polanski had propositioned a Swedish model in his presence with the line that he could make her into 'another Sharon Tate'.

The *Vanity Fair* article was one defamatory story too many. With his name and his reputation all-but restored because of *The Pianist*, Polanski was in a better position to take action against the implied slur on his character than he had been for some time. He demanded an apology and a retraction from editor Graydon Carter. Carter refused and told Polanski that the magazine was standing by its story. Polanski decided to sue – but in a British court, where offences of libel are treated with particular gravity. The action was commenced in August, 2002, but there was one snag: Polanski could not appear to prosecute his case in person, for fear of extradition proceedings being brought against him; his counsel would have to apply for a dispensation which would allow him to give evidence via video link from Paris, the first time ever that such an arrangement would have been acceded to in a British libel case. Permission was granted without demur.

Faced with the prospect that they would only be able to cross-examine Polanski via video link, *Vanity Fair*'s lawyers appealed the decision to offer him the facility. While the appeal was being heard by the Lords Nicholls, Slynn, Hope, Carswell and Baroness Hale of Richmond, Polanski embarked on the preparations for his 17th feature film.

With the unalloyed success of *The Pianist* at the 75th Academy Awards ceremony, the cinematic world was once again Polanski's oyster. From a combination of French, British and Czechoslovakian sources, plus the US distribution muscle of Sony-Tristar, he was able to amass a major $50 million-dollar budget for his next project, which fell into a genre which no one previously would have thought of interest to him, least of all himself: the 'family film'. 'I would never think of doing a movie for children if I didn't have any,' Polanski said. 'I relate to all the sufferings much more now that I have kids. Children have this capacity for resistance, and they accept things as they are, maybe because they have no other reference.'

With that, and the nostalgic aspect which had informed *The Pianist* (in terms of his 'orphaned' childhood in war-torn Poland) in mind, the subject in question was almost a natural. Polanski picked up the phone to screenwriter Ronald Harwood; 'Ronnie,' he opened. 'I have only two words to say to you: *Oliver Twist*.'

The surgeon leant over the body, and raised the left hand. 'The old story,' he said, shaking his head: 'no wedding-ring, I see. Ah! good night.'

The medical gentleman walked away to dinner; and the nurse, having once more applied herself to the green bottle, sat down on a low chair before the fire, and proceeded to dress the infant.

And what an excellent example of the power of dress young Oliver Twist was! Wrapped in the blanket which had hitherto formed his only covering, he might have been the child of a nobleman or a beggar; – it would have been hard for the haughtiest stranger to have fixed his station in society. But now he was enveloped in the old calico robes, that had grown yellow in the same service; he was badged and ticketed, and fell into his place at once – a parish child – the orphan of a workhouse – the humble, half-starved drudge – to be cuffed and buffered through the world, despised by all, and pitied by none.

Oliver cried loudly. If he could have known that he was an orphan, left to the tender mercies of churchwardens and overseers, perhaps he would have cried the louder.

Charles Dickens, *Oliver Twist, or, The Parish Boy's Progress* (1838)

Dickens's *Oliver Twist, or, The Parish Boy's Progress* was published originally as a serial in *Bentley's Miscellany*, a monthly magazine of which Dickens was editor. It ran from February 1837 to April 1839 in a total of 24 instalments, and it was first published in book form in November 1838, in three volumes, while the serial was still unfolding in *Bentley's*. What began as a thinly-veiled attack on the unjust 1834 Poor Law Act of Parliament soon grew into one of the great adventure stories of all time, as Oliver is enticed into a den of thieves by the wily Fagin and his brutish accomplice Bill Sikes. The character of Oliver Twist is alleged to have been based on that of Robert Blincoe, an orphan of the poorhouse who spent part of his childhood in the St Pancras workhouse before being found employment as a mill-worker in Nottingham. In 1828, he penned his recollections of a life of hard labour and penury in Regency England as a serial, entitled *A Memoir of Robert Blincoe: Horrors of a Cotton-Mill*; it saw further publication as a pamphlet in 1832, only four years before Dickens started out on *Oliver Twist*.

The character of Fagin, the story's deceptively seductive but infinitely malevolent Jewish gang-master, was also drawn from the life. Fagin was long thought to have been based on a notorious Jewish 'fence' named Ikey Solomons, who jumped bail and fled to Europe in 1831, after having been held in Newgate prison on a charge of receiving stolen goods; in fact, Dickens's model was more prosaic – that of a work-mate named Bob Fagin in Warren's 'blacking' factory in London, where he had been forced to toil at the tender age of 12 after his father was committed to a three-month term in prison over an unpaid debt. The real Fagin took the young Dickens under his wing and eased his passage into industrial grind by teaching him the tricks of the shoe-polish trade, for which the future author was naturally grateful, immortalising his childhood protector in print when the opportunity arose: 'I took the liberty of using his name, long afterwards, in *Oliver Twist*,' he wrote – though endowing one of literature's wickedest villains with the name of a well-meaning associate was not without irony; the educated Dickens had entered into acquaintanceship with this savvy example of London's working poor with considerable reluctance.

According to Polanski, he decided to make *Oliver Twist* after reading the novel to his two children: 'I made the film very much for them [because] I realised that there's nothing they can relate to in the movies I've made so far. I thought it was time to film something for them – something that they could watch without saying, like they did after seeing *The Pianist*, that Harry Potter is much better...' To support the contention, both of them were given roles to play: daughter Morgane was cast as the daughter of a farmer who turns Oliver from his door, while son Elvis was to be the recipient of a clip round the ear from an Artful Dodger on his way to pick pockets. 11-year-old Londoner Barney Clark became Polanski's hand-picked Oliver. 'Roman... made it easy,' he said. 'I loved staying in a hotel with a swimming pool and room service.'

Polanski's *Oliver Twist* represented only the second occasion on which its director had chosen to embark on a project which had a cinematic precedent. The screen is not exactly littered with *Oliver Twists*, but there had been several silent versions (one of which had featured the 'Man of a Thousand Faces' Lon Chaney as Fagin), as well as a 1933 sound film directed by William Cowen that, while not especially notable in itself, started a trend in Hollywood for adaptations of Dickens which did produce memorable versions of *David Copperfield* (1934) and *A Tale of Two Cities* (1935).

The best-remembered and arguably definitive version of *Oliver Twist* did not come along until 1948, under the auspices of J Arthur Rank and British director David Lean. The star of the film was Robert Newton (as Sikes), though it is often thought retrospectively to have been made as a starring vehicle for Alec Guinness, whose controversial portrait of Fagin formed perhaps the most iconic aspect of the production; Oliver himself was played by John Howard Davies, whose subsequent career took him into production at BBC Television Centre. Lean's *Oliver Twist* took all of its stylistic cues from German Expressionism, and designer John Bryan's Pinewood studio set of the villains' Jacob's Island warren in Rotherhithe stands to this day as the finest cinematic recreation of London squalor from the early years of Victoria's reign. Lean had the added advantage of a sterling repertory company of British character actors on which to draw, all of whom had been tutored in Dickens in their school years and were almost born to play the various comic grotesques with which the pages of the novel are peppered. Add to this the luminous chiaroscuro cinematography of Guy Green – never bettered in a British film, before or since – and it is easy to see why Lean's version of Dicken's first and most famous novel was always a hard act to follow. Comparisons may be odious, but in the case of *Oliver Twist*, they also happen to be unavoidable.

Dickens's stereotypical portrait of Fagin as the satanic Jew of medieval mythology was controversial from the very beginning. The tale's 25-year-old author was no more anti-Semitic than the next man of his time, but he was subject to the same historical prejudices as the rest; here is how he describes the wily old fence when Oliver first comes upon him: 'In a frying-pan which was on the fire, and which was secured to the mantel-shelf by a string, some sausages were cooking; standing over them was a very old shrivelled Jew, whose villainous-looking and repulsive face was obscured by a quantity of matted red hair.' This picture of a red-headed Fagin, pitchfork in hand, was embellished by original illustrator George Cruikshank to include a straggly beard and a large hook-nose, in the style of Shakespeare's Shylock or du Maurier's Svengali, and this was the Devilish image which Lean and Guinness went after in 1948.

It is perhaps surprising that such an outrageous racial caricature should have been deemed acceptable only a few years after the discovery of the Nazi death-camps which had claimed some six million lives as a result of similar bigotry; in fact, no connection was made between the two: Dickens's *Oliver Twist* is a classic of English literature, and an eminent British production of the novel was never going to meet serious complaint in the UK, despite its alleged ethnic shortcomings. In the States, however, the film was held up in release for three years and shorn of a full ten minutes of Alec Guinness.

Polanski's official line on Fagin was espoused in interview while his version was still in production: 'I hated the way Alec Guinness played Fagin in David Lean's film. They stuck that awful enormous nose on him. It was so anti-Semitic. You could not do that these days.' For *his* Fagin, Polanski had chosen his *Death and the Maiden* star Ben Kingsley, who had his own ideas for the character: 'I have some very fond childhood memories in Manchester of a man who ran a junkshop with mountains of umbrellas and pots and pans. And I remember looking at him when I was Oliver's age and being fascinated by this man who wore a coat tied together with string – and my Fagin wears a coat tied together with string. That's not research, it's mosaic,' he said. But however 'the Jew' was to be treated on this occasion, the fact that writer Ronald Harwood was Jewish, Polanski was half-Jewish, and Kingsley also was of Jewish extraction appeared to make it unlikely, if not impossible, that a charge of anti-Semitism could be levelled at the production. Notwithstanding, American critic Saul Austerlitz managed to express his continuing disappointment at the latest incarnation of Fagin after the film's opening in the US: 'While Fagin is bleached of his explicit Jewishness, he is still outfitted with a comically-exagerrated proboscis... Fagin may not be wearing a yarmulke, and no one in Polanski's film calls him a Jew, but on a slightly more subterranean level, this *Oliver Twist* still engages in some rancid physical stereotypes.' Proof, if any were needed, that some people will see racial slurs even where none are intended: the 'comical proboscis' of which Austerlitz complained was Kingsley's *own* nose.

> *There was a lad once, just like you; I was a father to him. He ran away, like you. He, indeed, went to the police, and can you guess how he ended up? – They 'anged him...at the Old Bailey. Certain evidence was made available, not all of it precisely true but all of it necessary to provide for my own safety and that of my friends. Yeah. Poor boy. 'Anged... It's a terrible thing, 'anging, Oliver: dawn... the gallows... the rope... the noose. You don't always have to be guilty, you see, Oliver... They 'ang you for anything, these days. That's 'cause they're so very fond of 'anging...*
>
> **Fagin (Ben Kingsley)**, *Oliver Twist* (2005)

Orphaned 'parish boy' Oliver Twist (Clark) is ejected from the workhouse which is his lot in life after asking for 'seconds' of gruel. He is apprenticed to an undertaker, but he escapes after a fight and makes his way south to the teeming city of London. Hungry and penniless, Oliver is taken pity on by the Artful Dodger (Harry Eden), a pickpocket in the employ of Jewish gang-master Fagin (Kingsley), who provides bed and board for his crew of young felons in return for a little petty theft; other denizens of the criminal fraternity into which Oliver is introduced are housebreaker Bill Sikes (Jamie Foreman) and his partner Nancy (Leanne Rowe). On an outing with Dodger to learn the tricks of his new trade, Oliver is separated from his companions when a robbery goes awry, and he finds himself arrested and hauled up before the beak. He again is taken pity on – this time by Mr Brownlow (Edward Hardwicke), intended victim of said robbery, who decides to become his benefactor. When he is sent on an errand by Brownlow, Oliver is abducted by Sikes and Nancy and returned to Fagin's lair; the gang force him to help them break into Brownlow's house – but this burglary also goes wrong: Sikes escapes, but Oliver accidentally is shot in the arm during the fracas.

Fagin nurses Oliver back to health but Sikes is determined that the boy will have to be disposed of, to prevent him from telling the authorities what he knows. Overhearing their plan, Nancy arranges to meet Brownlow under London Bridge, with a view to cutting a deal for Sikes and herself in return for Oliver's life. But Fagin has had her watched and reports the betrayal to Sikes. Enraged, Sikes bludgeons her to death. The hue and cry is raised on the discovery of the murder and the hunt is on for Nancy's killer. The gang is forced to retreat to an old warehouse on Jacob's Island, a dockland slum. Sikes arrives, but his former comrades have now turned against him. He grabs Oliver and heads for the rooftops. As he swings from one ledge to the next by means of a knotted rope, he is suddenly unnerved by his dog Bullseye and he loses his footing; the rope settles around his neck, the noose tightens – and he is hanged in full view of his pursuers. The rest of the gang are arrested, and Fagin is sentenced to death for his villainy.

In an epilogue to the dramatic events, Oliver and Mr Brownlow pay Fagin a visit in prison on the day of his execution. Oliver prays for his forgiveness, but the old Jew has almost lost his mind in fear of the hangman. They take their leave, and Fagin goes to the gallows while Oliver goes on to a new life as Brownlow's adopted son.

*　　*　　*

Once again recruiting almost all of the team which had helped him to put together *The Pianist*, Polanski and his crew decamped for 16 weeks of principal photography to the huge Barrandov Studio on the outskirts of Prague in July, 2004, and onto the largest outdoor set ever constructed in Europe. So authentic was Allan Starski's production design for Dickens's 1837-ish London that even the names on the Kings Street shops were accurate to the period, mirroring establishments which still exist to this day. The set was comprised of five major streets, as well as side streets and market squares, and it occupied 40 square kilometres and took nearly three months to build. 'We used more than two hundred construction workers plus the workshop people,' Starski said. 'I used eleven different types of brick for finishing the houses because we took some moulds and casts from London and made the copies in Prague.' 'There were more than 85 buildings, as well as five streets and a little stretch of river,' *Pianist* cinematographer Pawel Edelman recalled. 'It was really amazing!' (Even more amazing was the fact that filmmakers who spend so much time and energy ensuring the accuracy of items such as the facades of shops can still manage to make the simplest of mistakes: both the Lean and Polanski versions of *Oliver Twist* spell Bill Sikes's name as 'Sykes'.)

Polanski chose to eschew the heightened sense of melodrama and abundant comic caricatures with which the Lean version is littered and go instead for realism; the result remains true to the spirit of Dickens, if not the letter. Ronald Harwood pared Dickens's convoluted plot down to its bare essentials, as John Brownjohn had for Polanski with Pérez-Reverte's *El club Dumas*, and he deprived it of several notable characters in the process – the most obvious (but also the most dispensable) being Oliver's half-brother,

Monks. Of the main players, it is Fagin who is afforded the most sympathetic treatment by Harwood, a revision which curiously alters the emotional tempo of the film, turning it into a tug-of-war for Oliver's soul between his two surrogate fathers, the amoral old Jew and the philanthropic Mr Brownlow. This gives a new and refreshing reading to a story with which everyone imagines themselves familiar. Whereas the literary Oliver is a cipher in a polemic which urges social reform, Polanski's orphan is flesh-and-blood and roped into a right of passage. If Brownlow is the voice of conscience, Fagin is the primal force to which Oliver is attracted by virtue of his status as an outsider. As with so many of Polanski's films, the shift of emphasis is subtle, and the viewer is barely aware of it until the tale has unfolded and the whole begins to unspool again in memory.

Polanski had the same advantage on *Oliver Twist* as he did on *The Ninth Gate*, but not on *Tess*, in terms of the benefits of CGI when it came to the painting-in of English backgrounds. But with the largest set ever built on a European stage at his disposal, he and set designer Starski decided to utilise it only minimally. Polanski's aversion to such effects notwithstanding, *Oliver Twist* would have done better to rely less on large-scale sets of a small section of London and more on digital views of the city as a whole. Five years before, the same Prague studio at which *Oliver Twist* was shot had played host to another large-scale London set, in the form of Jack the Ripper's Whitechapel for the Johnny Depp starrer *From Hell*. That film had been enhanced by computerised vistas dotted with familiar London landmarks. The Lean version of *Oliver Twist* also had opted for some scene-setting cityscapes, based on the engravings of Gustave Doré (which the new film employs behind its end-credits). Against such evocations, all that Polanski produces by way of London landscape is a single computer-generated image overlooking the city's rooftops, as Oliver gazes wistfully from the window of his attic prison in Fagin's den. It is not enough, and somewhere between the clutch of extras who wait to watch Fagin swing in *Oliver Twist* and the impossibly huge armies who rush to do battle in films like *Kingdom of Heaven* (2005) must be a fairer compromise for director and CG artist alike. Executions outside Newgate jail, according to Dickens's own testimony, were attended by as many as 30,000 people; Polanski is at his best at close quarters, but he shows his age – or his obduracy – in his reluctance to embrace digital expedience in a story which so clearly would have benefited from it.

If the film has a fault, it is that there is too much light and radiance in lives that in their Gothic origins were dark and blighted, just as the streets of London, authentic as may be, are rather too shiny and new for a thousand-year-old city filled to overflowing with immigrant labour (despite the weeks that the crew spent 'ageing' the buildings). At an earlier juncture in his career, Polanski might have made more of the fact that sex, rather than the promise of riches, was the inducement which drew many a young boy into a life of crime in Victorian London. The role of adolescent seductress was one which 'chicken doxies' like Nancy were allocated automatically, and Dickens confessed to the fact that his heroine was indeed a prostitute after author Anthony Trollope had criticised his reticence in portraying her as such in the novel. (The film's Nancy is at least made to *look* like Dickens's serialised depiction of her, before she became more conservatively attired in subsequent revisions.)

Oliver Twist is at odds with expectation in another aspect of its design: Bill Sikes is one of literature's greatest villains – a psychopathic brute, whose callous murder of his mistress has been one of the high water marks of popular fiction for 170 years. Robert Newton's towering performance in the role in 1948 is as difficult to combat in any new interpretation as that of Guinness's Fagin, and this version's Jamie Foreman quite fails to cut the mustard. Polanski is not a director who favours his actors greatly because he indulges in few close-ups and he tends to avoid the conventions of cinematic grammar, such as low-angles on the likes of Sikes. The incipient menace of the man has therefore to be conveyed by other means more natural. Forman is the son of East End hard man and former Kray twins fixer Freddie Forman and he certainly looks the part – which in line with Polanski's casting whims and the actor's heritage, is hardly surprising, but his vocal intonations have neither the rasp of the inveterate lag nor the timbre of authority, nor is he mad of eye (as was Newton) or particularly imposing of stature (as was Oliver Reed in his uncle Carol's musical adaptation of 1968, *Oliver!*). Harwood adds to these deficiencies by having him tumble backwards into the Thames after the failed burglary at the Brownlow house, much to the ribald amusement of Toby Crackit (Mark Strong), while Nancy's bludgeoning is also contrived with a minimum of violence. (Prior to the formal submission of the film for certification in the UK, Universal was advised that the strength of the beating delivered to Nancy by Sikes was unlikely to be acceptable in the PG category; the episode was reduced accordingly in the submitted version.) Sikes is as much a figure of fun in *Oliver Twist* as of malice – devious, perhaps even potentially deadly, but no mythic 'monster' this time out (despite the Dodger's shouted accusation to the effect at the climax) – only banally and bumblingly evil. This reduction in Sikes's importance to the narrative feeds Polanski's fondness for demystification and a more realistic approach, but it denies the tale its soaring dramatic finale on the gambrel roofs of the Jacob's Island rookery.

The 1933 version of the film stayed true to Dickens by having only Sikes, Crackit and the other members of the gang of burglars besieged at Jacob's Island, but the Lean adaptation felt that Fagin's complicity in the capital crime would be better served if he were to be among those arrested in the dockside warren; consequently, Fagin is already in hiding at the Island when Sikes arrives, after having tried to dispose of Bullseye. Fagin's absence from the thieves' den for the climactic confrontation with the mob was one of many errors of plotting which Dickens made in *Oliver Twist* in his haste to meet the serial's monthly deadline, and Lean screenwriter Stanley Haynes was adroit in correcting it. Harwood adopted the same strategy in Polanski's version. The constraints of geography to which Dickens felt obliged to bow do not impede on films in the same way, and little seems amiss to the average viewer if Fagin packs his bags in Holborn only to open them again in Rotherhithe a moment later, just as the East End of London was merely a trot away from the West in *From Hell*. The gang is thus arrested en masse, which offers a clearer narrative line to the scene in which Oliver visits Fagin in Newgate than Dickens was able to provide.

When Oliver and Brownlow attend the condemned felon, they find him in a state of despair and extreme mental anguish, his composure shattered and his box of baubles, collected from a lifetime of thieving, now useful only as a tool with which to barter for his life. Oliver once more thanks Fagin for his kindnesses and then begs the distraught man to pray for forgiveness, but he is too deranged with fear to heed his visitor's pleas. Oliver and his guardian exit the prison with Fagin wailing in torment at their heels, and their coach passes what Dickens describes as 'the black stage, the cross-beam, the rope and all the hideous apparatus of death' – the gallows, in other words, being readied for duty that morning. They trundle on towards the green fields of Pentonville, their carriage illumined by dawn's breaking light.

Given that this episode is anti-climactic at best, Polanski spends considerable time and effort upon it. The endless prison doors which Oliver, Brownlow and the jailer are forced laboriously to traverse hint disquietingly of his own experiences in Chino, while the passionate outburst with which the usually subdued Oliver abdures Fagin to repent also smacks of expiation of a sort. Despite all the temptations which were offered him – 'This is a pleasant life, ain't it, my dear?' Fagin had earlier insisted – Oliver found the path to righteousness in the end. He may have been thought 'fit only for hanging' in the view of the parish board, but he was good at heart – a fact which Brownlow recognised and which enabled

Oliver, in his turn, to see the good in Fagin; if artists find it easier to express themselves through their art, then Polanski found something more personally profound in *Oliver Twist* than Dickens ever intended.

> *It's all in* The Chronicle. *You're in it; Bill's in it; Oliver's in it...*
> *'More information has reached your correspondent concerning the foul and bestial murder which took place in Spitalfields and which has shocked and appalled the citizens of London. It is believed the victim, a young woman, now identified as Nancy, was brutally beaten to death by one William Sikes, a well-known dangerous villain. The motive is as yet unclear, but your correspondent has learned that the murdered woman had informed on an associate and on an infamous fence, Fagin, who is now wanted for the abduction of a young boy, Oliver Twist. Neither Fagin nor Sikes are presently in custody, but the police are engaged in searching for them throughout the city and beyond. Sikes, according to police, is usually accompanied by a fierce, white dog.' How about that, eh?'*
>
> **Toby Crackit (Mark Strong)**, *Oliver Twist* (2005)

In July 2005, as the finishing touches were being put to *Oliver Twist* in readiness for the verdict of the public, another verdict became pending: Polanski vs Condé Nast Publications Limited finally reached the High Court in the Strand. *Vanity Fair's* appeal against Polanski being allowed to give evidence via video link had been dismissed the preceding February and the combatants were now at liberty to slug out their differences in full public view. Acting for Polanski was John Kelsey-Fry QC, and for the magazine was Thomas Shields QC; the presiding judge was Mr Justice Eady and the affair was to be conducted in the Old Bailey's Court number 13.

At issue was a passage in an article by A E Hochner about Elaine's restaurant in New York, which had appeared in the July 2002 edition of the magazine. In the piece, Lewis Lapham – who himself had been editor of *Harper's* since 1976 – was quoted as saying that on the very day of his wife's funeral, Polanski had appeared at Elaine's and seated himself beside a Swedish model who was in the company of himself and his friend Edward Perlberg; he had then 'slid his hand inside her thigh' and made advances towards her, which had ended with the promise that he would 'make another Sharon Tate out of her'. Polanski had denied the accusation in its totality. 'This was the worst thing ever written about me,' he eventually was to tell the jury. 'It's absolutely not true. I was in shock when I read it. But I think it was particularly hurtful, because it dishonours my memory of Sharon. It's all lies. That's not the way I behave...'

Right at the start of proceedings, Shields was forced to concede that the quote attributed to Lapham had contained at least two errors of fact. Beatte Telle, the model in question, was Norwegian not Swedish, and the meeting at Elaine's between he, Perlberg, Telle and Polanski actually took place some two weeks *after* the funeral of Tate, around Wednesday August 27, and not on the day alleged in the article. Minor points, perhaps, but if *Vanity Fair's* fact-checkers were capable of being slipshod over something as fundamental as the nationality of the woman at the centre of the storm, so ran the argument of Polanski's counsel, what other aspects of the story might they have been less than scrupulous about?

Shields, nevertheless, stood by the proposition that the article was substantially true and he based the case for the defence on Polanski's character – or lack of it. Referring to what he christened as 'Roman's law of morality', he said, 'This law knows of no rules – only violations of civilised conduct which, it appears, can be readily excused. As to whether Mr Polanski's reputation is capable of being damaged, sadly, we would say, it is beyond repair.' In a pre-emptive strike against Polanski's upcoming testimony by video link, he added, 'An honourable man would come to this court, an honourable man would return to California, an honourable man would not behave in the way he behaved, even in the Swinging Sixties.'

To support his contention that the facts of the article were broadly correct, Shields proposed to call Lapham and Perlberg to the witness stand – but not, significantly, Ms Telle. Lapham recounted his version of events that day in Elaine's: 'He began to praise her beauty and speak to her, romance her,' he said of Polanski's fateful meeting with Telle. 'At one point he had his hand on her leg and he said to her: "I can put you in the movies. I can make you the next Sharon Tate". I was impressed by the remark, not only because it was tasteless and vulgar, but because it was a cliché,' he concluded.

Edward Perlberg was more voluminous. On the third day of the hearing, he told the jury that a 'strange kind of quiet' had descended on the restaurant when Polanski made his entrance. 'I looked back and I saw Roman Polanski,' he elaborated. 'I knew it was Roman Polanski because his picture had been in the newspapers due to the unfortunate happenings in the few weeks before that. Also I was a kind of film buff.' He then went on to explain how Polanski had sat between himself and Telle, and that he had 'seemed most interested' in the Scandinavian beauty. 'As I was viewing this, I began to see that she was somewhat flustered,' he said. 'She arose and looked at me and said, "Ed, we're leaving". This was very unusual.' As Perlberg remembered it, Telle then told him that Polanski had suggested that she should 'come to Hollywood' for a screen test, and that he would 'make another Sharon Tate' of her. 'I thought this was generally creepy and it bothered me,' he said. 'I said, "You know, that's strange, but perhaps he could be excused because he just suffered such a massive shock", but that didn't seem to lessen her anxiety. We wound up agreeing that he had behaved improperly, and I think words that he was a twerp or to that effect were used.'

Shields turned his attention finally to Polanski himself. Over two days, the director was questioned about his predilection for 'fresh-faced, nubile' girls, his dalliances with air hostesses, his three-in-a-bed romp with Nastassja Kinski, the willing students at the finishing school in Gstaad and, in a further effort to use the testimony of his own words against him, his inability to tell the difference between 'fantasy and reality', as espoused in the opening paragraph of his autobiography. Polanski stayed calm throughout, merely reminding those watching him in the court that there were different strokes for different folks, and that for him, solace at his loss came in the form of casual sexual encounters. But not until some four months had elapsed after Sharon Tate had been laid to rest. 'I never sought to seduce anyone at Elaine's,' he declared. 'That would have been callous indifference to my late wife's memory.'

The last witness was Mia Farrow. The now-60-year-old actress had been Polanski's dining companion on the day and was happy to give evidence on his behalf. Recalling their meeting at Elaine's, she said that the only thing that Polanski had on his mind was the murder of his wife. 'He was in really bad shape at that time. He was unable to talk about anything else. When we walked around and around, he kept saying "Why?" and "Who could have done this?".' Shields pressed her on the fact that Polanski admitted to having had casual affairs in the wake of Tate's death, but Farrow was sympathetic: 'I feel there's a big distinction, especially for a man, between relationships and having sex. I could never pass judgement if someone in that frame of mind seeks comfort in any way that does not harm anyone,' she said.

Vanity Fair had done its best to defend the action, which amounted to the supposed recollections of two individuals against the professed denials of two others, but it had failed to produce a smoking gun. On the benches where Sharon's sister Debra Tate had sat impassively for much of the trial, Emmanuelle Seigner now sat as Kelsey-Fry began his summing-up. 'The burden is on the defence to prove their case,' he told the jury. 'The most obvious witness to call if their case is true, and she supports it, is Beatte Telle. You have heard not one word of evidence from her...'

On Friday 22 July, after deliberating for more than four hours, the jury of nine men and three women reached a unanimous verdict in Polanski's favour. Consequently, he was awarded libel damages of £50,000 and Graydon Carter, editor of *Vanity Fair*, was presented with a legal bill which was estimated to amount to some £1.5 million. Polanski was elated: 'It goes without saying that, whilst the whole episode is a sad one, I am obviously pleased with the jury's verdict today. Three years of my life have been interrupted. Three years within which I have had no choice but to relive the horrible events of August 1969, the murders of my wife, my unborn child and my friends... Many untruths have been published about me, most of which I have ignored, but the allegations printed in the July 2002 edition of *Vanity Fair* could not go unchallenged.'

Ever the gracious loser, Carter read a prepared statement to the assembled media waiting outside the court. 'I find it amazing that a man who lives in France can sue a magazine that is published in America in a British courtroom,' he said. 'As a father of four children – one of whom is a 12-year-old daughter – I find it equally outrageous that this story is considered defamatory, given the fact that Mr. Polanski can't be here because he slept with a 13-year-old girl a quarter of a century ago. Nevertheless, it is interesting to see how the wheels of British justice move. I wish Mr. Polanski well. Now, if you'll excuse me, we have a magazine to put out...'

If anyone else was in doubt about the validity of the verdict, support for Polanski's version of events came now from an unexpected quarter. Unlike *Vanity Fair*'s defence team, the *Daily Mail* had managed to track down Beatte Telle to her home in a suburb of Oslo and it had offered her the chance to put the record straight. 'Roman Polanski came over to the table where I was eating and it was as if he tried to say something but didn't,' she stated. 'He never said that he would make me "another Sharon

Tate" or that he would make me a star. He never spoke to me at all. Polanski just stood there. He just stared at me for ages. Perhaps I reminded him of Sharon Tate. If Ed says that Polanski spoke to me or did anything at all to me or upset me then he is confused.'

A last, magnanimous gesture from Ms Telle affirmed Polanski's faith in a judicial system which had left *Vanity Fair*'s Graydon Carter perplexed: 'I am pleased for him,' she added. 'I'm smiling. He didn't touch me, he just didn't.'

Three months later, *Oliver Twist* opened in cinemas across the world.

When critics make career-defining statements in relation to a director and a single film, such as Philip Kerr's about *The Pianist* in the *New Statesman* ('One has a strong sense that this is the film that Polanski – himself a survivor of the Krakow ghetto – was born to make'), one cannot help but think that anything which comes after must of necessity be anticlimactic. So it was with *Oliver Twist*.

The film was released in America on 30 September and in Britain a week later, on the same day as Nick Park's Hammer pastiche, *Wallace & Gromit in The Curse of the Were-Rabbit*. Critics on both sides of the water found its attention to detail meticulous but its tone too reverential. Todd McCarthy in *Variety* was typical – 'Without his name on the credits, it would be difficult to identify the latest version of *Oliver Twist* as the work of Roman Polanski' – while Cosmo Landesman in *The Sunday Times* was merely foolish: 'I can't remember when I last saw a film that was so haunted by another film,' he began – although it turned out that he was referencing the musical, not the version by David Lean! 'I know it's not fair to expect Polanski's Nancy to sing "As Long As He Needs Me" the way the wonderful Shani Wallis did in *Oliver!* – but Polanski doesn't have a song of his own. This film bears his name, but not his signature.' Philip French in *The Observer* was more learned but no more impressed: 'Behind the opening and closing credits of Roman Polanski's *Oliver Twist* are Gustave Doré's steel engravings of London and its inhabitants. They are elegant, appropriate and suitably atmospheric. What comes between them is much less satisfactory.' 'There are no great flourishes of cinematography, no novelties of interpretation or design other than to put Fagin closer to the centre of the story and make him a little more sympathetic,' Peter Bradshaw appended in *The Guardian*. '*Oliver Twist* does not flag or lose its way and it is always watchable, but the book's original power and force have not been rediscovered.' Under a headline of 'Please, sir, can we have more heart?' *Daily Telegraph* Critic of the Year Sukhdev Sandhu levelled a charge at Polanski which genuinely has haunted him from the first: 'This *Oliver Twist*, almost as cold as many of its characters, is a film far easier to admire than to love.' As though to prove that for every critical opinion, there is an equal and opposite critical opinion, Jenny McCartney in *The Sunday Telegraph* felt that particular attribute to be to the film's greatest strength. 'The director's purging of sentimentality has allowed him greater freedom to explore oft-overlooked parts of the novel. The scene in which Oliver visits Fagin's death cell in Newgate prison in order to forgive him, for example, is both indefinably disturbing and oddly moving.'

With *Oliver Twist*, Polanski had returned to the territory of *Tess* – a timeless and well-loved classic of English literature. The critics had expected him to etch something singular onto the sprawling canvas of Dickens's masterpiece, but his concern, as ever, was merely to render a faithful adaptation of the novel for a new audience to whom previous versions are not even a memory. The most rewarding aspect of *Oliver Twist* is that which most reviewers treated with disdain – its respect for its literary source. When a film veers wildly from the novel on which it has been based, critical voices are raised in outrage; when, conversely, it adheres too closely, the same critics decry the makers' lack of invention – yet Polanski had stated at the outset that his purpose was to make a film which his children could enjoy. John Irving, author of *The Cider House Rules* and himself an Oscar-winning screenwriter, was more comprehending of the motive behind the film, and he could not find enough in it to praise when he was asked to contribute a review to *The Guardian*: 'Polanski's *Oliver Twist* is by far the best [version] I've seen or hope to see. If there is a better writer-director collaboration than Ronald Harwood with Roman Polanski, I am unaware of it; both men are now in their 70s and have had other triumphs, but this *Oliver Twist* is a milestone of a movie.'

If a milestone it is, then it is in more ways than one. *Oliver Twist* represents the last outing to date for a director whose career has spanned almost fifty years – now possibly the last work of his oeuvre. If Sony, *et al*, had thought that they were onto a winner with Polanski's name attached to a film that in an age of digital Golums and high-definition Martian war machines might more suitably have found a home on Hallmark than in the local multiplex, they were soon to be disabused of the notion – *Oliver Twist* played to empty houses and took in barely enough revenue to meet its promotional budget, let alone that of its production. The film accrued a total of a mere \$1.9 million, or some 4% of its cost. For Roman Polanski, 2005 was another triumph, another disaster: the story of his life.

> *Oh fortune, this is too much for me. A poisoning and a wedding, all in one day!*
>
> **Jozef Papkin (Roman Polanski)**, *Revenge* (2002)

When it comes to the story of his life, Polanski's tragedy has been that in the minds of the public, his foibles have become inseparable from his art. He is as responsible as anyone for that perception: in his autobiography, for example, he spends as much time on his sexual conquests as he does on his films. In his attitude to women, he has shown himself to be a chauvinist at best. With some notable exceptions, women seem to have been little more than playthings to a man to whom the whole world became a plaything once he had managed to flee the grey conformity of Communist Poland. Like 'a kid in a candy store', Polanski was seduced by the decadence of the West at a time when East and West were polar extremes, and the

West was becoming more decadent by the day. That he sold out to success – and excess – there can be no doubt. That his actions in the wake of a tragedy which would have been unendurable to many primed him for a fall is equally indisputable. Roman Polanski was the architect of his own misfortune. He lost sight of the idea of moral conscience. His was a world of acquisition and attainment, be it for personal gain or public glory; it was a world which revolved around *self*, and the name of the game was survival. It had been from the beginning.

But in his formative years, when nothing should have marred the flight of the sweet bird of youth, Polanski was instead forced to watch from the shadows as love and trust and decency and humanity were all of them consigned to the gas-ovens.

There are those in the media (particularly in the US), drunk on their own piety, who still expect Roman Polanski to say sorry. Why? To whom does he have to apologise, other than himself? 'I have no intention of apologising for my life. I won't do that. I never have and I never will,' he has said. All of us make mistakes in life; some of them are easily remedied, while others, it seems, can never be remedied at all. In Polanski's case, the mistake he made in 1977 has, ever since, denied him the opportunity to be present and to pay his respects at the grave of his second wife, as well as that of his unborn son.

When Polanski first set foot in Britain in hot pursuit of a career in films, the then-Minister for War, John Profumo, had been forced to resign his post for having lied to Parliament about a brief liaison with a society call-girl. He spent the rest of his life doing charitable work in relative obscurity, eventually dying in 2006 at the age of 93, his name forever associated with a scandal which was brought about by a lapse of judgement in a situation of moral laxity. Polanski's sin may have been the greater as, unlike Profumo's, it did not involve consenting adults, but if his victim nevertheless has forgiven him, why cannot the rest of the world do the same? The sum of a man's life has to be weighed in the

balance of *all* that he does, and any objective consideration of
Roman Polanski's must surely find it in surplus. He was, and is, a
great filmmaker, if sometimes somewhat less a man. He was, and
is, one of cinema's favourite sons. He bestows a formidable legacy
on the creative community which he chose to serve. It was
wrought from a turbulent and troubled life, but it is the more
unforgettable for that. 'It's a miracle he's alive,' Ben Kingsley has
said of him. 'He deserves to be happy. He's been through two
Holocausts in his life.'

'I have a very happy relationship with my wife, and that
satisfaction has mellowed me a little. It's one of the longest
periods of happiness, of being settled, I've had, to the extent that
I sometimes ask myself whether it wasn't actually worth going
through all those difficult times to reach where I am now; after
all, without those times, I wouldn't have ended up here, in this
relationship,' Polanski reflected in September 1992, before the
birth of his first child, and three years into his marriage to Seigner.
That marriage is now 17 years and two children, to the good, and
there is nothing to indicate that the Polanski of today feels any
differently to the way that he did then.

Now 73, and a doting and devoted husband and father, the
former *enfant terrible* of international cinema seems finally to
have settled down. Filmland's 'prince of the dark' has finally
come into the light. All that remains is for the American justice
system to be seen to practice the Christian principles which it
professes to uphold and grant the errant director a belated
pardon for his 30-year-old transgression. His 'victim' has done so
already, which surely should be good enough for any presiding
authority supposedly overseeing the process of crime and
restitution. Ripe to the last, Polanski voiced his feelings about
America to *Libération*, shortly after the release of *The Ninth
Gate*: 'It destroyed me, but now it's destroying itself with its own
Puritanism. It reminds me of a painting of Dali's – *The Virgin
sodomised by her own chastity.*'

*'Though I speak with the tongues of men and angels, and have
not charity, I am become as sounding brass, or a tinkling
cymbal. And though I have the gift of prophecy, and understand
all mysteries, and all knowledge; and though I have all faith,
so that I could remove mountains, and have not charity, I am
nothing.'*

Johnny McQueen (James Mason), *Odd Man Out* (1947)

Roman Polanski's 45-year contribution to the art of cinema is too
wide-ranging, too significant and way too influential for his name
to be sullied indefinitely by the obduracy of the US courts. To err
is human, and Polanski's humanity is unarguable; he has lived
many lives, not all of them agreeable to right-thinking people down
the years. But he has done far more good than harm and he has
challenged, cheered and changed the world through which he has
passed – indisputably for the better.

While America continues to cavil over a 29-year-old
misdemeanour, the European Film Academy announced that it
planned to honour its prodigal son with a lifetime achievement
award, to be presented to him at a ceremony in Warsaw on 2
December. Rumours were also rife over the summer of a
return to acting for Polanski, with a cameo in Brett Ratner's
Paris-based *Rush Hour 3*, alongside franchise-team Jackie Chan
and Chris Tucker. 'I created a part for him,' Ratner told Devin
Faraci of CHUD.com, prior to the commencement of filming.
'We're shooting in Paris, so it's perfect.' At time of writing, neither
event could be confirmed but either would be very welcome.

Polanski is a film artist – actor, director, producer – *par excellence*.
Like any great artist, he deserves our tolerance when it comes to
the fleshly tapestry through which that art is filtered. If artists did
not live extraordinary lives, their art would be ordinary indeed. Or
simply no art at all. That is not a plea for license in the name of
art, but for a modicum of comprehension that the one invariably is
required of the other. It is part of the price.

Roman Polanski has long since paid the price for any sin which he once committed. He should now be thought of only for his legacy to the development of film as art-form – an extraordinary body of work, from a supremely gifted and wholly extraordinary individual.

Appendix
CAST AND CREDITS

1953

Three Stories
(Trzy Opowiesci)
• *Selected Cast*
Lech Pietrasz, Tomasz Zaliwski, Bohdan Kobiela, Jan Bratkowski, Antoni Lewek, Jerzy Kaczmarek, Ryszard Karpinski, Zbigniew Korepta, Stanislaw Michalski, **Roman Polanski (Genek 'The Little'),** Irena Szramowska, Ryszard Waldeck
• *Selected Credits*
Directors: Konrad Nalecki, Ewa Poleska, Czeslaw Petelski/**Writers:** Ewa Poleska, Czeslaw Petelski, Bohdan Czeszko, Andrzej Wajda/**Cinematographers:** Zbigniew Czajkowski, Jerzy Lipman, Stefan Matyjaszkiewicz, Czeslaw Swirta/**Music:** Tadeusz Kiesewetter/**Production Designer:** Wojciech Krysztofiak/**Editor:** Joanna Rojewska
Poland 108 minutes

1955

The Magic Bicycle
(Zaczarowany Rower)
• *Selected Cast*
Józef Nalberczak, Teodor Gendera, Bernard Michalski, Wlodzimierz Skoczylas, Ignacy Gogolewski, Wincenty Grabarczyk, Julian Jabczynski, Boleslaw Plotnicki, Aleksander Sewruk, Stanislaw Libner, **Roman Polanski (Adas),** Aleksander Bentczak, Czeslaw Byszewski, Jerzy Felczynski, Michal Gazda
• *Selected Credits*
Director: Silik Sternfeld/**Writers:** Jerzy Suszko, Bohdan Tomaszewski/

Cinematographer: Tadeusz Korecki/**Music:** Jerzy Harald/**Production Designer:** Roman Mann/**Editor:** Zofia Dwornik
Poland 71 minutes

A Generation *(Pokolenie)*
• *Selected Cast*
Tadeusz Lomnicki, Urszula Modrzynska, Tadeusz Janczar, Janusz Paluszkiewicz, Ryszard Kotas, **Roman Polanski (Mundek),** Ludwik Benoit, Zofia Czerwinska, Zbigniew Cybulski, Tadeusz Fijewski, Zygmunt Hobot, Cezary Julski, Bronislaw Kassowski, August Kowalczyk, Jerzy Krasowski
• *Selected Credits*
Director: Andrzej Wajda/**Writer:** Bohdan Czeszko/**Cinematographer:** Jerzy Lipman/**Music:** Andrzej Markowski/**Production Designer:** Roman Mann/**Editor:** Czeslaw Raniszewski
Home Vision 83 minutes

1956

Nikodem Dyzma
• *Selected Cast*
Adolf Dymsza, Urszula Modrzynska, Tadeusz Gwiazdowski, Kazimierz Fabisiak, Ewa Krasnodebska, Lech Madalinski, Andrzej Bogucki, Edward Dziewonski, Stanislaw Milski, Kazimierz Wilamowski, Tadeusz Fijewski, Halina Dobrowolska, Zygmunt Chmielewski, Krystyna Ciechomska, Jerzy Bielenia, **Roman Polanski (Boy at Hotel)**
• *Selected Credits*
Director: Jan Rybkowski/**Writer:** Ludwik Starski/**Cinematographer:** Wladyslaw Forbert/**Music:** Jerzy Harald/**Production**

Designer: Anatol Radzinowicz/**Editor:**
Czeslaw Raniszewski
Pol-Ton 107 minutes

1957

Murder *(Morderstwo)*
· *Selected Credits*
Director: Roman Polanski/Writer: Roman
Polanski/**Cinematographer:** Nikola Todorow
Criterion 2 minutes

A Toothful Smile
(Usmiech Zebiczny)
· *Selected Cast*
Nikola Todorow
· *Selected Credits*
Director: Roman Polanski/Writer: Roman
Polanski/**Cinematographer:** Henryk
Kucharski
Criterion 2 minutes

Breaking Up the Dance
(Rozbijemy Zabawe)
· *Selected Credits*
Director: Roman Polanski/Writer: Roman
Polanski/**Cinematographers:** Andrzej
Galincki, Marek Nowicki
Criterion 8 minutes

The Wrecks *(Wraki)*
· *Selected Cast*
Zbigniew Józefowicz, Zbigniew Cybulski,
Urszula Modrzynska, Jadwiga Prolinska,
Janusz Klosinski, Lech Madalinski, Adam
Kwiatkowski, Mieczyslaw Gajda, Roman
Klosowski, Czeslaw Piaskowski, **Roman
Polanski**, Kazimierz Wichniarz, Jarema
Stepowski, Juliusz Lubicz-Lisowski, Stanislaw
Michalski
· *Selected Credits*
Directors: Ewa Petelska, Czeslaw Petelski/
Writers: Ewa Petelska, Czeslaw Petelski,
Bohdan Czeszko, Janusz Meissner/
Cinematographer: Karol Chodura/**Music:**
Mateusz Wolberg/**Production Designers:**
Roman Mann, Roman Wolyniec
Poland 89 minutes

End of the Night
(Koniec Nocy)
· *Selected Cast*
Zbigniew Cybulski, Ryszard Filipski,
Adam Fiut, Marian Gorczynski, Jadwiga
Andrzejewska, Anna Ciepielewska, Józef
Kalita, Katarzyna Karska, Jerzy Kozakiewicz,
Ryszard Lomnicki, Tadeusz Ordeyg, **Roman
Polanski (Little One)**, Barbara Rachwalska,
Eugeniusz Szewczyk, Ewa Zdzieszynska
· *Selected Credits*
Directors: Julian Dziedzina, Pawel
Komorowski, Walentyna Uszycka/**Assistant
Director: Roman Polanski/Writers:** Julian
Dziedzina, Pawel Komorowski, Antoni
Bohdziewicz, Bohdan Drozdowksi, Marek
Hlasko, Jerzy Wójcik/**Cinematographers:**
Jerzy Wójcik, Henryk Depczyk, Krzysztof
Winiewicz/**Music:** Jerzy Kurczewski/**Editors:**
Wieslawa Stanek, Krystyna Tunis
Poland 90 minutes

1958

Two Men and a Wardrobe
(Dwaj Ludzie Z Szafa)
· *Selected Cast*
Jakuba Goldberga, Henryka Klube, Andrzej
Kondratiuk, Barbara Lass, Stanislaw
Michalski, **Roman Polanski (Bad Boy)**
· *Selected Credits*
Director: Roman Polanski/Writer: Roman
Polanski/**Cinematographer:** Maciej Kijowski/
Music: Krzysztof T Komeda
Criterion 14 minutes

Call My Wife
(Zadzwoncie Do Mojej Zony)
· *Selected Cast*
Wienczyslaw Glinski, Barbara Polomska,
Josef Bek, Hanka Bielicka, Jarmila Beránková,
Zygmunt Chmielewski, Jadwiga Chojnacka,
Bronislaw Darski, Frantisek Filipovský,
Waclaw Jankowski, Stanislaw Jaworski,
Ireneusz Kanicki, Andrzej Kopiczynski,
Andrzej Kostenko, Marian Lacz, Zdzislaw
Lubelski, Ignacy Machowski, Stanislaw
Milski, Artur Mlodnicki, Adam Mularczyk,

Leon Niemczyk, Ewa Pachonska, Jerzy
Passendorfer, Jirina Petrovická, Halina
Pienkiewicz, **Roman Polanski (Dancer)**,
Edward Radulski, B Rendl, Witold Sobocinski,
Jarema Stepowski, Eugeniusz Szewczyk,
Natalia Szymanska, Robert Vrchota
• *Selected Credits*
Directors: Jaroslav Mach, Halina Garus,
Lech Lorentowicz, Frantisek Matousek,
Jerzy Passendorfer, Elishka Vojtova, Marian
Zietkiewicz/**Writers:** Jaroslav Mach, Jan
Fethke, Václav Jelínek, Zdzislaw Skowronski/
Cinematographer: Boguslaw Lambach/
Music: Wladyslaw Szpilman/**Production
Designer:** Anatol Radzinowicz/**Editors:** Jirina
Lukesová, Vlasta Rubasova, Jadwiga Zajicek
Ceskoslovenský Státní 93 minutes

1959

The Lamp *(Lampa)*
• *Selected Cast*
Roman Polanski (Passer-by)
• *Selected Credits*
Director/Writer: Roman Polanski/
Cinematographer: K Romanowski
Criterion 8 minutes

When Angels Fall
(Gdy Spadaja Anioly)
• *Selected Cast*
Barbara Kwiatkowski, **Roman Polanski (Old
Woman)**, Henryk Kluba, Andrzej Kondratiuk
• *Selected Credits*
Director: Roman Polanski/**Writer:** Roman
Polanski/**Cinematographer:** Henryk
Kucharski/**Music:** Krzysztof Komeda/
Production Designer: Kazimierz Wisniak
Criterion 21 minutes

Lotna
• *Selected Cast*
Jerzy Pichelski, Adam Pawlikowski, Jerzy
Moes, Mieczyslaw Loza, Bozena Kurowska,
Bronislaw Dardzinski, H Dzieszynski,
Wieslaw Golas, Henryk Hunko, Tadeusz
Kosudarski, Irena Malkiewicz, Artur
Mlodnicki, Ludwik Pak, **Roman Polanski**

(Musician), Karól Rommel, Tadeusz Somogi,
M Wisniowski, Boleslaw Wozniak
• *Selected Credits*
Director: Andrzej Wajda/**Writers:**
Andrzej Wajda, Wojciech Zukrowski/
Cinematographer: Jerzy Lipman/**Music:**
Tadeusz Baird/**Production Designer:** Roman
Wolyniec/**Editor:** Janina Niedzwiecka
Pol-Ton 90 minutes

1960

Cross-eyed Luck
(Zezowate Szczescie)
• *Selected Cast*
Bogumil Kobiela, Maria Ciesielska, Helena
Dabrowska, Barbara Kwiatkowska, Krystyna
Karkowska, Barbara Polomska, Irena
Stalonczyk, Tadeusz Bartosik, Henryk
Bak, Mariusz Dmochowski, Aleksander
Dzwonkowski, Edward Dziewonski, Tadeusz
Janczar, Stanislaw Jaworski, Andrzej Krasicki,
Roman Polanski (Jola's Tutor)
• *Selected Credits*
Director: Andrzej Munk/**Assistant Director:**
Roman Polanski/**Writer:** Jerzy Stefan
Stawinski/**Cinematographers:** Jerzy Lipman,
Krzysztof Winiewicz/**Music:** Jan Krenz,
Andrzej Markowski/**Production Designer:** Jan
Grandys/**Editor:** Jadwiga Zajicek
POLart 92 minutes

Good Bye, Till Tomorrow
(Do Widzenia, Do Jutra)
• *Selected Cast*
Zbigniew Cybulski, Teresa Tuszynska,
Grazyna Muszynska, Barbara Baranowska,
Wlodzimierz Bielicki, Jacek Fedorowicz,
Roman Polanski (Romek), Eleonora
Kaluzynska, Tadeusz Wojtych
• *Selected Credits*
Director: Janusz Morgenstern/**Writers:**
Zbigniew Cybulski, Bogumil Kobiela, Wilhelm
Mach/**Cinematographer:** Jan Laskowski/
Music: Krzysztof Komeda/**Production
Designers:** Roman Mann, Ryszard Potocki/
Editor: J Niedwiecka
Poland 88 minutes

Innocent Sorcerers
(Niewinni Czarodzieje)
• *Selected Cast*
Tadeusz Lomnicki, Krystyna Stypulkowska,
Wanda Koczeska, Kalina Jedrusik, Teresa
Szmigielówna, Zbigniew Cybulski, **Roman
Polanski (Dudzio),** Andrzej Nowakowski,
Andrzej Gawronski
• *Selected Credits*
Director: Andrzej Wajda/**Writers:** Jerzy
Andrzejewski, Jerzy Skolimowski/
Cinematographer: Krzysztof Winiewicz/
Music: Krzysztof Komeda/**Production
Designer:** Leszek Wajda/**Editor:** Wieslawa
Otocka
Poland 87 minutes

1961
The Fat and the Lean
(Le Gros et le Maigre)
• *Selected Cast*
André Katelbach, **Roman Polanski (the Lean)**
• *Selected Credits*
**Director/Writer: Roman Polanski/Producers:
Roman Polanski,** Jean-Pierre Rousseau/
Cinematographer: Jean-Michel Boussaguet/
Music: Krzysztof Komeda
Criterion 15 minutes

Beware of the Yeti!
(Ostroznie, Yetti!)
• *Selected Cast*
Jarema Stepowski, Stefan Bartik, Ludwik
Benoit, Bogusz Bilewski, Anna Czapnikowna,
Mieczyslaw Czechowicz, Bronislaw Darski,
Wieslaw Golas, Zdzislaw Lesniak, Stanislaw
Milski, Józef Nowak, Bronislaw Pawlik,
Wojciech Pokora, **Roman Polanski (Driver),**
Czeslaw Roszkowski
• *Selected Credits*
Director: Czekalski/**Writers:** Andrzej
Brzozowski, Andrzej Czekalski/
Cinematographers: Henryk Depczyk,
Jan Janczewski/**Music:** Lucjan Kaszycki/
Production Designer: Jerzy Skrzepinski/
Editor: Krystyna Batory
Poland 77 minutes

Samson
• *Selected Cast*
Serge Merlin, Alina Janowska, Elzbieta
Kepinska, Jan Ciecierski, Tadeusz Bartosik,
Wladyslaw Kowalski, Irena Netto, Beata
Tyszkiewicz, Jan Ibel, Bogumil Antczak,
Edmund Fetting, Roland Glowacki, Andrzej
Herder, Zygmunt Hübner, Zofia Jamry,
Roman Polanski
• *Selected Credits*
Director: Andrzej Wajda/**Writers**: Andrzej
Wajda, Kazimierz Brandys/**Cinematographer:**
Jerzy Wójcik/**Music:** Tadeusz Baird/
Production Designer: Leszek Wajda/**Editor:**
Janina Niedzwiecka
Poland 117 minutes

Mammals *(Ssaki)*
• *Selected Cast*
Henryk Kluba, Michala Zolnierkiewicza
• *Selected Credits*
**Director: Roman Polanski/Writers:
Roman Polanski,** Andrzej Kondriatiuk/
Cinematographer: Andrzej Kostenko/
Music: Krzysztof Komeda/**Editors:** Janina
Niedzwiedzka, Halina Prugar
Criterion 10 minutes

1962
Knife in the Water
• *Cast*
Andrzej....................................Leon Niemczyk
Krystyna..................................Jolanta Umecka
Young Boy.....................Zygmunt Malanowicz
Krystyna (voice)................Anna Ciepielewska
Young Boy (voice)..................Roman Polanski
• *Selected Credits*
Director: Roman Polanski
Producer: Stanislaw Zylewicz
Screenplay: Jerzy Skolimowski, **Roman
Polanski**
Music: Krzysztof T Komeda
Cinematography: Jerzy Lipman
Camera Operator: Andrzej Gronau
Production Designer: Boleslaw
Kamykowski
Art Director: Jerzy Bossak

Editor: Halina Prugar
Sound: Halina Paszkowska
Sound Assistant: Jerzy Szawlowski
Production Manager: Josef Krakowski
Assistant Directors: Jakub Goldberg, Andrzej Kostenko, Maria Pietrzak
Makeup: Zdzislaw Papierz
ZRF 'Kamera' 98 minutes

1964

The World's Most Beautiful Swindlers
(Les Plus Belles Escroqueries du Monde)

• *Selected Cast*
Mie Hama, Jan Teulings, Gabriella Giorgelli, Guido Guiseppone, Beppe Mannaiuolo, Jean-Pierre Cassel, Francis Blanche, Catherine Deneuve, Sacha Briquet, Charles Denner, Arnold Gelderman, Jean-Luc Godard, Nicole Karen, Christian Lentretien, Jean-Louis Maury, Ken Mitsuda, Jean Seberg, László Szabó, Yatsuko Tanami, Philomène Toulouse
• *Selected Credits*
Directors: Claude Chabrol, Jean-Luc Godard, Ugo Gregoretti, **Roman Polanski**, Hiromichi Horikawa/**Writers:** Claude Chabrol, Jean-Luc Godard, Ugo Gregoretti, **Roman Polanski**, Gérard Brach, Paul Gégauff/**Producer:** Pierre Roustang/**Cinematographers:** Raoul Coutard, Tonino Delli Colli, Jerzy Lipman, Asakazu Nakai, Jean Rabier/**Music:** Serge Gainsbourg, Pierre Jansen, Krzysztof Komeda, Michel Legrand, Keitaro Miho, Piero Umiliani/**Editors:** Hervé de Luze, Jacques Gaillard, Agnès Guillemot, Rita van Royen
Continental 111 minutes

1965

Repulsion
• *Cast*
Carole Ledoux..................Catherine Deneuve
Michael...........................Ian Hendry

Colin...John Fraser
Hélène Ledoux.....................Yvonne Furneaux
Landlord................................Patrick Wymark
Miss Balch.............................Renee Houston
Madame Denise......................Valerie Taylor
John...James Villiers
Bridget...Helen Fraser
Reggie...Hugh Futcher
Mrs Rendlesham.....................Monica Merlin
Manicurist...........................Imogen Graham
Workman...Mike Pratt
Spoon Player...........................**Roman Polanski**
• *Selected Credits*
Director: Roman Polanski
Producer: Gene Gutowski
Screenplay: Gérard Brach, **Roman Polanski**
Associate Producers: Robert Sterne, Sam Waynberg
Music: Chico Hamilton
Cinematographer: Gilbert Taylor
Camera Operator: Alan Hall
Art Director: Seamus Flannery
Editor: Alastair McIntyre
Sound Recordist: Gerry Humphreys
Sound Mixer: Leslie Hammond
Assistant Director: Ted Sturgis
Makeup: Tom Smith
Hair Stylist: Gladys Leakey
Executive Producers: Michael Klinger, Tony Tenser
Compton/Tekli 107 minutes

1966

Cul-de-Sac
• *Cast*
George................................Donald Pleasence
Teresa.................................Françoise Dorléac
Richard......................................Lionel Stander
Albie.......................................Jack MacGowran
Christopher.................................Iain Quarrier
Christopher's Father.............Geoffrey Sumner
Christopher's Mother............Renee Houston
Philip Fairweather...................Robert Dorning
Marion Fairweather.......................Marie Kean
Cecil.......................................William Franklyn
Jacqueline.....................................Jackie Bisset
Nicholas....................................Trevor Delaney

• **Selected Credits**
Director: Roman Polanski
Producers: Gene Gutowski, Michael Klinger, Tony Tenser
Screenplay: Gerard Brach, **Roman Polanski**
Music: Komeda
Cinematographer: Gilbert Taylor
Camera Operators: Roy Ford, Geoffrey Seaholme
Production Designer: Voytek
Art Director: George Lack
Editor: Alastair McIntyre
Sound Editor: David Campling
Production Manager: Don Weeks
Assistant Directors: Roger Simons, Ted Sturgis
Makeup: Alan Brownie
Hair Stylist: Joyce James
Wardrobe: Bridget Sellers
Executive Producer: Sam Waynberg
Compton/Tekli 112 minutes

1967

The Vampire Killers

• **Cast**

Professor Abronsius...............Jack MacGowran
Alfred, Abronsius' Assistant.....Roman Polanski
Shagal, the Inn-Keeper........................Alfie Bass
Rebecca Chagal............................Jessie Robins
Sarah Chagal..................................Sharon Tate
Count von Krolock..........................Ferdy Mayne
Herbert von Krolock.......................Iain Quarrier
Koukol, the Servant.......................Terry Downes
Magda, the Maid............................Fiona Lewis
Village Idiot...................................Ronald Lacey
Sleigh Driver..........................Sydney Bromley
Woodcutters................Andreas Malandrinos/
            Otto Diamant/Matthew Walters

• **Selected Credits**
Director: Roman Polanski
Producer: Gene Gutowski
Screenplay: Gérard Brach, **Roman Polanski**
Music: Christopher Komeda
Cinematographer: Douglas Slocombe
Camera Operator: Chic Waterson
Production Designer: Wilfrid Shingleton
Art Director: Fred Carter

Editor: Alastair McIntyre
Sound Editor: Lionel Selwyn
Sound Recordist: George Stephenson
Production Manager: David W Orton
Assistant Director: Roy Stevens
Makeup: Tom Smith
Hair Stylist: Biddy Chrystal
Costume Designer: Sophie Devine
Executive Producer: Martin Ransohoff
M-G-M/Filmways 108 (88) minutes

1968

Rosemary's Baby

• **Cast**

Rosemary Woodhouse...................Mia Farrow
Guy Woodhouse...................John Cassavetes
Minnie Castevet..........................Ruth Gordon
Roman Castevet...................Sidney Blackmer
Edward 'Hutch' Hutchins........Maurice Evans
Dr Abraham Sapirstein.............Ralph Bellamy
Terry Gionoffrio.........................Angela Dorian
Laura-Louise....................................Patsy Kelly
Mr Nicklas.....................................Elisha Cook
Elise Dunstan.....................Emmaline Henry
Dr C C Hill...............................Charles Grodin
Grace Cardiff..............................Hanna Landy
Dr Shand......................................Philip Leeds
Diego.....................................D'Urville Martin
Mrs Gilmore.........................Hope Summers
Rosemary's Girlfriend.........Marianne Gordon
Tiger, Rosemary's Girlfriend....Wendy Wagner
Salesman..................................Bill Baldwin Sr
Mr Wees...............................Walter Baldwin
Sun-Browned Man.......................Roy Barcroft
Mrs Fountain......................Charlotte Boerner
Babysitter...Gail Bonney
Claudia Comfort.......................Carol Brewster
Sister Veronica............................Lynn Brinker
Argyron Stavropoulos............Sebastian Brook
Man by Pay Phone...................William Castle
Allen Stone............................Gordon Connell
Mrs John F Kennedy.......Patricia Ann Conway
Donald Baumgart.........................Tony Curtis
Dee Bertillon..................................Joyce Davis
Skipper...Paul Denton
Man...Duke Fishman
Nurse...Janet Garland

Pedro...Michel Gomez
Mechanic...................................John Halloran
Young Japanese Man................Ernest Harada
Dr Sapirstein's Receptionist...Marilyn Harvey
Sister Agnes....................................Jean Inness
Mrs Byron......................................Mona Knox
Portia Haynes................Mary Louise Lawson
Young Woman........................Natalie Masters
Young Man..............................Elmer Modling
Men at Party...........Floyd Mutrux/Josh Peine
Mrs Wees...................................Patricia O'Neal
Mr Fountain...........................Robert Osterloh
Rain Morgan................................Gale Peters
Patron...Jack Ramage
Pregnant Woman........................Joan T Reilly
Lou Comfort...................George R Robertson
Workman.................................George Savalas
Mrs Sabatini............................Almira Sessions
Pope...Michael Shillo
Mr Gilmore....................................Bruno Sidar
Man at the Party......................Tom Signorelli
Woman at the Party......................Sharon Tate
Taxi Driver.....................................Al Szathmary
Devil..Clay Tanner
Lisa..Viki Vigen
Hugh Dunstan..............................Frank White

• *Selected Credits*
Director: Roman Polanski
Producer: William Castle
Screenplay: Roman Polanski
   from the novel *Rosemary's Baby* by Ira
   Levin
Associate Producer: Dona Holloway
Music: Christopher Komeda
Cinematographer: William Fraker
Production Designer: Richard Sylbert
Art Director: Joel Schiller
Editor: Sam O'Steen, Bob Wyman
Sound Recordist: Harold Lewis
Production Manager: William C Davidson
Assistant Director: Daniel J McCauley
Makeup: Allan Snyder
Hair Stylists: Sydney Guilaroff, Vidal Sassoon,
   Sherry Wilson
Costume Designer: Anthea Sylbert
Stunts: Roger Creed, Frank Orsatti
Paramount/William Castle Productions
136 minutes

1969
The Magic Christian
• *Selected Cast*
Peter Sellers, Ringo Starr, Isabel Jeans,
Caroline Blakiston, Wilfrid Hyde-White,
Richard Attenborough, Leonard Frey,
Laurence Harvey, Christopher Lee, Spike
Milligan, **Roman Polanski (Solitary Drinker)**,
Raquel Welch, Tom Boyle, Victor Maddern,
Terence Alexander
• *Selected Credits*
Director: Joseph McGrath/**Writers:**
Joseph McGrath, Terry Southern,
Graham Chapman, John Cleese,
Peter Sellers/**Producer:** Denis O'Dell/
Cinematographer: Geoffrey Unsworth/
Music: Paul McCartney, Ken Thorne/
Production Designer: Assheton Gorton/
Editor: Kevin Connor
Commonwealth United 92 minutes

1971
Macbeth
• *Cast*
Macbeth...Jon Finch
Lady Macbeth........................Francesca Annis
Banquo...Martin Shaw
Macduff....................................Terence Bayler
Ross...John Stride
Duncan......................................Nicholas Selby
Malcolm....................................Stephan Chase
Donalbain....................................Paul Shelley
First Witch......................Maisie MacFarquhar
Second Witch................................Elsie Taylor
Third Witch......................Noelle Rimmington
Seyton..Noel Davis
Porter.......................................Sydney Bromley
Doctor....................................Richard Pearson
Gentlewoman..........................Patricia Mason
First Murderer........................Michael Balfour
Second Murderer..............Andrew McCulloch
Fleance..Keith Chegwin
Lennox....................................Andrew Laurence
Angus......................................Bernard Archard
Caithness.................................Bruce Purchase

Menteith...Frank Wylie
Lady Macduff............................Diane Fletcher
Macduff's Son..........................Mark Dightam
King's Grooms...........Bill Drysdale/Roy Jones
Cowdor...Vic Abbott
First Thane...Ian Hogg
Second Thane............................Geoffrey Reed
Third Thane..................................Nigel Ashton
Young Siward..........................William Hobbs
Old Siward..Alf Joint
Doctor's Apprentice....................Paul Hennen
Dancers...........Olga Anthony/Roy Desmond/
  Pamela Foster/John Gordon/Barbara Ann
  Grimes/Aud Johansen/Janie Kells/
  Dickie Martyn/Beth Owen/
  Christina Paul/Maxine Skelton/
  Don Vernon/Anna Willoughby
Old Soldiers...........David Ellison/Howard Lang
Hanging Man...........................Clement Freud
Soldier.................................Terence Mountain
Witch...Lynette Reade

• *Selected Credits*
Director: Roman Polanski
Producer: Andrew Braunsberg
Screenplay: Kenneth Tynan
  from the tragedy *Macbeth* by William
  Shakespeare
Associate Producer: Timothy Burrill
Music: The Third Ear Band
Cinematographer: Gil Taylor
Camera Operator: Alec Mills
Production Designer: Wilfrid Shingleton
Art Director: Fred Carter
Editor: Alastair McIntyre
Sound Mixer: Simon Kaye
Assistant Director: Simon Relph
Makeup: Tom Smith
Hair Stylist: Biddy Chrystal
Costume Designer: Anthony Mendleson
Wardrobe: Jackie Breed, Phil Pickford
Special Effects: Ted Samuels
Stunts: Ken Buckle, Russ Jones
Executive Producer: Hugh M Hefner
Columbia/Playboy Productions
140 minutes

1972

What?
• **Cast**
Alex Noblart..................Marcello Mastroianni
Nancy...Sydne Rome
Joseph Noblart............................Hugh Griffith
Priest...Guido Alberti
Tony..............................Gianfranco Piacentini
Young Oaf #1 in Car.............Carlo Delle Piane
Young Oaf #2 in Car..............Mario Bussolino
Catone..................................Henning Schlüter
Dresser..................................Christiane Barry
Man-Servant.................................Pietro Tordi
Chambermaid.................Nerina Montagnani
Germans........................Mogens von Gadow/
                                    Dieter Hallervorden
Nurse.......................................Elisabeth Witte
Edward...John Karlsen
Giovanni......................................Romolo Valli
Enzo...Franco Pesce
Ruth...Cicely Browne
Naked Girl with Hat..................Renee Langer
Charlie............................Richard McNamara
Jimmy....................................Roger Middleton
Naked Girl..............................Birgitta Nilsson
Mosquito...............................Roman Polanski
with Livio Galassi/Alvaro Vitali/Luigi Bonos/
  Carla Mancini
• **Selected Credits**
Director: Roman Polanski
Producer: Carlo Ponti
Screenplay: Gérard Brach, **Roman Polanski**
Music: Claudio Gizzi
Cinematographers: Marcello Gatti, Giuseppe
  Ruzzolini
Production Designer: Aurelio Crugnola
Art Director: Franco Fumagalli
Editor: Alastair McIntyre
Sound Mixer: Bernard Bats
Assistant Director: Tony Brandt
Makeup: Giuseppe Banchelli
Costume Designer: Adriana Berselli
AVCO Embassy 112 minutes

1973

Blood For Dracula
(Andy Warhol's Dracula)
• *Selected Cast*
Joe Dallesandro, Udo Kier, Arno Juerging,
Maxime McKendry, Milena Vukotic,
Dominique Darel, Stefania Casini, Silvia
Dionisio, Inna Alexeievna, Gil Cagnie, Emi
Califri, Eleonora Zani, Vittorio De Sica,
Roman Polanski (Man in Tavern)
• *Selected Credits*
Director: Paul Morrissey/**Writer:** Paul
Morrissey/**Producers:** Andrew Braunsberg,
Andy Warhol/**Cinematographer:** Luigi
Kuveiller/**Music:** Claudio Gizzi/**Production
Designer:** Enrico Job/**Editors:** Jed Johnson,
Franca Silvi
Ariel 106 minutes

1974

Chinatown
• Cast
Jake 'JJ' Gittes...........................Jack Nicholson
Evelyn Cross Mulwray...............Faye Dunaway
Noah Cross...................................John Huston
Lieutenant Lou Escobar................Perry Lopez
Russ Yelburton........................John Hillerman
Hollis I Mulwray.....................Darrell Zwerling
Ida Sessions...................................Diane Ladd
Claude Mulvihill.............................Roy Jenson
Man with Knife.......................Roman Polanski
Detective Loach.........................Dick Bakalyan
Lawrence Walsh............................Joe Mantell
Duffy...Bruce Glover
Sophie..Nandu Hinds
Lawyer..James O'Rear
Kahn...James Hong
Mulwray's Maid............................Beulah Quo
Mulwray's Gardener...................Jerry Fujikawa
Katherine Cross......................Belinda Palmer
Mayor Bagby................................Roy Roberts
Councilmen............Noble Willingham/Elliott
Montgomery
Irate Farmer at Council Meeting............Rance
Howard

Barney, the Barber......................George Justin
Banker at Barbershop........ ....Doc Erickson
Mulwray's Secretary.........................Fritzi Burr
Morty...Charles Knapp
Boy on Horseback................Claudio Martínez
Cross's Butler.........................Federico Roberto
Clerk at Hall of Records.............Allan Warnick
Farmers in the Valley...................John Holland
Jesse Vint/Jim Burke/Denny Arnold
Curly...Burt Young
Curly's Wife.........................Elizabeth Harding
Mr Palmer....................................John Rogers
Emma Dill.......................................Cecil Elliott
Policemen............Paul Jenkins/Lee de Broux/
Bob Golden
Driver......................................Richard Warren
• *Selected Credits*
Director: Roman Polanski
Producer: Robert Evans
Screenplay: Robert Towne
Associate Producer: CO Erickson
Music: Jerry Goldsmith
Cinematographer: John A Alonzo
Camera Operator: Hugh K Gagnier
Production Designer: Richard Sylbert
Art Director: W Stewart Campbell
Editor: Sam O'Steen
Sound Editors: Bob Cornett, Roger Sword
Sound Mixer: Larry Jost
Production Manager: CO Erickson
Assistant Director: Howard W Koch Jr
Makeup: Hank Edds, Lee Harman
Hair Stylists: Susan Germaine, Vivienne
Walker
Wardrobe: Richard Bruno, Jean Merrick
Costume Designer: Anthea Sylbert
Special Effects: Logan Frazee
Stunt Coordinator: Hal Needham
Stunts: Jim Burk, Steven Burnett, Alan Gibbs
Paramount 131 minutes

1976

The Tenant
• *Cast*
Trelkovsky...............................Roman Polanski
Stella...Isabelle Adjani
Monsieur Zy...........................Melvyn Douglas

Madame Dioz................................Jo Van Fleet
Scope.......................................Bernard Fresson
Madame Gaderian.......................Lila Kedrova
Husband at the Accident.......Claude Dauphin
Neighbour..................................Claude Pieplu
Georges Badar.....................................Rufus
Simon....................................Romain Bouteille
Cafe Owner...............................Jacques Monod
Robert.................................Patrice Alexsandre
Policeman............................Jean-Pierre Bagot
Office Worker.........................Josiane Balasko
Scope's Neighbour......................Michel Blanc
Madame Zy................................Florence Blot
Wife at Accident.........................Louba Chazel
Patron.................................Jacques Chevalier
Stella's Friend...............................Jacky Cohen
Witness at Accident......................Alain David
Bar Waiter.........................Bernard Donnadieu
Begge...Alain Frerot
Priest...Raoul Guylad
Madame Gaderian's Daughter.....Eva Ionesco
Office Clerk................................Gérard Jugnot
Head Nurse..........................Héléna Manson
Lucille.....................................Maïté Nahyr
Cafe Waiter............................André Penvern
Drunk......................................Gérard Pereira
Simone Choule..............Dominique Poulange
Tramp.....................................Arlette Reinerg
Jean-Claude..............................Jacques Rosny
Philippe.......................................Serge Spira
Martine....................................Vanessa Vaylord
Police Sergeant........................François Viaur
The Concierge........................Shelley Winters
Neighbour....................................Albert Delpy
Peeping Tom.................................Alain Sarde

• **Selected Credits**
Director: Roman Polanski
Producer: Andrew Braunsberg
Screenplay: Gérard Brach, **Roman Polanski**
from the novel *Le Locataire Chimérique* by
Roland Topor
Associate Producer: Alain Sarde
Music: Philippe Sarde
Cinematographer: Sven Nykvist
Camera Operator: Jean Harnois
Production Designer: Pierre Guffroy
Art Directors: Claude Moesching, Albert
Rajau
Editor: Françoise Bonnot

Sound Editor: Michele Boehm
Sound Mixer: Jean-Pierre Ruh
Production Manager: Marc Maurette
Assistant Director: Marc Grunebaum
Makeup: Didier Lavergne
Hair Stylist: Ludovic Paris
Wardrobe: Mimi Gayo
Costume Designer: Jacques Schmidt
Executive Producer: Hercules Bellville
Paramount 125 minutes

1979

Tess
• *Cast*
Tess Durbeyfield....................Nastassja Kinski
Angel Clare......................................Peter Firth
Alec d'Urberville.........................Leigh Lawson
John Durbeyfield.............................John Collin
Mrs Durbeyfield...................Rosemary Martin
Miriam......................................Carolyn Pickles
Vicar of Marlott....................Richard Pearson
Reverend Mr Clare.................David Markham
Mrs Clare.........................Pascale de Boysson
Izz..Suzanna Hamilton
Retty.....................................Caroline Embling
Parson Tringham.........................Tony Church
Girls in Henhouse.....................Lesley Dunlop/
Marilyne Even
Mrs d'Urberville.....................Sylvia Coleridge
Dairyman Crick.............................Fred Bryant
Farmer Groby.......................Dicken Ashworth
Landlady.................................Patsy Rowlands
Old Dairy Hands.......John Barrett/Ann Tirard
Girls in Meadow.................Brigid Erin Bates/
Jeanne Biras
Housekeeper....................................Patsy Smart
Felix Clare..John Bett
Cuthbert Clare..........................Tom Chadbon
Children....Géraldine Arzul/Stephanie Treille/
Elodie Warnod/Ben Reeks
Bailiff...............................Jean-Jacques Daubin
Yokel at Barn-Dance..............Jacob Weisbluth
Harvesters...Jacques Mathou/Véronique Alain
Mrs Crick..................................Josine Comellas
Mercy Chant.........................Arielle Dombasle
Parson at Wedding..........Gordon Richardson
Pedler.......................................Jimmy Gardner

Landlord...John Gill
New Tenant.......... ....Forbes Collins
Possmen................Keith Buckley/John Moore
Constable..............................Graham Weston
Carter...Reg Dent
with Lina Roxa
• *Selected Credits*
Director: Roman Polanski
Producer: Claude Berri
Screenplay: Gérard Brach, **Roman Polanski**,
  John Brownjohn
  from the novel *Tess of the d'Urbervilles* by
  Thomas Hardy
Co-Producer: Timothy Burrill
Associate Producer: Jean-Pierre Rassam
Music: Philippe Sarde
Cinematographers: Ghislain Cloquet,
  Geoffrey Unsworth
Camera Operator: Jean Harnois
Production Designer: Pierre Guffroy
Art Director: Jack Stephens
Editors: Alastair McIntyre, Tom Priestley
Sound Editors: Peter Horrocks,
  Hervé de Luze
Sound Mixer: Jean-Pierre Ruh
Production Manager: Paul Maigret
Assistant Director: Thierry Chabert
Makeup: Didier Lavergne
Hair Stylist: Ludovic Paris
Wardrobe: Thérèse Ripaud, Frederic Vieille,
  Caroline de Vivaise
Costume Designer: Anthony Powell
Executive Producer: Pierre Grunstein
AMLF/Columbia 190 minutes

1982

Chassé-croisé
• *Selected Cast*
Pascal Greggory, Arielle Dombasle, Pierre
Clémenti, Alexandra Stewart, Rosette, Eric
Rohmer, Marie Rivière, **Roman Polanski**,
Christian Marquand, Jean-Pierre Kalfon,
François-Marie Banier, Geoffrey Carey, Hervé
Duhamel, Youssef Baccouch, Pierre-André
Boutang, Maya Brando, Carita, Philippe
Collin, Edwige, Huguette Faget, Gérard
Falconetti, Nathalie Guérin, Isabelle Illiers,

Sabine Korté, Alexandre Matzefils, John
Mitchel, Sandrine Moisson
• *Selected Credits*
Director: Arielle Dombasle/**Writer:** Arielle
Dombasle/**Cinematographer:** Jacques Robin/
Music: Arielle Dombasle, Jean-Louis Valéro/
Editor: Christine Aya
Olympic 80 minutes

1986

Pirates
• *Cast*
Captain Thomas Bartholomew Red................
........................Walter Matthau
The Frog (Jean-Baptiste)............Cris Campion
Don Alfonso de la Torré........Damien Thomas
Boomako..Olu Jacobs
Captain Linares............................Ferdy Mayne
Surgeon...David Kelly
Spanish Officers.........Anthony Peck/Anthony
  Dawson/Richard Dieux/Jacques Maury
Master at Arms.....................Jose Santamaría
Commander of Marines.........Robert Dorning
Pepito Gonzalez..............................Luc Jamati
Angelito................................Emilio Fernandez
Jesus.....................................Wladislaw Komar
Pockmarked Sailor...................Georges Trillat
Padre.....................................Richard Pearson
María-Dolores de la Jenya de la Calde............
  Charlotte Lewis
Duenna...............................Georges Montillier
Carpenter...John Gill
Cook...David Foxxe
Boatswain...................................Brian Maxine
Armoury Guard Raouf.....................Ben Amor
Hunchback.............Eugeniusz Priwieziencew
Moonhead..................Roger Ashton-Griffiths
Meat Hook..Ian Dury
Ginge..Bill Stewart
Diddler.....................................Sydney Bromley
Lawyer................................Cardew Robinson
Dutch..Roy Kinnear
Hendrik...................................Daniel Emilfork
Surprise................................Carole Fredericks
Fiddler..Allen Hoist
Sailor...Denis Fontayne
Sentries........Michael Elphick/Angelo Casadei

Governor...Bill Fraser
Palace Guard.......................Antonio Spoletini
Jailer..Bill MacCabe
New Duenna....................Smilja Mihailovitch
Passenger.............................Bernard Musson
Passenger's Wife...................Josine Comellas
with Gina Calabrese

• Selected Credits

Director: Roman Polanski

Producer: Tarak Ben Ammar

Screenplay: Gerard Brach, John Brownjohn, **Roman Polanski**

Music: Philippe Sarde

Cinematographer: Witold Sobocinski

Production Designer: Pierre Guffroy

Editors: William Reynolds, Hervé de Luze

Sound: Jean-Pierre Ruh

Production Managers: Pino Butti, Vittorio Noia

Assistant Director: John Lvoff

Makeup: Jean-Pierre Eychenne

Costume Designer: Anthony Powell

Special Effects: Antonio Corridori, Franco Ragusa

Stunts: Ryszard Janikowski, Richard Graydon, Zbigniew Modej

Executive Producers: Mark Lombardo, Thom Mount, Umberto Sambuco

Cannon 124 minutes

1988

Frantic

• Cast

Dr Richard Walker......................Harrison Ford
Sondra Walker............................Betty Buckley
Michelle.........................Emmanuelle Seigner
Taxi Driver................................Djiby Soumare
Desk Clerk...........................Dominique Virton
Gaillard..Gérard Klein
Bellboy...........................Stéphane D'Audeville
Hall Porters...Laurent Spielvogel/Alain Doutey
Le Grand Hotel Manager..........Jacques Ciron
Bellboy 2..................................Roch Leibovici
Tourist.......................................Louise Vincent
Hotel Detective Le Grand Hotel..........Patrice Melennec
Restroom Attendant...............Ella Jaroszewicz

Florists......Joëlle Lagneau/Jean-Pierre Delage
Cafe Owner...........................Marc Dudicourt
Waiter................................Artus de Penguern
Wino..................................Dominique Pinon
Desk Cop...................................Richard Dieux
Inspector..Yves Rénier
US Security Officer..................Robert Ground
Marine Guard...........................Bruce Johnson
US Embassy Clerks................Michael Morris/ Claude Doineau
US Embassy Official.................John Mahoney
Shaap...................................Jimmie Ray Weeks
Bellboy 3......................................Alan Ladd
Blue Parrot Barman....................Andre Quiqui
Rastafarian.........................Thomas M Pollard
Dede Martin.....................................Böll Boyer
TWA Clerk..............................Tina Sportolaro
Peter....................................David Huddleston
Edie....................................Alexandra Stewart
Irwin.......................................Robert Barr
Man in Leather..................Patrick Floersheim
Man in Tweed............................Marcel Bluwal
Houseboat Owner....................Isabelle Noah
The Kidnapper...........................Yorgo Voyagis
The Bodyguard................................David Jaul
Dead Driver..................Jean-Claude Houbard
Dr Metlaoui...........................Raouf Ben Amor
with Stéphane Copeau

• Selected Credits

Director: Roman Polanski

Producers: Tim Hampton, Thom Mount

Screenplay: Roman Polanski, Gérard Brach, Peter Gethers

Music: Ennio Morricone

Cinematographer: Witold Sobocinski

Camera Operator: Jean Harnois

Production Designer: Pierre Guffroy

Editor: Sam O'Steen

Sound Editors: Laurent Quaglio, Jean Gouldier

Production Manager: Daniel Szuster

Assistant Director: Michel Cheyko

Makeup: Didier Lavergne, Sophie Harvey

Hair Stylist: Jean-Max Guérin

Wardrobe: Germinal Rangel, Laurence Guindollet, Françoise Marechal, Bernard Minne

Costume Designer: Anthony Powell

Stunt Arranger: Daniel Breton

Stunts: Vic Armstrong, Rémy Julienne, Wendy Leech

Warner Bros 120 minutes

1991

Back in the USSR

• *Selected Cast*

Frank Whaley, Natalya Negoda, **Roman Polanski (Kurilov),** Andrew Divoff , Dey Young, Ravil Issyanov, Harry Ditson, Brian Blessed, Constantine Gregory, Alexei Yevdokimov, Boris Romanov, Vsevolod Safonov, Yuri Sarantsev, Oleg Anofriev, Nikolai Averiushkin,

• *Selected Credits*

Director: Deran Sarafian/**Writers:** Lindsay Smith, Ilmar Taska/**Producers:** Lindsay Smith, Ilmar Taska/**Cinematographer:** Yuri Neyman/**Music:** Les Hooper, Rena Riffel/ **Production Designer:** Vladimir Philippov/ **Editor:** Ian Crafford

20th Century Fox 87 minutes

1992

Bitter Moon

• *Cast*

Nigel	Hugh Grant
Fiona	Kristin Scott Thomas
Mimi	Emmanuelle Seigner
Oscar	Peter Coyote
Mr Singh	Victor Banerjee
Amrita Singh	Sophie Patel
Steward	Patrick Albenque
Bridge Players	Smilja Mihailovitch/ Leo Eckmann
Dado	Luca Vellani
Partygoer	Richard Dieux
Bandleader	Danny Garcy
Bus Inspector	Daniel Dhubert
Girl in Boutique	Nathalie Galan
Cook	Eric Gonzales
Thai Maître D'	Jim-Adhi Limas
Oscar's Friend	Boris Bergman
Cindy	Olivia Brunaux
Basil	Heavon Grant

Hooker	Charlene
Neighbour with Dog	Geoffrey Carey
Flight Dispatcher	Robert Benmussa
Model	Claire Lopez
Housewife	Shannon Finnegan
Brunette	Frederique Lopez
Eurasian Girl	Yse Marguerite
Tran Mayor	Claude Bonnet
Beverly	Stockard Channing

• *Selected Credits*

Director: Roman Polanski

Producer: Roman Polanski

Screenplay: Gerard Brach, John Brownjohn from the novel *Lunes de Fiel* by Pascal Bruckner

Co-producers: Alain Sarde, Timothy Burrill

Music: Fausto Fawcett, Carlos Laufer, Vangelis

Cinematographer: Tonino Delli Colli

Camera Operator: Jean Harnois

Production Designers: Willy Holt, Gerard Viard

Editor: Herve De Luze

Sound: Daniel Brisseau

Sound Editors: Roberto Garzelli, Laurent Quaglio

Sound Mixers: Ray Merrin, Bill Rowe

Production Manager: Jean-Jacques Damiani

Assistant Directors: Eric Bartonio, Michel Cheyko

Makeup: Sophie Harvey, Didier Lavergne

Hair Stylists: Lolita Avellanas, Alain Bernard

Wardrobe: Anne Dunsford-Varenne

Costume Designer: Jackie Budin

Special Effects: Jean-François Cousson, Pierre Foury, Martin Gutteridge, Benoît Lestang, Jean-Louis Trinquier, Paul Wilson

Stunt Coordinator: Jean-Louis Airola

Executive Producer: Robert Benmussa

Columbia 138 minutes

1994

A Pure Formality
(*Una Pura Formalità*)

• *Selected Cast*

Gérard Depardieu, **Roman Polanski (Inspector),** Sergio Rubini, Nicola Di Pinto,

Tano Cimarosa, Paolo Lombardi, Maria Rosa Spagnolo, Alberto Sironi, Giovanni Morricone, Mahdi Kraiem, Massimo Vanni, Sebastiano Filocamo,

• *Selected Credits*

Director: Giuseppe Tornatore/**Writers:** Giuseppe Tornatore, Pascal Quignard/ **Producers:** Mario Cecchi Gori, Vittorio Cecchi Gori/**Cinematographer:** Blasco Giurato/**Music:** Giuseppe Tornatore, Ennio Morricone, Pascal Quignard/**Production Designer:** Andrea Crisanti/**Editor:** Giuseppe Tornatore

Sony Pictures 108 minutes

Dead Tired (Grosse Fatigue)

• *Selected Cast*

Michel Blanc, Carole Bouquet, Philippe Noiret, Josiane Balasko, Marie-Anne Chazel, Christian Clavier, Guillaume Durand, Charlotte Gainsbourg, David Hallyday, Estelle Hallyday, Gérard Jugnot, Dominique Lavanant, Thierry Lhermitte, Mathilda May, **Roman Polanski (Himself)**

• *Selected Credits*

Director: Michel Blanc/**Writers:** Michel Blanc, Jacques Audiard, Bertrand Blier/ **Writer/Producer:** Daniel Toscan du Plantier/ **Cinematographer:** Eduardo Serra/**Music:** René-Marc Bini/**Production Designer:** Carlos Conti/**Editor:** Maryline Monthieux

France 92 minutes

1995

Death and the Maiden

• *Cast*

Paulina Escobar....................Sigourney Weaver
Dr Roberto Miranda....................Ben Kingsley
Gerardo Escobar........................Stuart Wilson
Dr Miranda's Wife........................Krystia Mova
Dr Miranda's Sons..................Jonathan Vega/
Rodolphe Vega
String Quartet Players...........Gilberto Cortes/
Jorge Cruz/Carlos Moreno/
Eduardo Valenzuela
String Quartet Manager............Sergio Ortega
Alvarado

• *Selected Credits*

Director: Roman Polanski

Producers: Josh Kramer, Thom Mount

Screenplay: Rafael Yglesias, Ariel Dorfman from the play *Death and the Maiden* by Ariel Dorfman

Co-producers: Ariel Dorfman, Bonnie Timmermann

Associate Producer: Gladys Nederlander

Music: Wojciech Kilar

Cinematographer: Tonino Delli Colli

Camera Operator: Jean Harnois

Production Designer: Pierre Guffroy

Art Director: Claude Moesching

Editor: Herve de Luze

Sound Editor: Laurent Quaglio

Production Manager: Patrick Gordon

Assistant Director: Michel Cheyko

Makeup: Linda De Vetta, Didier Lavergne

Wardrobe: Germinal Rangel

Costume Designer: Milena Canonero

Special Effects: Gilbert Pieri

Stunts: Jean-Louis Airola, Alain Grellier, Guylaine Juillot, Janet Pharaoh, Anne Rossner

Executive Producers: Jane Barclay, Sharon Harel

Fine Line 103 minutes

1999

The Ninth Gate

• *Cast*

Dean Corso..................................Johnny Depp
Boris Balkan.............................Frank Langella
Liana Telfer...Lena Olin
The Girl............................Emmanuelle Seigner
Baroness Kessler......................Barbara Jefford
Victor Fargas.......................................Jack Taylor
Pablo & Pedro Ceniza/1st & 2nd Workmen....
Jose Lopez Rodero
Liana's Bodyguard.......................Tony Amoni
Bernie..James Russo
Andrew Telfer....................................Willy Holt
Witkin..Allen Garfield
Old Man............................Jacques Dacqmine
Old Man's Son............................Joe Sheridan
Daughter-in-Law.......................Rebecca Pauly

Concierge.........................Catherine Benguigui
Secretary................................Maria Ducceschi
Gruber.....................................Jacques Collard
Desk Clerk.......................Dominique Pozzetto
Baker.......................................Emmanuel Booz
Hotel Porter..................Lino Ribeiro de Sousa
Cabby..Asil Rais
Cafe Owners.........................Bernard Richier/
                                    Marinette Richier
American Businessman...............Christopher
                                      Goodman
with Jacquelyn Toman

• Selected Credits
Director: Roman Polanski
Producer: Roman Polanski
Screenplay: John Brownjohn, Enrique Urbizu,
  Roman Polanski
  from the novel *El club Dumas* by Arturo
  Perez-Reverte
Co-producers: Mark Allan, Antonio Cardenal,
  Iñaki Nuñez, Alain Vannier
Associate Producer: Adam Kempton
Music: Wojciech Kilar
Cinematographer: Darius Khondji
Camera Operators: Malika Mazauric,
  Stephane Verriere, Jean Harnois
Production Designer: Dean Tavoularis
Art Director: Gerard Viard
Editor: Herve de Luze
Sound Editor: Laurent Quaglio
Production Manager: Laura Stuart
Assistant Directors: David Campi Lemaire,
  Christopher Gachet
Makeup: Paul Le Marinel, Liliane Rametta,
  Jean-Luc Russier
Hair Stylists: Jean-Pierre Berroyer, Michel
  Demonteix, Bettina Miquaix
Costume Designer: Anthony Powell
Special Effects Coordinator: Jean-Louis
  Trinquier
Special Effects: Gilbert Pieri
Stunt Coordinators: Dominique Fouassier,
  Patrick Cauderlier
Stunts: Michel Bouis, Andre Cagnard,
  Remi Canaple, Rémi Canaple, Patrick
  Cauderlier, Jean Girard, Jean-Pierre Janic,
  Pascal Mercuri, Jean-Loup Michou,
  Alison Parson, Leslie Rain, Catherine
  Robert, Alain Saugout, Jean-Pierre Suchet,

Francis Terzian, Fred Vallet
Executive Producers: Michel Cheyko,
  Wolfgang Glattes
Artisan 133 minutes

2000

Tribute to Alfred Lepetit
(Hommage à Alfred Lepetit)
• Selected Cast
Thierry Berbezy, Jan-Claude Brialy,
Laetitia de Fombelle, Jake Eberts,
Gérard Guët, Sophie Lack, Elsa Lepoivre,
Stéphane Massard, Mathieu Mathclin,
Roman Polanski, Charlotte Rampling,
Eddy Rousselot, Edith Vernes
• Selected Credits
Director: Jean Rousselot/**Writer:** Jean
Rousselot/**Producer:** Laurence Braunberger/
Cinematographer: Pierre Barougier/
Music: Jesse Cook/**Production Designer:**
Simon Verner/**Editor:** Françoise Garnault
France 9 minutes

2002

Zemsta *(Revenge)*
• Selected Cast
Roman Polanski (Papkin), Janusz Gajos,
Andrzej Seweryn, Katarzyna Figura, Daniel
Olbrychski, Agata Buzek, Rafal Królikowski,
Lech Dyblik, Cezary Zak, Jerzy Nowak,
Tadeusz Wojtych, Henryk Golebiewski,
Jerzy Slonka, Magdalena Smalara, Grazyna
Zielinska
• Selected Credits
Director: Andrzej Wajda/**Writers:** Andrzej
Wajda, Aleksander Fredro/**Producers:**
Michal Kwiecinski, Janusz Morgenstern/
Cinematographer: Pawel Edelman/**Music:**
Wojciech Kilar/**Production Designers:**
Magdalena Dipont, Tadeusz Kosarewicz/
Editor: Wanda Zeman
Vision Film 100 minutes

The Pianist
• *Cast*

Wladyslaw Szpilman...................Adrien Brody
Captain Wilm Hosenfeld....................Thomas Kretschmann
Father..Frank Finlay
Mother................................Maureen Lipman
Dorota...Emilia Fox
Henryk...Ed Stoppard
Regina..Julia Rayner
Halina...............................Jessica Kate Meyer
Jurek.......................................Michal Zebrowski
SS Slapping Father.......................Wanja Mues
Mr Lipa....................................Richard Ridings
Feather Woman.........................Nomi Sharron
Man Waiting to Cross.............Anthony Milner
Street Musicians.....................Lucy Skeaping/ Roddy Skeaping/Ben Harlan
Schutzpolizei........................Thomas Lawinky/ Joachim Paul Assböck/Rafal Mohr
Itzak Heller......................................Roy Smiles
Yehuda..Paul Bradley
Majorek.............................Daniel Caltagirone
Benek................................Andrzej Blumenfeld
Child at the Wall........................Darian Wawer
Customers with Coins.......................Zbigniew Zamachowski/Lejb Fogelman
SS Officer....................Detlev von Wangenheim
Rubenstein..Popek
Woman with Soup...............Zofia Czerwinska
The Soup Snatcher..............Emilio Fernandez
Schultz....................................Udo Kroschwald
SS Shooting the Woman...........Uwe Rathsam
Woman Shot in the Head........Joanna Brodzik
Wailing Woman..........Katarzyna Bargielowska
Woman with Child.............Maja Ostaszewska
Dr Ehrlich.....................................John Bennett
Mr Grün...Cyril Shaps
Boy with Sweets.................Wojciech Smolarz
Fellow Worker........................Lech Mackiewicz
Janina...Ruth Platt
SS Shooting Benek..........Frank-Michael Köbe
Zig Zag...Torsten Flach
SS Making a Speech..........Peter Rappenglück
Janina's Husband.......................Ronan Vibert
Gebczynsk.....................Krzysztof Pieczynski
Neighbour.............................Katarzyna Figura
Dorota's Husband..................Valentine Pelka
Szalas.......................................Andrew Tiernan

Dr Luczak.....................................Tom Strauss
Lednicki..................................Cezary Kosinski
Polish Workman.......................Pawel Burczyk
Russian Soldier.................Dymitr Leszczenko
Prisoner...........................Andrzej Pieczynski
Girl.......................................Morgane Polanski
German film crew.................Maurycy Zylber/ Xawery Zylber
Polish Woman........................Nina Franoszek
Women in Ghetto....................Anna Gryszka/ Dagmara Sieminska/Izabella Szolc
Polish Officer...............................John Keogh
Jew Working on the Bulding Site........Ryszard Kluge
SS Officer.........................Ireneusz Machnicki
Men in Ghetto.................Pawel Malaszynski/ David Szurmiej/Jacek Wolszczak
German Soldier in Ghetto........Adam Malecki
German Soldier, Rummage Bags....Axel Prahl
Boy in Warsaw Ghetto...........Daniel Szpilman
Young Gestapo...............................Borys Szyc
with Grzegorz Artman/Adam Bauman/ Zbigniew Dziduch/Marian Dziedziel/Jerzy Goralczyk/Jaroslaw Kopaczewski/Patrick Lanagan/Dorota Liliental/Norbert Rakowski/ Piotr Siejka/Weronika Szen/Andrzej Szenajch/ Tomasz Tyndyk/Andrzej Walden/Zbigniew Walerys/Maciej Winkler/Andrzej Zielinski

• *Selected Credits*
Director: Roman Polanski
Producers: Robert Benmussa, **Roman Polanski**, Alain Sarde
Screenplay: Ronald Harwood from the novel *The Pianist* by Wladyslaw Szpilman
Co-producer: Gene Gutowski
Music: Wojciech Kilar
Cinematographer: Pawel Edelman
Camera Operators: Volker Gläser, Marek Rajca
Production Designer: Allan Starski
Art Directors: Sebastian T Krawinkel, Nenad Pecur
Editor: Hervé de Luze
Sound Mixer: Jean-Marie Blondel
Production Manager: Oliver Lüer
Assistant Director: Ralph Remstedt
Makeup: Waldemar Pokromski
Costume Designer: Anna B Sheppard
Special Effects Supervisors: Alister

Mazzotti, Hans Seck
Stunt Coordinators: Jim Dowdall, Zbigniew Modej
Stunts: Zofia Bachleda-Zolnierczyk, Janusz Chlebowski, Piotr Cichon, Robert Cichon, Jacek Dlugosz, Ryszard Francman, Jacek Jelen, Jacek Kadlubowski, Stella Kuczynska, Pawel Pliszka, Tomasz Przybysz, Jacek Ryniewicz, Rene Schobess, Jozef Stefanski, Sylwester Zawadski
Executive Producers: Timothy Burrill, Henning Molfenter, Lew Rywin
Studio Canal 150 minutes

2005

Oliver Twist

• *Cast*

Fagin	Ben Kingsley
Oliver Twist	Barney Clark
Nancy	Leanne Rowe
Toby Crackit	Mark Strong
Bill Sykes	Jamie Foreman
Artful Dodger	Harry Eden
Mr Brownlow	Edward Hardwicke
Mr Limbkins	Ian McNeice
Mr Bumble	Jeremy Swift
Mrs Bedwin	Frances Cuka
Mr Sowerberry	Michael Heath
Mrs Sowerberry	Gillian Hanna
Magistrate Fang	Alun Armstrong
Workhouse Master	Andy de la Tour
Dining Hall Master	Peter Copley
Hungry Boy	Joseph Tremain
Workhouse Boys	Andreas Papadopoulos/ Laurie Athey/Filip Hess
Charley Bates	Lewis Chase
Barney	Jake Curran
Noah Claypole	Chris Overton
Unkind Board Member	Richard Durden
Parson/Old Man with a Punch	Timothy Bateson
Mr Garmfield, The Chimney Sweep	Andy Linden
First Magistrate	John Nettleton
Charlotte	Teresa Churcher
Farmer	Gerard Horan
Farmer's Daughter	Morgane Polanski
Old Woman	Liz Smith
Nicky	Levi Hayes
Bet	Ophelia Lovibond
Boy with Hoop	Elvis Polanski
Bookseller	Patrick Godfrey
Woman in Street	Anezka Novak
Policemen	Andy Camm/James Babson
Elderly Officer	Frank Mills
Bullseye	Turbo
Policeman in Court	David Meeking
Mr Grimwig	Paul Brooke
Other Women in Street	Andrea Miltner/ Kaeren Revell
Woman at Window	Kay Raven
Barmaid	Lizzy Le Quesne
Man in Pub	Robert Orr
Barman	Paul Eden
Inspector Blather	Nick Stringer
Warder	Richard Ridings

• *Selected Credits*

Director: Roman Polanski
Producers: Robert Benmussa, **Roman Polanski**, Alain Sarde
Screenplay: Ronald Harwood from the novel *Oliver Twist* by Charles Dickens
Co-producers: Timothy Burrill, Petr Moravec
Music: Rachel Portman
Cinematographer: Pawel Edelman
Camera Operator: Marek Rajca
Production Designer: Allan Starski
Art Director: Jindrich Kocí
Editor: Hervé de Luze
Sound Mixer: Jean-Marie Blondel
Sound Editor: Jean Goudier
Production Manager: Daniel Champagnon
Assistant Director: Ralph Remstedt
Makeup: Linda Eisenhamerova, Didier Lavergne, Ivo Strangmüller
Hair Stylists: Linda Eisenhamerova, Ivo Strangmüller, Jean-Max Guérin
Wardrobe: Vera Mirová, Peter Paul, Richard Pointing
Costume Designer: Anna B Sheppard
Special Effects: Supervisor Martin Oberlander
Stunt Coordinator: Robert Lahoda
Stunts: Adam Kulhavy, Ladislav Lahoda, Paul Lowe, Tomas Tobola
Sony 130 minutes

BIBLIOGRAPHY

There have been many books written about Roman Polanski over the years, from the academically esoteric to the lurid and downright sensational. As with any such work which is undertaken while the subject in question is yet young and productive, most of them are now limited in their scope. By far the best single volume on Polanski's life, up to a point, is his autobiography of 1984; it is my earnest hope that this present volume might go some way to filling the subsequent gap. The remainder of this list is comprised of ancillary publications which were instrumental in aiding me with the task. My thanks go to their authors and creators.

Chinatown • Robert Towne/*Grove Press/New York/1997*

Cinema Of Roman Polanski, The • Ivan Butler/*Zwemmer-Barnes/New York, London/1970*

Death And The Maiden • Ariel Dorfman/*Nick Hearn Books/London/1991*

Dumas Club, The • Arturo Pérez-Revert/*Harvill Press/London/1996*

Helter Skelter • Vincent Bugliosi, Curt Gentry/*W W Norton/New York/1974*

Johnny Depp: A Kind Of Illusion • Denis Meikle/*Reynolds & Hearn/London/2004*

Master and Margarita, The • Mikhail Bulgakov/*Harvill Press/London/1967*

Oliver Twist • Charles Dickens/*Bentley's Miscellany/London/1836-38*

Pianist, The • Wladyslaw Szpilman/*Gollancz/London/1999*

Polanski • John Parker/*Gollancz/London/1993*

Polanski: His Life And Films • Barbara Leaming/*Hamish Hamilton/London/1982*

Polanski: Three Film Scripts • Roman Polanski/*Lorrimer Publishing Ltd/London/1975*

Repulsion: The Life And Times Of Roman Polanski • Thomas Kiernan/*Grove Press/ New York/1980*

Roman by Polanski • Roman Polanski/*William Morrow/New York/1984*

Roman Polanski • F X Feeney, Paul Duncan/*Taschen/New York/2006*

Rosemary's Baby • Ira Levin/*Random House/New York/1967*

Step Right Up! I'm Gonna Scare The Pants Off America: Memoirs Of A B-Movie Mogul • William Castle/*Putnam/New York/1976*

Tenant, The • Roland Topor/*Doubleday/London/1966*

Tess Of The d'Urbervilles • Thomas Hardy/*The Graphic/London/1891*

What The Censor Saw • John Trevelyan/*Michael Joseph/London/1973*

www.minadream.com/romanpolanski/ (Roseanna Lawrence)
www.variety.com

INDEX